It's a Dodger's Life

It's a Dodger's life

The autobiography of

Jack Wild

Foreword by Billie Hayes
Epilogue by Claire Harding-Wild
Afterword by Clive Francis

fantom
publishing

First published in 2016 by Fantom Films
fantomfilms.co.uk

Copyright © the Estate of Jack Wild 2016

A catalogue record for this book is available from the British Library.

Hardback edition ISBN: 978-1-78196-266-4

Typeset by Phil Reynolds Media Services, Leamington Spa
Printed and bound by CPI Group (UK) Ltd, Croydon, CR0 4YY

Jacket design by Will Brooks

'These are the bits that I've remembered and this is how it all seemed to me!'

Foreword

THE FIRST TIME I SAW JACK WILD was in the movie *Oliver!*. Aside from being adorable, his performance was brilliant. When I learned later that we would be doing *H.R. Pufnstuf,* a children's television series, I was thrilled. Then it crossed my mind: what if he was a spoiled brat with a monumental ego? But then we met.

With his cockney accent and my midwestern one we did nothing but laugh. There was not a trace of what had previously crossed my mind. He was down to earth, great fun and a true professional; and yes, he was adorable. After its completion Jack returned to England, and on occasion would visit the States. They were always joyous reunions. That is when I met Claire Harding. Jack had found his soulmate and I had found a wonderful friend. This book is a heartfelt autobiography of a gifted young man whom I shall cherish always.

Billie Hayes
October 2016

Chapter 1

MY EARLIEST MEMORY IS BEING WRAPPED UP IN A BLANKET in front of the coal fire. The days were often so foggy that the street lamps stayed on all day. As my Uncle Harry said, 'The birds are walking it's so foggy!' You couldn't see people clearly, but the sound of their wooden clogs on the cobbled streets paid tribute to the industrial town. My father, with nearly everyone else at the time, clip-clopped his way to the cotton mills – the mainstay of our way of life.

I had chicken pox, I was ill and didn't like it, and I could see no way of stopping it.

For company I had a teddy bear, handed down to me from my brother Arthur. (He had handed down the chicken pox as well.) He was a year older than me and so when he was done with the bear, I was given it and by the time I'd finished with it I'd pulled its eyes out, and its legs and arms off, so it was looking pretty ill too, and we sat dejectedly on the settee together.

It wasn't long, however, before I was swept up in the whirlwind that was my mother. She was a tiny woman and a bundle of nervous energy. Looking back on my childhood I don't ever remember my mother sitting down. She ran the house and all of us in it with a vengeance: 'living on her nerves'.

'Come on Jackie. Let's get yer washed and ready for nursery.'

I hated that name. And out came the tin bath in front of the fire. I was dunked and scrubbed and rubbed and dressed and left standing in the front room bemused and cold, and reached for my dummy for comfort.

Now, the year before, Arthur had been cajoled and persuaded into throwing his dummy on to the fire as he was now growing into a 'little man'. My parents wistfully believed I would show the same sense of maturity and follow Arf's lead. In place of Arf's sense of maturity, however, I had developed a sense of stubbornness!

'You don't want to take that wi' yer surely,' me Mum said as she whisked it from me, wrapping me in my coat and bundling me out of the front door.

We walked up the street to catch the bus to the cotton factory where Mum worked as well, and my brother and I were deposited in the factory's nursery. I waited in the cold between Arf and me Mum. Mum grasped my hand tightly and Arf held my hand reluctantly. The bus came and we were swept up into the warmth and noise, Mum calling to the people we knew. And in this safe, cosy haven I reached into my pocket and pulled out my trusty *spare* dummy.

'Oh Jackie,' Mum sighed, 'what am I gonna do wi' yer?'

*

Miss Vera Boardman (me Mum) married Jack Wild Senior (me Dad) on 6th August 1949. Dad had just returned from two years' service in Germany working in the salvage unit of the RAF ('five and a half years in th'airforce and never went in a bloody plane'). After they were married they moved into number 425 Shaw Road, Royton. Royton was a small town nestled in between Manchester and the Pennines, in an area that boasted more manufacturing mills to the square mile than anywhere else in England.

My Gran and Grandad lived across the road from us at number 338 and Auntie Emma lived four doors away at number 330. Auntie Emma had no blood tie, but was loved and cherished within our family. Being looked after by her was considered a real treat as she let us get away with murder. She was also the closest link we had to showbiz at that time, as her best friend was said to know Eric Sykes!

In 1951 Arthur was born at Oldham Royal Infirmary, and on 30th September 1952 I entered the world with rather less ceremony at 425 Shaw Road. I suppose the house was quite small, only two bedrooms, but there was a garden at the back with an air-raid shelter where we used to play until I cracked my head on it one day and we were told by my father 'keep out of that or there'll be trouble'. I managed to stay out of the shelter, but not always out of trouble.

We ventured further afield to where the grass was about five feet high, and as we weren't nearly that tall we played hide and seek and built houses with the hay by 'The Red River', so called because of the colour of the sand at the bottom. Looking back it was actually just a rather feeble stream, but to us...

I remember lots of silly little things about my childhood. One in particular was that, when I was about four years old, my mother took us into a wet fish shop and there was a huge fish in the window. It must have been twice the size of me and while she wasn't looking, I climbed in the window, dragged out the fish and stuffed it in her shopping bag. As we went to leave the shop, Mum realised the bag was too heavy and had a look. She couldn't believe what she saw.

'Oh, Jackie – you'll be the death of me.'

Living in Royton you got used to it being cold, damp and grey, but life was fine and sunny for me and Arf. I remember vividly on very special days going to the cinema in Oldham. There wasn't a cinema in our town so we had to travel about five or six miles by bus – we didn't have a car – and it was a real adventure. The first film I saw was *Bambi* and the second one was *Gulliver's Travels*. I remember them as though they were yesterday and to see these films on the big screen was like going into another world. It was incredible.

Then suddenly it was announced that we were going to move to London. I learned years later that there had been 'trouble at mill'. Me Mum had had a disagreement with management, Dad went to 'sort it out' and stated 'if she's off, I'm off', and so we were all off. But we were off to London where Uncle Brian and Auntie Sylvia lived. When Uncle Brian had come out of the forces in 1959, the cotton mills were closing, so his brother-in-law had got him a job at Firestone Tyres in London; and we were to follow the trail he had blazed.

As Auntie Emma walked us to school on the day of the announcement (we had to cross two main roads, so we weren't allowed on our own) I just couldn't believe we were going to the capital of England! I didn't really have any idea what the capital would be like, but two thoughts jostled in my mind: it must be so much more exciting than Royton – even more exciting than Manchester – and certainly, it must be much, much warmer!

So in the summer of 1960, Mum, Arf and me caught the No. 2 bus to Stephens Square to catch a train to London. As we reached the main cross-roads in Royton we saw our two school classes gathered together with an assortment of relatives to wave us goodbye. I was moving up in the world!

I was seven years old and Arthur was eight when we moved down to 28 Munster Avenue, Hounslow. The house that my parents bought was on one of the flight paths to Heathrow and, until we'd come to London, we'd never ever seen an aeroplane before. Me and Arf shared the back bedroom and when it had gone dark we would open the curtains and see the aeroplanes flying in and it looked as though they were going to land on the roof. It was incredible! We'd get so excited and then we'd hear:

'Get back inta bed or Edgy Dark'll get yer!'

With that threat we'd fly back into bed sharpish! Edgy Dark was an invention of my Uncle Harry. I don't know who or what he was but he sure as hell was frightening. He would supposedly punish you in unbelievable ways.

Edgy could not, however, diminish our fascination with aeroplanes and we started to collect the numbers they had on the back. Me, Arf and all my friends would have this little manual with all different numbers of aircraft in and as soon as you'd seen the actual aircraft, you'd either cross it off, or underline it, or something. There would always be bets on who would finish the book first; although nobody I can remember ever did finish the book.

We couldn't stay plane-spotting forever, and at the beginning of September we started our new school, Grove Road Junior. On that first day, me and Arf stood out in the playground. We had on the uniform, but I suppose we looked different somehow. Some people thought we were twins when we were younger as we looked quite alike; except that, while Arthur always looked pristine, as long as I had my tie wrapped around my neck somehow, it didn't really matter. On that first day, though, we didn't belong. A mess of boys surrounded me and Arf, surveying the two new curiosities.

''Av yer nowt better t' look at?' Arf said.

Arf's challenge provoked surprising hilarity, and it was played back to us over and over again, throughout the day and indeed that week. Not only did we look out of place, we sounded all wrong too. We threatened them with Edgy Dark, but somehow he seemed to have lost his power. Our status as outsiders was confirmed. Talking differently was obviously not a thing to be proud of, as me Mum had suggested. So me and Arf imitated the boys' accents and quickly learnt the lingo and after the first couple of weeks (or maybe a couple of months) they tired of that particular taunt and just picked on us for our size; but we weren't bullied too much and as me Mum said, 'They don't make diamonds as big as stones.'

The other alarming fact that dawned on me was that everybody else seemed to be that much further on in their education. Up north we were using pencils and down here they were using pen and ink! That made me feel very... not up to standard. They were even doing joined-up writing! And I was still doing... not-joined-up writing.

Still, they were very happy days at school and at least I had me older brother who would stick up for me whenever he could. Though once I had this argument with this one kid. I can't remember what the argument was about, but I started saying something to the effect of 'If you don't shut up, I'll smack ya in the mouth!' (I'd perfected the dialect by then). But he called my bluff, and so I had to stand up and I started throwing punches at him. For my size, I was very, very quick but not necessarily powerful, so there's me doing the 'Ali shuffle' throwing punches right, left and centre, but not hitting him at all. And, for a while he couldn't get anywhere near me.

Finally, he grabbed hold of me and sat on me. He was only about my size, maybe a bit podgier, and he sat on me and nutted me on the forehead; but, fair do's, he only nutted me once. It's not as though he carried on nuttin' me and trying to kill me. It was over and done with very quickly, but it didn't half hurt. I had a headache for a week.

As we were walking home that night I said to Arthur, 'Why didn't you drag him off me and stop him from mullering me?'

'Look,' he said, 'if I'd've done that, they'd have all turned round and said you couldn't fight your own battles.'

We walked along in silence.

'Anyway,' he said, 'you shouldn't have been so cocky in the first place, should ya!'

I wasn't prepared to admit it, but as me Dad said, I was all mouth and no trousers. Another time I can remember my trousers being tested was when I was collared down an alley by a bunch of Hell's Angels. I was walking this girl home with Terry Field, one of the ginger twins from down our way. This was after *Oliver!* had been released and I'd have been sixteen years old. We were walking down this long alleyway from the High Street in Hounslow and we heard this commotion behind us. There were about six Hell's Angels, three or four years older than me. They'd recognised me and they were having a go. I can't remember exactly what they were saying; but the finish of it was, one of them grabbed hold of me and pushed me up against this wire fence. As this happened my mate shouted out to them, 'Don't touch him because you know who he is and he'll sue you for… whatever!'

One of them turned round and said, 'Oh, shut up!' and punched him in the mouth. I remember thinking, 'Oh, shit! I'm really gonna get done over!'

I don't remember what happened, but suddenly it was all over. I think I must have talked my way out of it because my face was still intact. I guess I acted my way through whatever was necessary to get away with it. I do remember feeling sorry for Terry because he was trying to help me out and he got a smack in the mouth for his trouble. It did frighten me. I took the girl home, but I didn't go down that alley again.

Soon after we arrived in London, me Mum's Mum and Dad came down from Manchester and moved in with us. They were plump and jolly and spoilt us rotten. 'Don't tell yer Mum, Jackie,' Grandad Boardman would say, slipping me tuppence, as Gran watched the Saturday afternoon wrestling. The other good thing about them being down was that Grandad could start cutting our hair again. When we first moved to London, Mum had taken us to a barber's and asked for a short front, back and sides. The merry barber took her at her word and Arf and I emerged a little later, shaved and scalped and pulling the grimliest faces.

'Oh lads, whatever has he done? I didn't ask him to do that.'

The demon barber popped his head – with his nicely cut hair – out of the door. 'You said short *front*, back and sides lady. Most people just want the regular short back and sides, but what the lady asked for, the lady got!'

'Oh boys, I'm ever so sorry,' she giggled, 'I've never had to ask for a cut before.' She tried to explain and tried to force her face into a look of concern. 'You both look very nice,' she said as her giggle bubbled up and escaped her again.

As well as taking care of our hair, Gran and Grandad also looked after the house when we went on our summer holidays, and in August 1962 we headed off to take our two weeks away. It was always two weeks and always in August, to Margate in Kent. I wasn't keen on this stretch of sea as it had so much heavy duty seaweed. I went into the water as soon as we got there, but it was like a great octopus was pulling me under. It really spooked me. I felt like John Wayne in *Donovan's Reef* – only not so brave.

Safely on dry land, we walked along the main seafront where there was this Western bar. A couple of cowboys stood outside firing Colt 45s at each other and passers-by. How fantastic!

'Can we go in there please?' I pleaded. Nowhere else could surely be as exciting. 'I don't care when, but can we go there one time?'

We carried on walking, but I knew we had to come back the same way. As we came past, I was watching the cowboys messing about and I thought: I'll wait for one to fire again, make out as though he has shot me and hit the deck. So I waited until he fired near me and then I threw myself on this table and chairs, knocking them flying, and fell to the floor where I lay dead still. The cowboy went white and immediately looked at his gun to double check that, 'Surely that was a blank that I put in there and not a real bullet?' and, as he ran over to me, the onlookers laughed and there was the faintest ripple of applause. I was hooked.

'Who does he tak' after?' me Mum said.

'Don't be so stupid, Jackie,' me Dad said. 'Come away wi' yer.'

When we returned home, I tried my new comic genius back at school. We were playing cricket one scorching hot afternoon and I was out on the boundary tired, thirsty and more than a little bored. The bowler walked back to deliver yet another ball. It arched, bounced, and whacked the wicket keeper squarely in the mouth; he fell to the ground, his face covered in blood. I think it might even have knocked out a tooth. I mostly preferred football as it was more exciting, but this had livened up the cricket match no end.

I ran to join in the excitement. Mr Parsons, the sports master, bent over the slain soldier assessing his injuries, after which he stood up, wiped his head and replaced his glasses. 'Come on, lad,' he said as he turned to walk back to school; but the boy was still on the deck. I wanted to make people laugh and this seemed like my cue. 'Well, that's one way of catching it,' I said. 'C'mon. Get up! You're not dying!' I added with a grin.

Mr Parsons turned back with a stony face. 'Any more remarks like that, Wild, and you'll be doing detention.' And I remember being so surprised. I couldn't understand his reaction at all because I thought I was dead funny. *Dead* funny.

I see that part of my childhood bathed in a particular light. I remember adventures in the green forest where only a few shafts of sunlight managed to penetrate the canopy of the trees. I remember bike rides through rivers, secret camps far from home, and the lake which seemed to be at the other end of the island. The sound of the waterfall, the smell of camp fires and excitement; happening upon a chase through the woods with cops and robbers. Fear and great stories. Lungfuls of fresh air and not a care in the world.

Chapter 2

Now, I NEVER WANTED TO BE AN ACTOR. I saw myself as either a footballer or a doctor – I had learnt all the bones in the body in preparation! I also played football in my local park with the kids in the road, me brother Arf, and an older, spotty lad who wasn't that good at football, Phil Collins. We hung about the park, and the smokes behind the sheds punctuated the endless games of football. We could spend all day there and, for me, it was a place to get away from me Mum's irrepressible need for cleanliness.

'Put your cars away, Jackie.'

'Have you combed yer hair this morning?'

''Ere, let me…' and out would come the hanky and the spit.

'Jackie, will yer turn down that record player – you'll be the death of me!'

So we went to the park to be noisy, to be muddy, to be boys, and to sniff glue.

The aim was to see how long you could keep sniffing glue without becoming unconscious. We'd get a brown paper bag that we'd had sweets in, put a few dobs of glue in, stick our mouth and nose into the bag and inhale. And that was that. Apparently, the older boys said you would get a buzz, but I never got a buzz: all I got was a headache. One day I thought I would keep going and keep going until I got this 'buzz'. I kept inhaling and I thought if I don't get something soon, I'm packing it in. The next minute, I'm out of it and when I came round there was blood everywhere – worse still, *my* blood. Sod that, I thought, I ain't doing that again. And I didn't do it again: I was so frightened of the same thing happening or worse. I never did get a buzz, just a bloody lip.

Phil Collins wasn't a regular, and not a member of our gang, but he would come for the odd game of football. We were minding our own business playing soccer one day, when Phil's Mum came to pick him up. She saw me and Arf and called over to us and asked if we had ever thought of being actors and being on TV.

'This woman's crackers,' I said to Arf as we wandered over to talk to her, just to be polite like.

'You can earn a lot of money, like a real job,' she persisted.

'Yeah, well, we've already got a job, lady – we deliver milk.'

'On, no, no, no!' she said. 'You'll earn far more money than that.'

So we went home and spoke to our parents about it.

'Mum, we met this lady in the park who said we could be on telly.'

'Don't be daft, Jackie. Wash yer hands'.

'She's having yer on, son,' me Dad helpfully added.

My parents were obviously going to need some convincing and so it was arranged that they would meet Mrs Collins at the Duke of Wellington pub. Me Dad stood at the bar suspiciously viewing the bartender. 'If I stand here I can watch them pump mi' pint and not jug it. I'm not having no bloody slops.' You can take the man out of Royton...

And so in the early summer of 1964 the two worlds collided: cotton mills vs. show business, and show business won. Mrs Collins suggested we should go to the Barbara Speake Stage School, where Phil went. 'I run the agency there,' she added, 'as most of the children work at the same time.'

'Well lads,' me Mum said, 'you do understand that we can't afford to send you to a stage school because that costs money and we don't have it, but if you really want to do it, we'll back yer, but you'll have to earn the money to pay for yer school fees and if you can do that then it's all right with us.'

So we thought, well, anything for a laugh.

'Don't know why anyone wants to bother wi' yer meself,' Dad helpfully added.

Mrs Collins got to work straight away, and said there were some auditions coming up for a West End musical called *Oliver!*. 'You can both sing, can't you?' she asked. We both sort of nodded, so we were put up for that and the landlord's daughter was enlisted to teach us songs for the audition. Arf had a better singing voice than me, so he learnt a ballad, 'Friends and Neighbours', and I ended up doing 'My Old Man's a Dustman'. We went for the audition during the summer holidays and I thought it was just a bit of a giggle. I think Arthur took it a bit more seriously than me, and was more nervous. At the time I didn't really think about it because I didn't know what I'd be missing if I didn't get it. We heard within a couple of weeks, and we'd both got it. Arthur started straight away, but I couldn't as you had to be twelve or older to be on stage in the West End, so I had to wait until my birthday – three months away.

A few days later Mrs Collins rang to say there was an audition for a movie called *The Little Ones* and would I go for it? 'All right,' I said. At the audition they felt there was a slight trace of my northern accent and they really wanted a cockney lad, so they offered me the job of the stand-in and gave the role to Kim Smith, one of the Barbara Speake Stage School boys.

So for the whole of my summer holidays I was working on my first film. It was shot mainly in the slums of Shepherd's Bush, West London, in some of the filthiest places I had ever been in. It was fantastic. I caught the 117 bus from the top of my street, it took me all the way to Goldhawk Road and Goldhawk Studios where the production office was. I'd get there at 8.30am and come home at 6pm. I wasn't being filmed: I would just stand in while they set the lighting and the cameras, and that was all I had to do, so it was just a laugh. And they were paying me which was just as well as I had to earn money to put towards a new school uniform. Mum and Dad had already bought my uniform for my senior school, but now, 'It's all been changed as I'm going to be an actor now!'

After I finished the film, I thought, I'm made now; I've earned an absolute fortune and I'm now ready to start in my West End debut. I thought it the most natural progression in the world. Before these heady days could begin, however, I had to endure a week at Smallberry Green Senior School. Speake's term didn't start for another week so I had to go to normal school for a week. Smallberry was only a secondary modern, but it was famed for its sporting achievements. Apparently the first twelve kids out of the class of thirty from Grove Road Junior went to a grammar school and the rest just went to Smallberry secondary modern. By some extraordinary turn of events, I came eighth in the class, but was sent to Smallberry because I was good at sports. Me Mum and Dad went mad – they would have loved me to be a grammar school lad. The way I looked at it though was, if I had gone to a grammar school it would have been a lot harder to convince my parents that I should change to stage school; and anyway, only swots went to grammar schools. What fun would that be?

So I started senior school on the Monday and finished on the Friday. The initiation test for this school was being thrown over a wall. The previous year at the start of the new term, a couple of lads had had their legs broken. Arthur had gone through the test and so I was forewarned. As I arrived at the school, I looked out for the bullies and told them jokes to try and get them to like me and not want to break my legs. I concentrated on trying to keep their minds off the fact that I was a new kid and a potential missile. I think my humour confused them and threw them off their game. I managed to survive the week and, on the Friday, left Smallberry Green with my legs intact, a few confused facts, and with the certain knowledge of how to make a proper crisp roll.˙

*

So at eleven years old, full of confidence, excitement and the highest expectations, I started at Barbara Speake's Stage School. Arf and me put on the regulation black cap, and the white shirt and orange tie. We each wore a black blazer, emblazoned with an orange star; 'BS' in black capital letters proudly declaring our allegiance. A black-and-white checked overcoat completed the picture. We also had a black jumper for dance, black tights for ballet, school shoes, tap shoes, ballet shoes and dance shoes... it all seemed a bit tarty to me.

Arf and I stood opposite each other in our full regalia.

'What *do* you look like?' I said to Arthur.

'Same as you, idiot,' he replied.

Except he didn't, as he wore long trousers and I, being a year younger, had the ignominy of wearing short ones. He also wore a shyness, and a more serious, apprehensive look than my irrepressible, idiotic optimism.

Going to Speake's was so different from going to your normal school. Partly because it seemed like you were doing half the amount of school work – mornings were devoted to academic stuff, afternoons were dedicated to performance – and partly because unlike normal school, everyone wanted to be there.

There was a huge spirit and enthusiasm that filled this massive school hall in Acton. Me and Arf were to spend three years on and off in this establishment; mostly 'off' as we were usually working to pay our way. But there was a wonderful sense of camaraderie and I loved going back in between jobs. In the first term, someone opened the emergency exit doors. Nobody owned up to it and so a flurry of punishment descended. The whole school was given one thousand dictionary words each, and detention in which to copy them out. I was pissed off about the dictionary words, but I wasn't bothered about the detention. We all enjoyed being at school so much, it didn't seem like a punishment at all. And I'm sure if I'd have opened the doors I wouldn't have owned up either.

˙ Remove bread from inside of roll, leaving outer crust, put crisps in crust casing, replace roll top and eat.

We got into trouble over smoking as well. I'd been smoking since I was about ten years old, and all the boys used to go in the toilets and have a fag. There was only one cubicle along with the urinals, and because this had a little window, we'd all pile into it. At any one time there would be up to ten people in the cubicle, but only two people with lit cigarettes. We'd been smoking in there so much that when you opened the door to go back out, some of the smoke went into the Hall and somebody sussed out what was happening. And again, nobody would own up to it. And again, the whole school got detention and a thousand dictionary words. That's how we were at the school: very musketeerish (now *that's* not a dictionary word). It really was us against the teachers, and that is why the school was so much fun.

The only blot on the otherwise sunny landscape was ballet. I hated it. I didn't think it was very manly and would do anything to avoid doing it. We had bought our dancing equipment from Barbara Speake's shop, owned by the family, but they didn't have jockstraps. So me Mum had to go elsewhere to get them. She brought them home and put them on the kitchen table.

'But Mum, they're pink satin!'

'Pink?' said Arf with disgust.

'Satin,' I said with more disgust. 'I ain't gonna wear one.'

'You'll 'ave t',' me Mum said. 'They're the proper ones, they are. I checked.'

'If it shows through, I ain't wearing it,' I said.

At our first ballet lesson I gingerly put the offending pink article on and pulled my black tights over it. (Nothing could have induced me to try it on before I really, *really* had to.) And it did show through! I really hated ballet. I ripped off my tights and threw the pink thing in my bag. 'I definitely ain't wearing that, Arf.'

'Jack…' the voice of reason began.

'I don't care Arf, I ain't wearing it and that's final.'

And I didn't. Although in truth I didn't really have that much to support anyway.

Barbara Speake had a contract with the BBC to provide stand-ins for camera rehearsals for the live children's TV series *Crackerjack*. The job wasn't paid, but I was always exceptionally keen to do it. When Miss Speake asked for volunteers my hand went up as fast as a rocket, only matched by Arthur's dog-out-of-a-trap hand-raise. Our eagerness was not to meet the guest stars on the show, or to work with presenters like *the* Leslie Crowther and *the* Peter Glaze, but for the fact that it clashed with ballet.

Just before the summer holidays, you would normally do your ballet exam: either your Grade 1 or 2 or Elementary. I was at Speake's for three years, and I never got above Grade 1. They got so embarrassed because I was still there with all the babies that they ended up pushing me up to Grade 2 anyway.

At the end of the term we'd always do a show, mainly for the parents and families of the kids. More often than not, it would be held at the stage school in the big Hall, and occasionally we'd do it at the local Town Hall in Acton. I always ended up doing either comedy song-and-dance numbers, or comedy sketches. A lot of the time, I worked with Phil Collins and we used to 'do' Peter Cook and Dudley Moore sat at the table having a cup of tea and chatting about what was going on in the world. Phil was Pete and I was Dud. It always seemed to go down well and I really did enjoy doing them. Phil had the same sense of humour as Peter Cook: very dry, he was always great at throwing away comedy lines. We'd found instant rapport and even played Ugly Sisters together.

Although everyone's parents would come along to see the show, we'd never get a lift home with them. We'd want to make our own way home in the evening, by train or bus. We'd take care to walk the side roads: twice the distance, and it took twice as long, but at least we could smoke and not be spotted doing something we weren't supposed to be doing. It was all such fun.

Chapter 3

WHEN I FINALLY REACHED THE AGE OF TWELVE at the end of September 1964, and was old enough to work in the West End, I was asked to go and see *Oliver!* a couple of dozen times to get to know the show. It had already been running for nearly four years. I would go along to the New Theatre in St Martin's Lane with Arf after school. Working on the show we were getting nine pounds a week – my father was earning twelve – and it seemed an incredible amount of money. We would leave our house at 7.30am; one bus, one tube and then another bus would take us to the stage school. After school, another tube would take us to the theatre, and home again by 11.15pm. It gradually dawned on Arf and me (not eighth in the class for nothing) that, although we were earning nine pounds a week, after paying bus and train fares, school fees (forty-five guineas a term) and agent's commission of twenty-five per cent, we were left with less money than we earned doing our milk round!

Still, we were in showbiz now, even though when I first started in *Oliver!* I was still in short trousers. This led to an argument with the guy who was playing Dodger, Leonard Whiting, who later went on to be in Zefferelli's *Romeo and Juliet*. Because he was taller than me (well, everyone was taller than me in them days) he said something detrimental to the fact that I was quite short for my age and I said to him, 'Oi! If you don't shut yer mouth I'll... Come outside and I'll break yer neck!'

Now that's big talk for short trousers.

I was a newcomer to the show and outrageously cocky for my size. Thank God, though, he didn't take me on, because I'm sure he would have mullered me. I might then have been getting a bit too big for me boots, thinking, my brother's here and he'll make sure I don't get hurt; but thankfully it didn't get that far. Lennie just thought, oh, silly old twozzerp, and we ended up not coming to blows or even going outside or anything. I think in those days I was very fortunate in the sense that although I might have been cheeky, I wasn't cheeky *enough* to get a smack in the mouth.

On my opening night of *Oliver!*, all the boys were on stage for beginners – the Workhouse scene – and everyone was wishing each other good luck, when the boy next to me said, 'I'll just tell you one thing, watch out for the red brick.'

'The red brick?' I said.

'Watch out for the red house-brick,' he repeated with emphasis.

'What are you going on about?'

'Well, there's a bloke in the fly tower who will watch everything you do and if you make a mistake he will throw a red house-brick at ya head.'

'Oh, right, thanks,' I said, squinting up at the flies.

So for the whole two-and-a-half hours I stood half watching what I'm supposed to be watching on stage and the other half looking to see if a house brick is coming towards me. Fortunately I don't think I did anything wrong, but if I did I must have got away with it, because I didn't end up with a house brick on my head; though I did have a stiff neck.

On the second night, as we waited for curtain up, I was relieved for not being got on the first night, so I asked the boy, 'Is that geezer with the red brick still up there, waiting for me?'

He started laughing and said, 'No, he only does it for your first night, and if you get over that you're alright.'

In my early days there, I remember innocently whistling in the dressing room, a cardinal sin for actors. A chorus of voices sent me out of the room, told me to run round three times, knock on the door, come back in and swear. Mrs Phelps, one of the chaperones, explained that sailors used to work in the fly towers pulling the ropes heavy with scenery. They communicated by whistles: 'So you should never whistle in a theatre, Jack, in case they bring something in early on ya head.' She knocked my head to emphasise her point and offered me a drag of her Consulate cigarette – she really was the best chaperone. The boys nodded with gravity; this was obviously a serious offence I'd committed. Still, I thought they were all crackers. But they did take the old traditions seriously – odd really, as we didn't take any of the acting on stage half as seriously as these old superstitions.

Clive Green played a workhouse minder. He was older than us and one night when we were waiting to go on he told me, 'Don't go in the prop room because there is a ghost in there.' The prop room was on the opposite side to prompt corner and was more like a long corridor than a room. It ran deep underneath a Victorian alley, lined with junk shops, just off St Martin's Lane.

'Show us where it is then,' I said. I wouldn't be happy until I'd seen this ghost. So the other boys took me down there and we went in.

The room must have been about thirty foot long and about seven foot wide. There were no lights on, but shafts of light shone through these thick pieces of glass in the ceiling. At night, with the street lights on, these beams were broken and changed by the people walking past, casting an eerie light into the room. Clive had told me that an old Victorian actor had hung himself in this room and that you could still see his head in the noose. I *felt* as though everyone went in there with me, but the next minute the door behind me closed. I was in there all alone, in pitch black, expecting a ghost to come out from nowhere any minute and kill me.

I was released from certain death by a desperate assistant stage manager. 'You should be on stage *now*!'

I flew onto the safety of the stage for the second Thieves' Kitchen scene in Act 2. It was a favourite scene of us boys. It ended with Fagin, played by Aubrey Woods – a respected actor with a CV as long as your arm – counting his money and 'reviewing the situation'. It was a quiet, introspective scene which we destroyed by having farting contests. We would put farting powder in each other's tea and when we were supposed to be asleep, all you would hear was these farts going off right, left and centre, mixed with stifled giggles. Some boys could even fart on cue and didn't need the powder!

After the show there would be a contrite procession of boys followed by a battle-worn stage manager to Dressing Room No. 1 – 'Sorry Mr Woods, must have been somefink we ate,' we'd say – and then, worst of all, early calls as punishment rehearsals. We hated that because we would rather be out creating havoc just around the corner in Covent Garden, our playground.

We'd often go to Covent Garden and have fights with rival gangs that lived in the high-rise flats just off the Strand. We'd use the rotting fruit and veg from the market as ammunition. We never ever had any proper fisticuffs at all, but we had loads and loads of battles with the mouldy remains. The traders and sellers tried to keep it tidy for the dustman, but it was far too much fun to resist, and rotten flesh designated our cobbled battlefield. 'Bugger off!' a trader yelled, calling us every name she could lay her tongue to. But we paid no heed – it was like an over-ripe tomato off a ruffian's back.

Round the corner, every corner, there would be gangs of entrepreneurs/ conmen/crooks. They worked the three-card trick: Find the Lady. Punters walked past and bet as to where the Queen was. They had look-outs keeping an eye out for any policeman. We watched them wait until a tourist had put a lot of money down. Then one of the look-outs would shout out 'Coppers!' One person would grab the cards, another would grab the money, someone would grab the table and they would disappear into the crowd leaving a bereft and somewhat poorer punter. We thought it would be funny to wind them up a bit, so we'd sit and watch them and shout out 'Coppers' and they would seize hold of their cards and run like hell. I'm sure they would have given us a right battering if they caught us, but we never hung about to find out.

On Tuesdays and Saturdays, matinee days, we weren't allowed out of the theatre between shows. If any of us wanted food, only one of us was allowed to go and bring some back for the rest from the local Wimpy. At weekends we'd meet up early (the afternoon shows didn't go up till 4.30), sometimes at Hyde Park, and hire some rowing boats. Because there were twelve of us we would have three or four boats, and then we would go and find some other kids and surround them in our boats and soak them.

'Here, let's go and feed the pigeons in Trafalgar Square!' someone said, and we were off on another adventure. We'd buy sixpence-worth of birdseed from the bird man, squeezed into his cubicle in the middle of the Square. They had lived side by side for so long that the man had the look of the pigeons, and the pigeons had the look of the man; their round, over-fed bellies contributing to their family likeness. The old geezer had been there for years making a good living from the tourists and the pigeons jostling and flapping around his stall. With *our* tin of seed we would gradually, inch by inch, entice the pigeons away. The crumpled man would go bloody mad, as his punters drifted away because there weren't any pigeons to feed. We took the birds up the Square to just outside the National Gallery. We'd then walk them all the way up the steps and all the way along until the man, freed from his cubicle, came chasing after us, skating and sliding in the pigeon muck. 'I'll get you little bleeders! I know where you're from! I'll get you, don't think I won't...' his voice trailing off on the wind as we made our escape.

One night when it had been drizzling, we had all arranged to get to the theatre before six o'clock, so we had a good hour as the show didn't go up until 7.30. We decided we were going to go to St James's Park and were running through Trafalgar Square, and because of all the pigeon shit it was very slippy underfoot. We were running through as quick as we could, I went arse over tit in my school uniform and was covered head to foot with pigeon shit. Me Mum was coming to pick me up that night to go home so I needed to get clean before then. I went back to the theatre to sort myself out and left the other lads to create mayhem in the park. In St James's we'd hide, shout out 'rape' and pretend someone was being battered to death in the bushes. We'd wait to see what reactions we would get from passers-by, although the majority of people didn't take any notice whatsoever. It was a shame to miss that, but I had to try and clean all this crap off my clothes. I did my best and think I got away with it; I'm sure the pigeons had a good laugh.

At the theatre, by the time of the half-hour call, all the boys had to be in on the dot. One Saturday, we'd had an hour on the boats in Hyde Park, soaked however many people and spoiled somebody's fishing, and we were running a bit late. Usually, we'd go back to Knightsbridge tube station and, if a train was there, whoever got down onto the platform first would hold the door until everybody got in. This one afternoon, as we were coming up the platform, we could hear there was a train in, so everybody was shouting, 'Get a move on, get on the train! We're late!'

We were flying down the escalator and if anyone had got in the way they would have been floored as we were all so close together. The first person who jumped on the tube tripped and everyone else went flying, and we all landed on top of each other. Everybody was on the deck, a pile of bodies with the door closing just as the last boy landed in. An anguished cry went out from somewhere in the middle of 'You've broke my last cigarette!' As we were under sixteen we paid half fare on the underground, but most of us smoked, which you weren't meant to do under sixteen. As we had children's tickets, we couldn't say 'I'm old enough to smoke' if we got caught. So anyone who wasn't a smoker (and there weren't that many), would always do a look-out for any guards. After the pile-up everyone was moaning because they had smashed their fags, and as the lookout was at the bottom of the pile he failed to see the approaching guard.

Around Bonfire Night our battles with the Covent Garden Gang took on mega proportions with banger fights. We'd put bangers in rotten fruit and throw them. It was hard to keep them in the fruit and they would sometimes fly out in the air, but it seemed as though we were having a proper war. After one great battle, we made a pincer movement through the arcades, where somebody picked up a small box of fireworks, and we went to a park for a display. The park was surrounded by factories, businesses, and a small paint store. We started off lighting the Roman Candles and Catherine Wheels – the bangers we kept for gang warfare – and all too soon we were only left with a couple of rockets. We looked around for old bottles or oil cans or something to launch them in, but none were about. Then somebody suggested we put a rocket on the bottom of a kids' slide pointing upwards, 'and with a bit of luck it will go up the slide and take off'. We thought this was a brilliant idea, but the first one we tried was a measly effort; it got just enough power to go up to the top of the slide, but then packed up, slipping back down again, shamefacedly. So we thought: if we do it with a bigger one, with that much more power, it will definitely take off. I think we only had two so this was our second to last chance to get it right. Excited hands placed it, received advice, and replaced it, received more advice, 'Sod off – I'm doing it,' and replaced it again.

Then we all stood silently, respectfully, waiting for it to go off. And it didn't even bloody move. Then all of a sudden it just went *whoosh* and although it didn't go a massive way up, it did get airborne; and with all the precision of an Exocet missile it gracefully arced in through an open window of the paint factory. If we'd wanted to do that, we couldn't have done it in a month of Sundays. A moment's euphoria was extinguished by all-consuming fear. 'It's gonna blow!' 'Run!' We ran like hell back to the theatre, never stopping, never looking back.

We agreed in urgent whispers that, just in case, we'd better stay away from the scene of the crime for at least three months. In the meantime we would try to find out through local papers if there was anything about a paint factory, or an explosion, fires, or plans for penal servitude for the perpetrators. We never found out anything and soon forgot it, but at the time we were absolutely terrified.

There were and still are a lot of strip clubs in Soho, not far from the theatre, and we would have wagers: whoever could get in the strip club and into the cinema or the actual room where the strippers were performing, whoever was the first one to do that, would win a fiver, half a week's earnings. No one ever got past the front door. I tried but my bottle went – I didn't even get as far as the kiosk to pay. I was terrified of being caught. You had to be over eighteen to get in there. Even when I *was* eighteen I only looked ten so I had no chance, did I?

At Christmas time, we decided we would try and earn some money for Dr Barnardo's. I don't know what gave us the idea, but with us playing orphans we thought it appropriate. We'd stand outside Leicester Square tube station and sing carols. We never had a sign saying 'We're Fagin's Gang, all donations to Dr Barnardo's' or anything like that; we just stood there with a bucket and started singing. When punters asked us where we were from we'd say, 'We're in the stage show of *Oliver!*' and this seemed to make a huge difference to our income. So much so that when we advertised it, our takings quadrupled. We sang our hearts out to such an extent that a lot of us started to get sore throats and lose our voices. So when the theatre found out, they stopped us doing it.

We did do it the following year. This time we were more organised and got placards saying we are the *Oliver!* boys, and that all proceeds were going to Dr

Barnardo's. We did raise quite a bit of money, until we were discovered and stopped again by the theatre.

When Arf, me and Phil started back for our second year in *Oliver!* all the teachers from Speake's sent a card to the three of us. This time, Arf went back in as Oliver – the first dark-haired boy to play the title role and an extra three quid a week – and I went back to play Charlie Bates, Dodger's right-hand man. I really wanted to play Dodger, but I was a very tiny child; I'm not much bigger now. I wasn't tall enough to play the part as they would never be able to find an Oliver smaller than me. But Phil played the part and he was great, really charismatic and the first blonde Dodger I think.

Still, I'd reached Charlie Bates, the highest you could get. The order of rank was, you started in the show as one of the boys and after the first three months you were given more when they saw how good you were and what bits you were suited to. Whoever was the cutest and smallest would be given the job of 'laugh and cry' and 'the lates'. 'The lates' was in Fagin's Gang and whenever we were going anywhere this person would always be the last. In 'Be Back Soon' 'the lates' would be kicked up the bum by Fagin to get a move on. Also, during the 'Pick a Pocket' number he would get caught stealing from Fagin and then get told off for getting caught.

The 'laugh and cry' was one scene in the second half where Mr Bumble and Widow Corney are arguing about what has happened to Oliver. During this, a workhouse boy sees Mr B being told off by Widow C and starts laughing and pointing at him. On seeing this, Mr B would turn round and clip him one round the ear and immediately the boy would walk off crying.

When I was doing 'laugh and cry' one night I got a round of applause for it. I felt on top of the world. The boys took the piss because it had never happened before, but I didn't care; and looking back on it I think this was the moment that the adrenalin rush set me on the path that I was to follow. Up until that point I could have walked away.

The other career path in the show was from boy to 'books' – to my eyes a rather serious and boring part of giving books to Mr Brownlow with no opportunities for getting a round. Arthur did 'books' after a couple of months of starting and then he went on to play Oliver. I never wanted to play Oliver, I always had my sights set on Dodger. Still, playing Charlie Bates I was one up in the pecking order – no more money but a named character in the programme. And, most importantly, individual recognition from the audience.

''Ere Fagin, these sausages are mouldy.'

'Shut up and drink your gin.'

Reaction, audience laugh, job done.

The set had two sections either side of the stage that would go forward and back and stop at certain positions during the show. There was also a revolve in the centre that turned around to change the scenery. Now, come the second half of the show, these things either side would hit a certain mark, and a section would come down and rest upon them, creating an imposing London Bridge, solid enough for people to walk across. So of course, we would try and stop it. We'd try to jam the thing that went forward and back, by stuffing in our shoes or what have you. One particular night, we succeeded and so when the bridge came down, it wasn't as solid as it should be. I heard Sean Kenny, the designer, had said, 'Actors should not have to stop acting while something changes on the set,' but perhaps he should have said, 'The set shouldn't have to stop for the actors...' Anyway, a few small boys had just wedged London Bridge. Come the finale, all the boys would come down singing 'Food, Glorious Food' followed by 'Consider Yourself'. We'd take our bow and then run either side, up the stairs and sit on the now precarious London Bridge with our feet dangling over the side. So we're sat there, and the next song after everyone's taken a bow is 'I'd Do Anything' sung by Oliver to Bet. Everyone would join in and we'd be swaying from side to side on the bridge. This was obviously too much for it and the bridge decided to tilt forward, throwing us off, and a cascade of boys landed on the stage twelve foot below. Thankfully, only one person was injured; and he only got a broken shoulder blade or something.

A few weeks later, me and Arf were told to go to Mr Woods' dressing room and we assumed we were in trouble again; but instead, he asked us whether we were members of Equity. Apparently he thought we would go far and that we should join the union. Because we respected him, we did. Later, when we told Miss Speake and Mrs Collins they weren't pleased at all.

'You shouldn't have done that without speaking to us first,' they said. I couldn't understand why they were so upset.

Then one Saturday night in November we were doing the scene where Bill Sikes has just killed Nancy. Sikes is trying to escape with Oliver and he's on his way back to Fagin's to try and get some money from him. I was in Fagin's Den on stage, waiting to open the door when he bangs on it to be allowed in because he's being chased by the police. After that, every night, he would climb up the set out of sight of the audience, and the Bow Street Runner would fire his pistol and shoot him. Then the ASM would throw this fake body down. So, I'm waiting in there, in the dark; and the next minute, this body falls in front of me and automatically I thought, they've dropped the body of Bill Sikes too early. But they hadn't. It was the actor who played Mr Grimwig, Claude Jones, who'd had a cardiac and fallen in front of me. He'd been in the show since it opened, an actor all his life and about the same age as me Grandad. They dragged him off stage and the show went on. 'Let me in, Fagin, let me in!'

In the wings his heart stopped, an ambulance was called, they got him back to life, but he actually died before they got him to hospital.

The show finished and I went home. I felt guilty for not having done anything other than look at the body. I didn't know quite what I should have done, but I felt I should have done something.

Chapter 4

A T THE STAGE SCHOOL, YOU'D GO IN, you'd have assembly, you would sing one hymn and then, after the assembly had finished, there would be an announcement as to who was having auditions that day. All your names would be read out and what time you were going, and that would be the first we'd hear about it. Afterwards you went to the office for details. We were told to always have some money ready: half a crown. It was either given to Mrs Collins in the agency or you carried it on you at all times. It was more than enough for you to travel into London from the school, do your audition and get back. I'd say that a week wouldn't go by without me attending a couple of auditions, at least. I never really got nervous before them because I thought, this is all a bloody giggle this, it's all a joke. I'm getting paid to do something that I enjoy so much that it's insane! How can everybody not want to do this?

Our contracts for *Oliver!* were for nine months split into three twelve-week periods. After every twelve weeks you would have three weeks' rest and then after the nine months was up, you would have to wait another twelve weeks before you could go back on stage. In my rest weeks from the stage, I started doing small parts on TV: *Dr Finlay's Casebook* in a really tiny studio at Hammersmith Riverside (that was my first break), an early *Z Cars*, when they still went out live, and all manner of commercials.

I would sometimes even do a TV while working on the stage show as well, so long as they didn't coincide with matinee days and I could get to the theatre on time. I'd finish the telly by 5pm and get to the theatre by seven, and then I'd do that as well. Most of my work was for the BBC, including things like *I'm Talking About Jerusalem*. It was part of a big trilogy of Wesker plays the BBC were doing at the time, but I don't really remember it: it was just another little telly job. And of course if I didn't have any work, I'd be trying to catch up at school.

'Here's a nice letter for your scrapbook,' Mrs Collins said warmly one day when I was back at Speake's. 'Oh thanks,' I said. I didn't have a scrapbook, but I stuffed it in my pocket anyway, without much of a glance. I didn't mean to be flash, but to be honest I got quite a few letters of commendation from directors saying how well I'd behaved and performed. So it got to the point where I didn't really take much notice of them.

'You might want to look more closely at this,' Miss Speake said rather less warmly, handing me my school report.

'Oh, and Jack,' Mrs Collins added, 'you got that commercial for Kunzle Cakes, well done.'

Well, two out of three, that's not bad, I thought; and anyway, my report probably wouldn't be that bad. They usually said the same thing:

Jack has the ability for work but is absent so much…

and *Jack has worked well in the few classes that he has attended*

or *A little erratic this term – possibly through tiredness.*

I stuffed it in my pocket as well and contemplated the cake commercial. At least that sounded positive. I normally did commercials for food that I didn't like. Once I'd done one for Bird's Eye Garden Peas. In Manchester we'd never had garden peas as they were too expensive: we just had processed peas instead. So I spent all day eating those garden peas and I hated them because I was so used to the cheap ones. I guess I must have been a bloody good actor to eat those; I'd have taken a letter of commendation for that!

Another one was for Heinz soup. There was a whole series of adverts where you'd have a little kid swinging from side to side like a pendulum to the tune of 'It's a Heinz Super Day, Heinz Super Day, Heinz Super Day!' and that was it. And one time, it was me. The only soup I liked in those days was tomato. And what did I get? Mushroom soup! I had to sit there all day eating mushroom soup. I hated mushrooms! Or was it chicken? Actually it might have been chicken, but I hated both of them. And it was one of them definitely!

So I was cautiously looking forward to Kunzle Cakes. It was to be shot over two or three days at a studio in West Drayton. When I got there, however, I discovered these cakes were all made with marzipan. I hate marzipan! I've never liked marzipan and I never will. I spent all morning eating them. And of course the director said, not unreasonably, 'Make it look as though you're enjoying it please.'

By lunchtime, I was desperate for a cigarette and something to take the taste away. My chaperone took me out of the studio, and we were eventually lucky enough to find a pub that did food and would allow in children. I had a quick fag while the chaperone ordered, and then a double egg and chips; it tasted like paradise!

The next day I was back at school rehearsing a number with three lads that we'd done before, at an end of term concert. Mrs Collins had found out about an audition for *Opportunity Knocks* and suggested we put our number to good use and do it again for Hughie Green. So the four of us – me, Phil Collins, Danny Grover and Phil Harris – ended up giggling our way through a rehearsal for it.

'Come on boys, *Opportunity Knocks* has twelve million viewers, you know?' Mrs Collins said, trying to instil a sense of order.

It was a song from *Maggie May*, Lionel Bart's other musical that was playing at the Adelphi when we were in *Oliver!* at the New Theatre. A comedy song called 'Same Size Boots', where you had a tall guy, a short guy, a thin guy and a fat guy and we'd all change clothes while we were singing. Everybody would then end up in clothes that didn't fit them and hopefully look hysterical! We thought it was a great song and it always went down well.

Op Knocks was filmed outside Manchester, at an old theatre in Didsbury, and of course because my parents had worked up there they let everybody in the mills know that we were going to be on, so they could vote for us. In those days there wasn't a phone-in, you just had to write in and the results were announced the following week. As far as we were concerned we'd got as many people in Royton as in Hounslow to vote for us, but we still didn't get anywhere near winning. We came in second place to Tony Holland, who won six weeks in a row and flexed his muscles to music! From what I remember, he seemed a very nice guy; but if you come second to *that* where the hell do you go next in this business? You might as well give it up as a bad job!

Still, we had another go with it on *Stubby's Silver Star Show* which was the only other talent show on TV at the time. The well-known American song-and-dance man Stubby Kaye hosted the show, although I'd never heard of him back then. I later found out that he was very popular in the States and had done lots of shows and movies, like *Guys and Dolls* and the movie of *Li'l Abner* with Billie Hayes. We still felt it was all a giggle really: if we won, great, and if we didn't, on to the next job that came up. Well, we didn't win! We came second *again*, in the grand final (after winning our heat) but this time it was to a guy who played the guitar and sang 'King of the Road'. At least he was an entertainer and not a geezer with big muscles!

Whenever I wasn't on stage, I was always doing TV, and the majority of them were bit parts. I might only have one scene with half a dozen lines, or if I had two scenes I'd have three lines in each or something like that. Because I did so many, I remember very few of them. I was sent a fan letter a while back from a guy who was doing some research on the writer Sir Arthur Conan Doyle. He sent me a cutting from the *Radio Times* about me playing the part of Jackie Finch in one of his stories called *The Black Doctor*. This was probably at Riverside or Lime Grove, but I don't remember where it was done – I don't remember doing it at all...

'So lads, what's the play about then?' It was some interviewer for the *Radio Times*. There were always interviews and publicity that you had to do for these things, except this one I was doing with my brother Arf.

'Well, em, it's about two boys...' I tentatively began.

'It's about two boys and they never 'ave much money an' they wanted some, 'cos they never 'ad an 'oliday...' Arf continued in an older brother sort of way. We were actually playing brothers who torment an old lady in *A Game, Like, Only a Game*. It was the first big part that I'd done on telly really and the first time me and Arf had worked for the BBC together.

'And so how did you get the parts?' the interviewer continued. I couldn't really remember. I couldn't remember auditioning for it; maybe we'd just been asked. I'd worked for the director a couple of times before, so maybe he did just ask for us, I reasoned.

'And you're brothers in real life, aren't you, lads; so how is it, working together?' the interviewer dared.

'Well, we did *Oliver!* together in the West End,' Arf said, 'so it's nothing new.'

'But are you enjoying working on the show?' the interviewer persisted, turning to me. 'Have there been any problems at all?'

'Well,' I said, 'the chips served in the studios are always cold.'

The truth was we did have arguments, quite sophisticated ones, like 'Shut up, I'm the older brother' from Arf and 'Shut up, just 'cos you're older doesn't mean you know everything' from me. Just bickering really. If anything we argued less on the set because we were working. It was one thing that had been instilled in us from day one at the stage school: it is imperative that you behave like a professional. Not behave like an adult, but behave like a professional actor. And that meant showing respect to everyone and everybody. I had the same attitude with Arthur as I did with anyone else I was working with. He weren't any different: he was just a fellow worker.

The woman who was playing our mum was an actress called Shelagh Fraser and she was very, very positive about me and Arthur. She was the most friendly out of everybody in the show and we got on really well and kept in contact with her afterwards. Again, we had a letter from Christopher Morahan, the director, saying how pleased he was with both me and Arf, and the reviews after the broadcast said our portrayal of the deprived and depraved boys was wholly convincing!

Money *was* short but we certainly weren't deprived at home. Me Dad worked at Firestone Tyres on the Great West Road in Brentford, and me Mum worked in a shop; but, probably because they'd made this massive move to come to live in London, money was still tight. In actual fact, me Dad wasn't earning that much more than me, but they didn't take any of mine or Arf's money; they always said that we shouldn't waste our money but should try and save it for a rainy day. As soon as we started working, Mum and Dad took us both down to open a building society account. I think, in those days, you couldn't have a bank account until you were sixteen. They set us up so we could put in whatever amount we had, although I must admit, we didn't in the first two years, as we barely covered all our expenses and fees. We certainly didn't go into any losses, because we would've had to give up stage school had we done that; me Mum and Dad couldn't afford to pay for us.

We went to a building society right outside Hounslow Central tube station and I felt very adult of course, because none of my friends had accounts. I'm not sure how me Dad felt about me earning so much money; I never asked him that so I don't know. My Mum and Dad never discussed how they felt about us working, and working with people that they saw regularly on telly. They never ever said what they felt about it, but would just ask: 'Do you get on well with everyone?'... 'Is the director pleased with you?'... 'Are you doing as you're told?'... and the timeless, 'Are you behaving yourself?'

'Well, as long as you boys are being good and you're happy...' me Mum said, adding with a grin: 'And anyway, Jackie, I'll see for meself on Saturday.'

Mum was going to chaperone me for this particular drama. Not for the rehearsals because she was working at the shop, but for the actual studio days at the BBC Television Centre. She'd been in a TV studio before to see me do *Opportunity Knocks* and *Stubby Kaye*, but this was her first time in to see a drama being made. It was about this scientist who believed that he could make his plants bigger and better by injecting them with different concoctions of chemicals, and I played the part of the boy who lived next door. The scientist injected the plants so that they looked a bit like a triffid, or really like overgrown tomato plants; and instead of them needing water to live, they would eat flesh! He fed the plants diced rabbits and massive doses of vitamins, and they would catch cats, or dogs, or birds.

The show, which starred Milo O'Shea (a lovely Irish actor, a fantastic actor actually) was called *Come Buttercup, Come Daisy, Come ...?* and was part of a series called *Out of the Unknown*. Mr O'Shea played the scientist, and I sat on the garden wall with my catapult firing at things in his garden; and of course one of these plants bloody grabs hold of me, and has a go at me, and tries to eat me.

Mum had looked at the script two weeks before. 'A comedy with a chilling edge,' she'd read out. 'I can see what it says, Jackie, but I just can't imagine how it'll look.' And now here she was, going to see it being made, and she thought it was hysterical. She giggled her way through it as she sat and watched 'all those big grown-up men, Jackie' crawling around on the floor, pulling strings to make these plants look menacing. When I was doing my scene, the stage-hands seemed to have at least a dozen different pieces of string on each hand and they were pulling them like mad to make these weird plants attack me; me Mum loved it.

The other thing me Mum loved were these couple of Chihuahua dogs that were in it as well, and they also got eaten. We'd never had dogs in our family and me Mum thought they were really cute. A lady called Barbara Woodhouse looked after the dogs and me Mum fell in love with them. When we got home, she told me Dad and Arf, 'If ever we have a dog, then we'll have to have a chihuahua.'

And for once me, Arf and me Dad were in agreement and we said as one, 'That's a lady's dog, that is!'

'It's alright for you to have it, Mum, but we don't want to walk down the street taking it for a walk,' Arf added. 'We'd feel awful.'

'If we want a dog, we want a nice big 'un,' I said.

We ended up getting a Yorkshire terrier: exactly the same size as a chihuahua only it had long hair. So that was that.

Doing *Out of the Unknown* was the first time I'd ever had to have any sort of serious make-up, and what *I* loved about the show was seeing how it was done. I enjoyed all the attention of an extra hour in make-up as both of my legs were covered in horrific wounds created by this bloody triffid. I was fascinated to watch them build up the skin with a plasticine-type gel; and the finished product made it look as if this plant had cut me in ribbons, as though it had a knife or something.

As soon as I saw it on though, the first thing I wanted to do was pick, pick, pick, pick, but you can't because someone has spent an hour and a half putting this bit of wax on your leg to make it look like an injury and it's more than that, it's a sculpture! And there's me seeing it, and wanting to go 'Aaaghhhhh! get it off!' and make blood come out from here, there and everywhere. The discipline of not playing with it was immense. I thought it looked quite cool. I sat and watched this thing appear on my leg and I knew out and out it's not real, but to all intents and purposes it looked like 'My God, he's got a bad gash there, have you got a bandage to put on that?' I did feel a bit like a war hero type, but who in the hell would go home and say they've been attacked by a tomato plant? That doesn't really sound very butch does it?

One show that I thought might carry a bit more kudos was *Z Cars*. I remember vividly one episode I did, as I got to hold a real gun. It was a twelve-bore shotgun and I thought I was John Wayne. I couldn't wait to tell the boys in my street when I got home.

'I held a gun today that could kill someone. It could kill anything. It could kill an elephant!' (Now that was better than a triffid.)

I waited expectantly, but they stood in silence kicking imaginary stones until one of them said, 'Are we playing football or ain't we?'

Well, if they weren't impressed with the gun, there was no point in telling them that I'd worked with James Ellis, a lovely guy, and a guy that everyone would have seen on telly because *Z Cars* was such a popular police soap.

'Yeah,' I said somewhat deflatedly, 'yeah, let's play football.'

Chapter 5

TOWARDS THE END OF MARCH 1966 I went for an audition for the Children's Film Foundation, and I got it. It was to do a film serial called *Danny the Dragon*. It was about this spaceship that lands on Earth and this dragon pops out and creates havoc. These three children find the dragon, befriend it, and try to stop it from being killed, harmed or caged depending on the perils of that particular week. It was nearly a four-month job, including the whole of June, July and August. It was going to be shot on 35mm, so a proper film; and I remember it because it was in the year that England won the World Cup.

At the time of the audition, however, I still had another six months to do in *Oliver!*, so I was told by the agency, 'We need to get you out of your contract, Jack,' and I was told to go to my local doctor and get a medical certificate.

'So what's going to be wrong with you then?' Mrs Collins cheerfully asked.

I tried to think of some debilitating, heroic disease, devastating but temporary in nature.

'I get a bit of eczema behind my knees,' I volunteered apologetically. 'But I do pick it until it bleeds,' I added proudly.

'Oh Jack, you shouldn't, but that'll do nicely,' Mrs Collins chastised and rewarded me in one sentence. 'Let's see how we get on with that.'

'Well ya see doctor, the trousers that I wear on stage, they finish right at the knee and they rub against my eczema,' I said, becoming less and less convinced that this was the best ailment to be presenting, 'and you know, it's a bit painful like...' I trailed off lamely.

'I think it would be better if you left the show then, so how about if I give you a medical note which will cover you?'

It was as easy as that.

'Oh Jackie,' me Mum whispered as we left the surgery, 'it's not right.'

But it was for *Saturday morning pictures*! Me and my mates always went to Saturday morning pictures, every week, and we had seen Batman and Robin, Superman, Rocket Man, and now we would see me!

'Yeah, but Mrs Collins said it would all be alright,' I insisted.

'You weren't brought up to fib, Jackie,' she said, frowning, as she bent her tiny frame around her cigarette to light it.

I just thought it was all a laugh.

We shot *Danny the Dragon* on location in and around Surrey: Esher, Oxshott, the River Wey and all that sort of area. One of the crew would pick me up in his Land Rover and take me to a place just off the A3 called West End village. I thought it was mad because instead of Leicester Square and Shaftesbury Avenue *this* West End was in the middle of Esher and it was gorgeous. It was your typical village really; the roads weren't busy, and there was a massive pond in the middle of this big, big green. You had a pub, a post office, a sweet shop, a church, and that was it. That was the village and it was so, so, quaint.

On the way to West End, we'd pick up my chaperone, Mrs Layton, one of the teachers from Speake's. I liked her and thought she was great. If the kids messed around, or made a noise in her class, I would stand up on the front desk and shout 'Shut up! The teacher's trying to teach!' I don't know if she found this helpful. Her husband was in show business too and managed the singer Dickie Valentine (a big-name star who would occasionally come to the end-of-term shows).

So, me and Mrs Layton would travel down to Oxshott in this open-back Land Rover. I'd either sit in the back in the sun, with the wind blowing on my face, or I'd sit in the cab with Mrs Layton and change the gears for the driver. It was bloody brilliant, it was.

Apart from the eponymous dragon, the main characters in the serial were these three kids, two boys and a girl. The other boy, Chris Cooper, was from Speake's, so I already knew him. He was in the same class as me and had done *Oliver!*. And the girl was Sally Thomsett, whom I didn't know.

The adults included Peter Butterworth who played a farmer, afraid of a Martian invasion. He was such a funny man who'd done loads of *Carry On* movies. Apparently he'd started acting as a POW in World War Two. Another *Carry On* star, Kenneth Connor, did the voice of the dragon; and Frank Thornton played the police sergeant, who gets blown up by fireworks and stuck on a bike that goes backwards. There was a lot of visual humour in

Danny the Dragon, very much like Charlie Chaplin, Marx Brothers type comedy, with lots of chases and things like that. There was also the constable, who kept putting on lots of daft disguises, played by a big, big guy with a moustache, called Patrick Newell.

A few years later I became friends with him, about the time when he was playing 'Mother' in *The Avengers*. We used to go out and meet and have drinks down by Teddington Studios. But at the time of *Danny* these people were well respected and very successful actors in comparison with any of us kids so we held great respect for them and treated them as they should be treated.

We did ten episodes, each one 17 minutes. We were very well-dressed kids in the film and the clothes we were given to wear for each episode were like your Sunday best; only we had to wear them all the time! *And*, we all had brand-new bicycles given to us as props. I'd never ridden a new bike before, and this had gears and all sorts, much better than my manky one at home. *It* just got me from A to B without having to walk, but that was it really. We did a lot of riding in the film, which was great fun. I did one scene where the dragon gives me the power to go super-fast on the bike, so I ended up riding mine a lot more than Chris and Sally.

One lunchtime, however, I found out that Chris was having more fun than me. He had been having secret driving lessons with the Second Assistant, Eamonn; he was a lovely Irish guy, maybe fifteen years older than us, and he'd been teaching Chris to drive in his green Mini. As soon as I found this out I said to Chris, 'Why didn't you tell me? I want to learn to drive!'

'Well ask him then,' he said rather pragmatically.

So I did, and amazingly he said yes. We were on the shoot for a long while, a lot of it off any main roads and on private property, so I couldn't get into trouble for driving; '… and if a police car turned up, they wouldn't be able to do ya, so it was okay,' I said to me Mum that night.

'I'll show you what to do,' Eammon said the next day at work, 'then you sit in the car and practise at lunchtimes for the next week, and then the following week I'll take you out and we'll see how you do.'

'Magic!' I said. I was well into this. I thought, I'll be able to drive by the time I finish this job! I was well into Formula One and all that business and I thought I'd be the new Stirling Moss.

I kept practising just in a stationary car, and when D-Day came the following week I said, 'Look, can I? Today's the day!'

'Let me have my lunch,' he said, 'and you have yours, and then we'll have a go along the lane!'

And it was just a dirt track so, off we go.

'Have you got it in first gear?'

'Yeah,' I said.

'Right,' he said. 'Slightly rev your accelerator and slowly lift your foot off the clutch.'

So I did that and I started with a bit of a jerk.

'Okay. Now, put your foot on the clutch and put it into second.'

So I did that, but he didn't say take your foot off the clutch. And so I'm not doing anything; I'm just revving the engine.

'Take your foot off the clutch!' he said.

But I got so sort of stressed and panicked about the situation that I looked down at me feet and said, 'What am I gonna do?'

The car was obviously still going, but I was looking at the floor, and we careered off the road and hit a tree. Well, maybe not *careered* as we were only doing about ten miles an hour, but we certainly left the road and definitely hit a tree!

I think we were both a bit surprised, and we just sat there for a minute. And then I began to feel so, so bad because I'd done damage to his car, and *then* I thought, it's gonna cost me a fortune! I'll probably have to pay everything I'm earning on this job to fix his car for him.

But he didn't go mad at all. He just laughed it off, totally accepting the situation and didn't have a go and didn't even charge me a penny. I think he just put it down to a bad day at work, because of me.

That was the end of my driving lessons. I hadn't the cheek to ask him again. I headed off into the bushes so I could have a cigarette and calm myself down a bit. I took two or three cigarettes to work with me every day, and would find somewhere to hide and have them. It was such a hot summer, however, so I had to be careful with dropping matches and all that because the place would go up in two seconds flat! I felt the day had been bad enough, without starting a fire as well.

It wasn't long before Chris found me. 'I hear you had an accident,' he said laughing.

'You ain't exactly Stirling Moss,' I said.

'Well, at least I did better than you did!' he said. 'Come on!'

And we headed off to play at the lake. When we weren't working we'd either play at the lake or in the haystacks where we'd make hide-outs with these bales of hay and play hide and seek. I used to suffer from hay fever really badly, but I didn't let that stop me and left with streaming eyes.

Sally didn't come with us. I don't remember her playing with us that much. I don't think she was that interested in us, and I don't think we were that interested in her. Sally just seemed to want to keep out of our way, and so we treated her like a sister, and kept out of *her* way.

After the lake we headed back to the unit and I realised that even if Eamonn wasn't going to give me a hard time about the car, I was still mad at myself. I shouldn't have allowed myself to get distracted, I thought. I comforted myself with the thought that it obviously weren't meant to be for this particular time, so, not to worry, I'll just leave it. But I'd lost a bit of faith in myself. Still, on the way back I saw a gold-crested newt – *a gold-crested newt!* So at least that was something positive.

Coincidentally, during filming, the news was full of the NASA Gemini missions; Gemini 8 had in fact ended soon after we started shooting. The mission had gained quite a bad reputation as a few had failed during testing and others had got problems straight after take-off. This was a challenge for the two astronauts, Neil Armstrong and David Scott; and our space traveller was equally tested, albeit in more modest terms. Jack Le White was the space-hopping dragon, and his biggest problem was the weight of the dragon suit. This, coupled with the heaviest boots imaginable, and filming perilously close to the River Wey, was not a happy combination. We worked hard to keep him well away from the watery perils and, as he couldn't see very well either, we would double-check before each take, in case a branch had fallen in his path that may trip him up and catapult him into the river. A further indignity was that the smoke that he puffed out of his nostrils was the sort used to get bees out of hives, and it stank.

My challenge was to climb up a rope to a window, at the top of a barn, about twenty feet up. (I was trying to get into the dragon's invisible space bubble!) Nowadays, I don't mind as much whether people like me or not, but I did then; so, trying to be flash, I said I would do my own stunt.

'Do you think you can?' the director asked.

'Yes, course I can,' I assured him with more confidence than was entirely sensible.

'Well, show us before we film it then,' he suggested cautiously.

Someone showed me how to hang on to the rope, and I set off, thinking I was James Bond. But I could only get so far and no further because I couldn't hold my own body weight. So then they showed me a foot thing which enabled me to hang on properly. Oh that's better, I thought, and I shot right up to the top.

'That's it Jack, great. Now down you come.'

But on the way down, flushed with success, my feet got out of time with my hands, and I slipped down the last ten foot, whilst still holding on.

'Are you all right Jack?' the director asked, looking at my hands. 'Oh Jack, that's a nasty burn.'

As I was trying to be James Bond, I couldn't show anyone the pain and just said, 'Nah, I'm all right, I can carry on.'

He was such a nice man, the director, Pennington Richards. He'd been in films and TV for years, having started as a cameraman, so he really knew the business. He asked me to talk posher and pronounce my 't's. That was alright as we'd done elocution at Speake's. He just made you feel that you were in charge of your performance and gave you such confidence; he was a lovely man.

They put plasters on my hands so I could do it again, and a safety wire on my back as there were no stand-ins. This time, I had to cup my hands a bit so the plasters didn't show when they shot the close-up.

And this time it went much better.

'Well done, Jack,' the director said at the end of the take; and I was exceedingly pleased.

It really was a fantastic job. As we travelled back to Hounslow in the Land Rover that night, the sun was still warm, I had half a fag left in my pocket, and I felt great. I couldn't be happier, I really couldn't.

Chapter 6

I N THE AUTUMN I DID A TELLY called *The Other Fella*, a few days on a soap called *The Newcomers* and went back to the school. Because I'd spent the summer outside in the open, me arms were like really, really brown and the girls at school said, 'Cor! Look at your tan!' I thought, oh, I'm well in here. This is really great! I'd never had that sort of attention before. Mostly, all girls wanted to do was cuddle me like a baby. But now I was fourteen.

Then one cold morning in January 1967 Miss Speake read out the auditions list. 'There's auditions today for Robert Bartlett, Peter Bartlett, Arthur Wild, Jack Wild...' ('Give us a fag for the trip, Arf?' I whispered) '... Kim Smith, Billy Smith, Robert Langley...' And so we all collected our half crowns which we kept at school for travel, and later that day went up to the production office of Romulus Films just off Park Lane in Mayfair. They were making a movie of *Oliver!* and there were thousands of people there. It seemed that everybody and their grandmothers were at these auditions; and so we all sang 'Consider Yourself', did a dance and went back to school.

A few days later some of us were called back; a few days after that we were called back again; and then again, and again. I was recalled to test for the Artful Dodger. It was one of the few times I had been for an audition knowing what the part entailed. I wanted it so much. I think I did about five or six more auditions, always playing the same scene: when Dodger first meets Oliver. I played the scene with what seemed like an endless stream of young boys, and I was getting fed up of auditioning and wished they would just decide.

I do remember possibly one of the last auditions that I did was with this shy, quiet boy called Mark Lester. We were now auditioning in an office suite with John Woolf, the producer, and Carol Reed, the tall director. We had done it a few times when the tall man said, 'Well now, I want you to change places. Jack, I want you to play Oliver, and Mark, I want you to play Dodger.'

At first I thought he was joking, but I wanted the part so much that I would have done anything this distinguished, kindly, proper gentleman asked. (Jack, I wonder if you could set fire to yourself? Yeah, sure, no problem.)

I can't remember how Mark played Dodger, but as I certainly didn't want to play Oliver, I acted it as though Oliver was really stupid and played it for laughs. And the tall man laughed.

And then I was told I'd got the part; I was to play Dodger and the shy boy was to play Oliver.

For two years I had been dreaming of playing Dodger in the stage show, but I wasn't tall enough. They said I would have to grow another foot to play the part, and as I was happy with the two I already had, the film seemed the only way. My original dream was just to play it on the London stage. In truth I would have been deliriously happy playing it in any theatre, in any town; but now I was to be playing it in a film that would be shown worldwide.

As it turned out, I wasn't really tall enough for the movie either. Although I was fourteen and Mark was only eight years old, he was the same size as me, which I thought was disgusting (how dare he make me look so small?). I had to have special boots made for me with lifts inside them to make me a couple of inches taller than him. I went up to Anello and Davide in Covent Garden to be measured for the shoes (I didn't even know you could get handmade shoes) which cost £25.

And so, with the help of Anello and Davide, I was to play the Artful Dodger. Dickens described him as 'a snub-nosed, flat-browed, common-faced boy enough; and as dirty a juvenile as one would wish to see; but he had about him all the airs and manners of a man. He was short of his age: with rather bow legs, and little, sharp, ugly eyes. His hat was stuck on the top of his head so lightly, that it threatened to fall off every moment – and would have done so, very often, if the wearer had not had a knack of every now and then giving his head a sudden twitch: which brought it back to its old place again. He wore a man's coat, which reached nearly to his heels. He had turned the cuffs back, half-way up his arm, to get his hands out of his sleeves; apparently with the ultimate view of thrusting them into the pockets of his corduroy trousers; for there he kept them. He was, altogether, as roistering and swaggering a young gentleman as ever stood four feet six, or something less, in his bluchers.'

I don't think I knew then how close the fit was; and I couldn't possibly have known how closely my image would be linked with his for the rest of my life.

*

And so rehearsals began. The coach would pick me up from the end of my road at 8.00 every morning to take me to Shepperton Studios, just outside London in the countryside.

'They will send a car to pick you up if you would like, Jack.'

'No thanks, Mrs Collins, I'd sooner go on the bus with everyone else.'

The door of the bus swung open and I leapt up the steps. Mrs Permenter, the chaperone, was perched at the front of the coach and my lot were all at the back. 'Morning Mrs P,' I called as I headed straight to the back. She was nice, but wouldn't let us smoke, well at least not in front of her. So we sat at the back with the windows flung open. And once we were safely out of each other's view I would relax and sneak a fag out to smoke – and so would she; both of us content in our pretence of innocence. It was always easier with a chaperone who was a smoker: because when they smoked, we did, so it was harder for them to detect the smell.

I'd done the stage show with several of the boys now in Fagin's Gang: Ray Ward, Billy Smith, Robert Langley, Bob Bartlett, Kim Smith; and when we got to the studio, we would all be sent to start the day in the school room. On a really bad day we would be there until home time, but more often than not we would be set free to rehearse, to record, and later to film. Time stood still in the school room and I found the school work even more boring than usual. The other lads didn't have much enthusiasm either, unless it was for the 'Canadian teacher with the short skirts and the big knockers'.

To be honest, we didn't do much work that you could talk about at all. It seemed like a particularly cruel trick to trap us in a classroom within the studios – particularly in studios where they had made *The Guns of Navarone*, *The Spy Who Came In From the Cold* and the comedy Bond movie *Casino Royale*. I found it hard to concentrate and show any interest in fractions and decimal points when 007 could be just around the corner and might need my help with a particularly challenging villain.

They only had two school teachers for everybody on the production; and, because there were so many children involved in the movie, they averaged out the ages of all of us, and then you'd either go in the higher class or the lower class. Ian Ramsey, one of Fagin's gang, was older than me by a couple of months and the same size, and I was the second eldest of all the kids, so me and him ended up doing school work that we'd done the year before, and in effect we missed out on a complete year of work. Not that we minded. Why would we mind? We couldn't see that it mattered. *We* were making a film!

I'd obviously been involved in the same way with *Danny the Dragon*, but this was different. This felt like 'real movie' time. I'd worked in studios before, like Goldhawk, but that felt more like a photographic studio; whereas at Shepperton… You could get lost at Shepperton! The *Oliver!* sets covered six sound stages and all of the vast backlot. Every space was used to rehearse simultaneously. It always seemed I was meant to be in more than one place at one time. Even so I wasn't really aware of the sheer magnitude of the production. It seemed to me we just picked a routine to rehearse, any routine, and learnt it. I wasn't conscious then of the huge machine and the meticulous planning that was involved in orchestrating the hundreds of performers and crew. We were just having fun.

We wouldn't always rehearse with Onna White, the main choreographer, but often with one of her assistants, Larry Oaks. I already knew him from the stage show. He had been the dance captain and responsible for rehearsals, and I think he may have been the Bow Street Runner who shot Bill Sikes. He was always well dressed, immaculate, had dark hair and darker glasses, and looked like a male model. He was not much older than me and we treated him like one of us. Another assistant was Tommy Panko, who wasn't as approachable. He was a broad-shouldered man, more at ease with the adults, and gave the distinct impression that he didn't like children.

Onna White was absolutely adorable. She was a small, blonde, vibrant ball of energy, with a great Texan drawl. She got on so well with everybody, even us; and I mean, the bunch of kids that she had to contend with – it couldn't have been easy. She rented a huge house in Holland Park and, because I became friendly with her daughter and son, I would go there at weekends.

Not that we took to each other immediately. On one of the first couple of days shooting, because there were so many kids involved in the movie and because I was so small, I thought: how can I cover myself here? There were kids from Corona Stage School as well as Speake's, so I didn't know everyone. My lesson from Smallberry Green, however, stood me in good stead, and so I was trying to make friends with the toughest ones. I was in the process of sizing them up when Onna White's son turned up on the set and started mouthing off. He was American, towered above us and was saying everything was bigger and better in the States. Ray Ward disagreed with him. I didn't catch all of it, but I ended up seeing Ray standing up to him. Although Ray was small, no bigger than me, he thought the American was being too flash and cheeky and smacked him in the mouth.

So I thought, well, he is the obvious choice! I'll have him. If I stay friends with Ray I'll be all right.

There was a certain rivalry between the boys from Speake's and those from Corona. Clive Moss was the same age as me and playing Charlie Bates, and as a Corona lad, he was the obvious choice to be the leader of one gang; and I was the other. *We* called ourselves the 'Black Fingernail Club' from one of the *Carry On* films we'd all seen. We were the first ones to start it and so then Clive came up with 'King Wallaby's'. Clive used to suck his thumb through his handkerchief and always had one in his pocket; Clive wouldn't be Clive without his handkerchief. But really we were *all* a gang, and a gang in the true sense of the word. Together we created something much bigger; the whole was definitely bigger than the constituent parts. We each had our roles to play which created the dynamic and personality of the gang.

We shot the whole film at Shepperton. The only scene shot outside the studios was when Oliver has decided to run off to London. He's walking down this country lane and a coach and horses goes past very quickly and flicks mud into his face. That and a quick insert shot of St Paul's were the only things not shot at Shepperton, so the actual sets in the studios were incredible! It was a massive area to film on. I particularly remember the set for the outside of Fagin's Den. Up all those stairs, with every detail perfect; when we all had our costumes on, it was just like being back in Dickensian London.

Every detail was recreated, from the whole of Bloomsbury Square down to the old clay pipes the gang smoked. Billy Smith usually smoked a pipe on set, but several of the lads had to use them in the movie. The pipes were very popular as props and when they were handed out there were plenty of cries of 'Oh, I wanna pipe. Let me have it. I'll smoke it.' One day, I overheard the prop guys, Chuck and Bobby, talking about the tobacco in the pipes. They always made me think of Laurel and Hardy and were great fun. They said it was herbal tobacco; and whether or not I heard this fully, the impression I got was that this tobacco was very good for you. I went over to the prop guys and said, 'Hey, can you give us some of that herbal tobacco? The gang and me, we wanna try it for real like.'

They gave me a paper bag full of it. I said to the gang, 'Right, lunchtime, we won't go over the forest, it'll be back to my dressing room, get the pipes out and away we go!' We then had the rest of the lunchtime to finish this big bag of herbal tobacco, and we tried to cram in as much as we could. There were about ten of us in my dressing room which wasn't very big. It didn't have a bathroom in it or anything as lovely as that. It was just a room with mirrors on the wall and lights around it, and a few coat hangers and that's it.

We didn't quite finish the bag, but took as much as we could take; when we walked out of my dressing room we were all green. We didn't do it again. After that, when the boys were told, 'Right, we want you to smoke a pipe in this scene,' they would say, 'Oh, no. I don't want to, he'll have it,' and, 'He likes it. Give it him.'

We really created havoc in that studio. We must have driven everyone potty. I don't know how we didn't get caught and told off more than we did. One lunchtime on one of the backlots where we shot 'Consider Yourself', we were coming back to the main part of studios to have lunch – a swarm of boys with me at the centre – and we found an old dilapidated Dalek, left over from one of the *Doctor Who* movies they'd shot there a couple of years earlier. We tried to see if we could get it to work; and when we couldn't, we tried to topple it over and destroy it. And we did what Doctor Who couldn't! A photographer came and took some pictures. There was always a press and publicity photographer around, taking our every marketable opportunity.

As we headed back to work Bob Bartlett came up to me and said, ''Ere Jack, look what I found!'

It was a small section of 16mm film, and when I held it up to the light I could see it was me in *Danny the Dragon*.

'Blimey,' I said. 'Where did you get that?'

'I just found it in the studios,' he said. It had been thrown away as waste, so they'd obviously been editing it here at Shepperton.

'Did you know, the bloke who played the dragon has a bit part in *this* as well?' I said. There were also lots of adults from the stage show of *Oliver!* who had bit parts in the movie: Robert Bridges, who'd played Bumble, and Harry Goodier who was Sikes when I was in it.

'Really?' said Bob. 'No, I just thought you'd like it.'

I meant to say 'thanks' as he give it me, but at that point Ollie Reed swept into the studios, and Ollie Reed sweeping into the studios was always worth stopping for.

Mr Oliver Reed, who played Sikes, would always arrive at the studios in a primrose yellow, E-Type convertible Jag. I thought this was too much. He was everything I wanted to be: successful, butch, strong and good-looking, a bear of a man that women adored, *and* he drove fast cars – could there be anything more? I wouldn't actually speak to him; in fact I don't think I had a conversation with him in the whole year we worked together – I was far too frightened of him to do that. We all were.

When we were shooting a scene outside Brownlow's house there was a two shot just of me and Mr Reed. I had to stand with Mr Reed on one side and Bullseye on the other. I'm not sure who I was the more terrified of. The dog would spend half an hour in make-up and would end up looking really evil. I was told if that breed of dog bit you, the jaws would lock and you'd be done for. I stood warily between the two. But to be on my own in a two shot with Mr Reed: I felt like the bee's knees. I felt like I was imbued with his power and presence.

I thought that Dodger would try to behave as tough as Sikes did; Dodger felt like a mentally older and stronger person than me and I tried to put that toughness into my performance. I'd watch Mr Reed on set; I'd watch him change from this well-spoken actor to an East End villain and I believed this change absolutely. I remember in one scene he grabbed Nancy around the neck. As his hand touched her throat, he grimaced as though her pain was his. It was so powerful; to me that was perfect acting.

We were all in awe of him and would be on our best behaviour in the shadow of his towering presence. We'd not speak unless we were spoken to; and only safely out of his sight, and reach, did he become fodder for our amusement in our own dodgy sketches.

I think it began when we were shooting the argument scene in Fagin's Den. Sikes starts the scene with: 'We got to get him back! D'you 'ear me?... *Three days* since I spotted 'im – and what 'ave you done about it. *Nothing!'* He threw the words out with such force it seemed as though a single noun could have killed you stone dead. His delivery made such an impression on us that, afterwards, we would put it into conversations wherever we could.

'How long have you been queuing up for, Bob?'

'Three days,' he'd snarl back.

'How long before we're due back, Ronnie?'

'Three days,' he'd growl.

We thought it was hilarious. We would use it to answer questions at school, in the cafeteria, anywhere; it was always guaranteed a laugh between us boys.

At the end of the *'three days'* scene Carol Reed wanted a close-up reaction shot from me. 'You see Jack, I think Dodger's a little bit in love with Nancy. In the book she's not that much older than him. So I think you'd be protective towards her; but be careful, because Sikes could kill you with one blow.' He always spoke with a quiet authority and made the direction so easy to understand. He'd walk calmly over as though he had all the time in the world and his pieces of direction felt like a quietly delivered gift.

Later, after we'd made the film, I learnt that Carol Reed had said that, to get the best performances from kids, 'it is very important that children do not get nervous... therefore you must never let them see that you are worried or that tension is gathering. They must think of filming as a game.' And what a game we had.

When we first starting filming in Fagin's Den, we were given a designated place in the alcoves on the set for our character to sleep in. Once it was decided who slept where, it was accepted that that would stay your little space; and when we were hanging around waiting for the next shot to be set up, we would often go and wait on our character's bed. To amuse ourselves we'd create sketches and imitate people who'd made an impression on us. Ollie Reed was featured, and Robert Langley used to do a brilliant Winston Churchill – we'd be in hysterics. Me, Bob Bartlett and Robert Langley also did a sketch about Hitler and the fact that his dustbins hadn't been collected and his rubbish was getting higher and higher.

Sometimes we'd perform our sketches at the end-of-term concerts back at school. We'd also tried our hand at a love song entitled 'I Want My Baby' and, in what can only have been a rush of blood to the head, we decided to use it for one of those concerts. On the whole, not a wise decision.

Before the concert we had a run-through. I'm on the piano, and I only know three chords: C, D minor and E minor. So I'd play those, then I'd go back to D minor, and back to C, and after that, I would do exactly the same again. We sang the one-line lyric to each chord going up, and then each chord going down. Dennis McGrath was strumming chords, but as he couldn't play the guitar he was miming instead; and Bob had to mime too, so I was the only one making any sound.

We did a rehearsal and we thought this was the biggest pile of rubbish ever heard. We said to Miss Speake, 'We want to cancel it.'

But she said: 'No. I gave you plenty of time to come up with a sketch and you've got to take responsibility. If you don't do that you will have to come up with something else.'

Well, there was no time to come up with anything else so we tried it through and it just sounded like an unstoppable dirge. It didn't come across well at all.

All our previous sketches had been 'different' up till now so we thought, we've got to do something unusual to help this 'song' out. So I said to Bob Langley, who was the lead singer, 'As you're singing an emotional song about losing your baby, you must go into the audience and tell them, individually like, how much you want your baby.'

It was our last resort really. I thought it might make it funny and that that would save us. Bob Langley was dead against it as he was embarrassed and worried about what Miss Speake would say. Nobody had ever got off the stage before.

'It's our only hope, Bob, of getting away with this gig and making it funny,' I said.

So come the show Bob Langley did it the first time through and then got off the stage and went up to Mrs Collins and sang 'I want my baby' to C, D minor and E minor. She seemed a little bit embarrassed but laughed along with it anyway. He then went to Miss Speake and sang 'I've got to have my baby', trying to show his emotional range, and I'm just playing the piano like a man possessed. 'Get back up on that stage, Langley...' Miss Speake growled with considerable menace, '... *immediately.*'

The last word propelled him back onto the stage with such force that only an imprint of Robert was left standing in front of Miss Speake; and that imprint fell to the floor in a heap.

Somewhat regrettably, I suddenly realised that we hadn't worked out an ending. I tried to catch Bob's eye to finish it, but he just stood there confused and stunned singing 'I want my baby'. I played C, D minor and E minor more and more desperately until eventually he turned around to me. So I went from C to D minor and E minor again, hoping he would understand what I was doing, and then stayed on C to end in an extraordinary climax, banging the C chord to an inch of its life; it was the loudest and most dramatic C chord ever heard. But then we got stuck on the C chord and no one knew how to get off it; and Bob didn't look so good, so I thought I'll just have to tinkle something two octaves up and then I banged the chord once more, for luck.

It wasn't our finest hour.

At work we were more kindly received, and Onna White would come and watch our sketches and indulge us with applause.

'All right, let's break for lunch, back at two please.'

We tore off the set – 'Waistcoat, please, Jack' – and headed off to lunch. Wardrobe never trusted me with my waistcoat over lunch, as it was the only one they had. I had doubles of the rest of my costume, but the waistcoat was an original. The rest I wore, including my top hat, to have lunch in and to play football. We had to have a quick lunch if we wanted to have time for a proper game of football and a fag. We hurried past the sound stages and the plastering shops. Much of the set was made from plaster, from the clay pipes to the cobbled stones; occasionally we'd look in, and be told to get out.

In the commissary we had a separate room, away from the other diners. Whether we were put there so as not to disturb people while they were eating, or whether we chose it and no one else dared venture in, I'm not sure. But we lorded it in our own banqueting hall.

'Joining us today, are ya' Jack? Steak too tough at the restaurant?' jibed Billy Smith. Yesterday, I'd been invited to have lunch with John Green, the musical director. We'd had starters and everything, and it felt like I was having lunch at Buckingham Palace. I was glad to get back to double egg and chips, and back to the lads.

'Sod off, ya noisy git,' I said. 'All I can hear in that scene is you and your bloody pipe,' I added, flicking a chip at him. Billy Smith was a nutter. I'd nearly had a fight with him the other night going home. We'd been sitting on the coach and were arguing about something. One of us had said, 'Well, let's get off and sort it out.' We got off and squared up to each other like Sonny Liston and Cassius Clay. Billy's large eyes seemed to get bigger – through fear or bravado, I'm not sure which. The large grin he usually wore had disappeared and things were beginning to look serious.

'Hi guys. How's the gang today?' Vince called to us, breaking the tension. He was a sparks and a massive giant of a man – he seemed to us to be at least seven foot tall. We all liked him tremendously and he seemed to share in Carol Reed's 'game'. Whenever he saw us together he would grab all of our hands and shake them all at once. We really liked him because he was so cool, and so knowledgeable, and because he called us 'guys' and not 'boys'.

Me and Billy greeted Vince, and got back onto the coach. Neither of us had been really committed to a fight and we were both relieved it hadn't come to blows; and Billy's grin reappeared.

Anyway, we all finished lunch and escaped our chaperone to have a fag. There was a river that ran through the studios, and on one side of the river, there was a forest for smoking in and stuff, and on the other side there was the green for football.

The chaperones sat on a bench by the green keeping half an eye on us, and fortunately for us not their good half. However, we weren't going to play football this lunchtime as we'd found some oil barrels and wanted to see if they'd float. We'd already had great success with a long Viking boat that we'd found abandoned and forgotten from a film already wrapped and printed. I had secretly thought that the Viking vessel wouldn't float, but me and Ray Ward convinced the others it would, and had launched them on their maiden voyage. Surprisingly they didn't sink. Flushed with this aquatic success, we decided to float the barrels. But to add to the drama we were going to float them through this concrete tunnel that the river ran through. Billy Smith was the captain, and straddled these two claret-red oil barrels roped together, and paddled down through this concrete tunnel wearing his broad smile and his red claret *Oliver!* costume.

Mark wasn't allowed to play with us in case he got too red and hot, or bruised and damaged. He had his own individual chaperone who was never further than six foot away from him. She was blonde going grey, wore glasses and took her responsibilities very seriously, taking rigorously good care of him. We only really saw Mark on set, as he was stored in cotton wool when he wasn't working. He was kept out of the sun in case he went pink; his milk teeth were stuck back in if they had the audacity to fall out; nothing was to ruin a hair on his head, or the continuity of the film.

When we first started shooting Carol Reed would often ask me to take care of Mark and make sure he hit his marks on cue ('See that he ends up *there*, Jack. You know what to do: you're an old man in short trousers') and so very quickly I found myself automatically looking out for him. In 'Consider Yourself' I moved a stray fish off the ramp he was about to slide down, in case he didn't like it. It's still there in the final edit. Well, he was half my age really, just a kid, so I tried to look after him when we were working. When we weren't working, us lads were kept away from him as if we had infectious and incurable diseases. I did feel sorry for Mark as his chaperone, Mrs Nelson, protected her delicate charge with all the attributes of a particularly ferocious guard dog. I was snarled at and bitten a few times when I tried to lead him astray, and she successfully kept his lily-white complexion under lock and key.

By September 1967, Shepperton Studios felt like a home from home and I think me and the gang knew every square inch of it; especially the inches we weren't meant to. It was my fifteenth birthday and we were shooting 'Consider Yourself'. It took just over three weeks to shoot the whole number. We'd already done the bit with the butchers, where me and Mark go through the meat market. For that section, they had strung together two legs of lamb and the butcher was supposed to chop it in time to the music on one swipe. Then me and Mark would walk through on the next beat. But with his first swipe he didn't fully cut it. I thought I'd better break the rest of it as I walked through it, to keep time with the music. The guy thought he'd better have another go and went to swing the axe a second time. We narrowly missed each other.

Today, we were doing the bit with the Bow Street Runners. I'd had a bad day so far. As it was my birthday I thought I might be given a present before we started work. My expectations had been set as Mark had had his ninth birthday on set in July. He'd been given a Porsche Carrera slot car and his own joystick. I thought it was a brilliant present and wondered if I'd be lucky enough to get one as well. I'd asked Fagin's Gang to keep their ears to the ground and let me know if they heard anything. 'Nothing mate,' Bob had told me that morning. Maybe they had forgotten.

I'd then spent part of the morning watching the fire-eater doing his take, only to discover that it wasn't done by magic at all, but just by taking a gobful of meths and spitting it out. I was really very disappointed.

Tea break came. Nothing. They had definitely forgotten.

Then, after morning tea, I was having trouble with a particular look Carol Reed wanted. In the shot, Mark and I narrowly avoid a group of Bow Street Runners, and on the first take I had instinctively given the look that he wanted. I tried to recreate it in the next take, but I couldn't get it. I then tried another three or four times but still couldn't get it. Mr Reed could see I was getting frustrated; I was used to getting everything right first time.

'Don't worry, Jack; you just flicked your eyes up to heaven as if to say, that was a close call. Just come and have a look at the video to see what you did.'

Oliver! was one of the first British movies to use video playback on set. I'd never seen it, or any rushes of my performance, before that and was never allowed to see any playback afterwards. But I watched that one take and saw what he meant, and eventually I managed to get the blasted look.

We broke for lunch, and of course they hadn't forgotten. They'd set up a table with a cake, there was a huge birthday card, and they'd bought me a brand-new Moulton Mini bike. It was metallic red with tiny little wheels and proper suspension. I'd never had a new bike before. I didn't even have my *own* bike for a long while; me and Arf had to share – and I seem to remember that, as Arf was the eldest, he did a lot more sharing than I did. I was hoping to get a slot car, but this was ten million times better. A brand-new bike all of my own: that to me was my primrose yellow E-Type Jag.

That night when I got home, I ran in shouting, 'Mum, Arf, you'll never guess what I've got.' I dumped my card and the sorry remains of the cake on the table. 'Mum, Arf,' I shouted again, knocking part of the cake onto the floor as a climax to the trail of crumbs I'd already created from the front door.

'All right, Jackie, we're here. Oh, careful with that cake Jackie. Tell us what you got then,' me Mum said with an excited grin as wide as the one I'd been wearing all day, so I could tell she already knew. Apparently they had called to check if it was all right to buy me a bike.

'Well, that's very kind of yer, but I'm sure he expects nowt really,' she'd said. Thankfully they hadn't listened to her.

I got a padlock for it, kept it at the studios and rode it all over the lot to get to the various rehearsals. Ray Ward used to ride on the back. I was his personal chauffeur, which was a small price to pay really for the protection he afforded me.

Filming *Oliver!* I started for the first time to look and watch, and learn the 'how' of making a movie; beginning with wides and then close-ups and reverses before finishing a particular set-up. I not only started to look at the technical side, but also at what the other actors were doing.

I watched Ron Moody playing Fagin. Everything that he did, from the way he talked, to the way he moved, from his facial reactions to the way he danced, was unique! He was just so inventive. He had created the role of Fagin in the stage show back in 1960 and it was mad to think anyone else could have been considered for the role, but apparently Peter Sellers was.

When we started rehearsals for the dance sequences it was hard to imagine what Ron would look like as Fagin. When we saw him on the set for the first time with full make-up and costume he looked fantastic, and we were transfixed by his presence. Charisma flowed out of him as he was transformed from Ron into this new person we'd not seen before. He seemed to be so tall out of costume and so bent in costume. Unconsciously I echoed his change in stature and so instead of being stood upright I found that I was bent over too. And as soon as Carol Reed would say 'Cut' he would be back to his normal self. He wouldn't be Fagin. The only time he stood up to his full height on screen was towards the end when Fagin has lost everything. I thought that was brilliant. He said he always loved working with us, partly because he'd never grown up himself. We all respected him, partly because he treated us not so much as kids but as fellow actors, and we did our best to respond in kind.

For my own part, the role of Dodger had always felt like a perfect fit. I felt that I knew him and his world. I remembered this scene in the stage show where Dodger is arrested by the Bow Street Runner after the death of Sikes. Dodger doesn't miss a beat, and protests his innocence like a lord with all the cocky confidence of any self-respecting child actor. 'Who do you think you are a-laying your hands on? Assault and battery, that's what it is! Wakin' a respeckable man up in the early hours of the morning. And what are all these people doing here? Shame on you! Shame on you! If only my attorney was here – but he's having breakfast with the Vice President of the House of Commons...'

He is dragged off and that would be the last you saw of Dodger in the stage show. The Dodgers would usually get a laugh, and once or twice a round on the exit. That bit sold it to me really, and I felt I understood Dodger.

He was a child with the demeanour of a man, trying to beat the adults at their own game. And he didn't seem to be doing anything very different to what I was doing. I was working in a grown-ups' world, being treated like an adult and getting away with it. I liked it. I liked having the best part, and being made to feel important, as everyone knew me. Dodger was the best at what he did; as Fagin tells Oliver, 'Just do everything that Dodger and Charlie do. Make 'em your models. Especially Dodger.'

There seemed to be synchronicity between actor and role; and as everyone was telling me how good I was, I developed a swagger – or had it always been there? It was easy to become blasé about the compliments and accolades: 'Jack, you did a great job there'; 'He's the next Mickey Rooney, he is'; and people, such eminent people saying how incredible you are – what a dangerous place to be.

And then somehow a year had passed and it was the end-of-film party. I needed a suit, so it was off to the tailors. *Bonnie and Clyde* had just come out, and so I had a dark blue, double-breasted, one-inch-pin-striped suit, made to measure to wear at the party. Beyond that I'm not sure about much else that evening. I do remember after the official party Mark and me were invited to Ollie Reed's dressing room for an unofficial party. And I know I was dead chuffed to be asked. I vaguely remember at one stage me and Mark being hidden in the bath when the production manager came round as we weren't supposed to be there. And I also remember running through the cafeteria where I tripped, fell and wrote off my brand-new suit.

Mark's chaperone had one glass of champagne and took him home. Mine had several glasses and I had several more, and I dimly remember arriving home completely drunk, escorted by my equally drunk chaperone.

Dad was working a 2pm to 10pm shift at Firestone Tyres that night and I'd normally be in bed when he got home. As he got to the front door me Mum stopped him.

'Now just be quiet 'cos Jack's not well. He's asleep on the sofa.'

'What's wrong wi' him?'

Me Mum explained the state me and Mrs P had arrived home in.

'Bloody hell. What did yer sa' t'chaperone?'

'Well, I didn't like to sa' anything. I was just worried about Jackie's health.'

'*Bloody hell fire!*' Dad bellowed.

'Shhh, Jack.'

'Bloody hell fire,' Dad spat out, quietly.

This was not going to be the last time Mum would come between me, drink and Dad.

In the early part of 1968 we started doing the post-synching, mostly at Shepperton and once or twice at some dubbing theatres just off Wardour Street in London. We re-recorded sections of the dialogue in sync with what was on the screen, and this was the first opportunity I had to see what I'd done. I just saw little snatches in black and white and I thought, yeah, that's not bad. It looks quite good. I'd had a wonderful year making it, but I still didn't think that this was what I'd be doing for the rest of my life, or as a career as such. But I suppose what I did know, even then, was that parts don't come any better than Dodger and that I had been involved in something quite special.

Chapter 7

S O IT WAS BACK TO SCHOOL AGAIN; back to Maths and English in the morning, ballet in the afternoon, smoking in the toilets, and punishments of a thousand dictionary words. I'd been out for a year making *Oliver!* and, because we'd spent so much time out of doors, I had a muddy tan again.

'That ain't a real tan, that's a fake one. You put it on this morning.'

'No I didn't.'

'Yes you did.'

'No I didn't – got any fags?'

It was good to be back.

I'd only been back a few weeks, however, when Mrs Collins called me into her office and said, 'Jack, we've got an appointment to go and see an American gentleman called Mel Tormé. He is a record producer and he wants to produce a record with you.'

'Someone's playing a joke on us, Mrs Collins.'

I couldn't be a pop star; I was only just getting used to being an actor. I'd been in the business just over two years and I didn't even know if I wanted to do this for the rest of my life. I was just having fun for now. I had made the decision, however, that while I *was* in show business I should behave like an actor even when I wasn't working. So I wore dark glasses all the time and when I attended auditions I'd say to the producers, 'It's alright, I've arrived now, so you can send the others home.' Surprisingly they gave me the roles and not a clip round the ear.

'No, Jack,' Mrs Collins assured me, 'I've just spoken to him and he's very interested in recording a single with you. He wants to meet up and play you some songs.'

So we went to Kensington.

'This is the one that I think would suit you, Jack.' He seemed to take it all so seriously. 'It's called "Golden Days"; have a listen to it.'

As it turned out, the backing track had already been done, so it wasn't like what happened a couple of years later when I had a proper, pukka recording contract.

'So whaddaya think?'

I thought, well, it's catchy enough; it's not going to make number one – I just couldn't see myself on *Top of the Pops* with the Beatles and Lulu, who am I kidding? And the Bee Gees, it was insane! But, I thought, if he's mad enough to pay me to sing it, who am I to say no?

'Yeah, alright, fine,' I said.

'Right, we'll go and do that then!' And he gave us the draft of the contract in a large, white envelope.

As me and Mrs Collins travelled back on the tube, Mrs Collins opened the envelope. 'Oh Jack, look! Look how much money you're going to get.' The contract was for a thousand pounds: a *thousand pounds*. It was incredible. It was daft. My Dad wasn't getting that for a year and I was getting it for one record. Three hours' work maximum. And I *thought*, this is bloody mad ('cos you couldn't swear in front of Mrs Collins). I'd never seen so many noughts on a cheque before. A thousand pounds. To me that was a million.

I took the contract home for me Mum and Dad to sign, but as we sat down to tea a row was brewing. Apparently Arf was in trouble with the law. 'We weren't nicking it, we only borrowed it to take it over to the Heath for a ride.'

'What do yer mean yer bloody borrowed it?' Dad said.

I occupied myself, banging away to 'All or Nothing' on the kitchen stool.

Me Uncle Ken had a drum kit and I quite fancied myself as a drummer. Uncle Ken had played in the pubs, and me Mum had played the piano – the only difference being me Mum played *before* the punters arrived, 'to amuse herself and annoy me', me Dad said. But she weren't that bad; the chords she played were very close.

I'd put the Beatles, or the Small Faces, on my mono record player and, although I only had one kitchen stool to play, I could make quite a bit of noise.

'Oh Jackie, stop that and come and have yer tea,' me Mum implored.

Arf sat at the table, glad of the momentary distraction, and I squeezed in beside him. We couldn't all sit down together as the table wasn't big enough, so we ate in shifts.

'He was in again today,' me Mum said, trying to ease the tension.

Me Mum worked at the butcher's counter in David Greigg's, the local supermarket, and 'he' was Charles Hawtrey (the little thin geezer with glasses in the *Carry On* films).

'He was in dead on twenty-five past askin' for scraps again. Miserable old sod,' Mum said, handing me a plate of potato hash. Mr Hawtrey would always come just before closing time to ask for scraps for his poodle.

But my father wouldn't be distracted from the matter in hand.

'What do yer mean, yer bloody borrowed it?'

Apparently Arf had been over to a mate's house. This guy had an aviary in his back garden with finches, budgerigars, canaries and all sorts of birds.

'And the motorbike?' me Dad reminded Arthur.

The gang had been walking back along this alley with their bikes, when they found what looked like a dumped motorcycle. They checked it out. Look! It's got a bit of petrol in it – we'll have a ride of it, someone had said. 'I can't remember who, but it definitely weren't me, Dad,' Arthur insisted.

'And the police?' me Dad said – he wasn't one for detail.

'Well, no sooner had we got it onto the heath, Dad, than we were surrounded by three Black Maria police vans. We were rounded up and slung in one van, our bikes in another and the motorcycle in the third. And they took us straight down the cop shop.'

They all got done for handling stolen property because apparently the bike had been nicked. Arf said that his fingerprints 'weren't even bloody on the bike', but he got done as a 'handbag to the crime'.

We waited for Dad's response – he'd been known to express his feelings with his fists before now. Only in his youth, mind, and never to us; but then neither of us had been arrested before.

'Well,' me Dad said, drinking his last mouthful of industrial-strength tea, 'I think the police were a bit bloody much charging him, don't you Vera?'

'Well, as long as he's learnt his lesson, Jack. That's the main thing.' Crisis over.

'Now then Jackie, what about you? How's yer day been?'

'Oh... well... I've got to make a record for some American,' I said despondently. Trust Arthur to be flash and be the first one to get a criminal record. He was having more fun than I was.

I got up from the table, and as I walked out of the kitchen I slipped one of Grandad's dog-ends into the palm of my hand. I'd smoke it later in the bathroom and think things over. I had to be careful, though, as last summer I'd thrown the remains out of the bathroom window and they had landed on the tent and set light to it. I'd said something about 'the heat of the sun must have caught it Mum', and seemed to get away with it. So I continued smoking the fag ends I'd nicked, in the bathroom with the door locked.

Arthur told me later that the gang had actually been more worried about being done for smoking. When the police arrived they quickly dimped their fags and threw them in the bushes. They went back to look for them the following day, 'but somebody had bloody nicked 'em!' Arf ended up going to court and got banned from driving, which was a bit mad as he wasn't old enough to drive anyway.

I recorded that single for Mr Tormé, and another called 'Number One'. I think we had another meeting just to go through 'Golden Days' before we went in the studio to actually record it, just to go over phrasing and that. And then I recorded it at IBC studios in Portland Place, and that was that! A thousand pounds, just like that!

They were made in acetate and, as I was the first one at Speake's to get a recording contract and all that rubbish, we had fifty made and sold them at school for ten bob each ('if anyone wants to buy one before it comes out'). We sold about two dozen and it was never released. I can't remember why. The song had a brief revival at the end-of-term concert with Philip Gadd on guitar, Martin Gadd on bass and Phil Collins on drums and then it was laid to rest.

Another consequence of doing *Oliver!* was that I would be requested for jobs and not have to audition; and in May, June and July of 1968, I was contracted to do *Junior Showtime*. It was a TV show that mostly went out live and was filmed at the City Varieties Music Hall Theatre in Leeds: a small narrow theatre that at the turn of the century would have had to accommodate five or six vaudeville shows a day, and now had to accommodate a collection of adolescents and kids. We crammed segments from all the biggest musicals like *Oliver!*, *South Pacific* and *Chitty Chitty Bang Bang* into this dinky space. You could barely get a piece of tissue between us as we squeezed these big numbers onto the postage stamp of a stage. It required military precision, drilled into us by the Fat General, Jess Yates. He produced the shows and ruled with the proverbial rod of iron, sacking kids who didn't make the grade. I didn't think he was ever unfair in his judgements, and in many ways it was exhilarating to be part of such a tight performance, but we were all still terrified of him.

'My grandmother could do better than that – do it again!' he bellowed.

Neither his authority nor his grandmother's dancing skills were ever questioned.

The guy who starred in it was Bobby Bennett, a tubby lad who always smiled like he had just got a saucer of cream. He had become popular when he won *Opportunity Knocks*. He was about seven or eight years older than me; I'd have been fifteen then, so he must have been early twenties. There were also Liverpool's modest version of the Osmonds, the Poole Family, and to complete the cast the Peggy Spencer Dance School – a mixed assortment of young girls and enthusiastic boys.

Rehearsals were incredibly tight; we had about seven or eight days to rehearse the half-hour show, and because it was going out live you had to know it backwards, inside out and upside down. On the filming day, our little theatre was stuffed full with the technicians focusing the lights and setting up cameras, the live band tuning up and playing snatches of the music and thirty nervous and over-excited kids. The theatre squeezed us all in like an old woman letting out her skirts to allow for the extra load. She creaked and groaned and our collective hearts beat faster under the strain of the day. We went out live and our slot was from five to five to twenty-five past – and that was it. It had to be absolutely perfect and we all held our breath.

After the transmission Mr Yates came in from the gallery.

'Okay, that's it. Fantastic job, Bobby, and the rest of yer got away with it again.' It might have been meant warmly but it was hard to tell as he didn't have a smile, just a collection of grimaces.

Later on in the series we did some shows at Yorkshire TV studios which, because of their vast size, meant that the show became more of a 'special'. The dances could be more elaborate, the sets were bigger and there was a greater ease about it as it was recorded and not going out live. We didn't desert our theatre completely, however, as depending on availability we still shot some shows there. So one week we'd be on a stage the size of a football pitch – the next week we'd be in a cupboard.

By now, within the business, rumours had been going round about how good I was in *Oliver!* and how good Ron was as Fagin. All these adults kept saying:

'You've stolen the film!'

'You and Ron Moody have such chemistry between you!'

'Everyone's going crazy about you!'

'Oh, you must be so proud…!'

I found it all a bit embarrassing and awkward really.

'Well, I don't know what you're talking about,' I said, ''cos I ain't seen it yet.'

I started to become aware of what it must be like to be famous, but I couldn't really begin to have any idea of what was to happen when the film was premiered three months later in September.

I wouldn't have minded if girls of my age had been saying, 'We've heard how good you are,' and wanting to talk to me and have a snog or whatever, but still all they wanted to do was mother me. But my stock was gradually increasing and one day, in Leeds, after we'd filmed a selection from *Half a Sixpence* and were waiting for the 'all clear' from the gallery, I asked a few of the dancers to come back to my hotel room: the girls for snogs and the boys for decoration. One of the older dancers whom I tried to ask, extremely casually, was a pretty blonde girl called Heather. When I saw her for the first time, well, I thought she was lovely. She was a year older than me, and as a lad you tend only to have dealings with girls your own age, if you're lucky enough to have dealings at all. I think Bobby Bennett had his eye on her straight away – well, all the boys had their collective eyes on Heather. At any rate, I asked her along, but she'd set her sights higher: I was four foot six and Bobby was five foot four.

I was beginning to discover the downside of working so much. My growing popularity meant I attracted *most* girls... but what to do when I'd got one! I didn't really have as much time as everyone else to chat them up and have snogging sessions and all that business, so (in my eyes) I was way behind compared to what I was hearing from my gang at home. They'd be boasting about their exploits with Lynne, her sister, Barbara, and Lesley from up the road or whoever it was. I doubted they were actually telling the truth, but even that thought didn't make me feel any happier.

Still, at least work was going well; and, while I was doing *Junior Showtime*, I was booked to do another TV show, *Knock Three Times*, a children's serial with Hattie Jacques. As I couldn't do both, it was back to the doctors again.

Only this time it wasn't so easy. My 'sickness' got me out of the contract but Mr Yates was furious, phoned me Mum up and barked his orders at her. 'But I didn't know what to sa', Jack,' she told me afterwards. 'Mrs Collins does all yer bookings, don't she? I didn't know what to sa'.' She lit her cigarette and drew on it deeply. 'Ooh, I were on pins Jack.' I was fuming to see me Mum so upset. I didn't mind being bullied, but no one was going to bully me Mum.

I did the TV show down in London and then a week or so later took the train back up to Leeds to finish the contract. I was going to say something, but somehow nothing was said and everything was as it had been before.

I came home towards the end of the summer and back into the *Oliver!* madness. During the making of the film there had been questions in the House of Commons about the employment laws for kids. Apparently the production company was breaking the 1933 Children and Young Persons Act. We had been told at Shepperton that there were people trying to get illicit photographs of us, and if anyone we didn't know approached us for a photograph we should report it to the production manager straight away.

Somehow, despite the security and clandestine filming, they did get a picture of me and Mark and it was released and printed in the newspapers. The press interest was huge and everyone asked us what it was like filming and how we were treated. Each time we were asked we gave the same answers – we had great fun and were treated brilliantly. Apparently when the filmmakers were questioned over the lack of definitive laws for the protection of the kids they replied that the boys didn't need protection, *they* did!

At some stage before the premiere, Mrs Collins asked me if I would sign up to her for her to act as my personal manager. She suggested I speak to Mrs Layton's husband, who managed Dickie Valentine. 'You can ask him whatever questions you want to ask, Jack, and he'll be able to explain what it's like to have a personal manager.'

So I went to see Mr Layton and he told me I was hot property, because of my performance in *Oliver!* He said that Mrs Collins and Miss Speake would want to get me under contract pretty quick and that I was in a potentially very powerful position.

Well, I thought, if Mr Layton thinks I've got some power, I might as well use it. So when I had a meeting with Mrs Collins at Munster Avenue in the front room, I said I would be happy to sign with her, but I didn't want to sign with Miss Speake as well. Mrs Collins said the contract was with CSM (Collins, Speake Management) and that I couldn't just sign with her. I asked her to leave Miss Speake and just work for me, but she said no.

'Oh,' I said. I guess Mr Layton had been wrong about my power – I didn't seem to have any at all.

So I went along with it and signed the CSM contract and Mrs Collins became my personal manager. After all it wasn't going to cost me any more money – I would still pay twenty-five per cent commission – but I would have my own personal manager, Mrs Collins explained.

That September was the Royal World Premiere of *Oliver!* I hadn't really any idea of what the film would look like as I hadn't seen any rushes during the making of it, and only snippets during post-syncing. The first time I would see my performance would be in a packed cinema with all my family, friends, celebrity guests and royalty; I was a little nervous.

I was having a dinner suit made at Stanford's in Shepherd's Bush: a very expensive tailor's that Dickie Valentine recommended to me. He had his suits made there; apparently all the celebrities did. My suit was a black two-piece, double breasted suit with a lining of gold silk. Imprinted on the silk lining were pictures of London tourist attractions like St Paul's Cathedral, Westminster Abbey and the Houses of Parliament.

Me Dad thought I'd completely lost my mind.

'How much?'

'Just a little bit more than the suit I had made for the *Oliver!* party, and you liked that didn't ya Dad?'

'How much more?'

'Five times more,' I mumbled, 'but I get a second pair of trousers and a waistcoat to match in biscuit. So really I've got two outfits like for the price of one.'

In truth, I was a little bit surprised by how much it had cost. It was £100, which would have been a month's wages for me Dad, but at the same time I did think I looked a million dollars in it. I'd had three or four fittings; and to go and have your clothes made – that, to me, was on the same level as the Beatles or Elvis Presley. And anyway, I was going to meet Royalty.

And then I thought, well, if I'm having clothes made, I might as well have shoes made as well. So I went back to Anello and Davide where I'd had my *Oliver!* shoes made and I got black boots with Cuban heels which were all the rage. I was so pleased with them, I wore them to school after the premiere. Some of the lads said I looked poofy as only women wore heels, but I didn't care; they were dead trendy and they made me at least two inches taller.

On the day of the premiere, 26th September, four days before my sixteenth birthday, a pack of Wilds came down from the north and me Mum made herself ill with worry. She was short of breath and wheezing.

'Are you all right Mum?'

'Yes, course I am Jackie. I just need to have a cup of tea and a fag. I've got that many things on me mind.'

Mum always said that if she had a cigarette, it would calm her down; she said she could just focus on that for a moment and ignore all of the goings-on. And there were a great deal of goings-on. Uncle Harry and Edna, Uncle Ken and Yvonne, Grandma Wild and Auntie June all arrived on our doorstep ably flanked by Auntie Rachel who had come all the way down to look after the children for the night. The London contingent was me Mum and Dad, Arf, Gran and Grandad, Uncle Brian and Auntie Sylvia; it was like Moses and the Exodus!

Amidst the bustle, me Grandad took me to one side. 'Now, this is a special day, Jackie. Something like this will never happen again, so take it all in and hang on to it.'

'Oh Jackie, aren't yer dressed yet?' me Mum said as she flew past, an iron in one hand and a fag in the other. 'Hurry up,' she threw over her shoulder.

'Have a think about what I said, lad...' Grandad whispered confidentially, '... and you'd better get that suit on,' he added as he caught sight of me Mum's growing agitation, the iron having been replaced by her inhaler.

I did have a think about it, but I did feel they were all taking it a bit too seriously. I ran upstairs to get changed. After all, I was looking forward to wearing my new handmade suit, and I couldn't wait to see the lads again and share all this madness with them. I slipped into me Grandad's room to raid his ashtray by the side of his bed for all his old dog-ends for later. I carried on smoking them until I got brave enough to bring my own fags into our house as opposed to finishing them before I came home.

'Cars are here, Jackie... ohhh, would yer have a look at them,' me Mum cooed and then coughed.

'Coming,' I called, tucking five cigarettes carefully into the inside pocket of my jacket and running down the stairs to get a good look at the cars.

Two Daimler limousines had pulled up outside our house – and indeed several other houses due to their outrageous length. Mum worried us all out of the house and into the attendant black beasts, although once inside they didn't seem quite so big as there were so many of us crammed in. As we majestically moved away, it seemed like the whole street had come out to wave us off. I don't think Munster Avenue had ever seen a limousine before, and I think Munster Avenue was impressed.

We left Hounslow behind and headed for the bright lights of Theatreland.

We pulled up outside the Odeon, Leicester Square, and before I'd even got out of the car the flashes of the cameras started. I stepped out on to the red carpet and I tried to remember what me Grandad had said and take it all in, but it was just so overwhelming. Everyone wanted a picture or a chat, and they were shouting: 'Jack, over here! Over here Jack!'

I remembered I'd been told to smile and I was trying to behave like a professional, like I'd done this a million times before. But it was hard to know how much to look and smile and chat and laugh; it was hard to know if I was doing enough or if I'd done too much. I didn't want to look as though that's all I'd come for.

'Jack, are your parents looking after your earnings for you?'

'Nah, Mum and Dad won't take a blinking penny of me money. Dad says I've earned it and it should go in a building society until I'm grown up.'

'Do you think you'll change now you are a movie star?'

'Nah, I'm just me. I tried taking lessons to talk middle class, but as soon as I do, all my personality goes, so I ain't doing it no more. I'll let it come by itself from meeting important people who talk proper.'

I'd never experienced anything like this before: the cameras, the attention, the noise; I thought I must be the fifth Beatle.

I stepped inside the Odeon where we were met by a Columbia representative who shepherded and introduced us to a seemingly endless stream of people 'who would love to meet you'.

'Nice to see you, I hope you enjoy the film,' I said to the nameless dignitaries. Then I caught sight of the gang across the foyer. They were all dressed in their costumes. What a laugh to see them all again dressed like that. 'Hey lads, *three days*,' I shouted as I took a step towards them, but the sheep dog snapped at my heels. 'Jack,' he growled, 'let me just introduce you to...' and guided me back towards more people who would love to meet me.

'Nice-to-see-you-I-hope-you-enjoy-the-film' I repeated, wondering when I would be able to sneak a fag.

I kept trying to catch the eye of Bob or Billy Smith, but we were kept apart by this unrelenting current of important people. After about an hour, or was it a fortnight, when I felt like I had been introduced to everyone and their grandmother, the foyer began to clear. Most of the audience had gone in and we were preparing for the arrival of Royalty.

We'd been briefed on what to do in their presence, but I hadn't taken much notice of it coming up to the day as I couldn't believe it was really going to happen. But here we were, and I tried to recall what we must do and what we mustn't do, and try not to confuse the two.

We were taken up to the Circle Bar and lined up in readiness. Mark was asked to give a small bunch of flowers to Princess Margaret, and: 'Jack, can you give this tape of the soundtrack of the film to Lord Snowdon.' Yeah, sure, I thought, no problem.

'And say something like, "I hope you enjoy the film, and please accept this on behalf of Columbia Pictures." But remember, before you start talking, you've got to bow. So as soon as they come over to you, bow, then speak and only speak when you are spoken to, and only answer the questions that they've asked you.'

My head was swimming. Bow then speak, bow then speak. *Now* I was terrified. Petrified. I was about to meet the most important person I would ever, ever, ever meet. It really was too much.

Fortunately, Mark was on my left so he had to do it first. I watched the adults to see what they did so I could remind myself what to do. And very soon she was talking to Mark right next to me. As I watched Mark and Princess Margaret out of the corner of my eye, Lord Snowdon came up to me. Bow then speak, bow then speak.

I hope I got it right; I'm not sure as it all went so quickly.

And then they all moved along and suddenly she was there in front of me. She had diamonds in her hair and she shone like newly polished furniture. She asked me if I enjoyed making films. And I said, yeah, it's really great Ma'am. It was all so unreal. And then she glided by and it was all over. I wondered if she noticed my suit and the Cuban heels on my shoes.

The newspaper headlines the next day were: MARGARET MEETS THE DODGER!

And then we went in to watch the film.

I thought it was all right, but I noticed immediately in some scenes I was mouthing Ron's dialogue back to him. I was disgusted with myself and I couldn't understand why they hadn't used another take where I wasn't doing it. I thought everyone in the cinema must be thinking, who is this amateur? The next scene to leap out at me was when I first take Oliver to meet Fagin. I stick my head up the chimney and shout, 'It's Dodger... Coming up!' There is a mid shot of me, and under the lapel of my blue jacket I could see a Mercedes Benz badge that I had clipped on, that someone had given me. I felt a wave of embarrassment. How could I have left that on? I felt so unprofessional.

A little bit of pride was restored, however, watching the final scene between me and Ron. We were singing the reprise of 'Reviewing' and I had to sing the harmony line on 'what a team'. Now prior to recording this I had thought there were singers, and then there were people who harmonised, and that harmony was so specialised you'd have to learn how to do it especially like. I was so chuffed after we had recorded it, and then to see it on screen – me doing harmony; I just hoped it made up for everything else.

As we came out everyone seemed to be very pleased with what I'd done; and if they were pleased, then I was.

Afterwards, me Mum and Dad and me and Arf went to the Savoy for the reception. As soon as we got there, I slipped into the toilets to have a few drags; I still had three and a half fags left. The toilets were so posh, I'd never seen anything like it – they even had gold taps. I didn't let that put me off, however, and undeterred I went into one of the cubicles for a few puffs. I had half of the half, carefully dimped it, put it back in my inside pocket and went out again.

It really was an incredible evening seeing all these celebrities like Roger Moore and Richard Attenborough, but I missed sharing this massive evening with my mates. I waved to them, but I never got to speak to them and that's the one thing I really missed about the night. I was jealous that they shared the evening while I was left speaking to the press or important people.

But it was an amazing evening and so very exciting that it became a blur – strange really, as I was trying so hard to remember it as me Grandad had said. I tried to take it all in, and ended up remembering not very much at all.

My suit and I, however, were to have other memorable evenings together as the premiere tour for *Oliver!* began. It was decided that Mark would do the Far East and I would go to America with Ron, and I think me and Mark shared Europe. It was all expenses paid, first-class flights, the best hotels and all that business.

Our first port of call was Brighton, in Sussex. 'Let's have a bit of a joke!' I said to Mark because he looked as bored as I was. We were waiting for the reception and had been waiting for ages. And *waiting* is pretty dull. The day had started well enough. We'd come on this great old-fashioned steam train called the *Brighton Belle*, which to me was as good as going on the *Orient Express*. Bob Beerman, the publicity guy for Columbia, had met us at Victoria Station: a lovely guy, always smiling, well liked by everyone and who'd some-how grown to resemble his surname. A pack of press had waved us goodbye and we'd puffed our way down to the coast. It was a one-hour trip on the train because it didn't go fast. We got down there and all the press were at the station and there was a limo there to take us to the hotel for the press reception and photographs and that.

But now we were waiting. We were stood around in this massive reception room and, while no one was looking, I grabbed Mark's hand and we slipped, unseen, underneath the table closest to us. They had very expensive linen tablecloths, trailing as near as damn it to the floor; and I got this funny idea that if we hid under this long table, we could sit and listen to everyone saying, 'Where are they? Where have they gone?' getting ready for the reception. We did that for about ten minutes and we heard everybody going bananas, including Mrs Collins who'd come down with me, and we thought it was hysterical! Mark had the same chaperone as on the film and she was going bananas as well, because she played everything by the book, Mrs Nelson did. As far as she was concerned, he'd been kidnapped!

While we were under the table I considered having a cigarette, but I thought that might be taking the mickey too much. If they'd seen smoke coming from underneath the table, they might have thought something was on fire.

Anyway, Mark didn't smoke, as he was still just a kid. I know I started about his age, but I was a ruffian and he weren't. So I thought better of the cigarette; and, while their backs were turned, we chose our moment and came out, as though we'd suddenly appeared from nowhere. They didn't seem at all pleased to see us and we got a good telling-off. I made out as though we'd just taken a walk along the seafront and left it at that. I didn't mind a telling-off; I hardly noticed it. I don't know how Mark felt, but at least he didn't look bored any more.

So come November it was the Dutch premiere. Me and Mrs Collins flew out to Amsterdam. It was the first time I'd been on an aeroplane and the first time I'd been to a foreign country. I was a little bit apprehensive and quite a lot excited.

It was raining when we left London and raining when we got to Amsterdam. But above the clouds there was a sunny day. I thought this was quite wonderful and wondered where all the rain had gone. I sat quietly contemplating this conundrum; and, with such thoughts to wrestle with, it seemed no sooner were we up than we were almost back down again.

As soon as I got over there, I couldn't understand it as everybody spoke English. That really baffled me because, at school, I'd learnt French and from that I thought that when you go to a foreign country, they would all... well... speak foreign. And the bikes! I'd never seen so many – at 5.30 it was full of bikes. What a strange place.

At the premiere in Paris, we were told that there was going to be some more Royalty – Prince Rainier and Princess Grace. I'd never heard of Grace Kelly, but me Dad told me who she was.

They wanted me to give Princess Grace a bouquet of flowers. I felt a bit stupid holding bloody flowers and anxiously watched for the Princess to come so I could get rid of them. I knew she wouldn't be wearing a crown because the last lot of Royalty didn't have any crowns on at all; but Princess Margaret was wearing a tiara, so I thought, this Princess'll probably do the same. So this woman comes round the corner and she's got a diamond tiara in her hair, so I thought, great, I'll dive in here. I bowed, stepped up to her and said:

'Princess Grace, please accept these on behalf of Columbia Pictures. I hope you enjoy the film!'

But before I'd completed the slick royal move of bow, talk, stand back, somebody suddenly grabbed hold of me and ripped the flowers away from the woman because it weren't Princess Grace at all! It was some bloody wife of some businessman. I felt like a right pillock. The lady said something in French that I couldn't understand and hurried away. I felt so stupid, but she really did look like a princess to me.

While I waited for the real one to turn up, a firm hand held me back from making another unscheduled delivery. Then the hand pushed me forward (with, I noted, a distinct hint of frustration) towards the real princess who I must admit did look very regal. I bowed, did the talk and stood back, but my timing was all off, and it was more like disposing of chemical waste than a presentation of flowers.

We went to see the film, and then it's all the stretch limos again to the reception; and I'm getting used to this now and I'm really beginning to enjoy this. And as it turned out me and Mark were on the head table with our chaperones. I think Mark had his Mum and Dad with him, and I had Mrs Collins with me, and we're all sat on the top table with Prince Rainier. I'd been to the loo at least four times since the start of the evening to have my half a cigarette.

We're watching all these waiters coming in and out with the food and what have you; and then, they brought in a suckling pig, with an apple in its mouth! I'd never seen anything so grotesque. It wasn't just one pig; they brought in one after another, after another, until there was a whole herd in there. The one nearest us looked like it had been glazed to within an inch of its life; well in fact it didn't look like it had ever actually been alive, and it certainly didn't look like something you'd want to eat.

'I don't know about you, mate,' I said to Mark, 'but I ain't eating that rubbish! I fancy double egg and chips meself and that's what I'm gonna order!'

'If you're gonna have it, then I'd like it as well please!' Mark said.

'Alright,' I said, 'leave it to me.' And as soon as I got the waiter's eye, I said to him: 'We don't like what's being offered; can we have double egg and chips? And can we have that twice please?' I said, indicating me and Mark.

'I'll see what I can do, Monsieur!'

About ten or fifteen minutes later they were starting to serve up what everyone else was having, and I'm looking at my watch and thinking, I don't think this is gonna happen! I think we're gonna have to eat this rubbish! And all of a sudden, the waiter came back and said, 'I'm sorry it is taking so long, Monsieur, but we've sent someone out because all the food has been pre-arranged and we didn't have the ingredients. But they've just arrived and we're preparing it as we speak!'

'Oh, great, magic. Thanks!' I beamed at the waiter.

'It's alright mate,' I said to Mark, 'we're quids in now! They've got the gear and they're doing it!'

We were sat within six foot of Princess Grace and Prince Rainier so I'm bloody damn sure that's the only reason why we got it. If we'd have been sat at any of the other tables they'd have said, 'I'm sorry, but this is what's on and that's it! Take it or leave it!'

But no sooner had everyone been served with the normal suckling pig and all that, than our double egg and chips arrived and it was lovely! We both tucked into that something rotten. The others on the table couldn't believe it. I mean, it was like turning up at the Savoy and asking for a Big Mac! It was outrageous! But we so enjoyed it, me and Mark.

December brought the premiere in New York. I was really looking forward to it, having heard how everything was bigger and better in America. It was like an adventure ten times bigger than Paris or Amsterdam, because in comparison, they were only just round the corner. *And* we were going to fly on my favourite plane – a VC10. I was very excited.

We flew BOAC, and me and Mrs Collins travelled first class. We were given cocktails, lunch and afternoon tea, and the adults were given liqueurs. Half the menu was in French and we were offered 'Caviar from the Caspian Sea' for lunch. I didn't have the caviar and felt more at home with the 'Tea Sandwiches' at teatime.

We were about half way through the flight when I asked Mrs Collins, 'How high off the ground are we?'

'Oh, it's not that high,' she said reassuringly. 'It's only about a couple of thousand feet!'

A stewardess walking past overheard this conversation and stuck her head down. 'In actual fact we're flying at thirty-five thousand feet,' she said, smiling. I thought, well, a couple of thousand feet don't sound a lot, but thirty-five thousand? That's as high as Everest that is. Or even higher maybe. I dunno, but it sounded way too much.

And suddenly, despite it being my favourite plane and despite it being first class, I began to dislike flying. I'd been alright going to Paris and Amsterdam but this was going on too long; plus the fact that I'm going over the sea and I ain't that good of a swimmer. I mean, I'm alright, but not three thousand miles from land!

I remembered we were given a little pamphlet of what we were having for dinner and what choices we had, so I wrote a little letter on the booklet to take my mind off the flying and planned to send it home from New York.

Dear Mum and Dad, Arthur, Grandma and Grandad,

As we were about to take off we saw you waving and we waved back but we didn't think that you would be able to see us. As you probably know we flew in a VC10. Gawd blimey. I told you about the take-off in a Trident but this was ridiculous. It went up vertical.

We was shown how to use our life jackets and oxygen masks. (What were they trying to imply?) We were travelling at an altitude of 35,000 feet. (Too near God for my liking. I saw one of his angels fly past the porthole playing his harp. Ron was scared out of his wits.) Actually Ron was sitting next to Dora

Bryan. He was pleased. This VC10 was very comfortable. We was told that the weather in New York would be cold. When you look out of the porthole all you can see is blue skies and underneath clouds (pure white). It looks as though you are flying over Antarctica. The dinner was beautiful. Good luck next Saturday Arthur. How about coming first and you will have a ribbon too.

Look after yourselves

Love

Jack

Mrs Collins sends her love.

PS As I went to the toilet on the plane, I opened the door and... A...H...H...

When I'd finished the letter I looked round for something else to do and I asked if I could go in the cockpit. I thought it might make me feel a bit better about flying, but I wished I hadn't as it really spooked me. I went in and I was struck to see all these millions of dials and instruments but the pilots weren't looking at them, they weren't even holding on to the steering wheel, they were just sitting there chatting. I didn't like that. I didn't like that at all.

Despite the chatting, we made it to New York which *was* cold and dark and wintery. And it snowed! In New York! I found that quite amazing! After the snow, the first thing that hit me was how tall the buildings were. All these skyscrapers! And to see the Empire State Building, that was just unbelievable. I bought a sealskin hat with ear-muffs because it was so cold and an old Chinese coin for good luck.

I'd been booked to do *The Mike Douglas Show* which was a TV chat show that went out in the afternoon. It was broadcast live from Philadelphia and me and Mrs Collins went down in a stretch limo with blacked-out windows. I'd never been in one with blacked-out windows before.

'So this is your first trip to America, Jack,' Mike Douglas began. 'What do you like about it? What's different to England?'

'Well,' I said, 'I was told that everything's bigger in the States and it really is 'cos the cars are bigger, the roads are bigger, restaurants are bigger – it's magic.'

'And what do you think of the food here? Have you got any favourite food since coming to the States?'

'Yeah,' I said, 'I was taken the other day to McDonald's and I loved it – it was great.'

'And I'm sure they'll love you too,' he said, laughing; and I wasn't really sure what he meant, but before the show had finished, a crate packed full of burgers had arrived for me at the studios. And if there was one hamburger there must've been a couple of hundred hamburgers – it was amazing.

I was thrilled. Free burgers. 'Anyone want a burger?' I said. 'Help yerself like!'

They all soon disappeared and, after my second or maybe my third, one of the producers came over and quietly said, 'You know, you're not supposed to give free advertising on American TV, so be careful; but thanks for the lunch, you must come again!'

Back in New York, we were walking down Broadway when we heard what sounded like a car backfiring. About a hundred yards in front of us this geezer flew out of a shop, and as we got closer we could see that he was bleeding heavily and that he was firing back into the shop with a handgun. My first thought was, they're making a film and it's not for real, and I was looking to see where the camera was. But then the geezer legged it as quickly as he could and disappeared round the corner. By the time we got up to where it had all happened, there was pandemonium because there were fire engines, police cars and all sorts, and we could see there was blood on the floor.

Mrs Collins ushered me away because she was obviously feeling that we might be in a bit of danger. Me, I was quite excited by it! New York was certainly living up to expectations. And to walk down Broadway in my suit... I thought, Wild, you have arrived! Everyone else must have thought, poor bugger! He can't have much money. He's only got *one* suit! That's all we've ever seen him in.

After the New York premiere we went to San Francisco. Mrs Collins took me to Chinatown which was the main thing that stood out for me. Going into a restaurant to eat how the Chinese eat, that was a big culture shock. We also went to Los Angeles, and one warm day I remember walking around Disneyland in my bronze raincoat, my shades and my sealskin hat with ear muffs.

In LA, me and Mrs Collins stayed at the Beverly Wilshire Hotel. It was very grand – a suite with a lounge, two bedrooms and two bathrooms – but much more impressive was a telegram I received whilst we were there from James Cagney. He said he was sorry he couldn't make the premiere but had had a private showing, and added, 'You're just like me, kid.' I was amazed and so, so proud. That telegram was priceless to me. Though sadly not priceless to someone else, who nicked it from my room.

Several times between September and December of 1968, at the various premieres of *Oliver!*, we met up with Mark's parents who kept saying how pleased they were with Mark's new business manager. Mark's Dad seemed particularly pleased with him.

'Although Mark is still at Corona Stage School, we've got John Daly looking after him and he's doing great numbers for Mark, Jack. You should meet him.'

Mr Lester had so much more experience than my lot – even Mark had been in the business longer than I had.

'I'll introduce you and Mrs Collins if you like, Jack.'

He was dead posh, Mr Lester. He had been a male model and was tanned and good looking. In fact the whole family looked to me like they went skiing every year and had a holiday home in Europe.

'It's made quite some difference, Jack, since John's been involved. Mark's earnings have gone up at least tenfold. You really should meet him.'

I respected his opinion, but even I knew that ten times as much money for doing the same amount of work had to be a good thing. I'd thought I'd be mad not to.

So it was arranged that me and Mrs Collins would go and meet John Daly at his offices in Mayfair. Since Mrs Collins had become my personal manager it had taken up a lot of her time so I guess from her point of view if Mr Daly became my business manager, it would allow her to concentrate on the school again. From *my* point of view, I had been speaking to other kids while I'd been working and I began to realise that Speake's was charging much more commission than other agencies. After paying twenty-five per cent commission and tax on top of that, fifty per cent of my earnings had gone before I even started paying expenses. And while it wasn't about the money, the more work I did, the more it began to matter. So when we went to meet Mr Daly I was determined not to pay more than twenty-five per cent *combined* commission. And finally from my Dad's point of view – 'I'll leave it to you June, whatever you sa', I'll go along with' – he didn't have one.

John Daly was originally a car salesman, then an insurance agent, and then he became friendly with David Hemmings and together they set up Hemdale Artists and Associates Limited. John and David both seemed to me to be every inch the men about town. I hadn't seen any of David's films but I knew he was a star. He was charismatic and engaging, he had nice clothes, nice cars – a Rolls Royce *and* a sports car – he did card tricks in the office, had every kind of gadget and seemed to be able to afford anything he wanted. Women loved him, fans loved him, I think we all loved him.

John was very driven; he worked hard and played even harder. He always wore a suit and a tie: even when we were at Malibu beach together he wore his uniform, and I imagined he went to bed in his collar and tie. I liked them both tremendously and wanted to be part of their world. And so the deal was done, and John became my business manager. I was very fond of Mrs Collins and in many ways she was like my second mum. Obviously she couldn't behave as friendly as that while she was in the agency at school because it wouldn't have been right, but I think she cared for me and looked out for me, and treated me like one of her own.

But at that time I wanted to go about with John. He seemed more like an elder brother than my business manager; I looked up to him and wanted to be seen with him, rather than with me 'mum'.

And Mr Lester's predictions were right: John was earning me a lot more money. Mrs Collins had me signed up to Columbia Pictures for another five films, over five years, for the same money as I was getting for *Oliver!* John got me out of the contract and agreed a new deal where I was to be paid the full five-year fee for just one film. It made me think, maybe Mr Layton was right as well: maybe I was hot property.

Chapter 8

A FTER THE *OLIVER!* PREMIERE, I started guesting on all the TV variety shows in England: the Jimmy Tarbuck show, the Bachelors show, the Val Doonican show, the Engelbert Humperdinck show, Liberace, Stewpot – variety was dead popular then. They were mostly all shot in the old ATV studios and were mostly the same format. I'd sing, dance, do a few sketches, rehearse for ten days and record it. I was doing at least two or three a month for well over a year promoting singles, or films, or me.

I enjoyed doing these shows a hell of a lot. I'd meet the same people doing the variety rounds – even if you weren't doing the same show you'd bump into them at the studios – and they were well paid.

The Liberace Show was particularly well paid, but I loved doing it because I was mesmerised by him. Liberace ('*you* can call me Lee, darling') was so wonderfully generous, kind and tanned; and a love of life, fame and everything oozed out of him. I'd never, ever met anyone like him. He behaved like royalty and we were all more than happy to treat him as such. He was the king and the queen all on his own, and yet it all seemed so natural.

I was rehearsing the show with Terry-Thomas (ever so nice but a bit unapproachable) and Engelbert Humperdinck ('Arnold George Dorsey, nice to meet you, Jack') when it was suggested that I should have a jacket made to match Lee's. Now I'd seen Lee's outrageously elaborate bejewelled jackets and I was worried. Lee said I'd look 'divine, darling', but I could only think what my mates would say. Still, I was measured, fitted and charmed into the jacket which made me look just like a slightly paler, mini Lee. It could have been worse: at least the jacket didn't light up, although it had used up the sequin supply for the whole of the western world.

Liberace's was such a good show to do because it was a co-production which meant that it would be shown in the States as well, whereas with the Tarbuck shows, the Bachelors, Val Doonican and all those, they were English shows that in those days weren't sold abroad.

When I was doing Dorsey's show, it was very much a family-type atmosphere and great fun because he wasn't that much older than me. He was tall, dark and handsome, a bit shy, but really down to earth with a great sense of humour; no wonder women loved him.

If we got back early from lunch, we'd have a game of hockey before rehearsals. The studio was our pitch. On the floor, there were different coloured tapes to mark the scenery, and the set doors were created with a pole, a frame, a diagonal piece of wood and a knob to open it. So there were lots of bits of wood around in these massive rehearsal rooms and we'd use them as hockey sticks and the reels of coloured tape as the ball. You'd get your bit of wood into the middle of the reel, drag it along the floor and then flick it to whoever was on your side. I whacked it across the room to get it past Dorsey, but he got the better of me.

'Right! You wait, Dorsey! I'll get ya next time!' I yelled.

The 'Engelbert Humperdinck' thing was an invention of his agent I think. As I understood it, Dorsey became famous doing a Royal Variety when he was a substitute for someone who pulled out at the last minute. They stuck him in, but they didn't have a name for him. His agent had sold him as a bloody good singer, which he was, and at the eleventh hour they struck upon 'Engelbert Humperdinck' – goodness knows how.

Funny though, I had the impression that he didn't really enjoy his image at the time and would much prefer being one of the lads. I don't know, I could be wrong. Still, he did have a voice like velvet and me Mum was in love with him!

Lunchtimes on the Tarbuck show were quite different. He was confident and friendly, always telling gags, and always had an eye out for new ones. We had such fun that he invited me to do two of his shows in one series.

I'd go and have lunch with him at Pinewood and I'd always have prawn cocktail and fillet steak. I also had my first taste of red wine when I was working with him and at the time I thought, this is great, but only because I wasn't supposed to be drinking yet. I actually thought the wine tasted awful!

Val Doonican was lovely too, but I didn't socialise with him as much as I did with Tarby and Engelbert.

While I was doing the second of Tarbuck's shows, someone – I think it was Mrs Collins' daughter Carole – arrived at the rehearsal rooms to tell me I'd been nominated for an Oscar.

'What's that then?' I asked.

There was a chorus of 'Oh, Jack!'s and they all looked ridiculously excited.

'What is it then?' I tried again.

They explained to me what it meant to an actor, first of all just to be nominated, and secondly, if you were lucky enough to actually win it, what it could do for your career. I found it all a bit hard to believe; they'd said the same thing the other week when they said I'd been nominated for a BAFTA.

I thought they were all winding me up and said, 'It's not that important, surely?'

Another chorus of 'Oh *Jack!*'

At the beginning of February 1969 I was invited to Paris to meet Frank Borman, one of the astronauts from the Apollo 8 mission. Apparently he was in Paris meeting Charles de Gaulle, and his kids wanted to meet me. They asked the American Embassy to arrange it and I guess the Embassy didn't have much else on, as it was duly organised and I was dispatched forthwith. I had watched the mission on the television with disbelief. It felt as if it couldn't be real – men orbiting the moon, reading from the Book of Genesis at Christmas. I remember the morbid fascination of seeing whether the thrusters would fire to allow them to leave the gravitational pull of the Moon and come back, or whether the astronauts would remain trapped in space forever.

They weren't; so me and Mrs Collins flew over to Paris to have dinner with the Borman family. And because it wasn't a premiere, I didn't take me dinner suit (it was having a holiday). I was just in a normal two-piece, double-breasted suit with a dual tone overcoat: green if you looked at one way, and bronze if you looked at it the other. We had dinner on the first platform up the Eiffel Tower and I remember something about a tie. I had to wear one to pass muster, I didn't have one, bought one worth a small king's ransom, didn't have to wear it in the end – their vision was probably impaired by the glare off my coat – and oddly, the tie experience stands out more in my memory than the meeting itself. I only hope I made more of an impression on them, as they paid for my trip. I'm sure I didn't.

The next morning John Daly called to say that there was a deal to be done in America. He was in talks with a production company for an American TV series in which I would be the star. Apparently a friend of Lionel Bart's had seen an uncut version of *Oliver!* and as soon as he saw me he said, 'We have to have that kid.' John said that they'd been looking for me for some time and now that they had found me they wanted to fly me out to see them straight away.

So out we flew. The friend of Lionel's was a guy called Sid Krofft, a creative, eccentric man who had made his name in the world of puppetry. In partnership with his brother Marty, they were producing a children's TV show for NBC and they wanted me to play the main character. Oddly, Marty had been a second-hand car salesman, the same as John.

'Let me tell you,' Marty began in his deep sonorous voice, his legs stretching well out beyond the confines of his desk, 'we've been in this business a long time.'

'We sure have,' his diminutive brother concurred. 'I did my first show when I was seven years old. I invited all the kids from the neighbourhood to my paper puppet productions. I wanted to charge them a penny but my family wouldn't let me so I charged them a button instead.'

This was going to be some negotiation.

'We loved your performance in *Oliver!* Jack, and we think you are so right for the part of Jimmy. Let us tell you about the show.' Sid's face lit up as he explained the concept, his energy overtaking the story, so that at times I'd stop listening to what he was saying and just watch him.

It was about a kid who gets trapped on an enchanted island where all the trees are alive and the mushrooms and the flowers are alive, everything is alive. The boy tries to escape but is constantly thwarted by a wicked witch.

They wanted me to be Dorothy.

There was to be one song-and-dance number per episode, '… which is why we want you, Jack. I've worked with Judy Garland and you're our Mickey Rooney; man, you're so like him,' Sid raved.

He bounced around the office showing us ideas for costumes and sets in wild psychedelic colours. 'We've got the West Wind that looks and sounds like John Wayne, we've got a talking skull like Boris Karloff and a Humphrey Bogart Mushroom. We're going to put people in the costumes and create a living cartoon. You're gonna be our hero, Jimmy, stuck on this crazy island.' It was mad. He spoke with the energy of an unrelenting steam train.

'Well, whaddya think?' he said, coming into the station at last. He beamed at us with the breathless expectation of a child. 'It's great, isn't it?' he enthused.

I felt like I'd just been through Dorothy's tornado.

We had a few more meetings after that and John spoke money with Marty. I was waiting for John to come back after one of these meetings and was hanging around the suite at the Beverly Wilshire Hotel. I turned off the telly as John came in.

'Well Jack, we've agreed the deal. You are now a millionaire.'

I couldn't speak.

'Come on Jack. I'm going to take you out and buy you a present to celebrate.'

I got my jacket and we headed off down Rodeo Drive.

'Are you joking, John?' I asked. All the deals before this had been in the thousands; how could this one deal now be for a million?

'No Jack, I'm not joking,' he laughed. 'They've agreed a five-year deal for a million dollars.'

'Bloody hell!'

'Oh, one thing though, they want you to have your teeth done.'

'Bloody hell.'

I'd been wearing an old Woolie's watch up till now and so John took me watch shopping. I ended up getting a white gold one with a crocodile leather strap by some designer called Patek Philippe for eight or nine hundred dollars. It was dead sophisticated and, I thought, just the type of thing John or David would wear. I was well chuffed. I'd never seen white gold before. I don't know what I'd done to deserve it really. It was John who'd done all the negotiations and I hadn't really done anything at all.

Was this when things started to change? It's hard to tell or to take a particular moment and say this was the crossroads where everything was decided. Did I make a choice, or did one thing just lead to another? I don't know. Not that I was complaining: I was having a ball.

When we flew back to London I was mobbed by the press at Heathrow. I hadn't seen so many photographers since the world premiere of *Oliver!*. I'd done loads of photographic sessions for teen mags and stuff, but this was something different. I was wearing a suede Stetson cowboy hat, a suede tasselled jacket and cowboy boots to match. David Hemmings had sent his white Rolls Royce to meet us and I had photographs taken inside the airport and more out by the car. I stood with one cowboyed foot on the running board, tilting my hat with my left hand so they could hopefully get a picture of my watch. I was in grave danger of posing myself to death.

The press shouted questions and I was more than happy to respond.

'What's it like to be a millionaire at sixteen, then, Jack?'

'Great thanks!'

'How was Hollywood, Jack?'

I wanted to tell them it was fantastic and did they know I was wearing a Stetson bought for me by Marty's wife who was a Playmate of the Year! But I just said, 'Really great, thanks.'

While we were back in England, there was the BAFTA evening to attend on 26th March 1969. *Oliver!* was nominated for several awards, including me for Most Promising Newcomer. It was held in a very, very posh London hotel (Grosvenor House), and was recorded for television, going out the following day. The programme boasted a full evening of activities: 8.00pm Dinner,

9.10pm Presentations, 10.00pm Dancing to Acker Bilk and his Paramount Jazz Band and Max Cherry and the Cherry Pickers, 1.30am God Save the Queen; with a discreet notice that Tombola prizes may be collected between 10.30pm and midnight.

On our table was me Mum and Dad, Arthur, John Daly, Mrs Collins, Miss Speake, Miss Speake's Mum and Dad, Grandma Wild, Grandma and Grandad Boardman.

Some of the other people there who may have been collecting Tombola prizes between 10.30pm and midnight were Ian Holm, Roger Moore, Dame Edith Evans, Billie Whitelaw, Stanley Kubrick, John Thaw, Earl Mountbatten, who was presenting an award, Richard Attenborough, who was the chairman, and a smattering of Lords and Ladies too.

My suit came with me that night, with five cigarettes safely stowed in the jacket pocket. Despite being repeatedly told that the BAFTAS were really important, to me it just seemed like another evening where you had to get dressed up and put on a bow tie, and the novelty of *that* was wearing off. I wondered if my suit would begin to fade because of all the flash photography at its every outing. Not that I was about to let it go; I'd only had it four or five months. It was still in its early days! It'd only just started getting used to the limos.

My main concern was that, if I won, I would have to make a speech. I hadn't prepared anything because I thought that would be tempting fate. I suppose I wanted to win; I mean, why not? But I certainly weren't having sleepless nights about it.

I had my prawn cocktail and a fillet steak, went and had a quick fag and waited till ten past nine.

The other nominees in my category were Pia Degermark in *Elvira Madigan*, Katharine Ross in *The Graduate* and Dustin Hoffman in *The Graduate*. I didn't win; Mr Hoffman did. I saw the film (when I was old enough to see it, which I wasn't at the time), and I thought he was brilliant – he deserved to win. *Oliver!* didn't win any awards that night, and I didn't even get anything off the Tombola, but Grandma Boardman got Roger Moore's autograph and it made her night.

Within the month, John and I were back in LA to finalise the Krofft contract, do some publicity and then stay out there for the Oscars.

I'd been booked to do a guest appearance on *The Joey Bishop Show*. I'd not done a proper chat show before, but it was easy enough; it was just like the news interviews I'd done, but longer and to a live studio audience. I didn't even have to sing or dance.

We met Marty the following day and he seemed really pleased with the show.

'Good show, Jack. You looked real cool and laid back.'

'Well, he was so so nice and genuine,' I said. 'What's he done like, before?'

'Don't you know who he is, Jack?'

'No,' I said, 'I don't know him from Adam.'

Marty explained he was a member of the Rat Pack with Frank Sinatra, Dean Martin and Sammy Davis Junior. He'd been an actor and was in a lot of Sinatra's films and was a big, big celebrity.

'Oh, right,' I said. 'Great.'

There were more press calls and trips to Disneyland, and then Mark Lester arrived at my suite a few days before the Oscars ceremony. I had a race track set up with two Hot Wheels cars and I was racing them round and round the suite. I had enough track to go from one bedroom into the lounge, into the other bedroom and back again.

'Wow! Where did you get that from?' Mark asked.

'It's easy,' I said. 'You just ring up downstairs and ask them to order things, anything you want, and they charge it to the room. Isn't that great?'

'Who pays for it then?' he asked.

'I dunno. Fancy a game?'

Before we left England I'd been asked by the organisers of the Oscars Ceremony if I would perform a song. At first I thought, well yeah, I don't mind, it might be a giggle. But when I got out there and they played it to me, I changed my mind. The lyrics weren't proper lyrics, they were just a list of all the nominations and it went through listing them all. I thought it was awful. I hated the lyrics, I hated the tune and thought the style was way too operatic for my voice. *And* I didn't think I could do a good job of it at all. So I said to John, 'Look, I don't want to do this any more. Can you get me out of it?'

'Jack,' John reasoned, 'this is good for business. You've got to do it because millions of people are going to be watching this worldwide. *Live.* It'll be great for you to be seen doing it.'

'I don't like it. I don't want to do it.' There wasn't even going to be a band accompaniment, just a poncey harpsichord.

'Look, Jack, you'll be on the same bill as Aretha Franklin and Frank Sinatra. *They* are singing. I think it would be really good for you.'

'I don't care. I don't want to do it.'

'No, trust me, trust me…'

And the more John pushed, the less I wanted to do it. I think I'd got used to having so much fun and I didn't want to spend time learning a boring old song. I just couldn't see the importance of it, but I obviously wasn't going to get through to John. I was banging me head against a brick wall there. So I thought, how can I get *myself* out of it. And I thought, the only thing I can do is, I'll keep doing it badly; and the more I do it, the worse I'll get. And that was my sort of plan.

Just before the dress rehearsal Pat Davis took me down to Tijuana in Mexico for a day out. Pat worked for the Kroffts; he was a hip guy, very laid back and seemed to like the same things as I did. We liked the same music, we both loved cars and both loved an adventure; I was looking forward to a day out with him. I'd been told Tijuana was a very dangerous place and that if you had enough money, you could buy anything you wanted there. I was *really* looking forward to going.

It was a long drive down there; I bought a sombrero, and we headed back. Just as we were coming to the border a thought occurred to me.

''Ere Pat, as it's a different country, shouldn't I have to have a passport?'

'Haven't you got it with you, Jack?' He looked at me and then back at the road. 'Oh.'

'Pat, does it matter?' I asked, a note of panic creeping into my voice.

'Look,' Pat said, assuming an authority I'd not seen in him before, which I found reassuring and alarming in equal measures, 'whatever you do, don't speak, just stay quiet and let me deal with it.'

On no, I thought. If they catch me trying to get back into America without a passport, they will lock me up in Tijuana, and they'll just throw away the key, because that's the sort of place it is. This didn't seem so exciting any more and I slid down in the back of his Buick Riviera hoping my outsized sombrero would afford me some protection.

As we drew close to the border, the vegetation grew sparser. 'See those hills on either side of the freeway?' Pat said. 'That's where the FBI sit and watch to catch drug smugglers and illegal immigrants. They can pounce on them from up there; there's no escaping.' I had visions of incarceration, torture and an ignominious death. I felt sick as my stomach turned over. My legs stuck to the leather seats and the sombrero scratched my head as I tried to disappear into it; the sound of my heart bounced around the hills like an Indian drumbeat calling to the Feds.

As we passed through the border I stopped breathing... and somehow, somehow, we slipped through undetected. We'd got away with it.

The next morning brought the dress rehearsal and that bloody song. And to go along with my 'doing-it-badly' plan, I thought I would take along my trusty sombrero as it had saved me the day before. It was about four foot wide and quite ridiculous. From the back of the auditorium you couldn't see me at all; it would have just looked like a singing hat.

Other than the hat, I hadn't really worked out what I was going to do; and while I was thinking, a tall, slender, well-dressed man called Henry Mancini started playing the introduction on the harpsichord. I found out later that he'd composed the music and was actually quite famous.

They'd got the lyrics written on idiot boards, but they were miles away and because of all the lights shining on me, and because of my hat and possibly also not helped by my wraparound sunglasses, I couldn't see the words at all. I started to get behind with the tempo and so my plan began to take shape. Each time I got behind, I stopped it and said: 'Hang on a minute! C'mon Henry, get it right! Let's start again!'

He was so gobsmacked, I don't think he knew what the hell to do. He didn't know whether to batter me or to ignore me. But with an extraordinarily heroic display of stoicism, he didn't ignore me, and he did go back to the beginning. Each time I stopped, he'd do what I asked. This cocky, arrogant, rude little bastard got away with it.

But the organisers obviously panicked, and they'd started phoning round trying to get a replacement. They must have thought, oh hell, this kid's useless. We'd better get somebody in who can actually do it because he can't. He can't even learn his lines! How they dealt with him on *Oliver!* God only knows!

So they got someone else and I'd got out of it: got out of singing with Frank Sinatra, got out of singing with Aretha Franklin, upset, angered and publicly humiliated an eminent composer and gentleman, not to mention the organisers of the ceremony.

And I was so, so, pleased. I thought, *yeessss!* I've done it!

It was a long, long time before I saw this for what it was; and even then I justified it to myself by saying, well, if I'd have liked the song I'd have done it.

I don't remember John Daly having a go at me or going mad at all. All he said as we were walking back through the foyer was, 'Oh, Jack, by the way, on the way back to London we've got to call in to New York because you're going to be presented with an award from the National Catholic Association of America for Best Newcomer. It's at Carnegie Hall and what they're going to do is put wires on you and have you flying in looking like an angel, to receive your award!'

I stopped dead and hurled my words at him. 'I ain't doin' that. Tell 'em to send it to me in the post, I am not going!'

'I've already agreed for you to do it!' he said without a break in his pace and an infuriating nonchalance.

'Bollocks, I ain't doin' it!'

He turned with half a smile, held my gaze, and walked on. He was winding me up: to make a point, to make a joke, I'm not sure.

'You bastard,' I said, running to catch up with him.

Mrs Collins and Miss Speake had also come out for the ceremony and were staying in the same hotel as me and John. When they arrived they called to say that they had the four tickets for the ceremony. 'You, me and Miss Speake will be in the stalls and John will be in the Dress Circle,' Mrs Collins said.

'No,' I said, 'I want John to sit with us in the best seats. Miss Speake can sit upstairs.'

'Jack, that wouldn't be right. We three have been in it since the beginning. John's only just joined us; he is the one who should be up in the Circle.'

I felt so angry. How dare they take my tickets and decide who sits where! I didn't want to be with two old ladies. I wanted to be with John. I wanted to be with someone who I could have a laugh with. I didn't want him to sit up in the Gods, on this night of all nights. I wanted Miss Speake to sit up in the Gods, and me, John and Mrs Collins to sit in the good seats.

I phoned Columbia Pictures. 'You get them tickets off Barbara Speake and June Collins and give 'em to me, otherwise I'm getting on the next flight home and I won't be at the ceremony!'

They must've spoken to Mrs Collins and Miss Speake, and Mrs Collins was so upset that she wouldn't come to my room. Miss Speake came, however, to give me the tickets and some unwelcome and un-listened to advice.

'The way you're behaving, Jack, is dreadful. Your mother and father won't be very pleased when they hear about this. Do you know how much you have upset Mrs Collins? We're only trying to look after your best interests, Jack. And anyway, John Daly was the last to join the team and it's only right that he sits in the Dress Circle and we three should sit...'

And I thought, I've had enough, I'm not having this. If it hadn't have been for me, none of these people would've been here anyway, and that's number one; and number two is, surely, it's what is going to make me happy that is the most important thing for this particular night. I listened to her going on, and at one stage, I very nearly said, 'Yeah, alright then.' But it wasn't alright. Why do I never spend these important evenings with the people I want to be with? I couldn't be with the lads at the premiere, I'll be damned if I'm going to let it happen again. Bollocks, No, I'm not putting up with it!

'Right,' I said, 'give me the tickets. Right, there's your ticket, Miss Speake, and that's for Mrs Collins, and that's it! I'm finished now! I am not coming back to the stage school, and I'm leaving you both when I get back to England. That's it, I've had enough!'

And she left.

On the night of the ceremony it was decided Mark and I should arrive together in the same limousine. When we got there, Mark went to sit with his Mum and Dad, and I went and sat with Mrs Collins and John and oh, you could cut the atmosphere with a knife! What a hollow, hollow victory it was. The ceremony went on for hours, and barely a word was exchanged.

All the nominees had to be reasonably close to the stage so that, whoever won, it wouldn't take them three quarters of an hour to get up there. But we were particularly close to the stage as I was tipped to win. Ron and I were such hot favourites that we'd been asked to film two sequences before the ceremony. We were dressed as Dodger and Fagin; and one version was of us leaving the building with an Oscar each that we'd been given, and the other version was of us running away as we hadn't won and had decided to nick them instead.

I was following each category in my programme, ticking them off as I went and seeing who I could recognise. And the evening went on and on and on. It lasted for hours. As it crept along I kept thinking, I'm sure I won't win, why should I win this when I'm not even from here. If I can't win one in my own country how can I win one abroad?

My other thought was that if I did win, I would have to make a speech and I had nothing to say and even if I did I wouldn't remember it or say it right. I kept looking for when the award for Best Supporting Actor would come, and the closer it got the more and more nervous I got. I pulled at my hated, oversized, black velvet bow tie as I became more and more uncomfortable, until it got to the point where I was hovering two inches above my chair waiting for the pronouncement. I didn't want to get up and make a speech, it terrified me. What would I say, what would people think of me? It all began to matter too much.

And then, as if someone had suddenly decided to fast forward a film, they were reading out my category.

'And now, for Best Supporting Actor, the nominations are...'

Can the body still function when your heart stops beating and your lungs stop breathing and your mind goes into free fall?

'Jack Albertson in *The Subject Was Roses*, Seymour Cassel in *Faces*, Daniel Massey in *Star!*, Jack Wild in *Oliver!* and Gene Wilder in *The Producers*.'

'And the winner is...'

As he opened the envelope at fifty frames per second I thought I really ought to start breathing again soon.

'Jack...'

Oh no, I thought, it's me! Out of the corner of my eye I saw the cameras turn onto me and I saw the little red light come on. So I stood up, and they said:

'… Albertson.'

I sat back down again quickly. Right, well that's that then.

We won six Oscars that night and I cheered loudly for each one. I didn't know then how important it was to be involved in a successful film; I was just pleased for the friends I'd worked with all year. So I cheered when Johnny Green got it for best score of a musical and John Box for the set designs and Carol Reed for the direction. And I really wasn't too disappointed that I hadn't won, not then, not yet.

The reception after the ceremony was at the Beverly Hills Hotel, but I didn't want to go. I wanted to go back to my hotel and play with my Hot Wheels. I didn't want to stand around talking to the adults. But we went, and we went by limousine, and stood around talking to adults. I escaped them briefly when I spotted Ron and I headed over to him.

'You should've won that hands down, Ron,' I said. I was disappointed that he hadn't won Best Actor. I thought he really deserved it. I used to watch Ron and Oliver Reed in most of the scenes that they did, and it's just they were both so convincing. That moment when Ron comes on with the quill stuck in his hair in 'I'd Do Anything' was worth an Oscar in its own right, I thought. He was just magical! The way he would use his face in conjunction with all his make-up; and he was the complete opposite of what Fagin was – a very nice, funny, enjoyable person to be with. He should have won. But he just brushed it aside and said, 'Oh, it doesn't matter. It's been a good experience.'

Later in the evening Carol Reed came over. 'You know, in my opinion you two should have won,' he said, placing a fatherly hand on my shoulder.

'Oh well,' I said, 'there's plenty of time yet.'

He smiled and squeezed my shoulder. I think he felt sorry for us, as he'd won one and we hadn't, and me and Ron were the only ones on screen who'd been nominated. 'Without you two, none of us would have won,' he said. That was nice, I thought.

And then so many people at the reception came up and said, 'Oh I'm sorry you didn't win,' and 'Oh, you should've won.' They just made so much of it. There seemed to be too many people saying the same thing. I just didn't think they meant it.

Oliver! was nominated for eight awards and received six; and, no matter what, I am immensely proud of the film and privileged that I was a part of it.

The following year when I was filming at Universal Studios in Hollywood, Jack Albertson was either working on something there or just visiting for the day, and he made a special trip over to my set. He apologised for winning the Oscar because he thought I should have won. At the time, I hadn't seen any of his work and I just accepted it as a fellow worker being nice and I thought, okay. Fine, thanks very much. It was only really again maybe five or six years later when I sat back and thought about it, that I thought, well, Christ! That was such a nice thing, for the guy to have come over said that. I never met him again. The next time I saw him work was in *The Poseidon Adventure* where he played Shelley Winters' husband, and he should have won an Oscar for that.

I went back home to England, but not back to school. It still felt like the right thing to do and I was determined to stick by what I'd said to Miss Speake on the Oscar night. My future was with John; the present was breaking the news to Mum and Dad.

'Oh Jackie, do yer think yer makin' the right decision?'

'Mum, you know I tried to stay with Mrs Collins,' I said, 'but she wouldn't have any of it. It's Miss Speake's fault, not mine.'

'Even so, Jackie...' me Mum tried.

'Any road, Vera,' me Dad ventured in a surprising show of support, 'you were the one who spoke out agen' Miss Speake at parents' meetings when no bugger else would. Yer know she always wants things done her own way.'

'Even so, Jack...' me Mum tried again.

But it was decided and I was off to Hollywood. And for a while we didn't talk about it again. The next few weeks were filled with Hollywood preparations: the compulsory interviews with the same ubiquitous questions, photo sessions, dentistry sessions; and I hardly gave the breakup another thought.

I gave myself over to Hemdale, and whatever people they used, I used. They had publicists, solicitors, accountants, record producers, cars on tap and Dougie-the-Stitch. I was coming up to seventeen and coming up to a thirty-six-inch chest, but I hadn't got there yet so it was hard to find suits to fit. I'd had special day suits made at Stanfords, but David and John had all their suits crafted by Dougie-the-Stitch in Mayfair. So naturally I called for a chauffeur-driven car and went there too. I was shown into a small dark office, inhabited by this small dark-suited tailor who showed me cloths and designs and spoke in very proper English. He had a young face on a strangely older body and wasn't that much taller than me. I had the impression he came from a long line of tailors: you could almost see the adjoining thread.

I must have had at least a dozen suits made at his place and I'd always use my chauffeur-driven car to get to the fittings, simply because I had an account with Focus Cars. I had been given the impression that the cars were a luxury that was given to me and I weren't actually paying for it. It did seem flash, but to be honest it was so difficult to use London Transport at this time as I was always being bothered, so I thought it was just easier and safer to be driven. I did see at the end of the year a bill from Focus Cars that had been paid on my behalf, but money was no object, so I didn't really take any notice of it. I knew I had lots of money so the bill was of no importance. John said it was important to maintain an image, so I'd often phone up Dougie-the-Stitch and say, 'I've just seen a geezer on telly and I want a suit like that, can I have an appointment please?' And I'd call a car which would take me up, wait for me and then bring me home again.

All seemed fine and I took these newly given luxuries as the normal state of affairs, because at that time in my life, it was. If I asked for something, I got it; if I just showed a passing interest in something, I got it. If I saw something in a hotel shop at reception, I would only need to say to whoever was around me, 'I want that,' and they'd go and get it for me and I wouldn't have to pay for it, I'd get it all for nothing. If I went to a restaurant, I'd get the best table; and there were always chauffeur-driven cars, always, to take me here, there and everywhere. It was only later that I learned that many of these 'gifts' weren't gifts at all and that I was paying for them myself. And it took me even longer to realise that for the times that I *didn't* foot the bill, for every pound spent on me to keep me sweet, someone else made ten.

And honey was poured into my ears: 'You're the next Mickey Rooney, you're James Cagney, you're brilliant you are.' It got to the stage where I thought, in actual fact, I'm better than they think I am. And if I've got all this power, why waste it? If I have the power to change things that I'm not happy with, why not do that? It seemed the most sensible thing to do. Obviously, I wouldn't want to do it maliciously, but if something needed changing, then change it would.

Before finally heading off to work in America, I had to go and swear to a judge that I was happy about going and not being pushed into it by me Mum and Dad, or anyone else. David sent his Rolls to come and pick us up and we all went up to the Hemdale offices to meet John.

'Now listen Jack, you've got to take this seriously because without the judge's signature you simply can't go,' John said.

David was showing me a new gadget that he just picked up in New York.

'Jackie, are yer listening to John?' me Mum worried.

'Yeah, yeah,' I said, not really totally sure what I'd missed.

We set off to the judge's chambers in Bow Street which was actually where Dodger is up before the magistrate before being sentenced to transportation. Outside it didn't look particularly impressive at all, but as soon as we walked in there, the musty air was thick with authority and power, and it filled my lungs. The judge sat behind his desk like a large Christmas pudding steeped in history, tradition and more than a little brandy. He leant forward to speak to me as though he was about to impart a state secret.

'Now young man, I want you to be completely honest with me and I want you to tell me if you are happy to go to work in the United States of America. This is very important; and, if you are not happy for any reason, you must tell me now.'

Fortunately I really did want to go because, despite my finely tuned ability to lie, I don't think I could have said anything apart from the whole truth and nothing but the truth to this man.

Chapter 9

S O WITH MY PAPERS SIGNED AND MY TEETH FILLED me, me Dad and Arf set off to Hollywood. Arf came to keep me company (John's idea), and me Dad came to settle us in and make sure we behaved (me Mum's idea). We were to stay at Marty's house with his wife Christa and their kids, and Marty said he would try and find a job for Arf. Arf had been in a theatre tour and had done a few episodes of *Coronation Street*, but was between jobs that May and so was happy to come out with me.

Me Dad booked the time off work from Firestone Tyres in Brentford (me Mum couldn't come as she had to work), and when Firestone Tyres learnt that I was doing my own TV series in the States, Firestone puffed out its chest and said, 'We are an American company you know, and our main plant is in Akron, Ohio which isn't far from where you are going. We will arrange for you to meet the Head of Firestone Tyres. And you may even be able to have a tour of the plant in Akron!' I was interested in cars, but I certainly weren't interested in how bloody tyres were made. But for me Dad it was bigger than Hollywood. 'I just work on the wire cord section, yer know, yer don't expect people t'want to meet yer.'

We were going to Cincinnati where Sid and Marty had a resident puppet show that played in a massive amusement park there called Six Flags. I think the six flags had something to do with the six states and the civil war, but I was a little sketchy on our own history, let alone anyone else's. One of the characters in the puppet show was this brightly coloured dragon who was very popular and 'goes down real well with the kids', Marty said.

The Kroffts had a huge following. They had created a chorus line of puppets that appeared regularly on *The Dean Martin Show* until they were axed because apparently they received more fan mail than Mr Martin. And before that they'd had a risqué revue show called *Les Poupées de Paris*. It was an 'adults only' show with partially clad marionettes with bare wooden boobs. The inspiration for the show was based on the irrefutable fact that you can't arrest a naked puppet. It played to packed houses.

They had also made the costumes for the Hanna-Barbera show *Banana Splits* until an executive at NBC said, 'Why the hell are you making costumes for someone else to make a successful TV series? Why don't you do that for yourselves?'

'And that's how *H.R. Pufnstuf* was born,' Marty told me, on more than one occasion, about how the show that I'd come out to do, came to be. And so I was to work with this luminous yellow and green dragon. This large, foam, fluorescent reptile was going to be one of my co-stars – he'd even given his name to the series.

Sid and Marty wanted us to see the show, introduce me on stage to all the kids and to do some publicity stuff – although we nearly missed that bit as we'd been given free passes to all the rides in the park. Me, Dad and Arf hadn't seen anything like it before. I'd been to Disneyland, but *they'd* only been to the South Beach at Blackpool. We lost track of time and had stopped for a drink at an outside bar, when suddenly a burly security guard, armed and dramatic, swept in on an electric three-wheeled bike like a sheriff coming to clean up his town.

'Mr Wild, please come with me, sir – you're needed immediately.'

We leapt up, spilling our drinks, and all squeezed onto the bike which sped away in a flurry of Arf's excitement, my terror, Dad's panic and onlookers' glee. I'm so glad we lost track of time.

Mr William Hanna and Mr Joe Barbera were also in Cincinnati on business and I was to meet them too. Me and Arf had watched loads of their cartoons at home like *Tom and Jerry* and *Top Cat*, but I don't think we were that excited, I don't know why. So we did the publicity, met Mr Hanna and Mr Barbera, met the puppets and puppeteers and other dignitaries and 'Mr Firestone' for me Dad.

When all that was done, we were limousined back to the airport to fly to LA. We were all sat in first class: me, me Dad and Arthur, Sid and Marty, Harry Krofft (the shy, quiet accountant, nothing like his brothers) and Pat Davis, and then the Hanna-Barbera contingent as well, so that our two parties took over the whole of the first-class section.

The adults settled down to champagne and anecdotes. 'When I was Jack's age I joined the Ringling Brothers' Circus,' Sid told my father. 'I was very frightened. I constantly, constantly called my dad and begged, crying, "Please can I come home," and he said you're in show business now and the show must go on.'

'Do you know, when our father died,' Marty added, 'he left us a note saying, "Dear boys, I had a good life, I loved you all, but I've left you no money; and by doing this, I'm doing you a favour. It'll give you guys a chance to be self-made men. Love Pa."'

'Well, when I was in Germany in th'RAF,' me Dad started, 'my Dad said t'me...'

The anecdotes flowed as freely as the champagne.

I had other plans. When Arf and I had passed through the airport, we'd stopped at the Avis stand to fill our pockets with tin badges as they were sure to come in handy. We'd grabbed handfuls of these things, which carried the motto WE TRY HARDER in red lettering on a white background in every language on the planet. At the top end of the badge the metal was so thin that you could just bend it over so that it would stick on anything. The game was, how many can you pin on one person without them realising that they are covered in badges.

'Right, I'll have Marty, you go for Sid and see how many you can get on him,' I said. I think Arf would have been more interested in chatting to the blonde air stewardess, but he went along with it, although I think she put him off his game as I won 15-11.

As we were coming in to land at St Louis, the clouds were very low. We were about a hundred foot off the ground when, all of a sudden, the jet engines go on full throttle, the pilot lifts the nose up and we're like Apollo 11! We were then thrown to the left as the pilot turned the plane sideways so that one wing-tip looked as though it was scraping on the ground.

'Oh, this is just like a big dipper, innit?' Dad noted through the champagne.

We found out, after we landed, that another plane was on the runway and was in the middle of taking off; and had it aborted its take-off we would've run straight into the back of them! So, to be safe, the pilot decided to go round again. But the thing was, he couldn't go right up and back into the queue again because he didn't have enough fuel to do that. So he did a sort of handbrake turn instead.

When we got down, they opened the door and everyone was starting to disembark, but Marty was going bananas. 'I'm not getting off this plane until I've got a... until I've spoken to the pilot and got a good explanation of why we nearly crashed!' he said.

The pilot came out and explained, adding, 'I'm sorry sir, but safety does come first and it was just too risky to land. The one thing to be thankful for, sir,' he continued, 'is that we were in a Boeing 707; it's one of the only planes flying today that could've done what we actually did, sir!'

I was terrified and happy to get off the plane as soon as possible. Marty left, still scowling, and me Dad left smiling. As he walked past the blonde air hostess she said, 'I see that you enjoyed the last bottle of champagne; here, take a bottle home with you!'

'Oh, thanks very much, very kind o'yer, I'll take it home to Vera,' he beamed. 'Here Jack,' he said, 'what a great flight.'

When we got to LA we first went back to Marty's house in Studio City. Me and Arf were to share one massive room at the back, and at the front of the house there was a games room with a pool table, a couple of pinball machines, and a selection of one-armed bandits. I couldn't believe it; it was like your own amusement park. It was just paradise on Earth! *And* there was a swimming pool with an adjoining outdoor Jacuzzi and two lemon trees. They surely couldn't be real? They sat in tubs on the paved area with tables and chairs for relaxing before you went further into the garden. There were a couple more lemon trees on the patio by the pool. At first I thought they were plastic ones but no, these were real too. To live in a house with not only a swimming pool but lemon trees as well: it was in my dreams.

We took me Dad down to Studio City, took a left into Ventura Boulevard and there was a motel called 'The Sportsman's Lodge' where he was to stay. On the way back we stopped off at the shops for me Dad to get something for his champagne head and for me to persuade Arf to buy me some fags.

'Get ya own bloody fags,' he said.

'I can't, they won't sell 'em to me.' I was old enough to smoke in England, but not in the US.

'I ain't come all this way...' Arf was interrupted by a chorus of police sirens, a couple of loud bangs and me Dad.

''Ere, you two, get in that shop now out of the bloody road.' A robbery was happening across the street and Dad pushed us hurriedly into a Mexican furniture shop. 'It's the first time I've been to America,' Dad said to the furniture in general. 'Yer know, I don't feel too clever about leaving you boys here,' Dad said to us.

'It's all right Dad, Marty's is half way up a bloody canyon,' I said.

We stayed tucked in beside a reassuring three-piece suite watching the police race after the criminals. It was soon all over.

'Right, Dad, let's go then,' I said. I still had me fags to get.

'No lads, let's get back up that canyon.'

'It's all right Dad, we don't mind.'

'I didn't know this is how things were done over here,' Dad said, addressing the furniture once more.

'No, we're all right Dad,' I tried again.

'Never mind *we're all right Dad*, I'm a bit concerned about me bloody self, let alone you and Arf. Come on!'

The first week was filled with costume fittings, scripts arriving and lots and lots of publicity. Fan magazines chased me all the time and when we didn't give them any material, they made it up. Fortunately, Marty had a publicity agent that took care of all that stuff. I'd done loads of interviews and photo shoots in England, but this was *Hollywood* and they seemed even more interested in me. Marty was driving me home one night after I'd done an interview with *Tiger Beat* magazine at Paramount Studios. We cruised along in a dark brown Rolls Royce with dark brown windows and a leather interior; it used to belong to Ringo Starr. I sat in the front seat which seemed like the driver's seat as it was right-hand drive, so although Marty was driving, he was really just in the passenger's side I felt. I had the window wound right down, me Polaroid sunglasses on and a fag in my hand. I thought, for goodness' sake, I've definitely made it now, this is too much. Me in Ringo Starr's car! We were driving down Sunset Strip when Marty said, 'Hey Jack, look at that.' I looked up at this giant billboard which shouted down HOLLYWOOD WELCOMES JACK WILD. I couldn't believe it, but there it was. I thought, this is mad.

'What's it there for, Marty?' I asked. I couldn't think of a good enough reason why it should be there. I felt proud, but I didn't really know why. I suppose I was proud of the fact that I was probably the only person in Munster Avenue who'd got their own billboard. And to have it on the Strip of all places: it was the hippest place to be in Hollywood. I'd seen the 'in' crowd strolling down Sunset on a Saturday night looking in at the trendy boutiques and amazing psychedelic clothes shops. I asked Pat Davis to take me back so I could take a photo of the billboard, which he did, and I later lost.

Before Dad went home, we went up to Big Bear Lake in the mountains to shoot the opening sequence of *Pufnstuf*. Big Bear was two hundred miles north of LA, surrounded by pine forests. We went up in a convoy of stretch cars, a strange choice and a strange car. They looked far too long for their own good and far too long for mountain passes, but Hollywood was going a-filming and a-shooting, and so we picked our way up the mountain road like a cowboy in stilettos.

It was the first time I'd been up a mountain and we must've been about seven or eight thousand feet up. It was beautiful; the air was sharp and crsip, though with less oxygen than I was used to.

'So this is when Jimmy is on the way to the boat…' It was Hollingsworth Morse, the director. Holly was a tall guy, about six foot two or three, fiftyish and with grey hair. He'd done loads of TV series over the years and was very experienced. He always seemed to say the right thing at the right time to everyone, and always gave the impression of having the patience of Job. He was a delight to work with. He reminded me so much of Carol Reed because he had the same quality of knowing what he wanted, and how best to get it. Holly's wife was there too: Sandra Gould, a well-known actress who was in the TV series *Bewitched*. I knew her face immediately as I'd seen the show in England. She was smashing.

'So, Jack…' it was Holly again, '… is that alright?' We were shooting the bit with me running down the mountain with Freddie the Flute, and then getting into the boat on the lake. They told me to watch out for bears, and rattlesnakes in the grass. I thought I would spot the bears, but I wasn't so sure about the snakes; so as they were filming me running down through the grass, I jumped high to avoid the snakes, in case they were there and I just couldn't see them. I thought I was a real cowboy – the only time I'd seen rattlesnakes before was in John Wayne movies. And all the buildings seemed to be made of wood so it really did look like the Wild West.

When we got to the bit on the lake, there were swimmers in the water, helping to keep the boat steady. I remember they got sunburnt bobbing about. The lake was full of fish, and me Dad asked the local sheriff how they caught them. ''Ave yer to be patient?' me Dad asked.

'Hell, no. We just wait till they're near the surface and shoot the bastards.'

Me Dad had to leave soon after we got back from Big Bear. When I'd first come to the States I'd been surrounded by people I had grown up with really; but this time, after Dad went home, it seemed very different. There were so many people there to take care of me and to make sure I was happy; there were even people *employed* to make sure I was happy. It felt like I was living in a huge amusement park where every ride was free. There were no queues, endless treats and not a single admonishing call of 'Jackie!'

We were soon to start shooting with the whole cast at Paramount Studios. I'd met Billie Hayes (the lady who was to play the wicked witch) and the puppeteers (who were to play practically everyone else) at various press conferences and at the read-through. Billie had just been working in Vegas with Betty Grable doing *Hello, Dolly!* I thought she was fabulous, full of life and energy, and so funny; she was like a dozen firework displays ready to explode at any minute.

I remembered, from an odd day I'd spent at school, I'd learnt something about sunspots. I think they were explosions that burst from the sun out towards us, and although they are millions of miles away they heat our planet by a couple of degrees and the effect lasts for as much as a whole year, just from a tiny little sunspot. Well, to me, Billie is a genuine sunspot; she is small and blonde and petite but, even after you've left her, you're still warmed by her presence.

Most of the puppeteers working on the series were little people, and when I first met them I felt a little bit awkward. I didn't really know how to behave in front of them because they were so tiny in stature, and all adults, apart from a young girl called Joy Campbell who was just a couple of years older than me. I suppose I was expecting them to be somehow different than I was. Of course they weren't; and they behaved so naturally towards me that they made me feel very relaxed, and in no time at all our friendships blossomed into random, free for all, guerilla warfare. I remember we didn't stop laughing from the moment we got on the set until we finally left.

And I must admit, I was also more than a little pleased not to be the shortest in the cast. While my height wasn't exactly an issue for me (I'd grown another four inches since *Oliver!*) I *was* now sixteen, and felt that I was more than ready to grow up on screen, not to mention in real life. What I hadn't quite appreciated, though, was that despite having left school, despite having an attaché case and a Dunhill lighter and despite being allowed to work on me own in England, in America I was still classed as a minor and therefore still had to have a chaperone. I was disgusted with that. But there was nothing I could do. She was tall and thin and Scandinavian and had the bluest eyes I'd ever seen, and unfortunately she was invincibly sensible. Thordis was a bit older than me Mum and had been with us at Big Bear where unfortunately I'd been her sole priority and I'd been dealt with with a steely kindness.

I'd been the only member of the cast at Big Bear, so I hadn't seen the rest of them since the read-through. I was looking forward to starting work at Paramount, partly to see them again, but mainly because I knew that they were shooting *Bonanza* there. I'd grown up with *Bonanza*, so much so that I felt that I was one of the Cartwright brothers. It seemed surreal that I should be working at the same studios as Hoss Cartwright.

I'd be up at seven and I'd be home by 5.30. The laws were very strict, and if you started at nine, you'd finish at five on the dot! Marty would drive me to work, and at 8.30 every morning we'd pass through the old studio gates. He would drop me off at my trailer which was right outside the soundstage, and then drive on to his offices which were further down the lot. My trailer was really just a glorified cream caravan, but it had my name on it and I needed it to change – and to smoke my cigarettes in – in private. I couldn't smoke openly at the studios as I had my chaperone and the law to contend with.

So I'd get changed, have a few puffs and go across to the set. Most of the cast would already be there; Billie always had an early make-up call and the puppeteers would be waiting in as much of their costume as they could bear. These wild, psychedelic costumes were like little-people pressure cookers and the puppeteers would leave their heads off for as long as possible. We'd rehearse the scene on set with their heads off and then shoot with heads, and as soon as Holly shouted 'cut', the lids would come off and three freshly steamed puppeteers would emerge.

All the voices for Living Island – for the good trees and bad trees, Ludicrous Lion, Stupid Bat, good mushrooms and evil mushrooms, Dr Blinky, Judy Frog, Cling and Clang, Orson and Seymour and all the rest – were provided by just three voice artists: Lennie Weinrib, Joan Gerber and Walker Edmiston. I'd met them at the read-through and thought they were incredible. It was amazing when they would give us a burst of each character's voice and suddenly there was Shirley Temple, Judy Garland or W. C. Fields. They put their tracks down in post-production though, so on the set we just had one valiant continuity lady sitting by the camera reading out all the voices, and a lot of headless puppets.

I learnt the voices for the different characters so that when we were shooting I'd be looking at the right character. It took me a while to get it; I'd forget and instinctively turn to the continuity lady who'd just said the line. When we came to shoot it 'with heads' Felix Silla, or Johnny Silver, or one of the others would wind me up by talking inside their costumes. Continuity would still read out the lines, they would work their costumes, but inside their costumes I would hear:

'What do you think of this new kid on the block then?'

'He's just a Limey, isn't he?'

However, revenge was easily attained. When they had their heads on, their visibility was down to an opportunistic minimum, so I'd try and trip them up. If you were quick you could get away with it as it was hard for them to see who'd done it.

'I know that was you, Limey,' Johnny chuckled. 'I'll get you back, matey.'

Pufnstuf was shot on a much smaller scale than *Oliver!* There was a much smaller cast apart from anything else, and it felt very comfortable, like a rather large and rather eccentric family. We had so much fun that time flew, and acts of sabotage and relentless ribbing were not confined to the cast: everyone got involved.

'How are you today, Limey?' George Radar shouted. I didn't have a witty comeback so I just asked if Joy was in yet.

'Not yet matey.'

I went to sit down and wait. And while George was finishing setting the lighting rig, Andy came and sat on my lap to tell me some more about Jesus. Andy Ratoucheff was a little old man, Russian by birth, a devout Jehovah's Witness and an asthmatic like me Mum. He perched on my lap, his glasses clinging on to the end of his nose, and he read to me from the Bible in his quiet, measured tones. He had a face full of the softest wrinkles, and strangely reminded me of my Gran. I thought it was all nonsense meself, the Bible stuff, but he never said anything negative and there was something very comforting about his homilies. They kept oxygen on the set for him for when his head got too hot and he couldn't breathe.

'Can I just have a chat, Jack?' Holly asked. Andy slipped off my knee and went in search of another soul.

'Jack, about your character in this scene...' Holly began. I was having a great time filming *Pufnstuf* but to be honest I didn't really think there was anything interesting to say about Jimmy.

'Don't forget Jack, you're the only human in the show so you need to play it for real. Just play against the whole production,' Holly said.

I was finding it hard. They had asked me to tone down my accent and to aim for a mid-Atlantic style by changing some vowel sounds. They seemed quite pleased with the outcome, but to me it sounded rather unbelievable. And it was hard playing against the large characters like Dr Blinky. He was played with the exaggeration of a silent movie star, and what with the accent and the acting it all felt a bit plastic and not what I was used to. I struggled to find the truth in it and I looked forward to doing the scenes with Billie as it was the only time I got human reactions to play off. I wanted to put more guts into Jimmy, and it took a long while to realise that in many ways I was the straight man to all the insanity on the island.

Technically it also seemed more difficult too, compared to what I'd done in the past, what with the voices and the heads and also the stop-motion filming for Billie's appearances. I'd not experienced that type of filming before and at first I couldn't understand how it would all cut together.

'Holly, if you've finished, can I sing Jack his song?' Les asked.

Les Szarvas wrote all the songs for the series and was blessed with the biggest moustache this side of Budapest, and the enthusiasm of forty people wrapped up into this one Hungarian hippy standing here in front of me.

'Yeah, sure Les, that'll be great,' Holly replied.

'I've just written you a new song, Jack,' Les started. 'I was just pouring out my muesli when zowie! It came to me! Just think: you in a top hat and tails! "*I* is a lonely word, *You* is a happy word, *We* is a friendly word I much prefer."'

He burst into song, exaggerating the pronunciation of each line as though I had some difficulty understanding English. '*He* is a simple word, *She* is a tender word, *They* is a mating of a him and her.' His huge moustache that cascaded down to his chin and his big brown eyes acted the song out for me. '*It* is a word that can mean anything. *It* can be either large or small. *Mine* is a selfish word. *Yours* is a thoughtful word, but *Ours* is the nicest word of all.'

As he came to the end of the song, he went on to describe how he'd come by this line and that line, and when he'd joined them together 'magic came upon us yet again, Jack!' Les felt he was born to write and he wanted to share it all, with everyone. I thought he was great.

We never seemed to have much time for the songs and we would go and record them as quickly as they could be done. I would then mime to the click track when we were filming, and sometimes we would work out the choreography on the day. I don't actually remember any great length of time in rehearsals for doing the choreography and songs. Mostly we'd get the songs maybe ten days before we were going to film it and then, while they were filming something that I wasn't involved in, Hal Belfer, the choreographer, would take me to one side of the set to rehearse the routines. The sets were massive at Paramount and you could easily get lost in one corner. The songs were only short, only about two minutes, but I loved doing them. I didn't know how the storyline would work out and it was only when Les sang me the songs for upcoming episodes that I would realise that I still hadn't managed to get off the island.

My new life settled down into a very comfortable rhythm. Every morning, Marty and I would drive through *those* gates in Ringo's Rolls, wearing our dark sunglasses and carrying our matching black Samsonite lockable cases. Marty had one first and I felt I had to have one too; I was dead impressed by it and knew none of my mates back home would have one.

I worked my set hours; Thordis wouldn't let me work a minute more, and we always finished dead on the dot. She made sure I had all my breaks and educated me in the correct form for insults.

''Ere Thordis,' I said, 'George keeps winding me up and calling me a Limey. What can I say to get back at him?'

'Well, Jack, if you go back to 1776 and the Boston Tea Party...' Her eyes really were the bluest I'd ever seen in a human being; in fact, they weren't really blue, they were more turquoise, I thought absently; '... so perhaps you could call him a "colonial".'

I didn't really understand it; I hadn't really listened, but I did think 'colonial' sounded very flash. So the next morning, when George called me a

Limey, I said, 'Oh shut up, you colonial. You're all the same, you!' And everybody laughed, even George. I was dead chuffed; I hadn't realised it would work that well.

The morning's filming flew by and then at lunchtime I went to get my bike; but I couldn't find it, anywhere. I looked all over the set and asked everyone I saw, but I couldn't find it. I grabbed the first assistant and said, 'Get the police, my bike's been nicked! Get the police!'

My bike meant an awful lot to me. Before the series began, Pat Davis had taken me to the showrooms of George Barris. Mr Barris made cars for the TV and movie industry and had created the Addams Family car, the Pink Panther car, lots of roadsters and dune buggies, all of them original, one-off cars. He'd also made the Batmobile which I'd seen on TV at home with my mates. I'd been lucky enough to sit in the Batmobile at his showroom. It was incredible and I felt like a real hit sitting in that car. When I got home later that year, I told the lads that *I* had actually sat in the Batmobile.

'No you ain't.'

'Yes I have.'

'No you ain't.'

'Yes I have.'

'Well prove it then.'

'I can't, I didn't get a picture taken, but believe me I really did.'

Nobody believed me.

Shortly after we'd started filming the series, a gift was delivered to the set for me from Mr Barris, with his compliments. He had built me a bike – a handmade bike! And a Chopper to boot. There were no Choppers in England at this time and this had to be a kid's highest aspirations for a bike. That's *got* to show the lads back home, I thought. My Chopper was fiery red with silver magnesium wheels, massive butterfly handlebars and black leather upholstery with a huge backrest. It had a gearstick on the middle bar and everything except a radio. In them days there was nothing like it – it was unheard of. He'd even inscribed it with 'H.R. Pufnstuf' on one side and 'Jimmy' on the other. I was thrilled and rode it round and round Paramount Studios. And I'd always be really careful about where I was leaving it and whenever I was in the studio working, I'd leave it in my eyeline; and I would never leave it outside, unless it was lunchtime in which case I'd chain it up outside the commissary.

I never questioned why Mr Barris should make me a bicycle; I was always being given gifts because I was so popular, Marty said, so I just accepted the bike with great excitement, but without question.

'What can have happened to it?' I asked with growing agitation.

'Leave it to me, Jack. I'll sort it out for you,' the first AD assured me. 'You go and have your lunch and by the time you come back, it'll all be sorted and we'll have it for you.'

I wasn't convinced, but I was keen to go to the commissary as you never knew who you might see having lunch there. They were shooting *M*A*S*H*, *Catch-22* and of course *Bonanza* and I'd been getting to know Dan Blocker who played Hoss Cartwright, so I wanted to catch up with him.

But by the time I got to the commissary, there was hardly anyone there, so I had a quick hamburger and went back to the set.

'Have you found it yet?' I asked.

'No Jack, but we've got all the studio security looking, they're searching the whole premises as we speak; I'm sure we'll find it.'

We carried on shooting, but my heart wasn't in it; it was my pride and joy, this bicycle. We broke for afternoon tea at 3.30 and I was getting more and more het up. I imagined it lost and alone, in a mangled heap.

'It must be here somewhere,' Joy said.

'It isn't – I've looked,' I answered crossly.

'Are you sure?' she asked in a way that on reflection sounded suspiciously like a hint. We started back, and in between shots I was looking everywhere where a bicycle could be; and even in places where you'd be hard pushed to hide a bicycle clip, let alone a bike.

'Holly, you've got another five minutes and then, I'm sorry, Jack's got to finish,' Thordis reminded him.

'Right. Fine. I'll make sure. No problem.'

Her authority was never questioned on the set, and no matter where they were Holly would always agree.

Five o'clock and still no bike!

I finished the last shot for the day and then someone suggested, 'Maybe your bike's in heaven, Jack.' Now that was definitely a hint.

I looked up: and forty foot in the air, hung from the rig and not a mark on it, was my bike.

I felt quite light-headed, either from looking up or from the relief, I'm not sure which. I laughed as I was so glad to see my bike again. They'd all been in on it, but of course, it was George's idea.

The next day we were having lunch in a restaurant just outside the studio gates; I'd left my bike chained up on the set with a 'bugger off colonial' note attached to it. We were in a little Italian bistro and I think I was there with Joy and Billie and Billie's partner Kay. It wasn't often that I managed to get out of the studios as there were press interviews going on all the time which were mainly at lunchtimes and mainly in the studios. So this was a treat. Dan Blocker was also there and had a table with about eight people in the middle of the restaurant. I also recognised Lorne Green and Michael Landon from *Bonanza* sitting at another table and some other people I'd seen around the studios. We sat in a cubicle on the side. I remember Billie and Kay commenting on my new sunglasses. Billie had bought a pair the previous week from 'Optique Boutique' on the Strip which were absolutely fab; she'd shown them to me and I'd thought, I've gotta have a pair of them, and so I had.

'You've gotten so Hollywood,' Kay was saying, when all of a sudden a young guy leapt up and grabbed hold of Dan Blocker's head shouting, 'You dirty son of a bitch! I'm gonna kill you!' I had half a mouthful of hamburger and was suddenly very glad we were in a cubicle. The crazy young man grabbed Dan's head, and Dan's toupee fled the scene. The man, only momentarily distracted by the flight of the toupee, quickly adjusted his position and grabbed hold of Dan's earhole instead. He picked up a knife from the table and went to stab him in the eye. The whole restaurant, as if as one, was seized by panic, and with a strange primeval instinct I dived under the table for safety. I seemed to know that chairs and all sorts were going to start flying at any moment.

The next minute, however, the noise stopped and it was deadly silent. I thought, right, he's dead, or somebody's dead, or everybody's dead. I ventured a look out from under the tablecloth and cautiously crept out. And as I looked up, everyone at Dan's table was sat down eating their meal and carelessly chatting as though nothing had gone on at all. And it had been a joke: a prank played on the whole restaurant. I sat back down on my chair, and as I retrieved a few escaped chips I was pleased to note that I hadn't been the only yellow-belly who had dived under the comforting tables. I didn't stop laughing about it for days afterwards. I thought it was brilliant and just so Hollywood.

Shortly after this, Marty came home early one evening after work and said, 'I've just been on the phone to a friend of mine who's a television reporter.' We were all around the pool and I was just about to do a massive bomb on Arf in the deep end. 'Apparently,' Marty continued, 'there's been a mass murder, not that far from us.' On reflection I thought the dive-bomb could wait.

Marty told us about a man called Charles Manson. Apparently he led a group of people who looked up to him like some terrible Messiah and carried out any horrific act he asked of them. He'd told his disciples to go out and kill people who'd got lots of money, and they had chosen a house just around the corner from where we lived. Marty told us in great detail that to my knowledge was never published. These people had been high on drugs and all sorts and had committed the most appalling acts of mutilation and murder.

I stood shivering by the pool, but it was because I was wet, nothing else.

That night Marty said he'd take us to 'the factory' to take our minds off it. I was a little nonplussed as me and Arf thought he meant the place where him and Sid worked in the valley. It was a nice place; at the front of the building there were administration offices, and at the back there was the workshop where they created, designed and built all the sets and costumes for all the Krofft shows and *Banana Splits* – a nice place, as warehouses go, but not necessarily the place to go for a night out.

But Marty had something quite different in mind. *The* Factory was a nightclub owned by Paul Newman, Peter Lawford, Sammy Davis Jnr and Anthony Newley. Apparently this was *the* place to be seen at and was the hang-out for Frank Sinatra, the Rolling Stones, Jane Fonda, Liza Minnelli and Ronald Reagan; although strangely enough, it was a converted old warehouse too, in an industrial part of Beverly Hills. If you weren't a celebrity, you were turned away. Even Aristotle Onassis had trouble getting in there one time. Thankfully, the half-dozen times I went, I never had any trouble.

Arf and me would celebrity-spot for a while: ''Ere, there's what-his-name. I know him. What's his name? He's famous.' And Marty showed me off like a prize cow. It was embarrassing because there's only so much you can say when everyone is telling you how great you are and I just got bored of it. You could never tell who was being genuine and who was not, so I thought it best to treat it all as rubbish and leave it at that. The best thing about the place was the music. They played all the best pop music and the DJs were fantastic.

When we got home that night, me and Arf were talking about the Manson murders in our room and I must admit we were a bit spooked by it. 'Don't worry, Arf,' I said. 'If they come to this house, I've got this dagger you give me. So we'll be all right.' Earlier on in the week, Christa had taken Arf to Disneyland and he'd brought me back a present which was a very decorative curved dagger that was a letter opener. I was practising my stabbing technique on the mattress and I said, 'Don't worry, they won't hurt you or me, Arf,' and made one last stab to make my point when the knife buckled and gave way, diving into a 360-degree bend.

'Bloody hell, Arf,' I said, 'you could've at least bought me something that could be useful.'

'I bought it to open letters with,' Arf sighed, and rolled over to go to sleep.

I straightened out the knife and put it under my pillow just in case, but I'm not sure that I was overly worried by it. It just felt so Hollywood.

Some time before the end of the series I was having lunch in the café part of the commissary; there was also a more expensive restaurant part, but I didn't go in there that often. Marty often did, and I saw him coming out of the posh section and he caught my eye.

'Come over and meet a friend of mine,' he said. So I followed him into the posh section. I'd been in there before to meet work friends of Marty's so I thought little of it. I presumed it would be an important faceless executive whom I didn't know and would never see again. But it wasn't, and of course I recognised Marty's friend immediately. I couldn't believe it. It was John Wayne. *John Wayne.* And he was just so big; he was massive. This huge prime fillet steak of a man shook my hand in his and it seemed as if my whole arm disappeared into his fist. And I suddenly thought of Vince's gargantuan hands and how he'd shake the whole of Fagin's gang's hands in his.

'Nice to meet ya kid! Are you enjoying yourself?' Mr Wayne said.

But I was gobsmacked and completely speechless. I think I was lucky if I said, 'Nice to meet ya.'

I really hope I said something, and I really wished I had asked for a signed picture at least. It had always been drummed into us by Miss Speake and Mrs Collins that you must never ask for autographs, ever, but maybe they may have made an exception for Mr Wayne. Sadly though, I couldn't form the thought, or the words to ask.

I'd become friends with Dan Blocker by this time and on the odd occasion when I wasn't working I would go and see him on his set. He'd even invited me onto his yacht in Marina Del Ray, although for some reason I'd never been. So to be friends with Dan Blocker and to have met John Wayne, surely life couldn't get any better? Well, other than meeting Cochise, but he was dead. So my new life seemed to fit me as well as a Dougie-the-Stitch suit.

We'd spend the weekends at the beach. Marty had a beach house on Trancas, one of the Malibu beaches, and we'd go there from Friday night to Monday morning and I spent most of my time in the Pacific Ocean. It was constant sunshine seven days a week. I mean, in England you were lucky if you had just one day a week let alone seven. It was like living in the Tropics to me.

But Hollywood is a funny place and the times were wild. One day and night there was a party at Mario Casili's house, an Italian photographer for *Playboy*. He oozed style and dripped gold and his skin fought to constrain his muscles. He had a beautifully perfect wife and beautifully perfect children and the most fantastically massive Georgian house that I've ever seen, ever, with a driveway that must've been half a mile long at least. Behind the white pillared mansion there was another building with a studio and gym and stuff which was where he photographed the nude women. He'd photographed Christa before and this place was bigger than a six-bedroom house in England; and this was classed as an outhouse. What must it be like to have an outhouse like that? I remember part of one party when Mario and Marty played a game of snooker for the loser's car. I couldn't believe Marty was risking Ringo Starr's brown Rolls Royce Silver Cloud, but the prize was a red Dino Ferrari. It was so exciting; a game of snooker for a car of your dreams – how impossibly Hollywood. Strangely enough I can't remember much more. Whether Marty or Mario won, or whether the game was abandoned, I don't remember. All I know is that we went to work the next morning in the Rolls.

Other parties were less friendly. They were all in or around Beverly Hills or Bel Air or Pacific Palisades, all the really exclusive, millionaire's-row-type places. Me and Arf were always the youngest there. The rest were actors and actresses, producers or directors, all in the business. The tables would be laden with bowls of drugs and you could take your pick of uppers or downers. Instead of Twiglets, crisps and peanuts, there was a buffet of drugs: one ashtray full of speed, another of cocaine, marijuana, LSD, everything, all there for your enjoyment.

Through English eyes it seemed like total debauchery, but I accepted it as part of Hollywood. I just stuck to a glass of wine when I was out and maybe a Bristol Cream sherry when I got home; I had a sweet tooth. Drinking seemed the lesser of the two evils because although I wasn't old enough to drink in the States, I was in England, so it was probably all right, I reasoned.

In the midst of all this John Daly rang to say I had been offered a star with my name on it outside Grauman's Chinese Theatre. But you had to pay for it, and then they put it on the pavement, and then people could walk all over it! After you've paid for it! I told John that I didn't want to bother, thanks.

And then there were problems with Arf. I stuck belligerently beside him. Well, he was my brother, and we were two strangers in an even stranger land. Marty offered Arf a job on set, or to go home, but Arf said no; and I said if Arf goes, I go. We both stayed. Soon after this, Marty decided that he wanted to stay at the beach house all week and so Les Szarvas moved in to stay with me at the house. 'And then you can come down with me on Friday night to Trancas and we'll have the weekend at the beach, Jack,' Marty said. 'If that's all right?' he added.

I didn't mind. Les was great and I loved hanging out with him. After work we would go swimming in the pool, or play pool, or the machines, go to the cinema or watch the TV with its zillion channels. Some nights Pat would take me go-karting and Les would cook. He was a brilliant cook and would go to so much trouble; but it was just so hot and spicy that I said, 'I would really rather just have a hamburger, mate, if you don't mind.'

And for some reason, I'm not sure why, I started buying fish tanks. I'd convert them by sticking coloured glass and ceramics on the outside and then putting lighted candles inside. I'd get my supplies from this huge art and craft shop: it was as big as a supermarket and there was nothing like it in England. I'd often sit at home and make them. I made one for Marty and Christa, and I think I made one for Joy.

I suppose I got on better with Joy because she was the closest to my age. She was only like two or three years older than me. I'd occasionally go over to her flat just round the corner from Paramount Studios. We'd have a meal, watch telly and tell jokes. She'd buy me cigarettes if I asked her. On her own she was very shy, but stick her in the costume and she became something else. I wasn't really interested in girls as girls at all. I don't know why, I guess I just wasn't ready for them. I was only interested in work and go-karting and that was it.

I gave myself a certain amount of dollars a week from my expenses and was saving for a Nikkormat camera. I'm not sure why I gave myself such a small allowance and why I made myself save when I could have just bought the camera outright. I had $250 expenses each week which I shared half and half with Arf.

A boost to my camera fund came when Mr Hanna and Mr Barbera asked if I would do a guest appearance on their show, *The Banana Splits*. I didn't get a great amount of time to watch TV so I wasn't really aware of how popular *Banana Splits* was; so, to me, it was just another part of the job. I remember these big characters in very bright costumes and I remember my entrance coming down this slide, but not much else. It was shot relatively quickly in a couple of hours, and that was that. With my fee, I bought the camera, and got it in time for the Apollo 11 moon landings. Amazing; and I took seventy-three pictures of it on the telly.

Marty said I should stay after we finished filming, but John wanted me to go home and start work on my album and I wanted to see my mates to tell them what I'd been up to. Of course there were things I was going to miss; after all, I was living in a house where I had my own swimming pool and if I wanted to get up at three o'clock in the morning and go for a swim, I could do it. Not that I ever did. I did think Beverly Hills just had to be paradise with constant sunshine, mountains one way, beach another, and desert if you wanted it. You could bathe, ski or do whatever you do in the desert. It was like going to the greatest adventure holiday place ever, where the money you had to spend on the rides was limitless. It seemed you could have any nationality of food you wanted, though to be honest I just had burgers, but the choice was there. I did have steak and prawn cocktail on high days and holidays and really any days I fancied it and that was magic! But I wanted to go home.

So it was arranged that we would go, but we'd stay at Marty's for the first showing of *Pufnstuf* which was on Saturday 6th September at 10.00am; and, because it was Arthur's eighteenth birthday on the Monday, we decided to stay and have a tiny party at Marty's.

We all sat around the television and watched the show. I wasn't over the moon about my performance, so really I was glad that we just watched it at home with Marty's family, Josephine the housekeeper and Poupée the dog; and Poupée had never really thought that much of me anyway. I watched Billie leap out of the screen and steal the whole show. And I loved Orson and Seymour and Cling and Clang. They all had such terrific gags and I felt disappointed that I was the straight guy to all the madness. I just didn't think I was funny enough. I wished I could have been part of the insanity.

But Marty was thrilled. 'You've done it again, kid. You've done it again!' he shouted. Christa hugged me: 'You're fantastic, Jack, and just so cute.' Josephine beamed as she brought me a coffee, but Arf and Poupée never said a word. There was no publicity to do that day or any Hollywood hoopla, but I didn't really mind as it meant I could get off to go-karting that much quicker with Pat. Arf had come once or twice before, but didn't really like it as much as me and Pat, so he stayed at home.

Me and Arf left for England shortly after that, and were home again for my seventeenth birthday at the end of September. The teen magazines had whipped themselves up into a frenzy with my impending departure so it was a relief to get away from all that madness.

Chapter 10

We'd got the record deal coming up in April so I started work straight away on my album: looking for songs, and arranging to record them in England, with my record producer, Brian Lane. Brian worked for Hemdale in the new music department that had just recently been set up. He lived in north London somewhere, was about fifteen years older than me, and drove a banana yellow Lotus 130 coupé. Every inch of him was immaculate: from his black curly permed hair to his impossibly stylish clothes, from his fashionable shoes to his manicured teeth and nails; his large nose sitting proudly on his face surveying the stunning effect of all this work. He was very flamboyant and very, very showbiz. He was a great laugh and I liked him tremendously.

It was through Brian that I got to know the guys from the rock group Yes. They were also involved with Hemdale and we used the same offices, the same publicity people, the same studios, the same car company for limos, and generally hung around the same places in Mayfair.

They were all very laddish. Jon Anderson, the lead singer, came from Lancashire and I hit it off with him immediately. He was the smallest, the bass player Chris Squire was the lankiest, Steve Howe the guitarist was the perfectionist. Tony Kaye on keyboards was the quietest and the drummer Bill Bruford was working on it! I enjoyed their company; they were just so cool, and they would invite me to their concerts wherever they were playing. Sometimes they would be in big venues like the Royal Albert Hall, and other times it would be in colleges or universities; but I'd always hire a limo and would always wear my Joe Cocker boots, flares and sunglasses looking like a real bona fide hippy.

My mate Andy Cobb would often come with me as well. Andy was a mate of Arf's who bought and sold cars, had a garage in Hounslow and he also owned a dozen black taxi cabs as well. He was a year older than me, had white blonde hair, teeth, but not that many, and very blue eyes. He really liked their music, and I must admit I thought they were fab as well. We'd go backstage and have drinks with all the band. Their hospitality was great and there'd be all sorts of different substances available if you didn't like alcohol. I thought this scene was really cool and enjoyed it immensely.

Occasionally I would have a bit of dope. I thought it was all right as these were my friends. I hadn't known the people taking drugs in Hollywood so it seemed wrong, but these were mates and I somehow felt less vulnerable in my own country. So I tried it, but I'd probably had a few drinks before I got there and so I didn't notice any effect at all and wasn't that fussed about it. I would be recognised at these gigs, which made me feel embarrassed because it wasn't my gig; I didn't want to take the limelight away from the guys. I think they understood that.

The following morning after a gig I was on the phone to Brian when there was a knock at the door.

'I'll have to call you back, Brian.'

'Don't call me back, Jack,' he said, 'I'll send a car to come and pick you up and then we can sort out some tracks for the album.'

I opened the door and it was Andy. He'd turned up on my doorstep with five hundred goldfish.

'The business next to me needed to get rid of them. I said you'd have 'em,' he grinned. I waited to see if there was any more of an explanation as to why he thought I might like five hundred goldfish. There wasn't. He just stood there grinning. He just seemed to find life endlessly amusing and was just such great fun to be with. I never knew what he was going to do next.

I took the fish and put them in me pond, but it was a bit crowded, standing room only. They didn't live that long.

The car turned up and I went into the Hemdale offices at 39 South Street, Mayfair.

'So have you had any ideas, Jack, about the sort of songs you'd like to do?'

'Well, I definitely want to do some Beatles tracks, Brian.' I'd always been a great fan of the Beatles, and as soon as I was told I'd got the recording deal I thought of doing some of their songs. I would have covered them all for the whole album if I'd been allowed.

'Okay Jack, we can look at some of those. Let me play you some tracks that I've got and see what you think of them.'

Brian played me some new songs from different up and coming artists, and I'd either say 'Yeah! I like them!' or 'No, I don't!' and we chose however many tracks we wanted to do. 'I'll sort out another day for you to meet up with the arrangers that we're going to use, Jack. Two great guys will be working with you, Don Gould and John Cameron. I'll come with you and we'll sort out the keys of the songs.' It was all done by the office: everything was arranged, from chauffeur-driven cars to studio time. I never did anything; *paid* for it, but never did anything. And that's how it worked.

I remember choosing 'When I'm Sixty-Four' and 'Maxwell's Silver Hammer' which were Lennon and McCartney and then we chose a couple of show songs as well. One was 'Fish and Chips' from a well-known musical. At the end of the day, it was really more like sixty per cent my choice and forty per cent Brian's; because I'd got to the point I think, where, if I didn't want to do something, I wouldn't do it. And that's the beginning and end of it! Not that that philosophy had stood me in good stead in the past; still, I saw no reason to change it.

'Before you go, Jack, can you pop in and see Melanie?'

'Yeah, sure, Brian.'

'And I'll call you soon.'

Melanie Mitchell ran my fan club in England. In the States Marty ran my fan club from his offices at the factory. They were separate fan clubs and both used to receive bags full of letters, parcels, packets and all sorts.

Melanie wanted me to sign some photographs; whenever I went into the office, which was at least once or twice a week, I'd always sign photographs. I could never really understand it, all the fuss. All the newspaper and magazine articles, interviews or whatever, would always start at the Hemdale offices and then they would either take me out to lunch, or go to take photographs in Hyde Park, or somewhere. Melanie said they were organising a studio to have my album photographs taken. I wasn't best pleased. I didn't like having my photograph taken as I rarely liked the result. And as the years have gone on they just seem to have got worse; I've just got uglier and uglier as far as I'm concerned.

'You might want to have at look at all that lot,' Melanie said, indicating bags and bags full of letters. What was the matter with all these people? It was nice to hear the things they had to say about stuff that I had done, but had they really nothing better to do?

I sat down on the sofa surrounded by the bags full of fan mail; as well as the letters and cards there was a Union Jack teddy bear, tapes compiled by fans 'of my favourite love songs for you, Jack', sweets, love-heart-shaped key rings, love-heart-shaped picture frames (some with pictures of girls, some without), toys, ornaments and lots and lots of beads, rings and necklaces.

Various people came through the office and at one point John Mills walked in, negotiating the sea of teddy bears that I'd begun to group. 'What's going on here then?' he asked, pointing at the pile of bags. I looked up and smiled but didn't answer as I was absorbed in a rather odd letter. It was a letter from the States about *Pufnstuf*; I presumed it was for me although it did start with 'Hey man'. It went on to say that he knew exactly what I was going through: '... because like, I talk to the trees too, man, and I don't get a word of good advice from these guys at all.' And I thought, what is he talking about? He must be crackers. But as I made my way through the mountain of mail I found more of these letters, all saying they enjoyed talking to trees and books and mushrooms as well. And, 'We really dig the show, man.' What *was* the matter with all these people? How was I to answer fan mail like that?

It wasn't until the following year that Marty explained to me that *Pufnstuf* had been a big hit with the college students who 'were probably stoned when they watched it. It's got a cult following, Jack; they get all tanked up, then watch all the psychedelic colours and they're tripping.' But sitting in the middle of Mayfair, on a crisp October day, I couldn't understand it at all.

I gave up with the fan mail, signed some things for John Daly and headed off. David's chauffeur was taking me to Hounslow in the Mercedes sports car, so that I could get some cash from the Midland bank. The majority of my money stayed abroad and did not come to England until the mid-seventies because the taxes were so high. It was put to me by Hemdale that to save money all my foreign earnings should go straight to my account at Hambros in Jersey and I agreed. The overseas branch of Hemdale collected the money and I never saw it as it just went automatically into my account. I felt really rich in Jersey as I had access to all my earnings whereas in Britain I didn't.

I thought it was very flash, having a bank account in Jersey. It was like you'd read in the papers about these people with money, having bank accounts at Coutts or whatever these flash banks are. So whenever I wanted a holiday, I'd take me and the family over to Jersey, go to my bank, get some money and pay for whatever we wanted. I never really knew how much was in there. I'd get twice-yearly statements as to where all my money had gone, not that I bothered looking at them.

Hemdale said, 'If you want to give yourself more than £5,000 a year you will go over into the next tax bracket.' I think the rate was seven shillings in the pound. So I decided to just give myself the £5,000 a year. I was happy with that. I didn't really have any spare time anyway to go out and spend money, as

I was constantly working. When I did go shopping I'd buy clothes and records and that was it really. If ever I ran out of money at the Midland, I would just go and ask John for another grand. It was easy. Every time I asked for a thousand pounds, by the time my tax was taken out of it I was left with around £750. This would last me on average about ten or eleven weeks and then I'd just go and get some more; if it ran out quicker I'd keep getting more until I'd spent the whole five grand.

Things were moving on apace with the album and we were starting to record the tracks. One morning, Brian came to pick me up to take me to Advision Studios near Great Portland Street, in his Lotus sports car; I loved that car. He was telling me about an idea he had for the album sleeve. His girlfriend was an art student at the time called Lynsey de Paul: 'I think it would be a great idea for her to draw a picture of you for each song. And then we can put the book of pictures with each album to make a bigger package.'

'I've had an idea too, Brian, of what to call the album.'

'Oh right Jack – let's hear it.'

'When I'm Six Foot Four!'

I thought it was hysterical.

'You know,' I pursued, '´cos I'm doing the "When I'm Sixty-Four" track.' He still seemed not to get it. 'You know, 'cos like I'm only four foot ten?' It was inspired, what was the matter with him?

'Well, let's think about it, Jack.'

Think about it? When I'm Six Foot Four! It's genius!

Brian commissioned Lynsey to do these cartoon-style pictures of me and they were great, she'd got me down to a tee. Brian took the pictures to Capitol and said this is what we want in the record sleeve, but they didn't buy the idea; and my first album was called *The Jack Wild Album*. Inspired!

But I loved recording the album. We'd always do it with a full orchestra because you weren't allowed in those days to just do a backing track and put your vocals on afterwards; it all had to be done at the same time. It reminded me of doing the *Oliver!* soundtrack. We'd recorded the tracks at Shepperton Studios in the sound stages with a forty- or fifty-piece orchestra; it was massive. It was mad to go into the studio and sing live with that many musicians when I was only fourteen; bloody mad. It gave me such a buzz. I knew so little about music at that stage, and I didn't really know what I was doing, I just did what came naturally; but to feel that power of leading the orchestra – it was amazing.

Now, on the album, we'd normally do at least a three- or four-hour session; and, because it was a production deal, we obviously wouldn't want to waste time in the recording studios. You'd be given a sum of money by your record company to produce an album and obviously this would be against sales, but it would be an agreed price and that was your maximum budget. So you'd keep it under that and make the record as quickly as you could.

After one of these sessions my voice was going a bit and somebody said to me that sherry was very good for your throat. 'Oh right, great, thanks,' I said, and on the way home that night I said, ''Ere Brian, let's just call in and get some sherry like for tomorrow.' After that there'd always be some sherry on hand for me, if my voice started to go. I was quite merry by the time I'd finished the session. Not that I was slurring my words, but certainly very happy, thank you very much! I was still struggling with the idea of me as a pop star. I'd always seen myself as an entertainer, not a pop star; but since I was, the sherry helped me in the studio. It weren't the fact that it was alcohol: not yet, not then. I just thought it helped me get the job done as best as I could.

For the Capitol contract, it was agreed that I would first release a single and see how that went, and sometime during the first year, I would release one album; and that was the basis of the five-year million-dollar contract. That would happen each year, as a minimum amount of recording. We'd not got a track yet for the single, but Brian had been approached by Gene Page, a cool black dude who had been involved in the music for *Pufnstuf.*

Gene's brother Billy had written this song called 'Some Beautiful' and it was arranged to meet up with Gene and Billy in LA. They played the track to me and Brian and we thought, yeah, this is really hip stuff this! And the brothers were just so cool, which made me want to do their track even more. They were both immaculately dressed; whatever was in fashion at the time they would be the first people to be wearing it. They wore quite a bit of jewellery and drove a Cadillac. They were just so hip. The tops. As cool as they come. I was to record it in LA, Gene would arrange it and an up-and-coming keyboard player called Leon Russell was going to be one of my backing musicians.

At the time I didn't know who Leon Russell was, but I found out how great he was a couple of years later when Brian took me to the film premiere of *Mad Dogs and Englishmen* in New York. It starred Joe Cocker and his band which included Leon Russell as a featured artist; a musician and a half if ever there was one.

So we flew back to England and then back out to New York in November '69 to do a big Christmas TV special with Wayne Newton for *The Kraft Music Hall.*

'I don't like all this flying, Brian,' I said.

'Do you know the lyrics for your song, Jack?' Brian asked, trying to distract me, I guess.

'Piece of cake, mate,' I said. 'It's the Beatles!'

They'd asked me what sort of song I'd like to do and I'd said 'With A Little Help From My Friends'. I really loved this song and, as it turned out, the gig itself was really one of my favourites because of the amazing set. In the studio, they recreated the ice rink in Central Park. I was a down-and-out and all 'my friends' were tramps. It was set in the winter with snow coming down and people ice-skating. It was so picturesque and I remember it so vividly.

We rehearsed all the dance routines for two weeks and then shot it in ten days. I didn't do much else while I was there as I still wasn't old enough to drink and my popularity made it awkward to go out. So when I wasn't working I mainly sat in the hotel, had some beers and cigarettes that Brian got for me, and that was it really. I don't know what the show finally looked like; I never saw it on telly as we were gone before it was broadcast.

I went home for Christmas and then flew out to LA on 30th December, to get ready to start filming the *Pufnstuf* movie. Me Mum and Dad came with me, and Arf stayed at home with Gran and Grandad. I always knew we were going to do a movie of the TV show because it was in my contract that it had to be made within the first year and so we only had until next May to do it. If they hadn't have done it, they'd have had to pay me anyway so it didn't really matter. But I was pleased that we were doing it.

It was me Mum's first time on an aircraft and she nearly caused a panic. We were flying over the Pole through the night, when she saw the reflection of the lights underneath the wings and said very loudly, 'The plane's on fire!'

It caused a bit of commotion and Mum was really embarrassed, but it all calmed down soon enough.

'Oh Jackie,' she said, 'I feel really stupid. I wish they'd all stop looking at me.'

'Don't worry Mum, they're not looking at you, they're looking at me,' I said, cross with the people looking.

Once we got there, Mum loved it, and on New Year's Day we went to the annual 'Rose Parade' in Pasadena. I had to go to do a promotion for the TV series. It was a massive parade and all the floats were covered in flowers which was a hassle because of my hay fever. Most of the *Pufnstuf* cast were there and we just had to stand on the float and wave to all the people, dressed as our characters. It was nice to see everyone again, but there was such a huge crowd and I felt on edge the whole time. I kept thinking that there only needs to be one person in the crowd who has a grudge against me or doesn't like my face and he could shoot me and get away with it. I kept thinking, any minute now

I'm either going to feel something hit me or see a gun pointing at me and I'm done for. The crowds were so big and I felt as if I had no control whatsoever and that's when it became frightening.

I looked around to see if anyone else felt as uneasy as I did, but all I could see was these great big ridiculous foam heads smiling back at me and waving. I waved too and wished for it all to be over.

After the parade we went back to Mario Casili's house and had a drink. I was still only seventeen, so me Mum and Dad would only allow me to have a shandy, but I was quite happy with that. They then all went off to the Rose Bowl Football Match, but I wasn't fussed as it wasn't proper football.

A couple of weeks later Brian came out, firstly to record 'Some Beautiful' and secondly because there'd been interest from the International Hotel in Vegas for me to do a cabaret season there. So in the January me Dad went with Brian to discuss all that business. I stayed behind at the Chateau Marmont on Sunset. I was supposed to go as well, but for insurance reasons Marty didn't want me to fly and wouldn't let me go. Strange, really, as he did let me go hunting with a Winchester rifle, a Colt 45 and live ammunition.

When Brian came back from Vegas, he stayed with us at the Chateau. We had a two-bedroom suite: one had a double bed in it and the other one had two singles which Brian and I shared.

A few days later, I was asked to introduce the singer Tiny Tim at the Troubadour Club in Hollywood. Tiny Tim was about ten years older than me, played the ukulele and had had a number one hit with 'Tiptoe Through The Tulips'. He was about six foot six, about five foot wide, had long straggly black hair down past his shoulders and the biggest nose you've ever seen in your life! It was even bigger than me. He could check the depths of swimming pools with it.

I went to the Troubadour in a lovely shirt I'd been given for my birthday: I think it was from Marty and Christa's housekeeper's daughter. It really was a favourite of mine and I was so proud of wearing this shirt. It had a light cream background, with small flowers, and a few black stripes thrown in for good measure. It was in my top three of shirts. But when they took me backstage to introduce me to Tiny Tim, he's only got the same shirt on as me! I could've killed him! And I said to Brian, 'I am not doing this! He's got the same shirt on as me! I can't go on with this!'

But Brian was in no mood to deal with my nonsense. When we'd arrived, he'd had an altercation in the car park with another man's leg. Brian hadn't quite got the hang of the hire car. It was big, a bright red Dodge Charger; although it was a two-door with a front seat that was like a bench, you could play soccer in the back! As he was trying to park it, he inadvertently jammed the driver's door and a geezer's leg against another car.

So he was not to be trifled with over shirts, favourite or otherwise.

'Look, Jack…' Brian began, but some resourceful person had found a cravat for me to wear.

'It doesn't go with the shirt,' I protested, as someone quickly wrapped it round my neck. 'It's as big as me!' I said, fuming; it practically covered my whole shirt.

'Jack…' Brian began again, and I had to wear it. It would've looked stupid for us both to be wearing the same shirt. Tiny Tim seemed oblivious to the wardrobe fiasco. I think he was out of it, on another planet: I don't think he'd have cared if I'd have turned up in a dress. But I was certainly not in a nice frame of mind to introduce, to a star-studded celebrity audience, someone who stopped me wearing my favourite shirt. I did introduce him, we watched the show, and then went home.

The high spot of the night was that I met Goldie Hawn. I was totally, madly in love with her at the time because she was in *Rowan and Martin's Laugh-In* which was very successful. I can't remember what I said. I was just looking at her in amazement. At least I was introduced to her pre-cravat, so she saw how good I could look, before I had to cover up my snazzy shirt! Not that she took any notice, but there you are!

The next day, I went with Brian to change the car. It had come off much worse than the unfortunate man's leg, and the driver's door was buckled.

'I'm sorry about this, Jack,' Brian had said to me Dad, but I think me Dad was pleased; he had had his own altercations with it. Once, on the way to the studios, Dad had had an incident with a traffic cop and a funeral procession; and once, at the studios themselves, Dad had nearly run over Robert Wagner.

The car had to go; and while Brian and I were out getting a new one, I bought a ukulele. I thought it looked easy to play and I wanted one, so I got one.

We shot the *Pufnstuf* movie at Universal Studios. I was so pleased as it was so much bigger than Paramount and therefore had so much more to explore. Along with all the costumes, Marty had looked after my bicycle at his factory too, and I'm sure during the eight to ten weeks that I was at Universal I must've cycled to every set they had. I didn't change at lunchtimes, except my shirt as I was such a messy eater, and after a quick bite at the commissary I'd be off. I'd see the trams and buses doing the studio tours and hear the guide saying, 'And there's Jimmy from *H.R. Pufnstuf* on his bicycle! Give us a wave, Jimmy!' You'd have to play up to that, which was a bit awkward, but I really was a poser on this bicycle. I thought I was 'Easy Rider' all over again; one freewheeling hippy without the drugs.

The studio complex was so massive, with sets from every different period, and I cycled through the Wild West, the Great Depression and right on up to the Sixties. I think twice I couldn't find my way back to my set: once they sent out security when I was lost on some Mexican set up in the mountains, and the other time I did get back ten or fifteen minutes late and they were about to send out a search party. They weren't happy with me. 'You must make sure that you get back on time and don't get lost!'

'Yeah, yeah, yeah,' I said, but I thought, oh don't be so silly! I never considered how much it was costing by the minute to actually shoot the movie.

Another attraction of working at Universal was the pursuit of black widow spiders. Mountains and wild brushland surrounded the studios and I imagined there must be all sorts lurking in there. As soon as I got there I asked Pat Davis what wild animals there were and how dangerous could they be?

'Well, Jack, up in the mountains further north you will get grizzlies, but that's hundreds of miles from here. You'll get the odd coyote living in the hills and they'll come down when they are hungry to raid the trashcans.'

'What about snakes?' I said. 'Y'know, venomous ones. Where can I find them in Hollywood?'

'Occasionally you get rattlesnakes that you have to be careful of, but not that often; but there is something much, much worse than that.'

I hated snakes, what could be worse than snakes?

'There are black widow spiders: their venom is fifteen times more poisonous than sidewinders and they can kill you.'

I needed to find one of those.

He told me the best places to look for the nests and I'd cycle around the studios keeping one eye on the hills for wild animals and the other looking for the lair of killer spiders.

I was glad to be back. I was having a ball, but it did feel like the spirit of the show had changed now that it had come to the movie. Just before we had started shooting I was a bit disappointed to hear that for the opening titles I had to sing a ballad called 'If I Could'. I hated singing ballads and much preferred upbeat numbers because I didn't think my voice carried a ballad that well. I hated that song and I don't think it was a coincidence that I had a sore throat on the day that we recorded it. The music was the responsibility of a new partnership, Norman Gimble (lyrics) and Charles Fox (music). I don't know why somebody different was chosen for the film, but I just think that musically speaking it lost its magic.

We also had two main additions to the cast: Mama Cass (from the Mamas and the Papas) who was lovely and fitted straight in, and Martha Raye (a big film star from the forties) who wasn't and didn't. I felt the atmosphere change and I thought she was a right old cow! She was to play 'Boss Witch' which to me was a joke because the only one who could be the boss of witches, in my opinion, well certainly of every witch that I've seen, has to be Billie! So how could Miss Raye come on the set and pretend to be the bees' knees? And I felt she tried to put Billie down. She was a big star with the biggest mouth I've ever seen, which produced an endless sea of complaints and moans. She'd done loads of movies, not that I knew her from Adam.

The storyline was that Boss Witch decided to come and have a convention to award 'The Witch of the Year'. She decided to have it at Witchiepoo's Castle, then fell in love with Freddie the Flute and spent the rest of the movie trying to get him from me.

Billy Barty was another addition to the cast, a confident little guy who was a well-known actor in the States and had done loads of movies. The rest of the team was the same so it was just like falling back into the same old ways: the same old problems with the costumes, the same old ribbing from George Radar and the same old delight at working together.

Mum and Dad would drop me off at the studios, go off for the day and then they'd come back and pick me up at five. They'd either meet Christa and go and have lunch or they'd go shopping, or more often than not they'd go down to Santa Monica and sit on the beach. They loved the beach even though it was winter and everyone used to think that they were mad.

'Mum and Dad gone sunbathing again?' George asked.

'Nah, Christa's taken them to a fashion show,' I replied.

'Yeah, it's a good idea; it would probably be too hot for them today anyway. Not good for that delicate Limey complexion.'

'Colonial old git!' I shouted.

It was good to be back.

I was grateful to Christa because she was always taking my parents out on adventures and 'always ordering champagne', me Mum told me.

'Who's bloody paying for this?' me Dad would ask.

'I've got Marty's credit card,' Christa said. Me Dad frowned. 'Don't worry, Jack, we always fall out at the end of the month,' she breezily reassured him.

Like me, my parents were having a ball; it was such a long, long way from the cotton mills. I really wanted to share it all with them: my success, and all the things that it bought. At the weekends, we'd take Mum to Disneyland or Knott's Berry Farm, another amusement park, and we'd take her shopping in

Alvero Street, the Mexican quarter of LA. Prior to my success she had always loved looking in shop windows, and most of the time dreaming of what she could buy, but now she could *shop*; and me Mum loved shopping, she loved shopping full stop. It was great. There was so much to do as you could go to the beach, go to the mountains, or go to the desert and all within an hour's drive. You had every possible choice you could think of, whereas in them days in England you didn't have that choice. America was great.

One weekend at about four o'clock in the morning a couple of the electricians from the set came to pick me up from the Chateau to take me hunting. We'd got chatting at work and they had said they were really into hunting and I'd said, so was I. I'd never actually been, but I was sure I must be.

We drove out along the road to Vegas towards the Mojave Desert. There was no one on the road and it was just so determinedly straight. We drove for miles and miles and miles along this barren, dry stretch and then suddenly it was snowing. Snowing in the desert: and for two hundred yards we drove in this snowstorm and then it was gone, just like that. We couldn't believe it. No sooner had we gone into it, than we were out of it again. There was snow on the cactus. Now that was definitely Hollywood.

When we got there we headed off in the manly pursuit of meat. I think what appealed to me about hunting was mainly the guns, and to feel the power of a gun in my hands. I'm totally against guns and they shouldn't be allowed: because of the power, because the power is exhilarating. We stalked our prey, toting our guns, and I'm sure I showed more than a passing resemblance to John Wayne. The electricians were having a great deal of success with rabbits. I was trying, but not having much luck and so far hadn't shot anything living. I wanted to do one killer shot because I didn't want the rabbit to suffer and be in pain: I wanted to kill it stone dead, really, really quickly. But I just wasn't fast enough and they kept bouncing by.

After a while the guys said, 'Look, because you're useless with this rifle, when we see our next rabbit, we'll whistle and it'll stop to see where the whistle's coming from; and as soon as it stops, you shoot it!'

I thought, right, fine. (I had this idea of me taking home a photograph of all these things I'd shot, holding them up like.) And so this rabbit goes flying past and they whistle and it stops. And I've got sights on this rifle and I've got the head of the rabbit right in the middle; and the expression on this rabbit's face, it was so 'please don't kill me', and I couldn't, so I didn't.

I felt really embarrassed because their kids who'd come along were doing it and I didn't feel like I was holding up the side as it were; as soon as they realised that I weren't gonna kill it, they did.

We also had an incident with a snake. They had seen it long before I had, but I heard them firing and thought, right, there's something nearby that needs to be shot, where is it? I looked around to find out where it was so that I could have a go too. It was a sidewinder; 'They're not as venomous as black widows,' I called, trying to lift my stock as a hunter. I had a rifle and a pistol in a Western-style holster so I certainly looked the part, but what with the telescopic sight and trying to hit this fast-moving target with a single bullet, it was very hard. I mean, if I'd had a shotgun I could have got it for sure, but the snake just wouldn't stay still. I fired my rifle, several times, but God knows whether I hit it or not.

Towards the end of the day when they'd shot quite a few jackrabbits, this coyote appeared on the horizon. I didn't see it because I was so mesmerised with these killing machines in my hands and not taking too much notice of what was going on around me. The first I remember of it was hearing somebody's gun going off and turning to see what it was.

Somebody had got it and the coyote was wounded, but still moving towards our group. I had visions of it munching everybody. *I'd* seen Westerns; coyotes could hurt you. They are like wolves and a whole pack of them could certainly do you in. I really thought it was coming for me and I started firing at it, but I was in such a panic I could've shot everyone there. It was three quarters dead by the time I started having a go and had been wounded by two or three other bullets. I couldn't say definitely that my couple of shots were the ones that actually made it stone dead, but they certainly helped it along; it must've had about ten bullets in it by then.

The electricians told me afterwards that because coyotes are classed as vermin, if you cut the tail off and take it into the local sheriff, you get a ten-dollar reward. I didn't; they said they'd sort all that out.

It's hard to describe but, in one sense, I was so pleased I was given the chance to go hunting and it was as exciting as I'd imagined; but as for actually doing it, I didn't have the bottle to kill things. It really needed for me to be in danger before I would do that.

*

'We're going to see *Hair* in LA. Do you wanna come?'

It was John Cowsill on the phone, a member of the pop-group family 'The Cowsills'. I'd previously met them doing *The Krafft Music Hall Show* in New York. The original band was the four brothers: Bill on guitar, Bob on organ and guitar, Barry on bass and John on drums. Later, their mother Barbara joined the group and then finally the other kids, Susan and Paul, completed the merry band. Dad (Bud) managed them. They were huge and had a big following. They were asked to do a TV series called *The Partridge Family*, but the part of the mother had already been cast and so they turned it down.

The kids were of similar ages to me, so we got on well. I'd been introduced to them at the start of rehearsals and they'd said the usual thing of, 'Oh, you're from England. When you come out to LA, you must come and see us – here's our phone number! Let's stay in contact.' And the *unusual* thing was: we had.

'So are you coming or not?' John said.

'Yeah, fine!' I said. I didn't know what it was all about but I liked John and thought it would be fun.

'There's a nude bit in it!' he added and I thought, oh my God. Alright then, yeah, fine!

Me Mum and Dad stayed at their house with their parents while I went out with the kids. One of the brothers had recently passed his driving test and had just got a brand-new car, and in his red GTO Coupé we flew up Sunset Strip like a speeding train on acid. I sat in the back of this car, pleased to be wedged in beside the other brothers for protection in case of what seemed to be the inevitable and imminent impact.

Against the odds we made it to the theatre and I had just started to relax after our successful attempt to break the land speed record. I was really enjoying the show and I thought the music was fabulous, when suddenly an American cop comes running into the auditorium firing his gun in the air and shouting, 'You are all under arrest for participating in lewd activities!' I thought it was for real and I dove under the seats just at the point that I realised it was part of the show. The brothers didn't even try to hide their emotions to save my embarrassment. They all of them screamed with laughter, absolutely screamed.

We'd often hang out as a family at the Cowsills' place. They lived in Bel Air, just off Sunset on the way to Malibu, in a millionaire's private estate. They had a massive swimming pool with a diving board and sunbeds all around; they had a tennis court, a trampoline, a bowling alley, and a room the size of a double garage full of snakes. If there was one, there must have been fifty of them.

'Touch one of them,' John urged.

'No, bollocks!' I said, 'you've got to be joking.' They made me feel cold all over, and I went back outside into the sunshine.

Brian, my record producer, was asleep on the sunbed by the pool. He would often come and spend the day with us, which showed a certain resilience as he was frequently the butt of our jokes. I remember particularly he once got a meringue pie in his face; and I was surprised now to see him so relaxed as earlier, when he had fallen asleep, he awoke to find himself mid-flight, en route into the swimming pool.

'Jack,' John called, 'come down here. We're just gonna feed the snakes, man.'

I didn't know how you fed snakes so I was interested and headed off back downstairs. It took a while for my eyes to adjust from the bright sunshine to being inside, but even in silhouette I could make out the awful truth that the 'feed' was still very much alive. I was flabbergasted to see little mice and day-old chickens, and oh, it was awful to sit and watch. It seemed to me that they must know their fate as they sat shaking in the corner of the tanks. And the snakes seemed to taunt and tease them. They'd slither up and take a look: 'I'll just see what I've got for dinner. Ahh, should I kill it now? Oh, I'm not hungry at the moment but I know where it is, I can smell it, and it can't go anywhere else. I'll just inject a dash of venom and come back later.' I'm damn sure the chick knew that its death was imminent, and I hated that.

There was some serious talk of me and the Cowsills recording something together as we both had recording contracts, but it didn't happen. We did demo a track together called 'Ain't No Way', but it didn't come to anything, I can't remember why. I think it was at the time I was offered a song by Neil Diamond. I said I didn't like it and didn't want to record it.

'It's a good song,' Brian said, 'why don't you think about it?'

'It's not that good!' I said. I don't know if that's what I really thought, but it very much depended on what sort of mood I was in. My career in many ways still felt like a hobby, so when anyone asked me to do something, if I didn't want to do it, I would say, 'Bollocks, no!' Maybe I never took it seriously enough, coupled with the fact that I had become very spoilt very quickly; but I should have leapt at these opportunities as, after all, I was just a novelty entertainer from England versus extremely polished commodities.

I eventually lost contact with the Cowsills and I don't know what happened to them; I think they were big for about the same length of time that I was, and then, I don't know, they just sort of stopped. But while I was shooting *Pufnstuf*, we spent a lot of time with them. It was so much more relaxing, being at home with the Cowsills, as my fame at this time made it hard to be out in public. We never spent a great length of time in any one place because it would always attract too much attention. It was a bit of a pain when you wanted to take time to have a good look around somewhere, but it just made it a bit awkward to do that because you were causing so much havoc. Walking down the street, I'd hear a cry from the other side: 'Oh my gosh, that's Jack Wild! Quick, we must go over and get his autograph!' And they'd shout at the top of their voices so that everyone would look round and come over.

I was told by business managers and personal managers, 'Make sure you don't have your photograph taken smoking a cigarette or with a drink in your hand, because it's not good for your image and you're an icon now. You must set an example. Even a soft drink, the papers could make out it's alcoholic, so to be safe never have a drink in your hand.' So really I didn't want to spend too much time in the public eye, and it became easier to relax behind closed doors where I could have a drink and a smoke and not worry.

It's not that I didn't go to places, but I'd mostly want to go with people I knew around me, and not stay too long. One evening Marty took me, me Mum and Dad and Christa to the Magic Castle. It's a fantastic place with a couple of restaurants and a massive bar area and rooms and rooms of magic. You could go into one room where there'd be a magician whose speciality was card tricks, and in another room there'd be one with cups and balls, and in another room there'd be something else, hypnotism, say.

The cards we thought were amazing because it was very close-up magic. You were literally within three foot of the person and you thought you could see everything that was going on, but they always made you look at the wrong places at the right time. I'd been there before with Arf when we were making the series. We'd gone to one of these sort of ESP psychic geezers who suggested that Arthur's record was going to get in the Top Fifty and my record was going to be successful. So he must have mistaken us for someone else.

Arf had signed with Hemdale shortly after me and, to help him get a record deal, we put his voice on some of the tracks that I was doing for my album and eventually he got a deal. His voice was much smoother than mine. I always thought mine was very gruff and hoarse. His only single 'Woman In My Life' came out on the Capitol label, distributed in England by EMI. They were also going to release another one called 'Boulevard Saint-Michel' but I don't think that one managed to escape from the factory. 'Woman In My Life' didn't chart but nevertheless he was proud of it and so in truth was I. We didn't really talk about our respective deals, but we were involved with the same people – the same arrangers, and Brian produced Arf as well – so if I didn't hear direct from Arf I knew what was going on from them.

When we arrived at the Magic Castle, Marty suggested that we first went for a drink. The bar was huge; about twenty-five foot long and about five foot high. There were individual stools that lined the length of it so that you could actually use the bar as it was so high. As me Mum was so small, they sat her on this one particular stool and Marty bought a round of drinks. We're all sat there drinking and talking when, the next minute, me Mum went to get her drink but she couldn't reach it. Over the last ten minutes her stool had been slowly going down and now the bar was a foot and a half above her and she couldn't reach her drink. She also realised she was looking up at people talking to her and she was sat practically on the floor. It was hysterical and she was crying with laughter. It was a lot of fun, but we couldn't stay there for long. We were attracting a crowd.

Very soon the job was over, and we were getting ready to go home. I found out later that another series had been commissioned but Marty and Sid had said no as they couldn't afford it.

Just before I went home, my single 'Some Beautiful' had been released and they'd arranged for me to do *The Johnny Carson Show*. The show was recorded in New York so me, and me Mum and Dad, after we finished the film, came back to England via New York. I was under the impression that it was just an interview and we were scheduled to stay in New York for several days to do it.

I went to the first meeting and discovered that not only did they want me to sing 'Some Beautiful' but they wanted me to sing two other songs and do a dance routine as well. It was like a fifteen-minute bloody cabaret, and I'm there on my own! I didn't have my record producer to make sure the backing track was all right, I didn't have any of the music for the song, I didn't even know what key I sang it in – it could've been Yale as far as I was concerned!

I said, 'I can't do it! I'll come on and be interviewed by all means, but I can't do any singing 'cos I haven't got me record producer with me, number one, and, number two, I can't choreograph myself for two other numbers as well!'

I was surprised that they didn't say, okay, well, I'm sorry there's been a misunderstanding somewhere along the line; as you're in town, we'll have you on and you can just talk about it then. But they didn't. So I got on a plane and came home.

That one stands out, because I *didn't* do it. From that time on, looking back, I find it hard to distinguish times, places, interviews, tellys. There were so many that they stopped standing out: stopped being significant, noteworthy or even memorable.

Chapter 11

'**G**OOD TO HAVE YOU BACK, JACK – there's lots on, so let me tell you what's happening.' It was John Daly.

'But I only got back last night,' I said.

'Yes, well that's show business, Jack. Now, firstly, we've got to talk about this new film that we are investing in, *Melody*, which we want you and Mark Lester to do. Secondly, *Fab 208* want you and Arthur to go on a week-long photo shoot in Majorca, and thirdly you've got to do a guest appearance on a pop show in LA singing "Some Beautiful".'

'But I only got back last night,' I said again.

And so it all continued. They wanted to film my single for the TV show on Catalina Island off LA so arrangements were under way to do that; meanwhile Arf and I flew off to Spain on 15th April 1970. I thought, well, it's a free holiday and I haven't been to Majorca before, why not? *Fab 208* had invited out a clutch of celebrities to have photographs taken all around the island. No one I knew, but among the group was a young actor called Robert Powell who had a TV show called *Doomwatch* and a couple of lads, Adrian and Alan, from the group 'Judas Jump' who we became very friendly with.

We all stayed in a tatty incomplete hotel in Arunel. The area was an up-and-coming part of Majorca, but it hadn't quite come up, quite yet. But we didn't spend much time there as we didn't really have very much time to ourselves. We seemed to be photographed morning, noon and night. I was probably the youngest of the group, seventeen, and still really only interested in music, go-karts and work although I was expanding my horizons and was taking a healthy interest in alcohol. The lads had a more established relation-ship with alcohol and were trying to establish relationships with girls. They met some 'up-for-it' ladies and there were some drunken parties at the hotel. I wasn't really interested and would have my fill of booze and then go to bed, leaving the rest of them to it.

One morning the production team said they wanted us to go on some horses to have photographs taken, but I hated horses and said I wouldn't go. I had history with horses. I loved them once and had even ridden one; but as I got off it, it kicked me from behind, maliciously, and I've held that against them all ever since.

'Don't worry,' they said, 'we'll find something else for you to do.'

They did.

They took me onto the beach with this model to have photographs taken in Spanish gear and I thought, I don't want be a model! Suddenly the horses didn't seem quite so bad. I had history with modelling as well. At the age of like twelve or thirteen we'd have these photographic sessions in studios where you'd have to wear these awful jumpers or cardigans for knitting patterns and I hated doing it. Me Mum had kept pictures of Arf on patterns but I made sure she didn't have any of me, so then I could deny it if asked. I wasn't proud of it and thought it was a poofy job and not at all manly. In truth, I don't think any of the boys at Speake's liked doing it, it just helped to pay the school fees.

As I had said no to the horses I didn't think I could say no to the modelling as well, so I had photographs taken with this girl in a poncho and silly things like that: sat on the beach, standing on a beach, playing on the beach, pointing out to sea on the beach... Perhaps my early modelling had stood me in good stead, but I didn't enjoy it. The poncho did make me feel a little bit like Clint Eastwood, but not quite enough to shed those early modelling memories.

Worse, of course, was to come. The following morning they said they wanted to take us to a bullring. 'It'll be great and we can get some fantastic shots,' they said. I was reluctant; I would like to say it was from a moral standpoint, but I think it was really from more of a fear standpoint.

But the other guys agreed and about eight of us walked into this bullring. The walls must have been about five or six foot high – two crucial feet higher than me as I was only four foot nothing. From there, seating stretched up where the production team sat.

'Yeah, you look great down there, really great.'

Yeah, great, I thought.

There were four places on the circular bullring where a small barrier stood say three foot away from the wall that bullfighters could go and hide behind, and that was your only defence from the bull, I noted. Still, *we* were only having photographs taken; no one actually had to kill a bull or anything.

Then suddenly the bloody gates flew open and a bull came charging out. It wasn't a fully grown one, but it looked angry and was a hell of a lot bigger than me; and it had horns.

'You've got to be bloody joking,' I said and started to run like hell. My early surveillance paid off; I knew I couldn't dive onto the wall to climb it, so the only place I could run was one of those four barrier things. But the floor was like a beach full of soft, soft sand and not at all conducive to a quick getaway. As I tried to run forwards, I just felt as though I was digging my own grave in the process. The barrier wasn't getting any closer and I was getting deeper like I was in some crazy cartoon.

Eventually I closed in on the nearest barrier, hearing a great deal of screaming and shouting. Maybe that was just me, but I was the smallest and I'm sure everybody was a little bit startled. They obviously wanted to get their money's worth and get us in every goddamn situation going. When things began to calm down they took some more photographs, but I wouldn't come out from behind my barrier. I think the others were more adventurous than me, but I don't know as I couldn't really see. I waited till they'd caught the bull and got rid of it; '… and then I'll come out, and not until!' There weren't any pictures of me with the bull. Well, if there were, they would have had to have been bloody quick.

The next day they took us shopping in Palma, the main town. We bought sombreros and castanets, anything Spanish really, and I bought a very stylish black hat.

In the afternoon we went to have some photos taken at a go-kart track. When we'd finished the session and were just heading off, the guys that ran the track said, 'You want to have wager? See who the best team – you or us?'

'Yeah, alright!' we said. We were all up for it and completely unable to resist the challenge. We all put in about a fiver each, so there must've been well over a hundred quid in the pot for the winning team.

We were, I would say, certainly as good if not slightly better at driving these go-karts, but it got to the point where it was coming close to the end of the race and whenever we got into the lead, we'd always be run off the track, literally, by the other side. They'd just crash into you even if it meant taking themselves out as well, but they'd do it so that one of their team would be in the lead. I'd been working my way up through the positions and when I got to the lead, there were about three or four minutes left to go. I thought, I've just gotta keep going as fast as I can so they can't catch me up and try and nobble me!

But they were playing for higher stakes. Apparently the pot of money up for grabs was about six months' wages for them. And these guys had worked on this track for so long they knew exactly what these go-karts could do, and the track and its corners, inside out.

I didn't see the one who had crept up behind me as I was just concentrating on keeping in front. And the next minute he caught the back of me and spun me around, going round a bend. It could've have turned me over, but thankfully I kept it from rolling and I thought, bugger it – I don't need a hundred quid that badly! I didn't bother trying to get back up front; and in the end they won. We didn't say anything to them afterwards, but just moaned in English, out of earshot.

We walked back to the hotel along the seafront and saw a shooting gallery where you could win bottles of champagne. That would cheer us up, we thought. There were about six of us and we worked out that it could cost us just over a quid between us to win a bottle of champagne; and we thought, that's cheap! This'll save us a lot of money, being as everyone's having these parties at night at the hotel. So we spent a good hour or so winning all this champagne on this shooting gallery and we thought, we've done well here. The following day, along the seafront, we saw the same champagne being sold for the equivalent of 25p a bottle. We'd been had again, but it didn't matter. In fact it seemed incredibly funny, and money wasn't really of any concern to any of us.

Arthur didn't last the week there as he had to come back early for an audition or a job or something. He flew into Gatwick in a Comet 4B, one of the first commercial jets I think, and fire engines chased the plane down the runway because it'd got dodgy wheels. He was fine, but they didn't tell me until I got home because they knew I didn't like flying.

*

I came home more peacefully, at the end of the week, and started work on *Melody*, a sort of 'Romeo and Juliet in Hammersmith'. I was looking forward to it as I'd be working with Mark Lester again so that would be fun; and the Bee Gees were doing the music so, in my mind, it couldn't fail. So much so that, when they said to me and Mark, 'Look, because it's a small budget film, we'd prefer to offer you a small fee and a large percentage, rather than a large fee and a small percentage,' I agreed. Mark, or rather Mark's Dad, wanted more money up front for Mark and so he agreed to the opposite. But I believed in the film a hundred and one per cent and happily went for the 'less money now and big rewards later' option.

For the first read-through and photocall I went up to Colet Court, an old school building in Hammersmith that was to be the production office for the film. Mark was there with his Dad, and Tracy Hyde who was to play Melody, and Waris Hussein, the director. Waris was a gentle, considerate, quiet-talking man. He always came to work in a long black coat and big, tinted glasses. He was very shy and businesslike and spoke very seriously about the character I was playing in the film. He also wore a metaphorical black coat and glasses as he was a very private man. I never really knew any more about him later than I did at that first read-through.

Years and years later, me, Mark and Waris did a TV chat show together – Kilroy I think – and I learnt more about Waris in those couple of hours than I had in all the time we'd been working together on the film. We laughed, joked and reminisced and it was great to see him again; I didn't remember joking with him at all on the film.

'Hi Jack, how are you?' Mark said. 'I like your jacket. Where did you get it?'

Good old Mark. A month or so before, I'd seen a jacket in a shop in Hounslow that I liked, but it was plastic. I went into the shop and said, 'I really like that jacket, but could I have it in leather please.'

'I'm afraid we don't do it in leather, it would cost too much and nobody would be able to afford it.'

'But could you make me one?' I asked.

'If we did, it would be a one off and very, very expensive,' he said.

'Yeah, that's all right,' I said. 'No problem. One in leather, please.'

I didn't know how much money I had in the bank, but I knew I had enough to buy anything I wanted, and I wanted that jacket, and I wanted it in leather.

I was so, so pleased with it when it was made, and I proudly wore it to the read-through. It was dark brown leather in a safari style with pockets everywhere and I had complemented it by wearing a brown, green and yellow paisley cravat.

A guy called David Puttnam was also at the read-through; he was one of the producers for *Melody*, or *S.W.A.L.K.* as it was also called. I thought he was a dead ringer for Paul McCartney who had a beard at this time. David came to work with black leather saddlebags that you would normally see in a Western and I thought that was so, so, cool. I thought, I've gotta get some of them. I did and I've still got them now, but they were nowhere near as good as his.

He was telling me about the location they were going to use for where Ornshaw, my character, was supposed to be living with his granddad. It was somewhere on the south side of the River Thames near the Elephant and Castle area. The actual house had been condemned by the local council and we were all advised to be careful because it'd been rat-infested and all sorts of bloody awful things.

'Have a bath every day otherwise you'll get nits or something worse,' David said to me.

'Every day?!' I said.

*

'Okay Jack, try and get into that strip club and we'll film you from behind and see what happens.'

We were in Soho, obviously, and filming 'a delicate and sensitive study of bittersweet childhood', *not* so obviously. Waris was keen to do a lot of un-scripted, impromptu filming: point the camera and see what happens. They were shooting a scene where me and Mark go into the West End for a day. There were about ten or twenty specific shots that Waris wanted to get – things like me and Mark in Trafalgar Square, me and Mark at the Houses of Parliament – and for the rest we would see what happened.

'When you're ready, Jack, off you go,' Waris said. I ran across the road and looked at the pictures outside the strip club. There was a big bloke standing by the entrance and as soon as he turned away I slipped in to take a closer look. But as soon as I slipped into the strip joint, I was thrown straight out again. My costume was a school blazer and I like to think it was because of that that I got thrown out and not because I looked ridiculously young for my age. Anyway, they got what they wanted and used it in the final edit. I thought it was all a right giggle.

'Okay Jack, you see that vagrant sitting over there?'

'That tramp leaning against the parking meter?'

'Yes, that's the one Jack. Can you go over to him, pretend you think he's dead and check to see if he's alive, okay Jack, and we'll see what happens.'

I went over to him and knelt down, and tried to see if I could feel his heartbeat. When I did that he sort of woke up and looked at me and I thought, bloody hell, and ran off.

'Cut', 'Print', 'Next set-up', 'Leicester Square'.

'Okay Jack, you see that busker, well can you try and creep up behind him and just copy whatever he does, and if you're behind him we'll hopefully get his reaction, okay?'

I'd first seen this busker five years before when I started in *Oliver!* at the New Theatre and we'd go and take the piss out of him then. He had a little record player or something that played music and he'd dance to it. He did these sand dances with a fez on, a moustache, short trousers, bare legs and big boots, and he just looked daft. They hid the camera and I went up behind him and started dancing; and he sees me and goes to hit me: 'Get out of it ya little bastard!' and I ran off. Just like old times. He died about twelve years later and loads of actors went to his funeral as he was so well known around Leicester Square and Shaftesbury Avenue. I'm glad he is immortalised in our little film.

We were doing one scene in *Melody* where we've made a bomb. One of the lads lights up a cigarette and I take it from him to have a couple of drags for meself while we're waiting to see if this bomb's going to work or not. It was my idea for a nice bit of business, but the act itself threw up all sorts of issues.

I hadn't told me Mum and Dad that I was smoking and in fact had been for the last seven years. Whether they knew or not, I don't know; but as far as I was concerned they were none the wiser. So should I smoke as though *I* didn't know how to smoke, but was acting like someone who *could* smoke; or should I smoke like my character can smoke, *but so can I* and this is like my coming out smoking and not just acting smoking? I wasn't altogether sure I could bring out all these different levels of subtlety, and even less sure that my parents would read them correctly. In the end I just took a few drags.

The only other time I smoked in a film was when I did *The 14* and by then I'm like ninety-five years old so it didn't really matter.

The bomb-making scene was on a patch of waste land at Nine Elms, near Battersea Dogs Home. After trying to make the bomb blow up and not succeeding, the next scene was of us running back to catch the bus. The camera crew was positioned several hundred yards in front of us and we had to run towards the camera, cross the road and stop at the bus stop which was about thirty foot from where the camera was.

I was running in front as I was the leader of the gang. They hadn't stopped the traffic or anything, and as I'm running I see this big removal van coming towards me. I'm running in the road and all of the kids are behind me, so I'm running and thinking, as soon as the van goes past me, I'll nip in immediately to get on the other side of the road. What I didn't know was that there was a sports car, directly behind this van, that I couldn't see. As I go to dive into the gap as the van's gone past, I see the car; but by now it's too late and I just manage to swerve my body enough not to get run over. The rest of them weren't as quick, or as cavalier, as me and kept on the left-hand side waiting for the car to go past.

'That was a close one, Jack,' Waris said. 'Print it.'

When we were filming inside Colet Court doing all the classroom scenes, or outside the Bursary or anything like that, at lunchtimes we would always play soccer. Out the back was this massive area grassed over which was perfectly flat. It was where we shot the sports day in the film, but at lunchtimes it was our football stadium. Because there were so many kids in the film, we'd play various fixtures dictated by who was in the first shot after lunch.

This particular lunchtime, however, Mark had brought in his Monkee bike that he'd been telling me about. I'd told him to bring it in and let me have a go on it. The Monkees used them for their TV show in the States and I guess that's how they got their name. They weren't actually classed as toys but were classed as motorbikes, and you needed a licence to drive them and L-plates and all that business, so that's why we planned to have a go out back.

'Come on then Mark, give it here.'

I was well pleased at having a go on this; it only went about thirty-five miles an hour, if that, but being so low to the ground with no crash helmet it felt like you were doing ninety.

I'd ridden round the pitch and was a few hundred yards from Mark and his chaperone: the same one from *Oliver!*, Mrs Nelson. She was sat on surveillance on this wooden bench and, although Mark wasn't as carefully packaged as he was in *Oliver!*, he was still treated, by Mrs Nelson at least, as fragile goods. Me and Mrs Nelson had history, so I was aiming for her, planning to swerve dramatically at the last minute. It did cross my mind, wouldn't it be funny if the brakes failed; and as I was getting closer I thought, right, I'd better brake now. I went to brake and Christ, they were very spongy these brakes; and basically I'd left it too late and smashed into the bench. I missed her by about three foot, but she nearly had a cardiac. I thought it was the funniest thing ever. I tried to apologise straight away, but couldn't stop laughing long enough to complete the sentence. I was screaming with laughter and apologising at the same time; but she was so strict on behaviour and all that, it couldn't have looked good.

'Oh, you are a stupid boy. You should know better than to mess about with dangerous things. Anything could have happened. You stupid, stupid boy.'

But to me it just looked very, very funny. Nothing was hurt or damaged; I probably shocked meself more than I did any damage to either the bench or the bike, or Mrs Nelson for that matter.

A few weeks back, someone had given Mark a packet of condoms and he was filling them with water and throwing them at people. I don't think he knew what they were. Mrs Nelson blamed me for that, even though I swore blind that it wasn't me. And it wasn't.

Me and Mark made our escape to my dressing room. It was a big room and I did use it mostly as a place to escape to, for me and for anyone who was friends with me. Anyone who wasn't really old enough to smoke, I'd obviously allow them to come in so that they could have a cigarette and keep the chaperones away.

It was also to get away from the girls. They spooked me somewhat. Miriam Mann was Tracy's stand-in. She'd been at Speake's and apparently had a crush on me. She really had no chance because I just wasn't interested in girls at that time, so she could've been the most beautiful woman on the planet but she still wouldn't have stood a chance. So I just felt awkward around her.

Not that I hadn't had girlfriends. Veronica Purnell was my first. She was from stage school and was Bet in *Oliver!* the same time as me and Arf were in it. She was in the film as well, in the 'Consider Yourself' number. But some girls seemed to take rather too much of an interest in me. Girls like Debbie King. She'd apparently got on the set as an extra in *Melody* through her parents who were agents at the time, *to be near me!* And I didn't like that: I didn't like that at all. I felt all sort of pressurised.

I'd already had an encounter with Debbie King some time ago when I'd been invited to her party. I was seventeen and I weren't really invited to many parties outside of the showbiz kind, the sort with producers and directors there, where you've got to behave yourself. I thought at this party there'd be people there that I actually knew and hadn't seen for a while as I'd been working abroad. Arthur was also going to take his girlfriend Roberta Tovey, an actress who'd been in the *Doctor Who and the Daleks* film, so I thought, on balance, I'd go. So, that night, I'd been doing a personal appearance at the Royal Albert Hall and I got the driver of my limo to drop me off at a tall block of flats near Marble Arch.

When I got to the party, it was well into the scene and everyone was enjoying themselves. I stepped in to the room, to get a drink; but, before I could, her mother took hold of me and said, 'Oh, it's so lovely to see you, Jack.'

I didn't know that she was an agent and I thought it was just this girl's mother. 'Oh, I've got to show you my daughter's room, she's madly in love with you!' she said and grabbed hold of my hand and led me upstairs into the daughter's bedroom. 'Look at that!' she exclaimed.

And the wall was covered with pictures of me. There might have been a couple of David Bowie and one each of David Cassidy and Donny Osmond, but most of it was me.

Mrs King was explaining how her daughter had got this photograph and where she got that still and so on. It was a bit of a shock to see quite so much of me in this girl's room and I couldn't understand it, but I was looking and being polite basically. The next minute the door closes and the woman's voice stops. I turned around expecting her to continue with what she was saying, but she had disappeared and the daughter was there instead. I didn't know what to do. She was twice the size of me. I got out of that room as quickly as I could and went downstairs. I stayed with whoever I knew at the party, and left fairly soon after that. The next time I saw her was on the set at Colet Court and that spooked me something rotten.

Still, I was safe in my dressing room with Mark and I had my own personal hi-fi. It was made by Sony and I think it was the first portable stereo cassette tape recorder that had detachable speakers (aside from the actual machine having its own speaker) which was unheard of. I'd bought it when I was doing the *Pufnstuf* series and I don't think this particular model was available yet in England. The other lads thought it was an amazingly flash gadget and so did I because it came in an attaché case, so it looked as though you were carrying something technical when you had it with you. I took it everywhere.

After lunch we were doing a scene where Mark has taken Tracy to the beach for the day and then when they come back to the school the following day everyone's taking the mick about them being lovers. When we all go for lunch in the hall he wants to sit next to Tracy, but everyone is geeing him up and so I go to rescue him and bring him back to our table. We'd done it a couple of times when Waris said, 'Jack, as you pass this young lad here, I want him to laugh at you and as he does that, I want you to tip his dinner all over him, okay?'

The 'laughing lad' was Colin Barry. I knew him from Speake's and he was very into his education, the class swot and a bit of a bore. He'd never ever done anything to me so I had no reason to dislike him at all but I thought, Y-E-E-E-S-S-S-S-S-S! I'll enjoy this.

'Is that all right then, Jack?' Waris asked again.

'Yes sure, if that's what you want,' I said nonchalantly.

I could have done it all day, poor bugger.

But what goes around comes around and the following day we were filming the sports day outside. In one scene me and Mark are talking, and during our dialogue someone was to throw a ball at me so I could catch it and throw it back, and they wanted to shoot this scene all in one long take. And for some reason, this particular scene, I hadn't learnt as well as any of the other ones, and so I was concentrating that much more on my lines and not remembering what else I'm supposed to be doing and had totally forgotten about this ball. And so I'm walking along, and I'm a big film star, and I'm doing my lines and all these people are around me and... *thwack!* Straight on the nose. Everyone laughed, and I imagined Colin Barry laughing hardest of all. The nosebleed soon stopped, but my pride took much longer to recover.

Me Dad would come and pick me up at the end of the day, and if we'd been at Nine Elms we'd sometimes stop off at a pub on the way back; it was a pub just past the Half Moon in Putney, I can't remember the name of it now, but I remember the moment. We stopped there on the way home, and I had a shandy; and, sitting there, I felt sheer contentment. They were happy, happy days. They really were. If there was a problem, it could easily be sorted out. *But there weren't any problems*. And if there were, there were hundreds of people there to sort them out for me, or I could do it myself.

There was one time, however, that I did throw a wobbly. It was one day in the middle of the very hot summer. We were at Nine Elms in an area where all the dressing rooms, caravans and catering were – the place where everyone would congregate when they weren't filming. I can't remember why I was angry; maybe I'd asked for something, and they weren't giving it to me, or something to do with my costume, I don't know, something stupid, but important to me at the time. I had my costume on and I said, 'Right, if you won't give it me, then I'm gonna roll on the floor and dirty meself up!'

The ground was bone dry and I threw myself on the floor and rolled in the dirt. I rolled around the floor like an over-indulged baby elephant and was deadly serious as I was doing it. I guess it was like a baby throwing a tantrum; it's just that I was seventeen. They looked at me and couldn't believe what they were seeing. I can't remember what anyone said, they just looked astonished; but it made me feel better, so I didn't care. I think they were perhaps as embarrassed as I should have been. It's the only time I remember doing anything so *childish*. I just needed a slap, that's what I needed. I think I wanted to remind people of my power, but probably I just reminded them of what a twat I was instead. Nothing was said of it and I think I might have got my own way; to be honest, I can't remember.

About six months after we'd finished making it, we were invited to a private screening of the first cut of the film in a preview theatre in Knightsbridge and me Mum and Dad came with me. I was so pleased because not only did the Bee Gees (who I thought were great) turn up, but also Lulu (who I adored) was there, and to top it off, Ringo. That was amazing! Me meeting Ringo Starr! I can't remember what I said to him or what he said to me, but I *met him*. After the screening I nipped into the loo before going home and *they* were in there, the Bee Gees, and I peed with the Bee Gees. What a night!

Also during this time, my first single charted in England. The B-side was a hit that Joe Brown had in England called 'Picture of You', which was always a favourite song of mine. The single was released on 2nd May and it stayed in the charts at number 46 for two weeks and then disappeared and was never seen again. Strangely, however, during those two short weeks I was asked to appear on *Top of the Pops*. 'Strangely' because, in those days, you couldn't go on *TOTP* unless you were in the Top Thirty. Dorothy Squires was at number 25 with 'Till' and she'd been booked to do the show, but for some reason they had decided to drop her and put me in, a mere 46-er! Ms Squires wasn't pleased and complained about it. I think she was very popular at the time, but it was more my parents' sort of music than mine. It was all played out in the papers and they contacted me and asked me what I thought about it all.

'Well, I'm a Beatles fan and I've always wanted to do *Top of the Pops* and I don't care,' was my considered response.

So Ms Squires was out and I was in. Me and Brian went to Television Centre in a limo to rehearse and perform the show which was recorded as live. Oh, I thought I was a big hit! Brian, however, wasn't very happy with the music: we'd recorded the single in the States and had used lots of Moog synthesisers which were in their early days and it was a very complicated track to reproduce.

So as Brian worked on the music, I got on with being a pop star. The official photographers on the show were Harry Goodwin and his assistant Ron Howard. I knew Ron really well as he took all the photographs for everybody at Barbara Speake's and he'd also taken some illicit ones of me as Dodger. During the filming either June or Miss Speake had said to me, 'Sneak your costume home at the weekend, Jack, and we'll get Ron to take some nice photographs of you.' I did and he had. I had loads of sessions with him over the years and always enjoyed them. He would tell me about his escapades as a photographer: how he'd go and photograph pieces at the British Museum, or how he'd go to London hospitals and photograph pickled body bits and all sorts of amazing stuff. He was so interesting and had the biggest eyes, maybe from all the things he'd seen. He was dead positive and always made me laugh. They were taking the stills during the last rehearsals and he was such a lovely guy. He kept saying, 'This is a really good song Jack – it's going up the chart for sure.' A lovely guy, just not always right.

Meanwhile Brian was creating havoc because the orchestra didn't sound close enough to the backing track for me to sing live. I kept out of it; I thought, I've got no input here because I don't know enough about it – it was all out of my league, so I didn't let it bother me. I just let Brian get on with it. There were lots and lots of arguments in the studio, and I heard years later that because of that I was blacklisted by the BBC for being too much trouble with all the aggro that was caused about my track. Whether that was the case or not I don't know, but I certainly didn't get much work for the BBC until five years later in *Our Mutual Friend*.

Still, Brian was pleased with the end result. I, on the other hand, couldn't hear any difference from when we first heard them play it, to when I actually did it. We recorded it and I wasn't particularly nervous – I felt on cloud nine while doing it – and then we went home.

After that I would go and do other TV shows where I'd sing live, like *Lift Off*, and having done it the first time on *TOTP* the novelty completely disappeared. I thought, I've done that now, so that's that. Ayshea Brough who lived with Roy Wood (which I thought must be fun) presented *Lift Off* and I must've done it four or five times, whenever I had a single out really. The producer, Muriel Young, was one of the top children's TV producers at Granada at the time and I used to work for her loads. I'd first met her doing *Stubby's Silver Star Show*, and I think perhaps she had a soft spot for me.

Chapter 12

'**I**'M NOT GETTING ON THAT PLANE. I don't like flying at the best of times and that, *that* is a bloody joke.'

Me and Brian were in LA and on our way to Catalina Island to film the video for 'Some Beautiful'. There were three ways to get there: you could either sail, fly on a normal plane, or you can go on a seaplane. We were just going there for two days and were on such a tight schedule that we didn't have time to sail, and I didn't fancy a bloody seaplane. 'Landing on the sea and all that? No mate, we'll just go on the normal plane,' I said.

So we go to check in and I remember getting to the counter and I said to the woman, 'Can I have a seat by the window please?' I liked to sit by the window so I could see what was going on. I still didn't really like flying and being able to see out made me feel slightly better.

'They're all by the window, sir,' she replied.

I looked at Brian and I thought, what does she mean they're all by the window? 'What sort of aeroplane are we going on?' I asked.

'That one over there, sir,' she said, pointing out onto the runway. And I looked and it had about eight or nine windows on the side of the plane and two propellers on the wings.

'I ain't going on that!' I said.

'We have to, Jack, if you don't want to go on the seaplane, and we're only up there for about twenty minutes.'

'But that's not a proper plane, Brian,' I said.

'May I assure you, sir, you'll be quite safe,' the lady at the counter volunteered, 'and can I just say how great you are in *Pufnstuf* – my kids just love the show. Would it be too much to ask for an autograph?'

'Er... no... sure,' I said, embarrassed, and signed her bit of paper.

'I ain't getting on that plane unless you get me a drink,' I said quietly to Brian. 'A good few drinks,' I added.

As we walked to the bar Brian said, 'You know, Jack, fourteen million people tune into *Pufnstuf* every Saturday – you're bound to be recognised.'

But it wasn't that that was particularly worrying me. 'Yeah, I know, Brian,' I said; and, just before we reached the bar, 'Bacardi and Coke please.' I still wasn't old enough to drink in California, so when we got to the bar, Brian ordered me a 7 Up and three drinks for himself. When we got to a table I had the two double Bacardi and Cokes and then downed the 7 Up for good luck.

Feeling only slightly more courageous, we got on the plane; and it didn't seem as though we'd gone fifty yards down the runway before we were up in the air. And I thought, oh fuck, I don't like this! You could see straight through to the cockpit – there weren't no door or anything – and they only flew at about a thousand feet, which looked like two hundred foot; and I thought, I don't like this, I don't like this at all. For the whole flight I kept my sunglasses on and my eyes tightly shut, silently bracing myself for disaster.

I was told when we got to the airport that there were only a couple of towns on the island and that they were all walled because: 'We've got buffalo running wild on the island and the walls are to stop them coming in, Mr Wild.'

'Wow, cool,' I said, still a little shaky from the flight, or the Bacardis, or both.

'Everybody who lives in the town has a pass key like a credit card to open the town gates.'

'I've never seen a buffalo before, so that'll be interesting,' I said.

'Welcome to the island, Mr Wild, I hope you enjoy your time with us; and can I ask you for your autograph – I'm your biggest fan.'

On the cab journey into town we saw all these lovely buffaloes and that was great – it was such a novelty. It'd been arranged that we'd meet the director in a bar that night to talk about the shoot the following day, so when we checked in to the hotel Brian asked the lady at reception for directions.

'Oh, that's a lovely bar with pool tables in there and, you know, it's a great place to relax and have a drink.'

Yeah, if I was old enough, I said to myself.

'So where is it?' Brian asked again.

'It's about a ten, fifteen-minute walk: just go left outside and down to the end of the street and you come to the seafront. Make a left and it's eight hundred yards down the road. Oh, and can I have your autograph please, Jack – I'm your biggest fan.'

As we walked out of the hotel I looked at me watch and we were running a bit late; at that time, it still mattered to me to be on time. We headed off down to the seafront and I saw this tandem parked right outside the hotel. 'C'mon Brian, let's get on this,' I said. Brian gave me a sideways glance. 'It's not locked up,' I said, 'and we're only on the island, we can drop it off again when we come back.'

He only needed a little bit more convincing.

'We're only going down there for an hour: it won't get lost, and even if whoever owns it comes out and looks for it, it'll be back where he left it in the hour, so don't worry. Anyway,' I said, 'I've never had a go on a tandem before, come on.'

'Right, you get on the front and I'll get on the back!' Brian said.

There's a way of getting started on these things, and could we get started? I'm not kidding, we were laughing so much that we could not get going without one of us falling off it. I was crying with laughter and my stomach was aching something rotten, and so was Brian's. There were tears pouring out of his eyes. It took us about half an hour to get to this bar because no sooner had we got going than one of us would either fall off because we were laughing or we'd lose balance. We were a little bit late when we got to the bar, so we said we'll park it outside but we mustn't be too long because we've borrowed the bicycle and we'll have to take it back.

In the bar we met up with the director who said, 'Great to meet you, Jack. Should we have a game of pool then?' As though this was what we had flown here to do.

'Yeah, sure,' I said. I had spent the whole of the previous summer playing pool at Marty's house so I thought, well yeah, why not, because I'm pretty good at this.

We played the first game and he won and I thought, blimey, I was unlucky not winning – my shots went haywire and he had a lot of luck to my misfortunes. So I thought, let's have a laugh, and said, 'Why don't we make this interesting: why don't we play for money?'

'Yeah, alright, if you want. Okay, fine,' he said.

In between shots we talked about the next day's shoot, mainly where we were filming it and at what time; the director didn't volunteer much more and I wasn't interested in knowing much more, so we just played pool and I drank 7 Up.

He didn't win any more matches, and ended up losing about thirty or forty dollars, not a massive amount of money, but it didn't please him to lose at all; as it wouldn't have done me.

'Okay mate, we gotta get back to the hotel now,' I said, 'if we're getting up in the morning to get an early start of shooting.'

So we said our goodbyes to the director, left the bar and went to pick up the tandem, but it had gone! No sign of it anywhere. 'Somebody's bloody nicked it,' I said. 'Oh hell, Brian, what are we going to do?'

'Well we can't report it, Jack, because we weren't supposed to have had it in the first place,' he said, so we didn't say anything and walked back to the hotel.

I loved the island and thought it was fantastic. The following morning we filmed the video in this town with this beautiful big bay. The water was so clear and it was all so very picturesque, and what with the town being completely walled and knowing on the outside that you've got all these buffaloes running around like lunatics – that was quite nice. The bay was really deep and the seaplane would come in and it looked as though it was going to land on the beach, but it would glide in, then turn to the left and come round and stop a couple of hundred yards offshore. I gazed transfixed at the seaplane heading towards the beach.

'So, if you're ready, Jack.'

'Oh yeah, sure, sorry,' I said. 'Ready.'

'Okay', 'Turn over', 'Speed', 'Mark it', 'Action'.

The video was basically me riding a bicycle, singing about my girlfriend, and then I meet 'pretty girl' along the way and give her a lift on my bike.

'Cut', 'Check the gate', 'Gate clear', 'Print that one'.

In between takes I'd go over to Brian and say, 'Any sign of that tandem yet?'

'No Jack, no sign at all.'

What was really surprising was that we didn't see any more tandems at all in the whole town; we didn't see anyone riding one, or a parked one or anything.

I didn't ever see the video till a few years ago and I thought it was a bit naff. I think I thought it was a bit naff at the time really. It's not that I wasn't proud of the song, and I did enjoy riding quite a hip bicycle and I was quite into all that posing lark, but I thought it was just not a very exciting job. I saw 'pretty girl' on the shoot as a fellow worker. I didn't flirt – I'd have been too embarrassed to do anything of that nature then.

We shot it in one day and that night we flew back to LA. I asked Brian if we could sail instead, but he said there wasn't time as we had to get back for some radio promotions. I needed a couple of drinks before the flight to calm me down a little bit: well, at least enough to get me on the bloody thing!

'Are you sure you need…' Brian began, but he could see by my expression that I wasn't getting on board without a drink. 'Oh, alright then… Bacardi and Coke?'

It wasn't to get drunk: I just found it helped me do the things I didn't want to do. Well no, that's the wrong description; it would help me forget whatever it was that I was doing, or anything going on that I didn't like. When there was the trouble with Arf in LA a couple of drinks helped me. I didn't understand all the ramifications of the situation at the time, but I knew that it was causing me unnecessary aggro, and with a few drinks I didn't care so much and thought of it less.

*

'So what was it like shooting *Pufnstuf*?' It was an interview for someone, somewhere – they were hard to distinguish as they all asked the same questions.

'Well,' I started, 'we shot *Pufnstuf* on film, not on video, so it was like making a movie over that four-month period. It was great fun and I loved working on the songs each week. I was told that the network wanted to get away from cartoons that were excessively violent and I think the music in *Pufnstuf* played such an important part in making it as popular as it is.'

'What was your favourite song from the series, Jack?'

'It's a toss-up between "Pronouns" and "Mechanical Boy". I think "Pronouns" is a bit of Cagney and anything to do with Cagney is fine by me. So if anything, I prefer "Pronouns". I can't remember each one of the seventeen songs that we did, but every one had a big chunk of magic. I would say my favourite upon favourite is Billie Hayes singing "Oranges, Smoranges". Now that is insanity at its best! Who the hell would think of writing a song about the fact that there's nothing that rhymes with oranges? I did a show recently, and two fans came up and they sang that from top to bottom, all the way through knowing all the words and everything. That is insanity as well!'

'Tell us a funny story, Jack.'

Now I had to be funny as well.

'Well,' I began, 'while we were shooting the *Pufnstuf* movie at Universal I'd been given some award for the *Oliver!* film. I'd gone to the ceremony and was given the award in front of this audience and had said thank you very much and what an honour it was and all that, but at the end of the ceremony as I was leaving they said, "Can we have the award back?"

'"Well, I thought I'd come here to collect it," I said – I'd put on a suit and everything!

'"No, we've got to get it engraved now."

'So I gave it them back and went home. They later turned up on set when we were shooting the scene where I've just dived off the evil boat to try and swim home. I'd just finished shooting and I was soaked to the skin and they said, "Here you are. Here's your award and can we take some photographs of you receiving it?"

'"What, now?" I said.

'"Yes please," they said.

'I look like a drenched rat but what do you do? You can't say no, can ya? So I had to agree, and they took the photograph of me in my dripping costume with chattering teeth. I've got a copy of that in my collection and it looks hysterical.'

Was this what they wanted? I don't know, I'll just plough on.

I mentioned the Chopper bicycle, getting lost 'because you know how big the backlot is at Universal. It sort of goes off into the mountains, doesn't it?'

And I talked of snakes and spiders and security.

'Wow,' the interviewer helpfully interjected.

'And I had my own little bungalow on the lot at Universal for my dressing room and it had a bathroom in it and a lounge, TV, stereo, the complete works. And actually, I don't know if Universal know but I did take my name-plate from outside my bungalow as a keepsake and I've still got it.'

Was that a funny story? I didn't know. I couldn't tell any more what they wanted to know, what was funny and interesting and what was not. The fan mags all seemed to want to know such rubbish – apparently my favourite dessert was interesting and newsworthy – and it all *seemed* funny at the time.

'Oh, it must have been a blast,' the interviewer laughed. 'Thanks so much. It's been really great having you on the show.'

Oh well, job done then. On to the next. There were endless radio promotions.

I loved going into the Capitol Record offices when I was in LA. It was this great circular building, made to look like a stack of records, and was known as the Capitol Tower. One thing that I always enjoyed about that was that I could go into the offices and pick up any number of albums that I wanted from whoever was on the label. One of my favourites on Capitol at the time was 'The Band' who were a great group. It was amazing to be on the same record label as them and Frank Sinatra, Andy Williams, Neil Diamond, Nat King Cole, Simon and Garfunkel, the Beatles, Blood, Sweat and Tears, Chicago... the names were endless: everybody who was anybody, and me.

To be able to come back to England with all these albums that none of my friends would be able to get hold of, let alone know anything about, made me feel super-cool. I could say, 'Well, these guys are on my label and oh, I bumped into the lead guitarist of that one and he played on my single and Leon Russell was on the keyboards.' That was about the one and only time that I would enjoy boasting about my exploits abroad to my mates. I was also quite proud of meeting 'Tonto' when I did *The Mike Douglas Show* a few years later. Telling them somehow seemed to make it real, even though they mostly didn't believe me.

Whilst we'd been filming *Melody*, John Daly had been having talks with Columbia Pictures to finalise the contract renegotiations that June Collins had originally signed me up for. John had got them to rip up the original contract and, for what I'd have got for five films, they agreed that I would do one film, *Flight of the Doves*, and I'd get the full amount of money.

I'd had a meeting with Ralph Nelson, the director. He was very popular as he had just directed Candice Bergen in *Soldier Blue*, breaking box office records everywhere in the US. A very violent film, I'd been told, but I hadn't seen it, as I wasn't old enough. I was looking forward to working with him as he'd directed the film from the American Indians' point of view, the first to my knowledge to have done that. I was a great fan of the American Indians, so I thought there must be an affinity between me and Ralph. Cowboys and Indians had been a huge part of my childhood. I'd quite liked being a cowboy, as I could then be John Wayne, but I was just as happy being an Indian. There was usually a greater demand for Indians as the other boys really just wanted to be cowboys and 'git those downright, ungodly savages and pump 'em full of lead'. Consequently, I had been a lot of Indians in my time.

There was a problem, however, that threatened my working relationship with Ralph. He was adamant that to play Finn Dove I would have to have my hair dyed red – ginger! – as I was meant to be half Irish. Well, I wasn't having that in any way, shape or form. Firstly, I thought it was poofy to dye your hair. Secondly, Kim Smith had had his hair dyed blonde, almost white, for his 'Golden Wonder' TV ad and he looked so stupid because they didn't bleach his eyebrows or anything. He had this almost white hair with black eyebrows and I thought I'd end up having black eyebrows and bloody red hair. And thirdly, I remember at school it was really not very good if you had ginger hair: John Champkin had ginger hair in the stage show of *Oliver!* and suffered for it, and I wasn't ready to join the cause.

I didn't put all this logic to Ralph Nelson; I just said 'I'm not doing it' and went off to Jersey for a holiday leaving John Daly to sort it out. I took me Mum and Dad and Arf and went to get some money, and when I came back, it'd all been arranged.

'Okay then, if you really won't have your hair dyed, we'll let you wear a wig and you'll have to go to Wig Creations in Covent Garden and have it fitted!'

Well, I thought, yeah, that's alright. I was just pleased that it'd all worked out. If somebody said to me now, 'You've got to have your hair dyed sky-blue pink!' I'd say 'Right, where's the bottle?' But things are very different when you're seventeen. So, during this short gap which could've only been about six weeks between finishing *Melody* and flying out to Dublin to start *Flight of the Doves*, I had one or two wig fittings in Covent Garden.

So it was off to Ireland to work with Ron Moody again, and Willie Rushton, Stanley Holloway, Dorothy McGuire, and Dana strangely enough. I was looking forward to working with them all, especially Mr Holloway and Miss McGuire as they were such established experienced actors. I'd seen Miss McGuire in *Old Yeller* at the cinema and cried.

But I'd made a big mistake. On the first day of filming at Bray Studios, just outside Dublin, I was presented with my companion for the next ten weeks – a companion I hated from the moment we met.

'Look at it!' I said. 'All I need now is a red nose and I'll be away.' It was my wig and it looked as uncomfortable with me as I was with it. It was not only red, it was permed – *permed* red hair. They were having a laugh, weren't they? I'd made a huge mistake. I should've agreed to have my hair dyed once I got over here, and then had it dyed back before I went home, then nobody who knew me would've seen it. That's what I should've done rather than being stuck with this abomination.

'Doesn't look that bad, love,' me Mum tried. 'Just imagine you're wearing a hat and you'll be all right.' But it was no good. We already hated each other. It squatted on my head in protest and we did our best to ignore each other for the rest of the film.

Me Mum and I had flown out from Heathrow to Dublin (Arf stayed at home with me Gran and Grandad), and me Dad had driven the car up to Liverpool to come over on the ferry. He was driving an Austin Westminster, automatic and with a full-sized sunroof – it was really nice. On the way he called in at his Mum and Dad's, and at Uncle Vincent and Auntie Kathleen's. They were me Uncle and Auntie on me Mum's side, a jolly couple; he was tall and gangly, and she had big, giggling eyes. They had a farm full of pigs and chickens and me and Arthur went a few times before things got too hectic with work. We helped them collect the eggs from the battery hens which we thought was quite a laugh, although now I think it's a bit cruel. And we would go into the hay barns for a crafty cigarette which we also thought was quite a laugh, although now I think that was a bit stupid.

We met up with Dad and got sorted in a lovely hotel; and then me Mum said she wanted to go shopping. 'Oh bloody hell!' me Dad said. Among other things she wanted to buy a birthday card, and so we popped into a little corner shop.

'Have you got any birthday cards for a nephew, please?' me Mum asked.

'Yes, of course, my dear,' the lady smiled. She handed me Mum a pile of cards, and there must've been about eighty of them, all for nephews. 'There you go,' she said.

Me Mum put them on the side of the counter and started looking through them. Eventually she pulled out the one that she wanted and put that to one side, and handed back the other seventy-nine to the lady.

'Now then,' the shopkeeper said, 'that's one and six, three shillings, four and six, six shillings, seven and six, nine shillings…' and she was adding them up! All seventy-nine *Happy Birthday Nephew* cards.

'Just a minute, love – I only wanted one,' me Mum said. 'I haven't got that many nephews!'

We left the shop giggling like two schoolkids. 'Shh, Jackie!' me Mum said, bubbling with laughter. I don't think me and me Mum stopped laughing for the whole time we were there. Silly buggers.

Having already met my wig I was introduced to my other companion: my stand-in, John. He was a young Irish kid from a working-class family. He had dark hair, dark eyes and the sunniest disposition in Ireland. He was five years younger and was really a child to me, but we got on well and I enjoyed his company. He was unworldly and so innocent on the set, having never seen the filming process before, and he was mesmerised by it all. He was funny to watch and we had a real laugh in the studio. At lunchtimes we'd grab a football and have a kick about. I had a good feeling about this film, or 'fillum' as John would say.

The film was about two young children (me and Helen Raye) who are constantly bullied by their cruel stepfather (Willie Rushton) and they decide to run away. They escape across the sea to Ireland, but their wicked Uncle Hawk (Ron Moody), a brilliant master of disguise, discovers the kids are heirs to a great fortune and if they die or can't be traced he will get all the money. 'Will the judge (Stanley Holloway) rule in their defence? Will they make it to their grandmother's house (Dorothy McGuire)? Will the evil Hawk catch his prey?' the publicity demanded.

He does; we do; and he has a change of heart.

The ten-week schedule was to take us all over Ireland and it was a great crew to be touring with. We were starting off on the east coast of Southern Ireland in Dublin, then going west to Athlone in the middle of the country, then all the way to Galway, then straight into Northern Ireland and Portrush and then finally back down to Dublin again to shoot the parade. We were mostly on location, often in the middle of nowhere, and there really was every shade of green going. It was so beautiful, and so were the people: so generous and kind and warm and friendly and 'the best sense of humour in the whole world', I said to me Mum.

In our first week there we were doing lots of night shooting. We wouldn't be called until maybe six or seven o'clock in the evening and we'd have to wait until it'd gone dark before we could start filming. We wouldn't finish until 4.30 in the morning, after which we'd go back to the hotel and sleep for the whole of the day and then get up at 4.30 in the afternoon to go back and do another night's shooting.

About the third night, when everyone was tired and ratty, Helen wasn't doing something that Ralph Nelson wanted and instead of talking the scene through and trying to be helpful he lost his rag and started shouting at her. I thought this was totally out of order and I said, 'Look, there's no need to be like that. At least be nice about it, for God's sake. She's only a kid.' She was only about eight years old and she just looked so upset. I did feel very quickly protective towards her as she was such a very little kid. I suppose it was the same way I felt about Mark in *Oliver!* I sort of felt responsible for making sure they were all alright.

Ralph made an effort to calm down and said to her, 'I'm sorry; you know, it's been a long, long night. Let's start again.'

After the series of night shoots, we did some stuff in and around Dublin itself. It was a relief to be working during the day at last. I had a late call around midday, and as I was leaving the hotel I saw Willie Rushton in the bar. 'Have a good day, dear boy,' he called, 'I'll see you tonight,' and I headed off in the car. We were filming a sequence at the Ha'penny Bridge with the famous Irish actor Noel Purcell, who played a rabbi. It was an interesting scene because I'd never been in a synagogue before. This was to be my first time. It looked antique and was small and dark, and I couldn't understand why all the cast and crew wore hats. It seemed funny that everyone *had* to wear a hat.

Noel had a whitish-grey beard and the deepest voice I've ever heard. He was six foot six – a giant to me – and a very private man. I didn't really get close to him; well, I couldn't, he towered over me. He did, however, have a very distinctive smell and I didn't know what it was as I'd never smelt it before. I thought maybe it was something to do with being Jewish.

When we got back to the hotel at about 6.30 Willie was still there, still in the same seat. 'Ah, the workers return! Had a good day, dear boy?' he called. I was walking in with the third AD who had come to give out the call sheets for the next day; there were quite a few potential recipients in the bar who were involved in the film. We both walked up to Willie and the third AD gave him his call sheet. Willie took it by the corner with finger and thumb and in an outrageously posh accent said, 'I don't want… this fucking… *rubbish!*'

He took the opposing corner with his other finger and thumb, his little fingers raised in disgust, and ripped the offending call sheet straight down the middle. 'This means nothing to me,' he said and tossed the two bereft pieces of call sheet into the air, threw back his head, and let the pieces float onto the floor of the bar like unwanted leaves on an autumn day. He put his hand heavily on the third AD's shoulder and said, 'Now. What are you having to drink, dear boy?'

The entertainment was so good I decided to stay in the bar; and we were soon joined by one of the camera technicians, I think he was the focus puller. His name was Johnny and he was quite an old guy – I'd say he was close on sixty – and he'd been in the business years and years. He'd done loads of well-known movies, from the Bond films all the way through the sixties to God knows what.

'Barman! A gin and tonic for this fine young man here,' Willie declared, 'and make it a large one.'

Anecdotes flew around for the rest of the evening until Johnny declared that he couldn't drink any more and he was off to bed. 'Two large gin and tonics for the road, barman,' he said.

'Who's the other drink for, Johnny?' I asked.

'It's for my friend!' he said. 'It's for Mary!' And with that he ascended the stairs with his two nightcaps held unsteadily aloft.

I was intrigued and, the following morning, having breakfast on the set before starting work, I asked one of the other technicians about Johnny's 'Mary'. 'Oh, it's a pigeon he's been feeding the whole time we've been here. It sits outside his bedroom window and he gives it bread rolls and gin and tonic.'

'She's a *she*, not an "it",' Johnny said as he walked past, obviously having overheard our conversation. 'And the lady likes a large gin and tonic before she goes to bed.'

That day we were shooting very close to the public courts and we had a lot of extras on the set. There must've been at least a dozen extras dressed as policemen, and during a break in filming they had set up a game of poker by the side of the road and were playing for money. I'd been kicking a ball about with Helen and I looked to see what type of game they were playing. I'd played poker since I was a kid, and I stopped a while to see what they were using as a wildcard.

The stills photographer saw me watching and said, 'Can I take a few shots, Jack?' He was constantly on set with nine hundred cameras wrapped round his neck, clicking away for all he was worth. 'This'll be a great picture of the Artful Dodger playing poker with the police,' he said.

'Yeah, alright then.' I said. Even though *Oliver!* was three years ago, I thought, but, yeah, sure, if you want to.

He took the photographs and sent one to the local papers in Dublin and they printed it with some silly caption like 'The game's up for Dodger'.

While he was taking the photos I smelt that smell again. Noel wasn't around so I wondered who else it might be. I asked one of the extras, what's that smell?

'Sorry mate, that's garlic, I had an Italian last night.'

'Oh,' I said. 'It smells bloody awful.'

I'd been told before coming to Ireland that they had the best salmon and trout rivers in the world, so I thought, right, whenever I'm not working I'll go fishing. I'd been strictly a 'stick, hook and fishing line' sportsman to date, but felt it was now time to get all the gear and make my mark on the angling world. So every time that I wasn't working, if I was near water, I'd get me rod out which I always kept in the boot of me Dad's car and I'd be there, fishing.

While we were based in Dublin we filmed on location in the Wicklow Mountains. We were up there one day and we saw a lovely river and I said to Dad, 'I wanna try fishing there.' So the first day I had off, we headed back there. I'm a dreadful fisherman, even now, but I was worse then. I stood, almost patiently, on the riverbank looking where to start. The river was only about thirty foot wide and the water was very, very, clear. There didn't seem to be much action on my side of the river; but I could see on the other side, about twenty foot to my right, a whole load of trout. So I thought, not to worry, I'll find the nearest bridge, get across the river and walk along to where the fish are.

So I walked all the way over and set myself up again. I wasn't fishing with live bait or dead bait because I don't like messing about with things like that, but I was using a spinner – something that's supposed to look like a fish or an insect, but is really plastic. Well, no sooner had I got the thing ready to throw in the river, and looked for where to throw it, than I could see that the fish had moved – moved back to where *I'd* just come from! Now, you can't tell me that fish are stupid 'cos they're bloody clever.

I thought, this is ridiculous. So, I walked all the way back and when I'd got back to where I'd originally started from, the fish were back to where they started as well. I thought, this is a joke this is. It's bloody stupid.

Foolishly, I'd told everyone on the film set that on my days off I would be fishing; and so consequently, and constantly, I was greeted by, 'Hi Jack, caught any fish yet?' or, from the comedians, 'Did it get away again then, Jack?'

Still, at least I could *see* the fish. I know they're there, I thought, so there's hope for me of catching *something*. I went back to this spot about three or four times to try my luck.

'Any luck today, Jack?' a member of the crew asked, *again*.

'No, not yet, but I'll get one before I leave,' I replied.

He asked where I'd been fishing and I told him about my spot.

'Have you got a permit, then?'

'Permit? What are ya talking about?' I asked.

'That's private fishing! That's very, very, expensive that permit is, to fish there. You're lucky you didn't get caught.'

'Well, I didn't see anything saying you've gotta have a permit!' I replied.

'So neither you nor the fish were caught that day,' he laughed. I laughed too, but steeled my determination to catch something the next day off I had.

The next time, I moved further up the mountains to where there was a massive lake. I thought, right, we'll get the old rods out; and I was having a go with these spinners. I was getting fed up because I hadn't caught anything (although I was making so much racket on the lakeside that I'd probably frightened the fish away), but I wasn't even getting a bite. I was despondently pulling it in again, but this time thinking, it's a bit heavy this! The water was reasonably clear and as I'm pulling it in, I looked: 'Bugger me!' I said. 'I've caught an eel!'

I'd just heard from somebody that eels, if you're not careful when you catch them, ain't half got a vicious bite! And I was thinking, what am I gonna do? How am I gonna get this off the line? And as I'm dragging it in I'm thinking and panicking; but as it came closer, it turned out to be a medium sized log. It really had looked like an eel.

Wicklow Mountains really wasn't working for me. I hadn't caught a single fish and had only a log to mount on my wall. Still, I'm not sure what I'd have done if I *had* caught something because I didn't like touching fish, and certainly not eels! In some ways I was glad I hadn't caught anything; if I had, I'd have bloody died with a cardiac.

The next day at work we were shooting a scene and the ribbing was getting worse. My fishing exploits were quickly becoming the running joke on the set. I'd find postcards on my chair or in my costume wishing me 'all the best for the day's fishing' or joke postcards about bad fishermen. Somebody else bought me a pottery figure of a hapless fisherman, and left it nestled with a prop postcard I was about to use. I picked up the postcard and the fisherman and looked around to see everyone beaming at me.

'Thanks very much,' I said, indicating the figure. 'You wait, I'll catch something before I go,' I added boldly.

We were shooting the scene when me and Helen first arrive in Dublin. All we've got is a picture postcard of our grandmother's house in Galway and we're trying to make our way there. We get off the ferry and we're hungry and strangers in the middle of Dublin.

We were filming in O'Connell Street, the main shopping street in Dublin, on the busiest day for shopping. So they said, 'Okay, this sequence starts with you stealing the pork pies, the stall holder will then shout "Stop thief!" and then a member of the Irish police, the Garda, will join in and this big chase will ensue!'

But then they said, 'Because there are so many people about, it'll be far easier to hide the cameras and just shoot it. There'll be loads of crew with walkie-talkies intermingled with the crowd along the street and they can tell you when we've cut!'

So, we do the first bit where me and Helen walk up to this stall and look hungrily at these pies, I go to grab them, and then we run off. We'd done it a couple of times and for whatever reason we were doing it a third time and this onlooker obviously hadn't seen the first two takes. He just happened to catch the third one and thought it was all for real. He saw me run off, heard the stall holder shouting 'Stop thief! Stop him!' and decides to join in the chase and rugby tackles me to the ground.

'Excuse me mate!' I said from the pavement. 'We're making a film.'

And the poor guy's face just dropped. 'Oh be Jeezus,' he said, 'yer making a fillum?' and he was so, so, embarrassed. He quickly looked to see if he could see the cameras and when he saw some of the people behind the cameras walking towards me, mainly to see that I weren't injured or anything, he disappeared into the crowd as quickly as he could.

One of the crew helped me up, and sensing an opportunity he started: 'Looks like you've been caught mate...' I could hear another fishing joke coming on. It was going to be a very long day.

We went into the bar after work that night. It seemed whatever time you went in there you would always find someone from the cast or crew already ensconced. As soon as you had one foot in the door, the call would go out: 'What are you drinking, Jack?' It was such a friendly bunch. I got half a pint of shandy in and went and sat with the production manager who was chatting to me Mum and Dad. We were in the last week of filming in Dublin, and when there was a gap in the conversation I asked what was happening about my stand-in, John, when we moved on to Athlone.

'He's only been booked for while we're here, Jack. We'll be getting someone else when we get to Athlone, and then someone else when we go to Galway and Northern Ireland and...'

'Why can't we ask him if he'd like to come with us, 'cos I get on really well with him; and, if he'd like to, I'd prefer to have him with me all the time than different people,' I said, adding, 'and I'm sure it'd be easier for the production company.' I wasn't that interested in the production company's needs, but I thought it would add weight to my argument. 'Can you see what you can do, mate?'

'We'll see, Jack,' he said.

'He can stay with me in my hotel rooms,' I said. 'I don't mind.'

'And we'll be responsible for him on the set and be his chaperone if you like,' me Mum added.

And so it was all sorted; and at the end of the week we were off to Athlone. There were so many of us we couldn't all fit into one hotel, so the cast and crew were spread around two or three different ones. But it didn't matter which hotel you were staying in as you'd be surrounded by at least two dozen people who were involved in the film. Me and John checked in at the first hotel, and went up to inspect our room.

'Oh, be Jeezus!' John said, 'this is fantastic!' We were all staying in whatever were the best hotels in the area and I suppose he'd never been in a hotel like this before in his life. 'Would you look at this,' he said, 'we've even got our own bathroom!' And he was so, so, happy. I got such a kick out of watching him, and I wondered if I'd been that bowled over when I first stayed in a posh hotel. He went around the suite inspecting drawers and cupboards, the telly, lights off, lights on, lights off, lights on, lights dimmed, lights... (*'John!'*) and ended up back at the bathroom.

'Here Jack, would you look at this.' He was looking down into the toilet at the disinfectant lump that was in a cage of plastic, hung from the rim. 'You'll never guess where they've put the soap!' he said.

I nearly choked!

Normally while we were working me Mum and Dad would go for a drive. One day the crew asked me Dad if he'd get them some crates of beer on his travels and bring them back to the set. He did; and that became quite a regular occurrence too. Me Mum and Dad would head off from the set with the orders, and sometimes with Willie as well. 'If you need me, I'll be in the pub with Vera and Jack,' he called to the first AD with a cheery wave.

One day when we were shooting in Shannon Bridge, the orders went unfilled and Willie stayed on the set, as they asked me Mum and Dad to be extras. They hadn't got enough locals to fill out a pub scene – appropriately enough. They wanted a crowd of people watching the news about the kidnap of me and my sister on the telly. There was nothing on the actual telly they were watching, just a black line going up and down, so Ralph Nelson would talk everyone through what was happening. He'd tell me Mum when he wanted her to have a drink and she sat there with her brandy and lemonade, smoking her fags as well. Me Mum used to say she couldn't drink too quickly because of her asthma (she didn't say couldn't *smoke* because of her asthma); but she kept at the drinking and, sure and steady, won the day.

'Drink now, Vera,' Ralph directed, and me Mum would oblige pretending she was watching a news report about me. 'Okay, and have another drink now, Vera.' Me Mum had a sip and the scene rolled on.

They needed several takes of the scene as there were several elements to it, and when they broke for lunch me Mum came over to me. 'Oh, that *was* fun Arthur... err... Jack. Jackie,' she giggled. She was half pissed and she loved every minute of it. She got the nickname of 'Mrs B and L' in honour of her prowess with the brandy and lemonade, and glowed with the attention.

We'd often film off the beaten track, frequently needing extra bodies, and after the pub scene success ('Not bad getting paid to get half cut, Jackie') me Mum and Dad would readily come in and earn an extra's day's pay. Sometimes me Dad would just be asked to drive a car up and down sporting a brown checked flat cap.

In Athlone we were filming the stuff with Dana. She played a gypsy girl who helps me and Helen, and me Mum and Dad really got on well with her and her parents and brothers. Dana had just won the Eurovision Song Contest with 'All Kinds of Everything' and was a national heroine in Ireland. She was about a year or two older than me, a very quiet, sweet, plain girl. We got on all right, but I think our parents were trying to push us together. I wasn't interested and to be honest I don't think she was interested either. She had her singing (she was very shy and only showed her confidence when she was singing), and I had my fishing.

I was now fishing on the River Shannon and it was a big river, about eighty foot across, and one afternoon I wasn't happy with how far I was throwing me line. So I thought, I need to throw a really big cast, and I threw the line way behind me, hooked my landing net and threw it in the river. Fortunately, no one saw. But all was not lost as, this particular afternoon, I'd decided to up my game in the fishing stakes and had brought with me this other sort of metal fish tracer. It was made of three different pieces, all nailed together, that meant it bent in the water, moving like a fish; it also had three treble hooks on it. I think it was for pike fishing and somebody had told me Shannon Bridge was well known for catching big pike.

So I've got this bloody thing that's about six inches long and I'm looking at the river and I thought, that looks like a good spot there where pike would be! (Not that I had the least idea.) I was aiming to cast the thing about seventy foot away but I couldn't get it anywhere near to where I wanted it. What I didn't know was, standing about eighty foot away from me was Ralph Nelson's son, a good-looking guy with curly, blondish hair, who was I'd say in his mid-twenties, about seven or eight years older than me.

'You're not doing that right!' he said. 'Do you want me to show you how to do it?'

'Flash bastard,' I said under my breath, not out loud, because he was much bigger than me. To him I said, 'All right, go on then. I want to get it over there. Can you do that?'

So he went and did all this number of looking like a professional fisherman. He went to cast it and, as he threw it in, it hooked on the side of his leg. All nine hooks on each of the three treble ones went in his trousers. I could not stop laughing, I was so pleased. After about ten minutes he got them out. He didn't injure himself but there were an awful lot of holes in his trousers.

After that, I went on to catch an old boot but it was manky and useless; I threw it back in.

Before we left Athlone I had two more meaningful encounters – and both were with livestock. We were shooting at Shannon Bridge, where we had shot many scenes before, and this one was of a funfair and market. It was a big, complicated scene to shoot involving the cast, extras, real market traders, chickens, geese, ducks, sheep, all manner of farmyard animals, and the cutest piglets you've ever seen. They were waiting patiently in wooden crates; then, inexplicably, there were cute little pigs out of their crates; and then there were cute little pigs all over the place. Cast and crew tried to catch these surprisingly agile and bloody fast little pigs, diving and weaving through the market on their podgy little legs; there seemed to be hundreds of them outnumbering cast and crew and extras alike. Seeing the pandemonium, I dived for my camera and captured it on film. I was mad about cine cameras and so pleased to have caught this piggy fiesta on film – although, now I come to look for it, it seems to have escaped too.

At another location we had to shoot a scene where we're being chased by Ron through a gang of cows. I was terrified, *terrified* of these cows. This was when I'm in disguise as a girl so perhaps I was just deeply in character. But I was so frightened of these cows because they were much bigger than me and three times the size of Helen. When we came to do it, I just grabbed her hand and sped through the beasts, Helen airborne behind me. I ran so fast and ducked and dived, it was enough to make any podgy little pig proud.

The next stop was Galway. Stanley Holloway and Dorothy McGuire were to join us here, and me Mum and Dad were so excited to meet them as they were both film stars of their generation. On one of their extras days, there was a bit where the gypsies have double-crossed me and my sister, and are shopping us to the police. The gypsies go into the pub where those ubiquitous drinkers, Vera and Jack, are, when in comes Dorothy McGuire. So for me Mum and Dad not only to *meet* her but to be in a scene with her – they were over the moon.

For me it was incredible as well to meet and work with these people who'd been in the business so long. They exuded so much confidence in themselves and their job that, in a funny way, it made me want to try harder with my part and up my game. John hadn't heard of them.

We went to check into our new hotel and I said to the receptionist, 'I want to make a phone call to London please. Here's the number and I'll take it in my room.' I was calling Gran and Grandad to ask whether Arf was coming over or not. He did come for the weekend and as soon as he arrived, he sticks his rod in at Galway and out comes a trout! The only thing I could put it down to was that he was using live bait and I couldn't be doing with worms. I still hadn't caught anything after trying for nine weeks! With hindsight I shouldn't have bloody called him.

Me and John went up to our room to wait for the call. I wanted to have a wash and brush up and John wanted to see if they had soap in the same place as before. I looked round for the phone but I couldn't find one anywhere. I had a wash and went downstairs to the reception. 'Oh, that phone call to London that I booked, I'll take it down here, thanks,' I said to the lady.

'Oh sir,' she replied, 'I was just trying to call you to tell you, there's no telephone in your room!'

I waited in the lobby with John, and we looked out at the river that ran right outside the hotel. We'd seen salmon in there that were at least three foot long.

'How heavy do you reckon one of them would be, John?' I asked.

'I dunno Jack – bloody heavy I should think, ten pounds?'

'They must be at least twenty or thirty pounds, I would've thought,' I said, adding, 'I wouldn't mind catching one of them.'

The manager of the hotel had been listening to us and after introducing himself he said, 'I know some good places to fish in, Jack. If you want, while you're here, I'll take you.'

'Right mate, you're on 'cos I've been in your country nine weeks and I haven't caught a thing yet!' I said.

He laughed and said, 'Don't worry, I'll take you somewhere where you'll catch something!'

A few days later we were out on a rowing boat: the fishing hotel manager, me and John. John was with me all the time now. I don't think he was that into fishing; he certainly hadn't caught anything. He mainly sat and watched me and laughed, I think.

The fishing manager was quizzing me about my techniques. 'What have you been using for bait? What sort of places have you been fishing in?'

I explained that I didn't like touching live worms or dead fish, that I'd fished wherever there was water and that so far I'd caught an old boot, a landing net, one cold and no bloody fish.

'I don't think you've been doing yourself any favours, because I don't think you've really been using the right tracers for the areas that you've been. Show us what you've got in your box.'

I'd bought my box in Ireland and it was filled with all sorts. I'd go in fishing shops and buy what I thought looked like very pretty replica fish, only to find out they were bloody useless at helping me catch live ones; either that or I was doing the whole thing wrong.

I showed him my box with justified pride.

'Right,' he said, and paused. 'Well, where I'm going to take you, these three will be the best to use,' he said, pulling out rather a plain selection. 'One of those three, and when we get there, we'll see what the weather's like and I'll tell you which one I think is best.'

This is brilliant, I thought, this man really knows his stuff.

So, we went up and down this river and I'm fishing the whole time that we're rowing up and down. The sun shone brightly on the river and I was slightly sweating, either from the heat or the prospect of catching a fish, I'm not sure which. A beautiful, and rarely seen, hot, sunny day in Ireland – it was surely a sign from the gods that today was my day. But I weren't even getting a bite, and I hadn't had a bite all the time that I'd been there. And because this had been promised me, I'd said to everyone, 'The manager's taking me fishing. He knows the places to catch fish so I'll definitely catch something!' So I'm thinking, Christ, I'm gonna be well in it if this happens and I don't catch something.

By now we've been out half a day and I haven't caught anything and we're miles from where we started off and he said, 'We'll have to start making our way back now.'

'Alright then,' I said, thinking that the dullard obviously had no appreciation for the seriousness of what we were trying to do. We started making our way back and I said, 'You must know somewhere where I can catch fish. I'm not fussy. Forget about the bloody salmon and the trout. Just let me catch something so I can either get a photograph of it or prove to someone that I've caught something.'

The compassionate manager picked up on my desperation and said, 'There's a couple of little tributaries going off the main river. I'll take you on one of those. They have a lot of fish in there.' We drifted into one and I sat silently willing the fish to throw themselves onto my line – surely it was the least they could do after giving me the runaround all this time. I mean, I like a joke as well as the next man, but enough is enough.

'You do realise that if I catch something,' I said, 'I won't be able to get it off the hook?'

'Sorry?' the manager said.

John was helpless at this stage; his mirth increased at the same rate as my desperation.

'If I catch something, I can't get it off the hook,' I repeated a little sternly. The pressure was beginning to tell and the sweating had increased.

'Well, you should do it yourself really,' he replied.

'Well, I can't,' I said. 'I want to catch something but I can't kill it or do any of that business. You'll have to do it, or John will have to do it. I can't do it.'

'Alright, don't worry about that, we'll worry about that if we get to that stage,' he said with a forced softness in his voice, as if he was trying to talk me down from the ledge of a tall building.

He gently took me through the thing to use and, to my amazement, I got a couple of bites. But obviously I'd sort of pulled it the wrong way and the fish escaped. But I was heartened by this and thought, well that's a lot better than I've been used to so far. There's hope for me yet.

And eventually I did catch three or four but they were like the size of goldfish, and we kept them in the keepnet. No mercy for tiddlers; they hadn't shown me any.

'Can you eat these?' I asked.

'Yeah,' he said dubiously, but it was enough for me.

'Well, can we take 'em back then and I'll have 'em tonight for dinner?'

'Yeah, I'll cook them for you,' the kindly manager replied.

So we took them back and ate them. It felt like the parable of the five loaves, two fishes and the great big miracle, even though they would only feed me and John, just. I returned home semi-triumphant and that night we were served up with the exotic supper. They had the look of red piranhas and they tasted bloody awful! If they had eaten me and John I think they would have had a tastier meal. All that trouble: ten weeks! And they were so small; I didn't bother taking photographs of them.

Of course they were much bigger when I was telling my fishing story the next day at work; of how we had netted our catch and how me and John had brought them home and feasted on what we caught. I was just glad to at last *have* a fishing story.

Early in the film, Willie throws our treasured model of Granny's house on the fire. When we arrived in Dublin and I saw the postcard of Granny's house I thought it was too beautiful to be real. I thought it must be a glorified prop. And so when we got to Galway and actually saw 'Granny's house', it was unbelievable: too beautiful to be real, and yet real. There it was, just down a few rolling fields and nestled at the edge of the world with the water beyond it, stretching out forever. I was told there were 365 islands on the lake that spread from the house and that it was stuffed full of trout. It was like landing in Oz – but, as Dorothy found, getting there was going to be a bumpy ride.

They wanted me to ride a horse, bareback, with a stuntman, down this not insignificant slope at speed, then jump over the stone wall to conclude.

They picked up me and Helen, and sat us on the front; I personally closed my eyes. It wasn't so much the ride down, although that was bad enough, especially so close to the front; it was the jump over the wall I was concerned about. I was not happy because these are big horses. I didn't enjoy that at all. Not in the least. The thing that sort of gave me bravado, if not actually courage, was that before we shot it my brother asked if he could have a ride on them before we shot the scene. He was jumping and all sorts. Flash git. He had learnt to ride in Hounslow at the stables where I got kicked. I'd got off the wrong side and as I was walking away I was thinking, this is great this! I'm gonna take this up as a hobby! And with that the horse goes *whack* right up my arse! And I thought, bugger that!

So having watched Arthur doing all this flash riding, when it came to me having to film it I couldn't turn round and say, 'Oh no, I'm frightened, I can't do that!' I had to be the big, brave one – the 'I-do-all-my-own-stunts' lark!

'You'll be all right, mate,' Arf said. 'Look at Helen, she's half your size and she's doing it.'

'Well, she don't know any better, does she!' I snapped.

We had to do three or four takes of the horse nightmare; it was the only time I stopped worrying about my wig.

In the bar that night after work I felt it was certainly the right time to have my first Guinness. Willie had been trying to get me and me Dad to try it since we got here. Me Dad had been more game than me and had tried it in the first week. I was still holding out. Willie loved the Guinness. 'You've got to taste it over here, Jack, because it's not like the stuff you get in England. This is the real McCoy – great stuff.' He finished his pint and ordered another one. 'It's like drinking wine, dear boy. Liquid gold,' he said, sucking the froth from the end of his ginger, comedic moustache.

He was great fun to be with: a very witty, clever man, and married to an even more bubbly redhead. Willie was always looking for an opportunity to crack a joke, and more often than not found the ideal place and cracked the perfect joke. If he thought he could get away with a funny line he would and did. In the film it was his idea to clutch Helen's teddy bear all the way through the film; this bear of a man clutching a teddy was inspired.

I used to shoot the hanging about between takes with my cine camera. Point a camera at Willie and he'd give you twenty minutes; mind you, so would Ron, and to be honest me as well – even little Helen. What's the matter with us all? But Willie always seemed to be very respectful of Ron and was careful not to tread on Ron's toes.

'Go on then, young Jack,' Willie said and passed me his Guinness to let me have a sip. It looked like very thick black soup, but after the day I'd had... so I tried it.

'Yuch, that's bloody awful that is,' I said. 'It's like drinking syrup.'

'You have to understand, it tastes better with a moustache,' he replied.

I left Willie in the bar entertaining the troops and went to look at my lines. I looked at the call sheet to see what we were going to be doing and learnt what I needed for the following day. I learnt lines very quickly in them days. It seemed as though I could just breathe them in.

We were soon to be heading up to Portrush, but before we left Galway we had a couple of parties. One was in the hotel – an 'end of Galway' party where I had a couple of Irish coffees and I got a bit merry. The other one was when Ron paid for the whole cast and crew to go to a 'medieval night' in a castle somewhere. They had hot mead and all that business and I got a bit merry then as well.

It was great to be working with Ron again. Such an amazing actor. His character, Hawk Dove, was a master of disguise and Ron had to play several characters throughout the film. He made them funny, sinister and a bit mad all at the same time. Only Ron could've done it like that, and sometimes you'd swear it wasn't him at all. His first character was a lawyer with whiskers; then a detective; and then the funniest of the lot, a woman reporter, a Marjorie Proops type. I'll never forget shooting these long dialogue scenes, with me and Helen in the back of this clapped-out Triumph Herald (the same car that I was in the back of in *Melody* with Mark), and it was so hard to keep a straight face seeing Ron: he was just hysterical. But he was such a deep-thinking clown; one minute I'd see him in serious conversation with Ralph about his different characters, the next he'd be messing about with Willie. I think he's a genius.

In Portrush the two main things that stand out for me were, one, the fact that I had toothache and a swollen face; and two, singing Irish Catholic songs in Protestant Northern Ireland. The majority of the crew were Catholic, and after we'd finished work we'd all go drinking in the hotel bar. The Irish crew would start to sing, and the hotel manager would go bananas. He kept coming up and saying, 'Can you please… *please* don't sing that type of songs here, *please*, we'll get in trouble!'

It's not that any of them were politically motivated, I think; they were just doing it for the 'craic'. Not that I understood anything about the politics of it at all. I didn't really know what any of it was about, but I thought it was hysterical. We were on tour, and holiday rules applied, we could do anything – we'd been making a film!

They were incredibly happy days in Ireland. It had been one big laugh from the day I landed on the island till the day I left. And the people are diamonds.

Chapter 13

THE NEXT MORNING I HAD A CALL FROM JOHN DALY. 'Hi Jack, it's John; I've just had a call from Bing Crosby's office asking you to appear on his Christmas Special in LA.'

'Great,' I said.

'*Bing Crosby's* Christmas Special,' he repeated.

'Yeah, I heard ya, great,' I said again.

'But Jack, it's a great honour to be invited. Bing always chooses the guests he wants on his Christmas show himself. It's a great honour,' he repeated.

'Great,' I said again. We didn't seem to be getting anywhere.

I was a big fan of the 'Road' movies with Bing and Bob Hope so I was looking forward to doing it, but if anything me Dad was more excited about meeting Bing than I was. I think it was the first time that I ever saw him really excited about going somewhere. *I* hoped I might get to see Bob Hope: I'd prefer to meet him as he was funnier.

So while we did the final day's shoot for *Flight of the Doves* on the Saturday in Phoenix Park, me Dad took the car back on the ferry 'to get it all sorted' so me and him could fly out to LA on the Tuesday. It was that quick of a turn-round, with only a matter of days between finishing the film and flying out to LA.

Me Mum wasn't going to come: 'I've been away so long, Jackie. I need to get back and sort out the house, and Arf, and me Mum and Dad... Anyway, I can't drive, Jack, and you'll need yer Dad to drive you around.' I think while all that was true, me Mum weren't feeling that clever either, what with her asthma, but she didn't say that.

'Get us an autograph, though, Jackie,' me Mum said. 'There's a good boy.'

So me and me Dad went out there and settled into the Beverly Hills Hotel which was on the best side of Sunset, where all the ten million dollar houses were. We were to be out there for a couple of weeks to rehearse all the singing and dancing for the hour-long show. I was involved in the Christmas Carols and in a mini-pantomime where Bing was the King and I was to play a pickpocket (as seemed to be becoming my destiny).

On the first day of rehearsals we arrived at the studios where there were fans outside clamouring for me. The teen magazines always seemed to know when and where you were going to be and *Tigerbeat* and *16* would shout about it to all the fans. The magazines would be on the phone every week wanting stories or photo sessions; and even if you were guarded about information, someone else wasn't. Most of what they wrote wasn't true, but it was all innocent harmless stuff. Apparently I had a pet mouse called Cassius and regularly wrote to Donny Osmond who was a great friend of mine. I'm sure he would be if I met him, but to date I never have. Only later did these lies and total disregard for the truth begin to matter. Even when I corrected an assumed and baseless 'fact' in an interview, when the article was published, there would be the rubbish in print, untainted by the truth. Years later a Japanese magazine reported my death, and I read the touching obituary.

So on this first day of rehearsals I was surprised to see quite so many fans outside the studios, but I was a big superstar. I got fan mail addressed to 'Jack Wild, England' and it somehow got to me. Even when the only part that was right was my name, it still seemed to find me. Maybe it was just a tribute to the GPO, but I thought it was more attributable to my great status. It's not like I was being big-headed: everyone was telling me how great I was, and not just fans, but journalists and fellow professionals as well. They can't all be wrong, can they, I reasoned. There must be something in me; I am, after all, a pretty sort of important person now. I graciously signed their pictures and escaped into the studio.

I was given coffee and a white script folder with my name on it and *The Bing Crosby Christmas Show 1970* on it in red lettering. I thought that was incredibly posh – things don't get any better than this, that's for sure. Me and me Dad were introduced to the other guest, a black singer called Melba Moore, who I'd never heard of, but I chatted to her and the technical people as we all waited for Bing and his family to arrive. It wasn't long before the doors opened and there he was with his wife and three kids.

I put my coffee down and stood up to say hello, because obviously he would come over to me first and say something like, 'Hi Jack, thanks for agreeing to do the show.' But he didn't. The first person he goes over and talks to is this woman who is just sweeping the floor. I instantly felt gutted. What an arsehole, I thought. Why ain't he coming over here? It's not that I think I'm better than anyone else; I mean, I'll talk to anyone, but he should've come over to me first, surely.

During the rest of the day I couldn't stop thinking about it. I had just done three films straight in a line and for that whole year I'd earned an absolute fortune and they were my fans out there, and yet, and yet he went and spoke to the cleaner first.

I watched him as we rehearsed and he seemed to have an aura around him, I can't describe it any other way. He knew everyone on the set by name and seemed to know all the names of their kids as well. As the days went on I tried to work out what it was that made him stand out. When he walked into a room I swear everyone went 'Ah-h-h-h!' and that was him, that was the effect he had. It was incredibly magical working with him, and his voice was so smooth it made velvet seem like coarse sandpaper. He sang 'White Christmas' live and it was perfect, exactly the same as the record, not a quiver or a scratch, and the world stopped. I felt very much put in my place by his skill and his humanity. I felt dead inadequate working with him, because he was just so good. And I wasn't good enough to perform with him. He could have invited anyone on the planet and nobody would have refused. And I was so honoured that he asked me.

It was September outside and Christmas Day, every day, inside the studio. The rehearsals were a joy to do, and although he seemed to be a very private man, the more we worked together the more relaxed he seemed to become; but the most relaxed I saw him was when he was singing. At the start of rehearsals there is always that apprehension, but as they went on, we settled into a rhythm and began to have fun with it all. He always remained the ultimate professional to work with.

I did like a laugh and I tried to get his kids to let their hair down and do things they shouldn't. I got them to play football which they seemed to enjoy, and they tried to teach me baseball. It was a wonderfully warm family atmosphere and it reminded me very much of the Cowsills and their family business. And I've never seen me Dad so gobsmacked as when he met Bing and had photographs taken with him.

I thought, I'm not at Barbara Speake's any more, I'll ask for an autograph. I did and I got Bing and his wife and his three kids to sign my white and red script folder and a signed photograph for me Mum.

When we weren't rehearsing I met up with Marty a couple of times, and it was also the month before my album was to be released so Brian came over and we had several meetings at Capitol Records. There was all the promotional stuff as well; and the fans followed us around, from the studios, to Capitol and back to 'Millionaires' Estate'.

It was a fantastic couple of weeks, but that one minute, that first minute of meeting him: when, despite all the phenomenal work he had done up to that moment, he was so, so humble that he could take the time to go and speak to the cleaning lady first. *That* minute stayed with me.

When we got home John Daly advised me that, one, I should invest my money in property and, two, because I was earning so much money, he thought it'd be a good idea if me Dad packed up his job and worked for me as my personal manager and travelled all around with me. Dad was a bit hesitant, but we all thought we might as well keep it in the family as pay someone else to do it. I said I'd pay him £5,000 a year, the same as me.

So we went house-hunting. We wanted everybody to have a bedroom: 'everybody' being me Mum and Dad, me Gran and Grandad, Arf, and me. So that was four bedrooms, and ideally if we have five we've got a spare room in case anyone wants to stay. And so just before my eighteenth birthday I bought my first house; my family came to live with me, and me Dad to work for me.

Our new home was 47 The Grove, Isleworth, London. It was a grand old house with five bedrooms, an oak-panelled hall and a gallery above. I chose the room above the garage as I was the loudest and it also looked out front and back, so I could see anybody coming. Arf chose the one next door to me and next door to him were me grandparents. Along the corridor was me Mum and Dad's, which was the biggest bedroom of all, and the last bedroom was the spare one which my mate Bob Bartlett used to use.

'Blimey Jack, that's quite something to buy the family home like that,' Bob said. I'd been at Speake's with Bob and we'd done the *Oliver!* show and movie together. He lived at home with his Mum and Dad and was working on *The Two Ronnies.*

'I mean, having your parents live *with you,*' Bob persisted.

But it didn't mean a lot to me really. It was nice to be living in a much bigger house with plenty of space, but apart from that, it didn't mean a great deal.

'Well, I suppose I'm just paying my parents back for doing what they'd done for me up to date, like,' I said. I think I did feel that, but in a very shallow way as opposed to deep.

I also saw it as a place to entertain directors and producers and people in the biz. 'If we wanna invite Bing Crosby over, say,' I said to me Dad, 'I need to be able to offer him any drink that's available and so we've gotta get a bar!'

I got a bar, and I sent me Dad down to the off-licence to buy a bottle of everything they had.

'Not everything, surely, Jack?' me Dad asked.

'Yes Dad, we've got to give people a choice.'

So me Dad got 'one of everything'; most of the stuff none of my family would ever drink in a month of Sundays, or anyone in their right mind for that matter.

While me Dad was stocking the bar, I got Brian to take me to the Edgware Road where all the best hi-fi shops were. I wanted him to help me to choose a top-of-the-range stereo for my room. I thought, him being a record producer he's sure to know the best stuff to get. I also wanted to get a brown leather settee for my bedroom. This was the first time I'd ever had my own bedroom, so I wanted it to be right. I got the settee from Roy Moore who used to rent props and furniture to film sets and TV studios, and I bought a bamboo chair, hung it from the ceiling and covered it in fairy lights. Sometimes I'd take a bottle of Blue Nun upstairs and sit in my bamboo chair, surrounded by my psychedelic lights, listening to Led Zeppelin.

Bob popped his head round the corner and saw me a little worse for wear swinging in my cage.

'Alright mate?' he asked.

'Never better,' I replied. 'Never better.'

'Won't your parents mind?' he asked.

'I'm eighteen, it's my house, what can they say?'

'True,' said Bob, slowly closing the door.

''Ere mate, don't say nothing, though?' I said.

'No, sure Jack, I won't say nothing. Goodnight.'

'Goodnight.'

During this time, my first album was released. I was asked to do pro-motions, TV shows, variety shows where I'd sing a song from the album, and lots and lots of interviews.

'So was the *Oliver!* movie your first job?'

'No, I did the stage show before that, and loads of telly and stuff as well.'

'Oh right, and what televison work did you do?'

'Loads really; I did a bit in a situation comedy called *George and the Dragon...*' I don't know why that popped into my head, but I decided to go with it anyway, '... with Peggy Mount and Sid James.'

'Sid James,' the interviewer said, joining in, 'and John Le Mesurier, yes of course. What did you do in that?' he asked.

'Well, there was me and two other boys and we were carol singers,' I said.

'And what was it like working with such big names?' he asked.

'Well, Sid James, he was such a character and I remember thinking, this is, ya know, a big star. He was great, a typical old-school pro like.'

'That must've been a wonderful experience; what else do you remember about that show?' the interviewer asked.

What I actually remembered was our chaperone Mrs Bertorelli, a dark-haired Italian smoker who let us smoke without her knowledge. She'd let us smoke in our dressing room but not anywhere else; she didn't know that we'd go and smoke in the loo as well. I didn't say that, though, and just said something about how lovely Peggy Mount had been.

I had learnt that it wasn't always helpful to say everything that comes into your head. When I'd done *Top of the Pops* at the beginning of the year I was doing one interview, for the *Daily Mirror* I think. I must've got out of bed the wrong way or something and I was in a dreadful mood. I was railing on about the music industry; how in 1969 Elvis Presley released 'Suspicious Minds' and what went to number one? Rolf Harris with 'Two Little Boys'; and, even more insane, the Beatles released 'Let It Be' just before my first release, and what went to number one? Lee Marvin with a song from *Paint Your Wagon*. 'Where's the sense in that?' I said. 'You tell me, 'cos I give up with that one.'

I went on to say how, although I was languishing at number 46, I thought if Lee Marvin can do it, anyone can. I continued with how I'd recently met Harold Wilson and the amount of tax I had to pay on my earnings was ridiculous. I finished the interview with: 'What is the world coming to when you've got Harold Wilson running the country and "Wand'rin' Star" is number one?' I think I even had a go at the Queen.

And for the first time, I was printed verbatim. When John read the article he told me to keep my mouth shut in future.

When the album came out a fan mag wrote: 'Jack's sing-along type songs are so groovy, and the songs he's chosen are lighthearted and warm, just like Jack himself. This is a must album for Jack's fans and for those who aren't sure yet, this LP will convince you of Jack's multi-talents!'

The *Daily Express* said: 'His voice lacks tune, but his projection of a young Cockney personality is first class. His version of "Maxwell's Silver Hammer" is enormous fun. In more romantic songs the standard slips, but one can't blame him for trying!'

Fortunately, I didn't take recording as seriously as I did my acting. I thought my acting was something that I enjoyed doing and wanted to have as a career; I didn't want to be a pop star. I didn't want that as a career ever. I thought, I'll let my idols get on with that because they're far better at it than I am, whereas I felt I could make a place for myself on the acting side. Looking back, I think it started being a career to me on the movie of *Oliver!*, because that was 'big time': I had a very good part, in a very good film, and so this was not to be messed about with.

*

'I really fancy Gaynor. I'm gonna try and get off with her tonight,' one of the lads said.

It was Christmas 1970 and a group of us were going to a party on the other side of Hammersmith Bridge. It was Gaynor Jones's party, a girl from Speake's. I'd thought she was a snob at school and a right stuck-up cow, but she'd obviously made a greater impression on one member of the group. As we walked along, I remembered seeing Gay's father pick her up from school in a green estate car and in the back of the estate where you would normally have a dog, they had a monkey, a capuchin. That was a bit different, I thought. Anyway, I'd found out about this party from friends at the stage school and it was arranged that everyone would meet at Hammersmith Tube and then walk from there, as none of us had cars.

'And you think you can do that, do ya?' someone challenged.

'Yeah, sure,' the confident suitor replied.

And I can't remember whether I said this or whether I was just thinking it, but I thought, I'll show you lot! I shall get her! And I don't know why, because she didn't really mean anything to me at that time.

I don't think this was part of any game plan, but at one stage I remember I was in the back kitchen helping Gay's father to organise the booze. The doorbell went and it was the police complaining about the noise. I offered to sort it out and went and apologised and promised 'to turn the music down immediately'. And at the end of the party I got Gay's number.

We went to several parties after that and somewhere along the line we started dating. Robert Barrett, a mate of mine, fancied Gay's best friend Fran and we all got a taxi together once, which helped things along a bit. We went to several music industry parties as Gay's father was trying to get her a recording deal and we met up with a couple of guys from a group called 'Tin Tin'. Really great guys, I don't know what happened to them, but I remember they both had Ovation guitars. I'd never seen them before and they were beautiful guitars: they had a wooden front and neck, with a rounded fibreglass back; bloody lovely, they were. Anyway, after a few months Gay got her recording contract, and me as a boyfriend.

At the beginning of 1971, my first album had long since died and gone to heaven. Consequently Capitol had not taken up the second year option on the five-year contract. But I wasn't complaining. I was proud of the fact that I had entered both the English and US charts with my first single. Plus I had made a lot of dosh, and besides Brian was off to New York to secure another contract. He soon came back with a new deal with Buddah Records, who had the likes of Melanie and Sha Na Na on their label; and so we started the search for songs, one to release as a single followed quickly by my second album. It was arranged that we'd record some songs and then go out and do a tour of the radio stations in the States to promote the single.

Brian had been looking for songs in New York and had arranged a meeting with a guy called Les Lido who had a song he thought would be good for me. So I flew out to meet him. Les was a charismatic guy who lived in New Jersey. He had broad shoulders, was tubby further down, and a big smile on top. I liked the song and so 'The Old Man Song' became the A-side, and the B-side would be a song called 'Working on it Night and Day' from *Melody* which was due out in early '71.

After a successful meeting Brian had arranged for us to go that night to a Simon and Garfunkel gig at Carnegie Hall. There were loads of industry people there and I think Brian planned to do a bit of business as well. Brian knew the drummer who was backing Simon and Garfunkel – he'd played on a few of the tracks on my first album – and I think it was him who had got us the tickets for the concert. Anyway, it was a fantastic evening because they played everything from their *Bridge Over Troubled Water* album which had just been released. It was amazing and certainly one of the best concerts I'd ever been to.

I had a great time, and Brian did his business, and over the next few days Brian played me some of the possibilities. Neil Diamond's publisher sent us a song, 'Ain't No Way', which sounded like a option. We went into the studios and recorded it with the Cowsills, but something wasn't right and we decided not to put it on the album. There was a Paul Simon song as well, but I didn't like it. I did record a Bee Gees song called 'The Lord' on the second album. I didn't know at the time, but it was a spiritual song, although the title is a bit of a giveaway in hindsight.

The search continued and meanwhile I recorded the single and got ready for the tour. Arthur came out to do the tour with me, and just before we left Les said to me, 'Look, Jack, I know how crazy you are about cameras; well, I've got a friend in New Jersey and if you tell me what camera you want and what sort of lenses you want, I can get it for you dirt cheap, no problem.'

'Oh right,' I said. I think he was pleased that we'd recorded his song and wanted to do something nice for us.

'Well?' he prompted.

I was well into these box cameras that had three-and-a-quarter-inch negatives. They were the tops compared to 35mm so I said, 'I want a Rolleiflex with a wide angle, a normal and a telephoto lens please!'

I was just being cheeky, I didn't really think anything would happen.

'Alright, that should be no problem,' he said. 'You leave it to me and by the time you come back after the tour, it'll be organised for you!'

And I thought bloody hell, that's good.

As we headed off I said to Arf, 'We'll have to buy him something for getting this camera for us.'

'I've got a better idea,' he said, 'let's buy his kids something instead.' And annoyingly, it *was* a better idea.

A guy from Buddah Records organised the tour and two Buddah guys flew with us, and a couple more would meet us at each destination. It was a hectic tour, and one day in particular we went on three different flights to three different cities and did at least three radio interviews. We even flew with Allegheny which was supposed to be the worst airline in America. Me and Arf had our photo taken to prove we'd been on three of their flights and survived. Still, at least we could have a drink.

Because I'd started to get a large following in the States it'd been arranged by Buddah Records that during the tour I'd also do personal appearances in these big superstores. The plan was to go in, sign a few autographs and leave. At the first one Arf came with me and the Buddah men, and I was signing away and talking to the fans in front of me. What I wasn't aware of was the number of people gathering at the back and their great desire to come to the front. Ron, one of the Buddah men, who was ever so nice and with us the whole time, leant forward and whispered in my ear, 'Look, there's too many people here and we're getting a bit concerned, Jack. We want to get you out as soon as possible; so when we give you the nod, we want you to run to the front of the store and there'll be a limo there waiting. Jump in it and off we go!'

So there's me and Arf, and he's staying close by me now and we're watching this guy for the signal. It's been arranged that Arthur will watch Ron for the nod because I'm busy signing the autographs, then when Arf says we've gotta go, we go! But I'm keeping one eye on the Buddah man as well, and one on Arf as I can see things are getting out of order and I just want to get out.

'Right Jack, we're going, come on!' Arf said and we start legging it to the front of the shop; and it's a good hundred-yard run to the front, if not two.

We get to the front of the shop and…

'Where's the fucking limo, Arf?'

And there's all these kids behind us, and I can see it now: they were just knocking everything over on the counters of this shop. And I wondered how much damage they were doing as hundreds of kids came crashing towards us.

'Now what are we supposed to do?' I shouted.

'C'mon!' Arf said, grabbing hold of my jacket, and we started off round the block. I felt like I was running two feet in front of myself and my stupid body couldn't keep up. No sooner had we got to the first corner than the limo turned up and the doors flung open. We flew in and the car drove off, the kids still chasing us down the street.

'Sorry about that, Jack,' the worried Buddah man said. 'Are you guys alright?' I looked at Arf and he looked as spooked as I was. 'Don't worry, we won't do that again without two or three bodyguards to protect you.'

We're doing it *again?*

'We hadn't appreciated the numbers and how popular you are, Jack.' He tried a laugh. 'But don't worry, we'll protect you properly from now on,' he said, wisely abandoning levity.

'Good,' I managed to say. I was still breathing hard from the running and the panic. I was shit scared; I'd had similar incidents in England but only with, say, thirty or forty kids and you can just about deal with that; but here it was two or three hundred and just me and Arthur and nowhere to run to… that was too frightening for words.

We had bodyguards everywhere we went after that.

*

'I wonder what that button does?'

It was another city, another interview and I'd been left alone. I was waiting to go and do *The Mike Douglas Show* again and had been left to my own devices for entertainment. I was bored and idly wondered what might be through that door. So I opened it. It was a control box. I'd been into the equivalent at the BBC Centre and recognised the layout of a dozen different TV sets all on one wall. One would be for camera one, another set would be camera two and so on. Only one TV had a picture on and the rest were switched on, but were blank. In front of the tellies there was a desk with millions of buttons, slide controls and all sorts.

I sat down and started pressing a few buttons and then a few more. I could see out of the corner of my eye one of these blank TVs; I pressed a button and a red blob appeared. Oh! I thought. Did I do that? So I pressed it again to find out and another red blob appeared. Cool! I started pressing more buttons and I got the red blobs to move onto the blank set next to it. I thought, this is great this! And I could see about five sets away there was somebody giving a news bulletin, or that's what it looked like; so I thought, I wonder if I can get these blobs over to where he is? By the time I'd got these blobs to the set next to where this guy was, I'd now changed the colour of the blobs to green. And I thought, I wonder if I can get them floating past his eyes. I was having the time of my life with all these buttons.

The next minute I've got these green blobs floating past this guy and I thought, this looks hysterical, but it was obvious that the guy couldn't see these blobs at all so it must be only what I was seeing.

By now, I'd been in there about fifteen minutes or so and the next minute this security guy comes in and says very politely, 'I'm sorry Mr Wild, but you've got to leave this room now please.'

'Oh, I was having a bit of fun here,' I said. 'I haven't done anything wrong, have I?'

'No, Mr Wild, come out now and come back to the green room and everything will be alright.'

I went back to the green room and then soon after that I was on. I went out and sang 'The Old Man Song' and was thrilled to be on the show with Tonto (Jay Silverheels) from *The Lone Ranger*! Oh, he was like an idol to me and although he was so ancient by now, you could still recognise him as Tonto, 'Kemo Sabe' and all that! It was amazing, it was really great. I was well chuffed to have been on the same show as him because as a kid, I'd sit and watch him every week, so that was really fabulous.

Before I left the studio I found out that my green blobs had gone out live on the news. I don't know how many million people saw these blobs, but it was a one-and-only show from 'the Wild fingers'!

Strangely, they invited me back again. I remember the last time I did *The Mike Douglas Show* I met up with Pat Davis's first wife Diana and she was lovely. She was either separated or divorced from Pat and living back where she was born on the East coast. She'd came up to Philadelphia to see us, and as we had a suite with more than one bedroom she stayed overnight with us.

The next morning we had bright and early press interviews in our suite and Brian was very worried about the fact that this friend of mine had stayed with us and that she was a beautiful girl. I say girl, she was mid to late twenties then which was a good ten years older than me.

'You know, it wouldn't look good for you, Jack.'

'She's just a friend, Brian,' I said.

'Yes, but people might not see it like that. She is *older* than you,' he persisted, but I still couldn't see why he was so concerned.

'People might think... well... you know... she is... professional?'

'Oh... *Oh!*'

Brian kept her hidden in the suite while we did the interviews, and I never saw her again after that.

And the tour rolled on from city to city to city.

And then on to Chicago... 'And what do you think of our city, Jack?'

'Freezing.'

'Yes, I'm sorry about the weather, Jack – it is mighty cold.'

'No, but it's great, and the lake, blimey mate! They told me it was a lake but I can't see the other side of it. Looks more like a sea to me. It's the only lake I've ever seen with waves on it.'

And then on to Houston... 'And what do you think of our city, Jack?'

'Great. Me and my brother went to Mission Control and saw the moon capsule.' I bought loads of space badges of all the different expeditions and a little gold sputnik for me Mum to go on her charm bracelet.

And then on to Georgia... 'And what do you think of our city, Jack?'

'Great. Me and my brother went to see your underground streets which were amazing and...'

I actually didn't like Georgia. There was a palpable feeling of hatred and racism that I'd never experienced in America before. I thought that the inequality was disgusting and I wanted to leave and get on another plane and go to another city.

'Got a letter here from a fan who said they loved you on *The Larry Kane Show*,' Ron from Buddah said, handing me a letter.

'Great. Did I do that show then, Ron?' I asked, handing back the letter.

'Must have done, Jack. Must have done.'

That night in our hotel room Arf asked me if I wanted some female companions.

'What d'ya mean, Arf?' I said.

'They want to know if you and me want some female companions.'

'Nah, I'm alright watching telly, thanks,' I said. Why would I want a woman I didn't know coming up to keep me company?

Arf sighed and left the room.

Me and Arf spent a lot of time in the hotel suites because you couldn't go into the bar and have a drink as there was too much hassle and too many people wanting a piece of you. It didn't bother me too much, being stuck in the suites, as I could watch telly or have a drink. If I wanted something else I could just call one of the Buddah guys and they'd be there if you wanted company, or food, shopping, or anything really. They were at your disposal.

While I was over there I had a meeting in Hollywood with Sam Fuller, a short stocky friend of Marty's who was a screenwriter and director. He had written a film that he wanted me and Ernest Borgnine to do. It was a fabulous script about an English lad travelling on a stagecoach which is attacked by Indians. The lad is the only survivor; Ernest Borgnine's character was to be an ex-gunslinger who finds him wandering about, and the film is about their relationship. The gunslinger has gotten too slow to draw to compete any more and too old to take on the youngsters. He is not, however, too old to teach the lad how to fire a gun and pass on his skills and prowess and the kid looks up to him, as indeed I did and would have. I'd never met Ernest before, but I thought he was a great actor and I'd seen him in hundreds of movies. He had a very lived-in face, and was a bit podgy. I remember watching his films and him mesmerising me with his eyes. *The Kid From Soho* was the working title for the film, but sadly it was never made. I think they didn't get funding or something. I was so disappointed when it didn't work out. To be in a cowboy movie at that time, that was my dream.

Eventually the tour was all over and we went back to New York. When we got back there, we went shopping for Les's kids and bought them these heavy plastic tricycles in kit form. They were amazing bikes: I mean, if I'd have been a kid of that size, I'd have loved having one of these. We put them together ourselves in the hotel, although Arf did most of it. If you could've seen these two kids' faces when we gave them their bikes already assembled, it was like we were giving them the world. It was lovely just to see that in itself. I can see them now, riding all the way along this corridor that was about a hundred yards long in the hotel, grinning from ear to ear.

So did you manage to get the camera?' I asked Les.

'Yeah, we just gotta go and collect it. I'll come and pick you up at the hotel tomorrow at five and we'll go and get it then.'

The following day Les drove us out to New Jersey and we ended up somewhere a bit suspect. We parked the car.

'Where are we going to meet him then?' I asked.

'Well, we'll wait here, and he'll be here soon,' Les replied.

The next minute, this stretch limo with blacked-out windows turns up and parks opposite to where we are like; and I said, 'I suppose that's him, is it?'

'Yeah,' said Les.

'Well, isn't he gonna bring it over then?'

'No,' he said. 'We'll go over to him.'

We all three get out and lock the car and walk across the road, and the chauffeur gets out of the limo and opens the door for me, Arf and Les to get inside; and I'm thinking, this is a bit funny! What's going on here then? And now I'm starting to question it.

So anyhow, in we gets and all I could see was this geezer who was a dead ringer for Marlon Brando in *The Godfather*, and he said, 'It's lovely to meet you, Jack. Here you are. This is what you ordered.'

It was all sort of boxed up and everything and I said, 'How much do I owe you for this then?'

'Oh, to you, a hundred dollars!'

I gave him the hundred dollars.

'Are there the three different lenses with it?' I asked.

'Of course, Jack, it's all there for you.'

'Oh, thanks ever so much. This is really good this!'

And this guy, he owned a pool bar in New Jersey and he said, 'Come in and see us.'

And I said, 'Alright then.' And the chauffeur opened the door, and we got out and crossed the road back to our car.

I was pleased as Punch with the camera. It must've been a thousand dollars' worth of equipment at least and I was getting it dirt cheap.

'Thanks Les,' I said as we drove back to our hotel. 'I've got a right bargain here,' I said to Arf.

The following day me and Arf walked down Fifth Avenue with my new camera. I'd put the film in and I was taking pictures of everything; but it was just awful, I felt so guilty. It was obviously nicked and I thought everybody on the street was staring at me. It felt as though everybody knew that I've got a nicked camera and they're all looking at me saying, look at him, he's a thief!

And I got back to the hotel after a very quick walkabout with Arf and I said, 'I can't do with this, Arf, it's driving me mad! I'm gonna get nicked. I've gotta get rid of this camera.'

'Give it back then,' Arf said.

'I can't just give it back, Arf; that geezer is a heavy-duty mafioso type. He'd've sent out his boys to the local camera store to break in just to get the one camera and lenses and left everything else there. That's what he'd've done. He would have said, "Here's my shopping list," to his gang members, "that's what I want. I don't want anything else, just go and get that and come back to me." It's robbing to order Arf, that's what it is. I can't just give it back,' I said, getting slightly hysterical.

'Well, why don't you give it Les and tell him to sell it, and whatever he gets for it, let him buy the kids something,' Arf sighed.

I got on the phone to Les. 'Look mate, I know you've done me a favour and all that, but I can't handle it. Please, just get rid of it and whatever you get for it, buy the kids some sweets or toys or whatever. I just can't deal with it.'

'Sure Jack, if that's what you want, sure man, no problem.'

He sounded surprised; I was relieved.

A few weeks later we found ourselves at the pool bar in New Jersey. Me and Arf were playing and Les was standing by to play the winner. I was contemplating my next shot when a dark figure loomed over the table.

'How are you doing with your camera, Jack?' he asked. It was the Godfather.

'Oh, it's magic!' I lied. 'Amazing. Thanks ever so much!' I said, chalking my cue industriously, desperately trying to think of a change of subject.

'I had the police on the phone to me the other day,' he said nonchalantly as he walked slowly around the table. Was this a change of subject? Or was it the same subject? I chalked my cue some more for comfort, avoiding everybody's gaze.

'They'd got a siege situation on 52nd Street and they needed to borrow some of my sub-machine guns.'

'Oh… right,' I ventured and carried on chalking, not sure what the right response was to that sort of information.

'Yeah, whenever they need ammunition or guns they always call, as I've got the best gun collection in New York.'

I naively thought that the police would have the best gun collection in New York, but kept that to myself and stuck with the 'Oh… right' response as it seemed to be working for me at the moment.

'Well Jack, if there is anything you need while you are in town, just let me know and I'll organise it for you,' he said, placing his hand upon my shoulder that sent a shiver down my spine, through my stomach and on to my boots; but I think he meant it kindly enough.

Soon after that we came home to England. It was reassuring to be back. As soon as we were home we started to promote my records that were out at the time. Within a month of getting back, I was on the phone to Gay one night and by now I was thinking that I really was an amazing human being. We were arguing on the phone, I can't remember what the argument was about, and I thought, does this woman realise who she's talking to here? She got so mad at what I was saying that she put the phone down on me. And I thought, who does this woman think she is? Putting the phone down on me! Right, that's it, I won't call her again, it's over. No one puts the phone down on Jack Wild.

*

'I've written a great song for your character, Jack; let me play it for you man.' It was Donovan, *the* Donovan, and he'd written a song for me. I'd bought his records and he was really an idol to me, and there he was singing this song. It was the summer of 1971 and I'd been contracted to do a film of *The Pied Piper of Hamelin*. David Puttnam was producing it and they wanted me to play the crippled boy, Gavin. A French guy called Jacques Demy was directing it and Donovan was signed to play the Piper and do the music.

I think Donovan's involvement had a lot to do with David Puttnam being so hip. Out of all the producers I'd worked for, he was the hippest, well into his music; whatever was in fashion, David had it. For *Melody* he'd got the Bee Gees to do the music, so for this movie to have the coolest, hippest music at that time it would have to be Donovan. I was glad to be working with David again: he was a real cool-looking guy and I thought that when I get to a proper adult age, if I can be like him, I won't be doing too bad. He was just amazing and I had two hundred per cent respect for him.

Donovan was a lovely guitarist and he played this song 'Riding Homeward' to me and it really was beautiful. He soulfully plucked out the last chord and looked up at me expectantly.

'Oh, I can't see me singing that on the screen,' I said, and his face fell: he looked so disappointed.

'But it's a beautiful song, Jack!' he said.

'Yeah, I know it is,' I said. 'I love it, but I can't carry that sort of song off. I really don't want to do that if I can get any way around it; please, let someone else do it, or you do it, or whatever. But please don't ask me to do it.'

I didn't have a great deal of confidence in my singing voice. I mean, I can fake it with an uptempo number, but I don't seem to do well with slow numbers. This song was gorgeous, but it was a ballad and I just couldn't see me doing it justice.

Of course I regretted it later. Donovan ended up singing it in the film and looking back I wished that I'd done it. It was one of my favourite songs from the film and it would've been nice to have such a beautiful song to add to my collection of 'songs never to be heard of again'.

We shot the film in Rothenburg ob der Tauber in Bavaria and in the Lee International Studios, Kensal Rise, London. In Germany we all stayed in the tiny little town of Rothenburg, nestled in next to the Tauber river. It was a very old medieval town set on a hill and completely surrounded by high walls. In the main market square there was an amazing clock that would chime on the hour and all these beautiful dolls and things would come out from walls and all sorts; it was real Hansel and Gretel time. The square was all cobblestones, and led down to the big wooden gates that protected the fairy tale within. The cast and crew were hermetically sealed within this town, which was so small you could walk all the way around it and in ten minutes be back where you started.

The first thing I realised when I got to Germany was that I didn't like the food, whatsoever. Up until now I'd been used to on-site caterers who would provide all sorts of food at every hour of the day and night. For *Pied Piper*, however, most evenings the principal cast and crew would have an evening meal at one of the local restaurants in the town. I don't know whether this was because of the numbers of people involved and whether we had loads of extras using the on-site caterers or what. Anyway, there wasn't such a close bond between us all as I had experienced previously on shoots. On *Flight of the Doves* and *Oliver!* and *Pufnstuf* it had been like being part of a wonderfully colourful family, all for one and one for all and all that. But for *Pied Piper*, the cast were in one group, the crew in another, the production side yet another; and I don't think I made things any better this one particular night…

A few of the cast had had a drink at my hotel before supper. It was a fabulous cast and seemed to me to be like the *Who's Who* of acting in England. There was Peter Vaughan, Michael Hordern, Diana Dors, Donald Pleasence, Roy Kinnear who I'd done *Melody* with, and John Hurt. Someone else was originally cast to play John's part, but in the first week of filming he hadn't managed to stay sober for any workable amount of time, so in came John. I was glad they'd got John in: I thought he was great and we shared the same hotel.

We eventually settled down in the restaurant at our segregated tables, and as the main meal was served I gave it the quick once-over. 'Thank God it's not veal,' I said with genuine relief. We'd been filming for about three weeks and all we seemed to have had was veal. Veal grilled, stewed, frittered, pied, diced, whole, stripped and stuffed. I didn't actually know what veal was, but I knew I was fed up of it.

I started to tuck in to supper when suddenly and without warning I found, hidden under a mountain of sauerkraut, bloody veal medallions.

I steamed over to Gavrik Losey, the production manager, who was sitting over at another table. 'This is getting beyond a joke, this! Veal again! You've even got to the point now where you've got to disguise it. It's getting that bad! Can't we have something other than veal or German bloody sausage?'

I could hear people in the background saying, 'Go on Jack! Go on my son!' I suppose they were just winding me up, but I took the bait and let fly.

I think I climaxed with, 'Why can't we have something bloody English?' and I got a round of applause – from my table at least.

Looking back on it, I shouldn't have done it. I should've gone over to him quietly and asked for something other than bloody veal. I was totally out of order, and I'd completely understand if he ever talked about it to his friends and said, 'That *arsehole* came over to me...' I should've apologised within the hour, that's what I should've done; but as it happens, nothing did change with the menu at all!

It seemed curious: on the Buddah tour just a few months before, if I wanted something I'd just pick up the phone and it would be there, whatever I wanted, even things I didn't know that I wanted. And now, *now*, I couldn't even get fish and chips.

We went back to the hotel for a drink afterwards. I stopped in at the discotheque opposite our hotel as I saw Cathryn in there. Cathryn played my girlfriend Lisa, and she was very young, about fourteen I think. I felt protective towards her and wanted to look out for her. The Stones' 'Brown Sugar' was pumping out into the night and I went in for a drink. When I got in there I could see Cathryn was with a group of people from the film so would probably be alright, I thought. I kept my eye on her though, and on Puttnam's kids who were also in the film. I don't know why. I don't know whether I could see what I was turning out to be and whether I wanted to protect them from it; I don't know. Not that they needed or even wanted my big-brother affections. After all, Puttnam's kids had their Dad, and Cathryn was Rex Harrison's granddaughter so probably knew more about the world and the business than I did.

Still, I stayed for Joe Cocker's 'Delta Lady' and 'Cry Me a River', but when it got to Middle of the Road's 'Chirpy, Chirpy, Cheep, Cheep' I finished my drink and decided to call it a night.

John Hurt was in the bar at the hotel when I got back so I settled down with him. He had a Campari and soda and because I hadn't tasted it before, and as it was about the only alcoholic drink I hadn't tasted by now, I gave it a go.

'Oh, fucking hell John, how can you drink that? It's like a gorilla's armpit!' I said. It really was awful tasting. He smiled laconically and I headed off to the bar where a comforting Bacardi and Coke was already waiting for me.

I'd got quite friendly with the barman and the previous week he had said to me, 'Look Jack, because you're going to be here for eight weeks or so, you will spend a fortune with these bar prices.' He leaned across the bar conspiratorially. 'I have some friends at the American army base near here,' he whispered. 'Let me introduce you to them and then you can get all your alcohol from them and I'll keep it behind the bar for you.' The thrifty barman smiled. 'And then, whenever you want a drink, all you would need to buy would be the Coca-Cola. You'll save a fortune!' he declared in triumph.

And the American army did me proud. It turned out they were *Pufnstuf* fans and so I went to the base, signed a load of autographs and came back with eight hundred cigarettes, a gallon of Bacardi for me and a gallon of brandy for me Mum.

I took my drink from the bar and headed back to John. On the first day of getting the Bacardi I went a little bit mad and had to leave John early and go to bed. As I'd left I'd said, 'You know what you are mate? A proper pro actor – you're from the old school. You know, you are every bit as much of a pro, although you are much younger, like what Michael Hordern is; and to me, Michael is exactly like Ron Moody.' Comparing any actor to Ron was the highest compliment I could give anyone. I made my way unsteadily upstairs and was tucked up in bed by eight o'clock, on a non-school night! Now, I was better acquainted with my bottle of Bacardi and took it steady.

Me Dad was staying in the same hotel, as he had come over to Germany with me for the first two weeks of night shooting. After that, Mum and my mate Andy Cobb flew over to be with me as well. On the day they arrived, me and Dad took a production car to the airport to pick them up with this lunatic driver. He drove like a maniac on the way out so we tried to get him to slow down on the way back, and he then stuck at ninety. But me Mum was still a little shaken up, so when we got to the hotel I introduced her to her gallon of brandy.

'It's like a giant pickle jar, Jackie; how in the world am I going to drink all that? You'll have to help me, love.'

'I've got me own, Mum,' I said.

'Well, how many ordinary bottles are in this then?' me Mum asked.

'Oh I dunno, maybe six or eight bottles,' I said.

'Had I better get started then?' me Mum laughed, 'or I'll never get it done.'

She ended up taking most of it home with her, but I finished mine.

Before I'd left for Germany I'd said to Andy, 'As I'm going out to do this film, if you fancy coming over for a holiday, I'll sort it all out for you.'

So he'd come over and was to stay with me in my suite while me Dad moved out into another hotel with me Mum.

The following morning a production car came to pick up me and Andy as I'd got Andy an extras job on the film for while he was over there.

'Nice car,' Andy said as we got into the Mercedes. We were going to the main location where the catering, wardrobe and make-up vans were at the other side of the town.

'Normally I'm picked up in a BMW,' I said. 'We're going upmarket today.'

'BMWs are nice cars though,' Andy replied.

'Oh yeah,' I said, although I'd never actually heard of a BMW before I got there. 'When I learn to drive and pass me test, I've definitely gonna get one of them 'cos they're really quick cars!' I said.

'Nice to be picked up in a BMW every day,' Andy said.

'No, it's downhill mate,' I joked. 'When I was in the States I went to work in a Rolls Royce every day, now I'm going to work in a Mercedes or a BMW. What's it gonna be in the next film, a bloody Mini or what?'

'You're getting top billing though, aren't you?' Andy asked.

'Oh sure, yeah,' I said, 'I'm still up there with the rest of them.'

We were passing by where they had built a set of the outdoor market in front of the main church and it was a fantastic set. It was very much like the *Oliver!* sets, only on a much smaller scale.

'Donovan's bought a top-of-the-range one of these,' I said, 'a Mercedes 300 SEL. A great car.'

'What's he like?' Andy asked.

'He's great,' I said. 'He's teaching me the guitar.' I'd bought an old acoustic in Rothenburg and he was showing me some more chords. Gay had already taught me a few chords, before we'd split up, and now I'd got Donovan to teach me a few more.

'Wow,' said Andy.

'Yeah, it's a lot of fun and he's teaching me chord sequences as well.'

I knew all Donovan's songs, and to be actually working with him was a big plus for me because I just thought he was great. I used to watch how he would pick up a guitar and make it talk. He seemed to do it with so little thought and so easily, as though he didn't have to concentrate at all. It was an extended arm if you like. I didn't say any of that to Andy; I just said, 'He's married to Brian Jones's widow, you know, the lead guitarist in the Rolling Stones.'

'Wow,' Andy said again.

We got to the location and went our separate ways. I did catch sight of Andy later and he looked outrageous. He was all dressed up in costume, and with his white blonde hair he just didn't look real. But he seemed to be having a ball. I guess because he didn't have anything to do with the business it was all new to him. He gave me a thumbs-up.

To be honest, work was going well for me too. Most of my scenes were with Michael Hordern and I thought he was an amazing actor. You could just sit and watch him, and whether you were learning anything at the time or not remained to be seen, but if you were a dedicated actor you would be learning; I drank him in and hoped something stuck.

When I agreed to do the film I was expecting the finished product to be like the old Danny Kaye films or *The Wizard of Oz*. I had a vision of Donovan playing his pipe striding towards the mist-covered mountain. In my mind, I saw it slowly opening up to swallow the Piper and the bewitched children, and then majestically coming back down again like *Thunderbirds* – only better. It would be a wonderful film. Real Disneyland time.

Occasionally my belief in the film was tested, like when they shot the exodus of the rats from the town. They'd used real rats in some scenes, but for this choreographed exit they needed something a little more trainable. Most of the scene was shot at night; and, inspired by the cobbled streets of Rothenburg, they came up with this device of having a sheet of nylon netting and they glued these plastic bodies of rats on it. Then they dragged it along the street with some strong fishing line and, as it went over the cobbles, the little models would move and make it look as though they were alive. I know things always look better in the finished product, but watching it as they filmed it I certainly had my misgivings.

'This is never gonna bloody work!' I said. 'It'll look like one of them cheap Hollywood sci-fi movies where they're supposedly dinosaurs but really they're iguanas with plastic horns on their noses. It'll look ridiculous!' I helpfully added.

My contribution to this magical fairy tale was as a cripple boy with a gammy leg. I tried to work out how best to do the limp because I'd never been asked to do that before. The nearest thing I could come up with was when me and Phil Collins used to do a Peter Cook and Dudley Moore sketch. I was the one-legged man coming to audition for the part of Tarzan, but he was hopping so obviously I couldn't do that as that would be a little over the top. Then I thought of putting something in my shoe, but I thought, well, that's not really painful enough to remind me! What else can I do? I ended up tying just a normal bandage on my left knee to remind me that that'd be my bad leg.

Next there was the issue of the stick. At the start of the film I have a crutch, but then that is broken by a soldier and I end up with just a stick. I decided to put my crutch on my left, to try and make it take the place of the leg, so that I could just drag the left leg along with me. That seemed to work pretty well, but then when my crutch gets broken, I felt I needed the bandage even tighter as I'd then got a chase sequence with just a normal walking stick. I had to use the leg that much more, with less support, and at the same time, try and keep the limp the same as it was with the crutch.

By lunchtimes, the bandage would've got a bit loose and I'd have to tighten it up again before we restarted in the afternoon. By the end of the day, my leg would be bright red because I've tied this thing so tightly and also, while I was putting it on, I tied it with my leg bent so then hopefully my leg would stay bent all day long and I wouldn't be able to straighten it up. Anyhow, I think it did the trick. I certainly felt like a cripple.

John looked at my swollen red knee as I unveiled it after shooting.

'Did you do that to yourself?' John asked.

'Yeah, good innit?' I replied. 'Here, John, isn't that counted as method acting or something?' I asked.

'Well, it would be if you actually injured your knee, Jack,' he said.

'I ain't that bloody serious about it, mate,' I said. 'Fancy a drink?' I said to him and people in the general vicinity.

I would generally invite people to the bar for a drink with me, which worked out well if they liked Bacardi.

We were tied to Rothenburg during those months, and on our days off we tried to get away from the town. One weekend we'd been told about a swimming pool that was about half an hour's drive away, so we escaped for a while. When we got there, however, they wouldn't let me in unless I bought a plastic hat to wear – my hair was very long. I plonked it on my head and I looked ridiculous.

'Oh mate, I can't wear this – I look like a Gonk,' I said.

'What are you going to do?' Martin, my stand-in from the film, asked. I wasn't entirely used to conforming, as he knew, but the attendants were adamant. Well, they didn't say *how* I had to wear it, I thought, and I kept it perched on top of my hair.

'In for a penny, in for a pound,' I said. 'I might as well look an idiot and at least it'll give someone a laugh if nothing else!' I added.

On our way home, we could see a storm in the distance and forked lightning illuminating our fairy-tale town. It looked really supernatural. I'd been told that Bavaria was well known for forked lightning and I thought that was very spooky. Rothenburg looked decidedly angry with us.

On our next day off we didn't try to leave the town, but there was to be a beer festival in this big field a short walk away. We thought that would be at least something different. I arranged to get there for midday with Andy, and me Mum and Dad. There were massive marquees and big, long tables that would seat about at least a dozen people. It was an all-day event with the traditional brass bands, with leather short trousers and all that business. And there were these women walking along, and they were big women these ladies, they were like wrestlers. They'd hold about six or eight litres of beer in each hand, and there was me struggling to lift just one. I couldn't believe it.

'Oh Jackie,' me Mum said, 'they only sell beer.'

'It's a beer festival, Mum,' I said.

'Don't worry, Vera, I'll go back to the hotel and get you a brandy and lemonade.'

'Oh thanks love,' she said, and me Dad went and brought her a drink back, in a carrier bag.

We stayed there for a good few hours. I drank two and was done for. It was strong stuff.

'That's me,' I said. 'I can't have any more!' And I do remember staggering back to the hotel where we bumped into John.

'Are you having a nice time, Mrs Wild?' John courteously asked me Mum.

'Oh yes, it's a lovely place,' me Mum said. '*And* I've found a little shop that sells sort of medieval knick-knacks and immediately when you go in, you're given a shot of brandy, whether you buy anything or not.'

'You'll have to tell me where *that* is,' John said.

'It's my favourite shop in the whole of Germany,' me Mum giggled.

I think David was aware of our Rothenburg battle fatigue, and so to entertain the troops he organised a football match: England versus Germany. He arranged for us to use the only football pitch in the town on our day off, and it had stands and everything. A lot of the crew were German and it was billed as a chance for the Germans to get their revenge for the 1966 World Cup Final. *I* thought it might be a chance for me to get away from my image as a cripple.

In the film I spend a lot of time chasing my girlfriend and shouting, 'Lisa, Lisa!' And now, whenever I went out, I'd be walking down the street whether it was on my day off, or at lunchtime, or in the evening when I'd finished, and if anyone saw me, *anyone*, they'd all start limping and shouting, 'Lisa, Lisa!' For a day or so, I thought, oh, that's really funny. That's quite cute! But after eight weeks of it, it was becoming a bit of a pain, as old and young alike hobbled along as soon as they saw me. Maybe a match to show my sporting prowess would stop it. We played the fixture one Sunday; everyone was there and it was a great match. But on the way home, passing some locals, the familiar cry went out: 'Lisa, Lisa!' they shouted, limping insanely by. 'Ha ha ha, yeah, that's very good!' I smiled. Ah well, at least it had been a great match.

After we'd finished location filming, it was arranged that we'd have a knees-up and a barbecue in this farmer's field just outside the town. The whole cast and crew were invited. As we had more filming to do in London, it was really just a party to end our time in Rothenburg. It started mid-afternoon with the cooking of the food and everyone having drinks, and as it got dark we had a disco. The highlight in the evening was Donovan, as he had agreed to do us a concert. He played his acoustic, and mixed his set with songs from the film and his old hits. It was brilliant. He'd also written one song especially for the continuity lady on the film. Her name was Zelda Barron, a lovely lady and great at her job.

'Zelda the Welder, she's a gas; Zelda the Welder, she's built to last; Zelda the Welder, my heart's working overtime, a union blast!'

His voice rang out across the fields. It was bloody great it was; even though he'd sung some of his hits, 'Zelda the Welder' was one of my favourites of the whole night.

'Bloody great!' I shouted. I was a bit merry by now and called out requests in an increasingly gruff voice.

'Hurdy Gurdy Man!' I yelled and if I shouted it once, I shouted it at least eight dozen times.

'Hurdy Gurdy Man! Mellow Yellow!'

At one stage he asked me to sing 'Riding Homeward'.

'Oh, please don't ask me to sing it, mate,' I said. 'I don't feel confident enough to do it.'

So he sang it, and sang it a million times better than I ever could do. I cheered and roared at the end. He then got Cathryn up to sing and I felt a bit stupid because I thought I really should do my bit as one of the stars of the piece, but I didn't have the bottle. It was unusual for me because normally I'd go on there and not give a toss about anything. I just think that I respected Donovan so much as a singer: I think if I hadn't have respected him, I'd have probably gone up there and done it. But it was a great evening and I joined in with all the songs, screaming through the whole concert. It was just as well that I didn't have to work the following day.

And so we packed up and came home. I gave the guitar that I'd bought to a boy who played one of the gypsies that I leave with at the end of the film. I'd wanted to get a guitar like the one Donovan had had in the film. An artist in Scotland had been commissioned to create a design for it to make it look like an old fresco-type painting from the fourteenth century. Donovan came up with the idea of starting at the main body of the guitar with sunlight, then through to daybreak and then as it goes up the guitar it goes to night-time, then the whole neck of the guitar is just stars and planets. I think it was done in oils and it was done so magnificently, and varnished all over to protect it. As soon as I saw it I decided to get one, if only to hang on my wall because I thought it looked beautiful; but I never got round to organising that. I don't know why, because I knew I could have afforded it.

When we got home we did another month in the studios to finish off a lot of the inside stuff and everybody was involved in that, although I never got to meet Donald Pleasence and I was a bit disappointed about that. I always rated him as an actor and I thought he was very, very, frightening.

Watching the way it was being filmed and the way the director was interpreting the scenes it was hard to tell what the end product would look like. I remember during the making of *Oliver!* and *Melody* they were such fun and the final cuts were even better than I had imagined – the energy and happiness bounced over on the screen. When I saw the final edit of *Pied Piper*, the energy from my point of view didn't seem to show. I felt incredibly disappointed, having worked on the film for three or four months, to then see the finished product so far from what I thought it would be when first reading the script. To me, it seems so heavy duty, trying to point out that politics were just as corrupt then as now, if not worse, and that pollution was dreadful and medicine was awful, everything depressing... and it's a kids' story! I felt it should be fantasy, it should be Danny Kaye, the Brothers Grimm, Hansel and Gretel time.

Not that I had warmed to the director, Jacques Demy, from the start. He was very aloof and only spoke to you if you were doing a scene. Even the film seems very detached, as it's mostly long takes with hardly any close-ups. I think I'd been used to so many people being nice to me, it struck me when someone wasn't, and he wasn't; and I took a dislike to him, more perhaps than he deserved, but I avoided him like I'd avoid a plate of undyed tripe.

I did do some promotion for the film later on and attended the Cork Film Festival in Ireland. On stage and in front of a big crowd I was asked, 'Where did they get all the rats for the film from?'

'Well, we brought them all over from England!' I replied, which was true: they'd brought about two hundred of them over; and I got a huge round of applause. I couldn't understand the reaction and asked me Dad why, but he didn't know either.

I didn't find out until afterwards at dinner. Joseph Locke, the singer, was there, and Noel Purcell who I knew from *Flight of the Doves*, and Susan George, who was there for one of her films. I thought she was great; she was blonde, voluptuous and charismatic – I really fancied her! Over dinner, I asked again why I'd been cheered for saying about the rats, and someone said it was because of all the problems with the Irish and their history about England. Apparently the Irish called the English rats for doing whatever they did, whenever it was.

'Yeah, but we *did* bring all the live rats over from England to Germany,' I said, and everyone laughed again.

We were having a lovely time when, also over dinner, someone told me that Cork was the main area where the IRA had started. It made me feel uneasy, and by the following morning that uneasiness had grown into full-blown paranoia. I thought that the IRA might be following me to kneecap me, or worse. The feeling wasn't helped by the fact that everyone looked at me wherever I went. The sideways glances and the whisperings intensified my feelings of alarm. I was very wary for the rest of the time I was there and was glad to come home again.

*

In August 1971 we were preparing for the release of the second album, and the fan magazines in England, and there were quite a few, had whipped themselves up into a frenzy. There was *Jackie*, there was *Mirabelle* and there was *Fab 208* which was the biggest. *They* had phoned up at the beginning of the year and said, 'We want to run a competition and the prize we want to give them is you!' More precisely the first prize was '*A Day Out In Paris With Jack Wild!*' And the runners up would receive a '*super chiffon scarf!*'

'Is that alright?' they asked.

John advised me to do it, and to be honest it seemed no different to me than just another photo session. So I said, 'Yeah, okay'. I'd say yes to anything.

I weren't really thinking that far ahead, and anyway, it was ages away, not till August. But August came, and it was arranged I'd meet the winner at Heathrow and off we flew to Paris with a photographer and a reporter to catalogue everything that happened on this romantic date! We drove through Montmartre and visited Notre Dame and I think we had lunch at the Eiffel Tower. I'm not sure, but it was all very... well, you couldn't really relax. We were constantly having photographs taken, and every so often I'd have to stop them to have a fag. I'd been told from day one by John Daly that I had a responsibility to my fans. 'They're young kids, Jack, and they're very im-pressionable, so if they see you smoking, they'll want to do the same.'

'I want to have a fag now, so don't take any photos!' I would say, and I did that for years and years. So you had to be on your guard and be aware of what shots were being taken; and I thought Paris would have been lovely, with someone you knew.

But anyhow, it was just work, and I tried to be as nice as I could to the girl. 'Imagine what a fantastic companion he'd be walking up the Champs-Élysées,' the magazine had twittered; I don't think I was. I did give her a signed photograph and a kiss on the cheek at the end, but I think she would have been happier with the super chiffon scarf!

When we got back to London, I got into the limo and I said to the driver, 'There's a shop just off Marble Arch going down Park Lane that I'd like to go in.'

By now I'd had a few drinks and, with a warm glow that Paris hadn't given me, I went and bought an Afghan coat. When I got home me Mum thought I'd gone mad.

'Jackie, what have ya bought that for?' she said.

She wasn't impressed with me at all. But I thought it was smashing. I could go to all my pop concerts in it now looking like a real hippy. I was well into it and practically lived in it to be precise!

'So anyway, how did it go love?' me Mum asked.

'All right,' I said.

'Ahhh, did you hate it, Jackie?' she worried.

'Well, I could've thought of far better things to do other than that, Mum, but it's part of the job innit?'

'I suppose so Jackie,' me Mum said, a look of concern hovering around her eyes.

To be honest, I'd really nearly forgotten it already; it's what you've got to do, so don't complain, just get on with it. And after all, *I'd* got an Afghan – I could sense *this* was the start of a beautiful relationship.

'It's great, innit?' I said as I tried it on, checking out the pockets.

Mum looked unconvinced. 'It smells terrible, love.'

Later that week I bought me Dad a new car to drive me around in: a Daimler Sovereign 4.2, red with doeskin leather upholstery and electric windows. It was beautiful and only about a year old. We wanted a new one and I had plenty of money. And we wanted a different one, so that's what we got.

I also popped over to Jersey to get some money out. Me Mum and Dad, Arf and his girlfriend Roberta came with me. I wanted to go before heading off to do a promotional tour of England. The tour was for the release of the second album and single, and was due to start in September. I got some money and I bought a Rolex watch, and what with that and the Daimler, I was ready to go!

Chapter 14

THE TOUR TOOK UP MOST OF THE REST OF THE YEAR and then I came home and started work on my third album. In the January of '72, John called to say Nippon Herald, a film distributor in Japan, wanted me to attend the premiere of *Pied Piper* in Japan in June. I'd planned to have finished the album by then and, as I wasn't doing anything else, just a few tellies and stuff, I thought, why not? Mark had said how much he had enjoyed Japan, and Mark's *Dad* had told me how much *money* Mark had made out there.

Because of the success of *Melody* in Japan, I was doing as many photographic sessions and interviews for the Japanese fan and film magazines as I was doing for England and America. So I guess I was quite popular over there, but I didn't think that much about it really.

What I *did* think about was the twenty-hour flight! On the way out we were to refuel in Moscow, and in Anchorage, Alaska on the way back. I hated the idea of flying for so long, but Nippon paid for the flight, it was first class and me Dad came with me. For twenty-odd hours the stewardess asked, 'Can I get you anything?' and we drank the hospitality: me Dad had beer and champagne, and I had Scotch and soda: rather a lot of Scotch and soda, and after a couple of hours I began to feel quite happy about being sat there.

Gay had got a manager called John Foster who'd been in the business a long while; he'd started out with Cliff Richard and the Shadows. Whisky was John Foster's favourite tipple and, because we spent so much time with him, he obviously sussed that I enjoyed drinking and he put me onto Scotch and soda as well. He also put Gay onto a recording contract with York Records, run by a guy called Deke Arlon. In the end Deke didn't do much for Gay and he took up with Sheena Easton and made *her* a star instead which really pissed Gay off.

Gay hadn't had much luck, thinking about it. She did do a TV series with Ralph Richardson but I can't remember the name of it. This was while she was still at Speake's. After she left Speake's she went and did a whole course at the Lucy Clayton School: some sort of finishing thing where you learn how to walk and all that bollocks. Then she was trying to get record deals because she wanted to be a singer. At stage school anything to do with pop had been frowned upon and they would advise against that as a career to everybody. I don't know why, but this is the impression one got because when Phil said he wanted to be a musician they'd say, 'Oh, that's not a good idea!' It was the same for anyone wanting to be a singer: 'A dancer or an actor, that's fine; but singing, no.'

But Gay wanted to be a singer. There was always this argument at school amongst everybody as to 'who was the best singer in the school'. And it was always between Gay and this other girl called Kim Goody. I thought there was very little difference really, to be honest.

'Can I get you another drink?'

'Yes please,' I said.

I vaguely remember being told by Gay that her father had supposedly got Disney interested in signing her up and supposedly Speake messed it all up and it didn't come off. I remembered hearing something about that in the very early days of me dating her, but I wasn't sure; and anyway the air hostess was offering me my drink, so I abandoned that line of thought and took my Scotch.

I felt positively relaxed as our jumbo jet stopped off at Moscow. Maybe that was the trick with whisky: have a lot and then you don't get aggressive. I thought perhaps whisky had made me verbally aggressive in the past, but now I felt exceedingly mellow at Moscow. Until, that is, I looked out of the window as the plane was taxiing in to stop. All I could see were these soldiers with sub-machine guns surrounding the plane. An announcement came through the tannoy system to say we were stopping for an hour, so please listen for information and calls to reboard our flight. There was no mention of the army outside, as if their presence was the most normal thing in the world. I was a bit worried, but I said to me Dad that they were probably just counting how many people got off to make sure the same amount got on again.

'Come on, Dad,' I said, 'let's go and get a coffee or something. We may as well as nobody will recognise me here.'

We had a look around the terminal and went in the gift shops and I picked up one of them Russian dolls. I thought I'd buy it for me Mum and took it up to the counter to pay.

'You!' the assistant said as I handed over the wooden doll. 'You!'

She went on in very broken English to say that she enjoyed *Oliver!*. And I was so chuffed about that! I thought, bugger me! Somebody knows me in bloody Russia! I must be famous now! I must be!

I couldn't believe it. It really did make my day; even the army looked less sinister. Then it was back on the plane, and back on the Scotch and soda.

On the next leg of our flight, one of the flight attendants asked if I would like to go into the cockpit.

'No thanks,' I said.

'Yes he does,' me Dad said with a shove. So we both went and had a look and me Dad complained that the wings were flapping.

'They always flap a bit in the air, sir.' We were reassured and went back to our seats.

Despite the flapping we made it to Japan and, as we were coming in to land at Tokyo, I could see on the tarmac loads of what looked like photographers, and security staff holding back crowds of people. They were obviously expecting some dignitary or something and I said to Dad, 'There's somebody really famous on this plane! There must be a big celebrity or something. Let's watch everyone get off. If we stand here, we'll see everyone leave. Let's see if we recognise anyone!' So we waited and watched an endless stream of businessmen and families get off until there was no one left.

'Did you recognise anyone, Dad,' I asked, ''cos I didn't?'

'No!' he said.

'Oh, bugger it,' I said, 'let's get off anyway 'cos there'll be someone waiting for us, Dad.'

I stepped onto the stairway and all the heavens opened with all these flash-flashes of the cameras going. I instinctively looked behind me, but there was just a baffled Dad. So I thought – it must be for me then.

Bloody hell.

I was walking down the steps from the plane, but I couldn't feel my legs. I began to make out the kids lining the tops of the buildings, but bizarrely in a strange silhouette as the flashguns distorted my vision. I was like a pissed rabbit in headlights. As I got closer I could see a circle of bodyguards holding back these hysterical people, and through the screaming and shouting I could make out a vaguely familiar name that sounded very close to my own.

They had on T-shirts emblazoned with WELCOME TO JAPAN JACK WILD. I'd never seen Jack Wild T-shirts before in my life! (In truth I haven't actually seen them since.) And they had posters of me on placards and I thought, I could be quite happy with this. I could get used to this. I felt like Donny Osmond and I couldn't believe it.

Mum and Dad

Arf and me

Arf and Mum watch me watering Dad in the garden at home

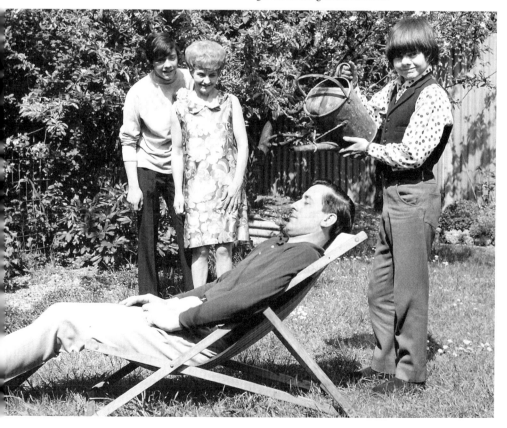

Danny Grover, Phil Harris, me and Phil Collins
on Stubby Kaye's *Silver Star Show*, 1965

Arf as Oliver, Phil Collins as Dodger, and me wishing I was tall
enough to wear the hat, backstage at the New Theatre, 1965

One of Speake's promotional cards: Arf and me are in the middle
at the top, Gay is top right (Photo © Barbara Speake Stage School)

ROBERT LANGLEY

ARTHUR AND JACK WILD

GAYNOR JONES

SUSAN ROYLANCE

THE
BARBARA
SPEAKE
STAGE SCHOOL
& AGENCY

HOU 6585
RIC 6615
SHE 2711
SHE 6096

OVER 200
CHILDREN &
TEENAGERS...ALL AGES.
MANY NATIONALITIES.

JEREMY WOOLSTON

JONATHAN DEANS

STEPHEN AND RUBEN BULLIVANT

VERONICA PURNELL

Chris Cooper, Sally Thomsett and me leaning on the 'invisible' space bubble in *Danny the Dragon*, 1966 (Photo © Children's Film Foundation)

A tense moment with David Daker in *Z Cars*, 1967

A lighter moment with Bobby Bennett and company in *Junior Showtime*, 1968

Me (in my Speake's blazer!) and
Mark Lester at Shepperton

Probably the best-known picture of me as the
Artful Dodger (Photo © REX/Shutterstock)

Dodger, Fagin and Oliver (me, Ron Moody and Mark)

Mark and me on set

Fagin's Gang on the back lot at Shepperton, summer 1967. Back: Ian Ramsey, John Watters, Billy Smith, me, Ronnie Johnson, Clive Moss, Nigel Grice. Middle: Jeffrey Chandler, Kim Smith, Robert Langley, Ray Ward, Mark Lester. Front: Chris Duff, Bob Bartlett, Freddie Stead, Nigel Kingsley, Stuart (Peter) Lock (Photo © Marvin Lichtner)

Ron's sketch of me as Dodger

My fifteenth birthday during filming of 'Consider Yourself' (Photo © John Brooke)

Final days at Speake's, before the falling-out! Above left, with Barbara Speake; above right, with
June Collins (Photos © Ian Tyas/Keystone Press Agency Ltd)

Hemdale managed Mark and me in
1969. They've made me look even
shorter than I actually was!

With Hattie Jacques and Sally Ann Jones
in *Knock Three Times*
(Photo © ITV/REX/Shutterstock)

Heading for Hollywood! The big contract with
Sid and Marty Krofft
(Photo © NBC/Sid and Marty Krofft)

With Marty and Christa Krofft

With the fabulous Billie Hayes in 1969…

…and still fabulous thirty years later

"Pufnstuf" is now a movie.

It didn't get much bigger than Bing's
Christmas Show (Photo © Kenny Lieu)

With Engelbert Humperdinck, Terry-Thomas,
and sharing Liberace's tailor!

On Val Doonican's show
with Michelle Lee

With Bruce Forsyth

Reunited with Mark in *Melody*

It looks as if Ron doesn't like my terrible wig either: on location for *Flight of the Doves*

On location in Rothenburg with Donovan for *The Pied Piper*. The town was much nicer than this picture suggests

A break in filming *The 14* with director David Hemmings (Photo © Keith Hamshere)

Arf and me (and a friend!) in Hollywood

On *Lift Off*, 1972 (Photo © REX/Shutterstock)

Teen pin-up material, Seventies style

Mobbed in Japan, 1972. I am as scared as I look!

With my old mate Tony Carpenter

With Gay and Johnny Whitaker during the
filming of *Sigmund and the Sea Monsters*

My spider monkeys, Billy and Bluebell

This was as undressed as I got in *Keep it Up Downstairs*, 1976. The moustache was definitely not mine!

Nineteen years old and playing a boy stowaway in *The Onedin Line*, 1972

Me as Mike and the wonderful Arthur English as my grandpa Sam in *Everyday Maths*, 1978

Showing the strain filming *Alice* in Poland, 1979, shortly before an attack of pancreatitis
(Photo © South Street Films/Hemdale)

Two publicity shots from my drinking career in the Eighties

…and back on track after getting sober. The perm didn't last long!

That's more like it!
(Photo © Katie Vandyck)

Made up to look done over for the *Lock Stock* TV series

With Clive Francis, Mike Melia and Victor Spinetti in *The Lavender Hill Mob*, 2001

A silent Baron Hardup in *Cinderella* at Worcester, 2004

Backstage with Claire, ready
for the opening scene of
The Lavender Hill Mob

A favourite picture
at home with Claire

But then as soon as they started to get a bit closer to me I started to get a bit worried and frightened because there were so many: there were just hundreds of people there. I was shepherded into the circle of bodyguards and me and me Dad got separated. Then one girl made a dive, the guards missed her, and all hell broke loose. They couldn't hold back the girls and someone said to me, 'Go and jump in that black car there!'

So the nearest black car I saw, I quickly scrambled into.

The door closed – peace again. I exhaled, turned around and then it began again. A Japanese woman was sitting beside me waving and screaming, gesticulating and shouting at me in Japanese! But *she* didn't seem so pleased to see me. I don't know what she was saying, but she was obviously upset and so I thought I'd better get out.

As I went to get out of the car, someone else grabbed hold of me and man-handled me into the *right* black car. I don't think my feet touched the ground. And I thought, what's going on? I mean, as far as I know, I could be being kidnapped or anything!

The guy who was sat in front, next to the driver of this limo, turned around and in very good English said, 'Welcome to Tokyo, Jack; I'm from Nippon Herald. Please don't worry, it's all under control!'

'Where's me Dad? What's happened to him?' I said, only slightly reassured.

'Please don't worry, Jack, he will have been taken care of in another car and he will be following us to Tokyo, but we must get you away!'

I sat back trying to believe the last twenty minutes, what had actually happened to me. I'd never experienced that before. It was amazing! I couldn't believe it!

The car took me into the centre of Tokyo and I didn't see me Dad then until I was in the reception of the hotel and I was checking in. Me Dad's face was a picture when he came into the lobby. He looked as flabbergasted as I was.

'Where've you been, son?'

'Riding around Tokyo,' I said.

'Bloody 'ell,' he sighed, sitting down on the steps.

'Where have *you* been, Dad?'

'I dunno lad, I just kept my eye on the bloke wi' cases. Bloody 'ell,' he sighed again.

Despite my father's vigilance some of the cases got lost. We went up to our rooms and I turned on the telly and flicked through endless incomprehensible channels.

Early next morning the round of photographic sessions, temples, TV shows, personal appearances and endless premieres began. It was all planned with military precision and our every minute was accounted for. We were given a Japanese lady to act as our field marshal. She was tiny, five foot nothing and spoke great English. 'I will be looking after you for the whole time you're here,' she said. 'Let me know anything you need.' Me Dad called her 'Sunshine' because she was always smiling.

On the first morning I said, ''Ere Sunshine, while I'm here, I must, at some stage or other, I've got to buy a Nikon camera! You've got to organise that for me, please!'

'Don't worry, we'll organise that for you, it's no problem at all!' she said. 'I know the best places to take you as well.'

Sunshine guided us through this strange new world. She guided us through games at Pachinko Arcade ('just like your bingo' she said); there was gambling and prizes and an awful lot of ball bearings, but beyond that I don't think I really grasped it. She taught us how to eat in a traditional Japanese restaurant where you sit on the floor, on matting. If you could've seen me Dad trying to eat with chopsticks, sat on the floor, it was hysterical! Not that I was any better: I kept getting cramp. In another amazing restaurant there was a fish tank right in the middle full of carp. I've never seen carp as big. They were like bloody whales they were! I just couldn't believe it. It was just ridiculous.

I was also told (though I thought they were winding me up), 'You've got to have some Kobe beef while you are here!' I love fillet steak, so I was interested.

'Well, what's different about that to normal Angus Scottish beef?' I asked.

'Well, we massage the cows with beer,' they said.

'Yeah, tell me another one!' I said as I tried to picture someone with a pint of lager rubbing it into this cow; but it did taste lovely.

Tokyo was the busiest place I'd ever been to. There were millions of people on the streets and there was so much noise and light and neon signs, and I couldn't understand anything I saw or heard. Thank goodness Sunshine was responsible for being with us everywhere.

And *everywhere* was an opportunity for a photo session. That's all it was, photographic sessions all the time, mixed in with going to premieres of *Pied Piper*, and I was getting a bit fed up of both. At one premiere, somewhere, they said to me, 'After the film's been shown, we'll get you up on stage and ask you a few questions and, through an interpreter, allow the audience to ask you a few questions if you wouldn't mind?'

So I thought, okay, fine! So, they'd seen the film and they introduced me and I came on to a big round of applause and all that and the guy asked me a few questions and then threw it out to the audience. 'If you've got any questions you'd like to ask Jack, hold your hand up and we'll get to you.'

This one kid, a cheeky little sod, put a hand up and said: 'Why, Mr Wild, have you such a big nose?' I wanted to say, 'The same reason why you've got a big mouth!' but it seemed too rude. I just laughed it off instead and carried on on the merry-go-round.

I wasn't on a daily rate or anything, and although I was doing lots of TV shows, I wasn't being paid for them. I remembered Mark's father Mike had said to me, 'When you are in Japan, they'll make you work like a pig without wanting to pay you, so make sure that you get paid.' Well, I'd been doing quite a few of these shows and I was getting a bit cheesed off because I weren't being offered any money at all.

So when we came to do this particular show, a late-night very hip chat show, I was determined to make a stand. When I got to the studio I said to Sunshine, 'Look, I'm getting a bit fed up now 'cos I'm not being... it's just that... I want paying if I'm gonna do this show.'

'I'm not sure that they even pay on the show, Jack, but I'll see what I can find out and get back to you.'

She came back and said, 'Well, they don't actually pay their guests but the producer has agreed to buy you something if you'll do the show.'

I thought, well, okay. I didn't really want to make too big of a song and dance about it because they were treating us generally so well. There was always somebody there for you and you only needed to ask for something and it was given. I'd said one day that I liked listening to music and the next day I got a Sony cassette recorder. I didn't know where it came from or who paid for it, but it was there, and it was given to me as a gift. It got to the point where you almost felt guilty at asking for things because that's what you would be given. I agreed to do the show, which was probably just as well for them as it was live.

One of the sponsors of the show was the leading brand of Japanese whisky, so there was plenty of that going on while we waited to do the show. When they got to my bit, and they'd said 'Welcome to Japan' and all that, they firstly asked, 'Who's come over with you?'

'Oh,' I said, 'I'm over here with me Dad – that's him over there!' and they swung the camera over and filmed him; and he was so embarrassed, me Dad was, because he didn't like anything to do with anything of that sort of nature. He didn't forgive me for that for a long while.

'Don't you ever do that to me again 'cos I didn't know what to sa', or do, or anything like that,' he said to me afterwards.

'If you annoy me, I'll do it again,' I said, 'so you'd better behave yeself!'

After I'd done my first bit, the camera went to this Japanese guy. I was still sat in my chair, quietly waiting for the camera to come back to me after he'd done his five minutes. He was small, dark haired, wore black-rimmed glasses and a big smile, and was very eccentric looking. I didn't know what his segment was about and he just started going on, talking ten million to the dozen. I couldn't understand a word of what he was saying and his facial expressions were going into overtime. It was every expression imaginable, every five seconds, and I was crying with laughter: tears were pouring out of my face listening to this guy. I didn't know what the hell he was talking about, but he was so, so funny. Even me Dad was in bits. I was wiping away the last of my tears as the camera came back to me and it went on and we finished up.

After the show the producer gave me a gold pendant of Buddha as payment; and okay, fine, I thought, that's alright, at least it was showing willing. I ended up giving it me Mum for her charm bracelet when I got back.

Then it was off to Kyoto, the religious capital of Japan, 'on our Bullet Train!' they proudly declared. At the time, I didn't know much about it. All I'd heard was that it went twice as fast as our ones did in England, so I was quite looking forward to it. The tour was organised down to the last second – *you've got ten seconds to get from this car, into this building and you've then got two minutes to get into this room where you're going to be photographed!* – and it was all done like clockwork. So we got to Tokyo station at the appointed minute to catch our train and I couldn't believe how futuristic it looked. We boarded the train and literally within two minutes of starting, it was thundering along the rails at God knows how many hundred miles an hour, and all you could see then for the journey to Kyoto was paddy fields flying past. During the journey people came along and sold us stuff. You didn't have to get up out of your seat for food or drink or anything. I found it really amazing that although we were going so fast, if you had a drink on the table – it stayed there.

Somehow the fans discovered what train I was getting and the same thing happened again at Kyoto railway station that happened at Tokyo Airport. The fans were there with the T-shirts and the posters and the scarves and the hats which was an amazing ego-trip for me; although, again, the sheer numbers frightened me: I hated crowds where I was the focus. It reminded me of when I did the St Patrick's Day Parade the previous year in New York. I'd just signed with Buddah Records and I'd been advised to do the parade, where they had me sat on top of this ten-foot snail, and dragged it from one end of Manhattan to the other.

I remember this as though it was yesterday, thinking, I'm gonna see a rifle barrel sticking out of one of these windows pointing at me! I know I'm gonna see it! The crime in New York was a bit horrendous to put it mildly and I was stuck on this bloody snail for about three or four hours, sat there for anyone to take a potshot at. Somebody did throw a coin which hit me on the head and my initial reaction was 'I've been shot!' But when I went to rub me head where the pain came from, and I didn't see any blood, I thought, I'm alright! It's okay, I can carry on, I'm not injured!

I hated putting myself in these positions, but it was hard to refuse to do these things. I was always strongly advised to do everything you can to keep up your popularity if you want to continue being successful. We changed our hotel three times in Japan because the fans kept finding out where we were and made it impossible for us to stay.

Kyoto was of course an opportunity for more photographs to be taken in exotic locations and *now* they were starting to give me clothes to wear. 'We'd like you to model these type of clothes!' I agreed to some and not to others, and then they said, 'As we're now in the religious centre of Japan you've got an afternoon off to see the sights.'

This was the only afternoon that we had off in the whole time we were there. So I said, 'Right, if this is my only free time, I wanna go and buy a camera!'

'Yes, yes,' they said, 'but we have to take you around the temples first.'

And I turned to me Dad and said, 'Bollocks to the temples! I wanna go and buy a camera!'

'You can't say that Jack, this is their bloody culture. You've gotta respect it and we'll have to do that first and then you can get your camera after that!'

'Alright,' I said, 'as long as we're quick though.'

We started touring temples, but you had to take your shoes off every time you went in. I was getting fed up of walking round, taking your bloody shoes off every five minutes, and we spent a good couple of hours going around about half a dozen of these different temples. I kept looking at my watch after each one to see how much time we had left. But Sunshine was as good as her word, and after it was all done she took me to the best place in Kyoto for camera shopping.

As we travelled back on the train I thought, I'm really glad that I did the temple tour; had I not, I'd have missed an amazing part of Japanese culture. The thing that I couldn't understand was that you'd walk round these temples covered in gold and jewels that were obviously worth an absolute fortune; and yet you couldn't see any security there to stop people saying, oh, I like that emerald and I like that diamond, I think I'll have it.

The next morning it was a paper-folding and flower-arranging demonstration. I said to Dad, 'For goodness' sake, if I fall asleep give me a nudge will ya?' and as it happened, we *both* fell asleep! And according to me Dad, he then reckons we flew to Sapporo city; I've got no recollection of it at all. I couldn't even have told you that it was in Japan. I felt as though we'd been photographed and interviewed in every inch of Japan so I imagine he is right, and I was photographed and interviewed there too.

And I wouldn't have missed the whole trip to Japan for anything, because it really was an amazing place; I'll remember it for the rest of my life. We came back at the beginning of July having earnt no money, but with three cardboard cases full of Japanese presents.

*

I think it was the beginning of September of '72 that I wanted to go back to Jersey and have a holiday, so we booked it all up and Gay came with me and me Mum and Dad, and I took her and showed her all my favourite places in Jersey. At some stage I'd got back together with Gay. I'd not really seen her after we'd split up for a good eight months as I was away doing my album and *Pied Piper*. She told me that when I was in Germany, she'd gone on holiday to Austria and was only about forty miles away, the other side of the mountain, but she didn't come and see me on the set although she knew where I was filming.

She also told me that after we'd broken up she used to tell Debbie King, my fanatical fan, when I was going to the Hilton Trader Vic's for a meal on a Saturday night so that she could go there and sit at another table. Gay said as soon as she knew my whereabouts she'd let Debbie King know to get at me. So when I did shows like *Top of the Pops* Debbie would get a ticket to be in the audience, and she did turn up more than once at the Hilton when I was having a meal. I'd go there a lot with Robert Barrett who liked fillet steak just as much as I did and I'd say to him, 'Why is it my luck every time I come for a meal, she turns up on the same day?'

Not only did we get back together, but in the early part of 1972, me and Gay sat down and talked about getting engaged. When we'd agreed to do that, we decided that we weren't going to tell anyone about it until we'd found the rings that we wanted. Then we'd go and tell the parents, then we'd have an engagement party, and then we'd let the press know. We spent days together hunting all the jewellery shops and were advised to have a look in Hatton Garden in London because that was the place to go, especially if you wanted something made. I really enjoyed all that and over the years I got friendly with one jeweller in particular and I would often ask him to make a pendant or a brooch for Gay.

Having toured the whole of Hatton Garden we ended up finding both rings in Michael Davis's shop. One was a diamond cluster for her with about a dozen diamonds in it, and mine was just a single half-carat diamond. We decided to have the engagement party at Gay's mum and dad's house because, at the time, they had the biggest house out of the two of us.

This was just before going to Japan, so John wondered if I should wear my ring because I'd got a lot of fans over there and he wasn't sure how they would react.

'Yeah, but I want to wear it. Can't I just say it's just a ring that I bought for meself?'

'I'm just thinking about your image, Jack.'

'They're gonna know sometime,' I said.

'Of course, Jack, it's just how we announce it,' John tried again.

'Well, I'm gonna wear it for now and say it's just a ring, until we decide how best to play it,' I concluded.

I didn't wear it in Japan.

At the beginning of 1973, I met up with a guy called John Velasco from United Artists Records in London. He wanted to produce me on record and so we got into discussions about getting a production deal for England. He was a funny, witty man who gave the impression that he knew everyone in the music industry. He had reddy-blonde curly hair that bubbled out of his head, but beneath this rather jovial exterior there was a ruthless businessman attached. He got me a recording deal with Pye Records. It was only a singles deal for the minute, and then obviously if we had a hit single they would want us to do an album; but with my history of making records that didn't seem like it was going to be a possibility. It felt like a very casual relationship to me, and certainly not as high-profile as with Capitol or Buddah. Buddah had been such a hip company to be involved with, with Cat Stevens, Mama Cass and Melanie on the label. And Capitol, well, Capitol was more mainstream and the biggest record company in the world; I mean, their base in LA was a landmark for goodness' sake. To be involved with Capitol was a constant thrill.

So in contrast to that, the contract with Pye seemed more of a game than a career move as such. I think they were known for R&B and soul music, so heaven knows why they should be interested in me. I certainly wasn't taking the contract or my pop career seriously. I took my singing seriously in films, but I just didn't see myself as a pop singer and thought I would just enjoy the game.

We'd done the usual looking round for songs, and a friend of John Velasco's, Scott English (a performer as well as a songwriter), had this song that we all liked called 'I Need More Loving'. So we headed off to a recording studio in the East End of London, near Petticoat Lane, to record it. I'd stopped on the way to get a bottle of sherry for my voice, and for this particular bunch of sessions I was buying Emva Cream.

'What the hell's that, Jack?' John asked.

'Emva Cream – a Cyprus sherry,' I said. 'Do you want some, mate?'

'No thanks, Jack; let me introduce you to the guys,' he laughed, shaking a few more curls up and out of his head.

'Howard, come and meet Jack...' he called. Howard was Howard Shepherd of Shep's Banjo Boys, a band that were on telly every week in a series called *The Comedians*, I think John said. And I guess they weren't doing anything else, so came in to record this with me.

We were going in not just to make one single, but to do four or six songs so that we had a choice and a mimimum of two singles out of it. So anyhow we went in there and realised we ain't got any B-sides. And one of the Banjo Boys said, 'Well, why don't you do an old Cockney song?'

That would be a giggle, I thought. I'd just bought an album of Alf Garnett's singing old Cockney songs like 'I'm Forever Blowing Bubbles' (he was a West Ham supporter), and one of the tracks on his album was 'Bill Bailey' so I said, 'Let's sing that one!'

'Yeah, great,' someone said. 'Does anyone know the chords?'

'Oh, and can someone help me with the words?' I said. Between all of us we worked out the words and chords and got it as near as damn it right. We recorded it and put it out as a B-side, I think. That'd be unheard of nowadays, to do business like that. This was one of those production deals where we were given an amount of money to come up with a minimum of two singles and obviously you'd need two B-sides as well. They gave us a guarantee as opposed to an advance against sales. They would release it, with a year's option, and obviously the cheaper we could produce it, the more money we'd have spare, John said.

We finished cutting the discs and waited for the release. I remember the excitement of having records out and waiting for the trade press to come out with reviews and playlists. But it was a strange world, the record industry, and it seemed to me people behaved very differently. It was so fickle that it made the acting business look like a stable job for life. And the drugs: the drugs were 'out of sight man'. Not that I was really interested in them. I was, however, interested in getting the rest of the money from the production company. We'd given them the finished product, but they hadn't yet paid us the remainder, so I decided to go and get our money. After all, an agreement is an agreement, even in *this* industry. It might be only a game, but I'd done the work and they owed me money.

So I said to John, 'You know, this ain't good enough! This agreement was entered into on a gentlemanly basis and they should stick to it. I'm not happy with this! I'm going in and demanding that they pay us what they owe us!'

John thought it wasn't necessarily the right sort of way to deal with the situation. I don't know how much previous business he'd done with this company, although I presumed he had done quite a bit and therefore knew the guys involved; but I didn't give a shit.

The offices were in Mayfair and were very expensive looking, and I went in and asked for the money. The guy was sat at this Georgian-type desk, just laughing it off as though it was of no consequence, as though I was talking rubbish. And as the meeting went on, I could see that I wasn't getting anywhere; so I said, 'Now, come on, be fair. That money, you know, the remainder of the money, it's only fair that it's given to us who made the record and so therefore, can I have my fifty per cent and can you write a cheque out for it please?'

And the guy just leaned to one side of his desk, opened a drawer and pulled out a gun. He flicked the barrel as if to make sure it's all working and cocked the trigger and as he was doing this he said, 'You don't really want that money, do you?'

Now I didn't know whether the gun was loaded or not. But as I said to John afterwards, 'Say if it had been loaded, what if the guy had a bloody tick or a bad night on the booze and had a bit of a twitch and I'd have been splattered all over the wall! That ain't funny! Is it, mate?'

So I decided to play it exactly the same way he was playing it and I said, 'No, I was only joking, it's alright, you can have it. I don't want it!' And as I said that, he opened the drawer and put the gun back inside, and I turned and walked out. I was bloody terrified and I never got the money; life seemed more important.

I didn't have any more to do with that company.

I stayed in contact with John Velasco for a while and got involved with his accountants, Shulmans, and some restaurants that John had shares in as well. John had so many irons in so many fires that he wasn't dependent on this deal or that deal coming off; *he* played a very clever game, and always kept himself covered. Still, we'd released two singles, and for both singles I'd done the TV show *Lift Off* in Manchester. I can't remember when I did the shows, but it was somewhere between when I bought my Toyota and the Berlin Film Festival. John came with me to Manchester, and on one trip we met David Essex. He had a single out and we travelled back from Manchester on the train together. We got on great and he said he was going to write a song for me.

During 1972 the number of film scripts that were being sent to me had started to slow down. In the early part of the seventies I was getting about half a dozen a week and that intensity lasted for a couple of years before the deluge turned into a steady flow of two or three a week. Looking back on it now, I did notice the change, but it didn't really bother me. After all, I was still working and still had plenty of money in the bank.

At the beginning of 1972, one of the scripts I received was from John Daly for a film called *The 14*. It was based on a true story. I'd remembered reading about it in the newspapers; it had been headline news at the time. There was a family of fourteen kids brought up in a big-city slum and orphaned when their mother died aged thirty-eight. The children fought to stay together despite the authority's attempts to foster them in separate homes and institutions. There had been a photograph of them on the front cover of one of the broadsheet's colour supplements. (The photo was later replicated with all the actors, to use for publicity for the film.) I remembered their vulnerable, determined, watchful eyes staring out like cornered stray cats.

David Hemmings was to direct the film and he wanted me to play the part of Reg, the oldest member of the family. I was pleased to be offered a part so close to my own age (I was nineteen and Reg was eighteen) as I was getting tired of playing kids' roles. This would be the first time in my career that I would play an adult and I thought that could only be a good thing as I could finally grow up on screen.

The character for my on-screen rite of passage, Reg, struggles with the responsibility of his large, unruly family; too old to be considered a child and too immature to take on the responsibilities of an adult – I thought I had kind of a handle on that! It looked like a great part and it wasn't a period piece either, so it felt like it was close to home.

I went to meet David and Frank Avianca, the producer of the film: a smooth, debonair, well-dressed guy flanked by two bodyguards which made me sure he worked for the Mafia. He was a tanned, fit, good-looking Sicilian man. He came from a rich Italian family that owned Avianca Airlines and always dressed absolutely five hundred per cent immaculate. He had two cockney brothers as his bodyguards who I remember as six foot six and five foot wide.

I'd just finished shooting an episode of *The Onedin Line*, and so had a few bob in the bank, and had been shopping on the way to the meeting. I'd bought a Stylophone which I took in to show David.

Frank talked about the film. 'You see, Jack, the welfare people couldn't find one foster home for all fourteen, much as they tried. The children were separated into children's homes, foster care and trade schools. They kept running away to try and reunite as a family and that's when they hit the headlines and when my co-producer Robert Mintz read about it,' Frank concluded. I nodded wisely as though he was the Godfather explaining about the importance of family. 'And profits from the film will go into a trust fund for the children.' Or did he say bambinos?

'There are no villains in the film. Only victims of the society we ourselves have created,' David added. A few more sage nods.

I said I had read the script and what a great part I thought it was, and mentioned that I had noticed that my character had a bedroom scene.

'Yeah,' said David, not registering my concern.

The meeting went on and eventually hands were shook and backs were slapped, but I left the meeting with mixed feelings. A lady called June Brown was to play me mum; and Keith Buckley, who I knew from *Pied Piper*, was to be a social worker, so that would be fun. But they wanted me to have my hair cut like the original character. I said I didn't want to, they said they *did* want me to. I said I wouldn't, and David said don't be so bloody stupid. I said I didn't want to do the film if I had to have my hair cut. They said they wanted me to do the film *and* to have my hair cut.

I think my parting comment was, '*And* I definitely ain't gonna be naked.' And I think David's was, 'Don't worry about the bed scene, have your hair cut and if I give you the money can you get me one of those Stylophones please?'

Luckily there was no horse's head on my pillow in the morning.

It was shot in a documentary style, mainly at Pinewood and on location in and around London. I think the other thirteen kids weren't from stage school, but were just ordinary kids ranging from three to fifteen years old and a baby! It was chaotic when all the kids were there. I remember one boy called Wayne Brooks who must have been five or six years old. He had the cutest face, big brown eyes, was always asking questions and as cheeky as hell.

Everything took twice as long when the kids were there and I think David sometimes found it difficult getting what he wanted from them. He blew up at them a few times and then one silly bugger broke his leg messing about on set. David had to come down on them hard as filming was delayed and then we had to shoot round the boy's plastered leg.

David blew up at me once too: I'd forgotten to take off my chronograph Rolex watch.

'What are you doing wearing a fucking watch? Reg couldn't afford a fucking watch. You've been in the business long enough Jack, there's no excuse.'

'Anyone can make a fucking mistake. No one's perfect. I'm sorry and it won't happen again,' I shouted back.

They were the only heated words we had and were forgotten straight away. I understood that because David was trying to catch magic moments from the children that they might not be able to reproduce, it was important that everything else around them was right every time and not ruined by someone who'd forgotten to take their watch off.

It seemed every film I did, I had kids to look out for and now I had thirteen of them! I thought David was very good as a director, but perhaps with not as much patience as Carol Reed. David inspired confidence; he gave the impression he knew exactly what he wanted, but wasn't always sure of the best way to go about getting it. This was his second film and I looked up to him. I thought maybe I would direct one day: I was already involved in a project called *Caterpillar Taxis*, so I watched and listened to what David said.

'Once you've committed yourself to films you've got to end up wanting to be a director. I love painting and I like gadgets and people and business and if there's one form that encompasses all of this it's undoubtedly directing. I'd like to act again – but I'm not really bothered, if I can continue to direct. I had to decide what I wanted to be: the mod madcap guy or David Hemmings, serious film man.'

I guess we were both going through a transition of sorts – mine was having a stab at adulthood. I'd got Peter Bartlett (Bob's twin) the job as my stand-in; and, as I was trying to align myself more with the adults, and what I saw to be David's way of life, Peter and I would often go into the restaurant at Pinewood and have a lump of steak and try a nice red wine with it. I felt I related well to the kids on set, and I'd play soccer with them when we weren't filming, but at the same time I wanted to be seen as a grown-up and quite separate from them and their antics.

But sometimes it was irresistible.

An early scene in *The 14* is where the mother dies and we shot it at the new Charing Cross Hospital in Fulham. June Brown played me mum and she was such a giving actress, she wanted everyone to be good. She also wore these white plastic knee-length boots in the film. We always joked about them and constantly tried to find gags about white plastic boots. She said, 'When I die I want to be buried in them!' The hospital hadn't opened yet. It was only just being finished and they were putting all the insides in. There was a lot of hanging about, but me and the kids used our time well and had chariot races in the wheelchairs up and down the corridors. We made a right racket and left skid marks on the newly polished floors. A right mess it was. Years later I was back there to see a German psychiatrist when they thought I needed help with drinking. I did, but I think she was madder than I was; although I must have looked pretty odd, surreptitiously looking for our old skid marks.

While we were making this film, one of Frank's bodyguards came on the set one day and showed me this replica gun. You would swear blind that it was a real gun because it was just the right size. It wasn't made of gunmetal, just some cheap alloy, but for all intents and purposes it looked exactly like the real thing; and seeing this I said, 'Oh, I've got to have one of these!'

I had a driver on the film, Bill (short, fat, late fifties), who picked me up from The Grove, and he was a lovely old guy. If we were on location, he'd have cans of beer in the boot for me, so if I wanted a beer, I could just leave the set and get one. Anyway, I got the address where they had these replica guns and I phoned them up and asked them if they had this particular Beretta in stock.

'Great, well keep it in the name of Jack Wild and someone will come and collect it now,' I said. And I sent Bill out to get it for me. As soon as he came back with it I was showing it off; and as soon as David saw it, he sent his driver out to get him one too.

On the way home Bill would drop me off first, then he'd drive Peter to his home as that was near to where Bill lived. That night I was sat in the back of the car and so pleased with this toy gun. I thought, if I point the gun at Bill, I wonder if anyone will notice? I whispered to Pete, 'Let's see what happens!'

So, I'm doing all this and I was getting well pissed off because as far as I could see, nobody was taking a blind bit of notice of me with this gun held at the driver's head.

We were slowing down for a set of traffic lights and I thought, okay, surely someone will see me now. We pulled up alongside a battered old car, a tattered bumper sticker declaring FORGET OXFAM – FEED TWIGGY. We sat next to this car and I thought, hold still – we'll get a reaction now. But nothing. *Nothing*. What's the matter with everyone, I thought, it's not like we're in New York.

I got home that night and then went over to see Gay at Holland Park. But somebody *had* seen the gun and they'd phoned the police. The police went to Peter's house to check up on the story. They'd gone to Bill, but he didn't know anything about it and they'd gone to my house but I weren't there. Me Mum and Dad were, however, and they went bloody mad when I got home. I was almost twenty but I was behaving like a kid and they really did tell me off something rotten.

The next day was to be a big one as I had my driving test first thing and then we were to film the bed scene: I'm not sure which I dreaded more. The bedroom scene was with Cheryl Hall; she was the girl who played Robert

Lindsay's girlfriend in *Citizen Smith*, but she was married to him then and we'd only just met. She was lovely: small and wrapped in an appealing layer of puppy fat; shy, but very giving as an actor. I was doing press interviews during the making of the film and they were saying, 'We've heard that you have a bedroom scene, what do you think of that?'

I don't know if they were expecting me to behave like a typical red-blooded male and say, 'Yeah! I'm really looking forward to it. She's a tasty bird!' and all that, but I was more than a little apprehensive so I said, 'Yeah, it'll be interesting. I've never done one before.'

I'd already said to David Hemmings, 'I'm not appearing naked. You can forget that for a start!'

'It's alright Jack, it won't affect you in that way at all, don't worry about it!' he'd said, but I was.

But the driving test was first.

I'd still continued to have a go at driving whenever I could; I'd turn me Dad's car round in The Grove because the drive was big enough to do that. When I was old enough to learn how to drive properly, I was mostly too busy working and I didn't have the time. It's only really when the work started to slow down a bit that I had time to learn to drive and take my test during *The 14*.

Gay had passed her test; so I'd thought, if I buy a car, she can sit with me while I'm learning. I went to the garage in Hampton and bought a brand-new white Toyota Corolla 1200cc coupé. I bought it outright and stuck on L-plates to drive it off the forecourt to take it home. Originally I was going to buy a 1600 Toyota Celica but me Dad said, 'No, that's too powerful for you. You'd be better off getting the smaller one for now, and getting a bigger-engined car after you've had a bit of experience.' And for some reason I listened to him.

I'd drive every spare moment with Gay sat in the front seat. Every weekend, I'd say to Bob, my mate Tony Carpenter and his girlfriend Chris, 'C'mon, let's go out for the day.' I drove them all thousands of miles in that first four or five months to get a bit of practice in. Bob thought it was outrageous learning to drive in a high-performance sports car. He was right, of course.

'Listen mate,' I said, 'the garage sold both Toyotas *and* Scimitar GTE cars and I really fancied one of them 'cos that's a three-litre sports car, so this is nothing in comparison. *That* would've been ridiculous,' I said, momentarily thinking that maybe I should have got a Scimitar.

I'd foolishly told everybody at work that I had to have time off because I'd booked my driving test. We were filming in Kilburn on the day and because my test was early in the morning, I said to the film company, 'Send a car for me when I've finished my test and then I'll come straight to Kilburn.'

I was very nervous and regretted telling so many people: if I didn't pass everybody would know and I'd feel such an idiot.

Thankfully I passed; one hurdle down, now on to the next. Gay came up to where we were filming for lunch to find out how I'd gone on and after lunch I tried to calm my nerves with a few games of boules. Somebody had introduced us all to the game while we were filming a lot of the interiors at Pinewood. We'd set up a ninety-foot-long sandpit to be our pitch and had a contest. I can't remember who won, but I was knocked out in the quarter finals.

Boules couldn't protect me forever though, and eventually I was taken back to do *the* scene. I had to be in bed sort of covered up, and bare from the waist up. This I did, but I kept my jeans on under the bedclothes to be on the safe side. I remember vaguely David on the set discussing on a one-to-one basis with Cheryl about what he wanted her to do. At the time she was just wearing a top and I think David didn't want her to have any knickers on. She wasn't happy about this and I think she kept her knickers on. I don't know, because I didn't look down. It was only a short scene and after we'd finished filming, Cheryl said, 'I did feel awkward doing that,' which were the first words we'd really spoken about it. We hadn't talked about it beforehand as I think we were both far too embarrassed.

Still, at least it was done *and* I'd passed my test – a good day all in all.

That weekend a load of us decided to meet at Gay's parents' house in Claygate, Esher, to go in Bob Bartlett's minibus to Chessington Zoo. It wasn't exactly Bob's minibus: it was the Speake's Stage School bus. Bob used to drive it during the week to take the kids to auditions in and around London, and at weekends to take us lot sightseeing. I'm sure Miss Speake wouldn't have been impressed with me lording it up in her van, but I wasn't really thinking about that; I just thought, it's a vehicle to get loads of my friends together. It had about eight or ten seats in it and it saved us hiring a minibus.

When we got to Chessington, Gay showed me the type of monkey she had had as a child. She'd had to give it to the zoo when it had got to about four years old because it became too aggressive. She was supposed to be given a report two or three times a year, but this one time she didn't get one. She went to see what had happened; it had died, and she was upset because she never, ever, found out why. I remember her saying if ever she had monkeys again, she wouldn't get the same breed as apparently they were known to become more aggressive than others.

Another time we went to the Hellfire Caves in Bob's bus, but I think Chessington was our last outing. Apparently, I'd been seen in it at the zoo! Miss Speake had said that Bob could use it for popping about in and nothing more. She obviously didn't want him driving up to the north of Scotland and back on his days off, and obviously didn't want him driving me about; she almost sacked Bob for it, so after that we couldn't use it. Still, it had been fun.

Back to work on the Monday and after the bed scene, the rest of the filming sailed plainly by. Very soon we were wrapped and done and at the end-of-film party at Pinewood. It was a fabulous night. Everyone was drinking champagne and enjoying the lovely end-of-term party. Gay came with me and we were listening to Avianca giving a speech. Then, the next minute, in came two hoods with Thompson sub-machine guns and spread it all over the room. Everyone was diving to the ground, Hemmings and the two producers were all splattered with blood and the cake was in bits everywhere. Avianca walked over to the bodies and said, 'You should have read your contract.'

There was a roar of laughter and it had all been a bloody wind-up. They'd lined the cake with explosives, hired two actors to come in with the guns, and they'd rigged David and the producers up with bullet explosions coming out of their bodies. It was amazing! It was just like 'Al Capone come home!' It was brilliant!

It was almost too outrageous actually for people to be frightened. It felt like a film that was released maybe the year or two before, called *The Wild Bunch*. It was a western, where all the shooting was done in slow-motion. You'd see a bullet hit someone, the body would explode and blood pour out and this is how it seemed with the three of them. It was amazing, really good it was. And of course David had been instrumental in the whole thing.

At the end of shooting *The 14* Gay convinced me to go to her dentist in the Edgware Road. Because I'd had fillings in two teeth either side of my front teeth and they were looking a bit manky, she suggested: 'Why don't you go and get them sorted out for when the film comes out next year?' I hated dentists and agreed to do it only if he put me out the whole time. I had about four crowns put on and it ended up costing me a couple of grand: thirty quid a time was just for a shot of Valium to put me out. Still, I thought it was quite flash because I was told that one of his clients was Olivia Newton-John so that made me feel good if nothing else.

And because I'd got plenty of money in the bank after doing *The 14* and I'd passed me test, there was no point now for me Dad to have an expensive car to drive me about in. So I said to him, 'We'll get rid of the Daimler and put it in part-exchange for a BMW, like the one I was driven to work in on *The Pied Piper*, and I'll give you my Toyota!' So that's what I did.

At the end of that year I did *Lift Off* again. 'By popular request...' the *TV Times* enthused. It went on: 'How many times have you heard that? Well, in the case of Jack Wild it's true, for Jack makes his fifth appearance on *Lift Off* – by popular request – singing "Picture of You".'

Singing 'Picture of You', with better teeth and a BMW it should have said!

My other significant acquisitions for that year were two beautiful squirrel monkeys. Perhaps prompted by our Chessington Zoo visit, me and Gay had decided to extend our family.

I hadn't been sure where to find them so I'd looked in *Exchange and Mart* and surprisingly enough found a number for a guy in the East End. This was before the laws had been brought in to protect exotic animals so really anybody who had the money could buy whatever they liked. The first time we went to see the guy, he said that he could get us any animal we wanted. If we wanted a gorilla, he'd get us one. If we wanted a chimp, he'd get us one. If we wanted a lion or a leopard or...

'I just want two squirrel monkeys, please,' I said.

'I've got two in,' he said and took us to see this forlorn pair, who didn't look healthy at all. Now I'm older and have much stronger views about animals I would see that they had obviously been mistreated and that that needed to be addressed, but then I just thought they don't look healthy so I didn't want them.

He called us some time later and eventually we got two beautiful, healthy monkeys: Bilbo, whom we called Billy for short, and Bluebell. I was still living with the whole of my family in The Grove in Isleworth. So the monkeys stayed in a heated shed in Gaynor's parents' house in Esher. We'd got a radiator in there to keep them warm and I'd put my black-and-white TV in there as well. At night, me and Gay would go and sit in with them and watch telly. They'd come and go to sleep on our shoulders and that's how we initially got them used to us.

Chapter 15

I'VE ALWAYS DREAMED ABOUT BEING SHOT, always, as long as I can remember. I don't know why and I can never see who is trying to shoot me. I just keep running, but the buggers won't leave me alone.

'Jack? Jack? Are you listening to me?' It was John Daly.

'Yeah, sorry mate; what were you saying again?'

'We need to have a meeting with Harbottle and Lewis, soon; June Collins is taking us to court.'

'Yeah, right, okay mate,' I said.

I'd not seen Mrs Collins since the night at the Oscars, over three years ago. John had said there was a possibility that she might take us to court, and now she was.

The case from June Collins' point of view was that John Daly and me had illegally broken my contract with Collins Speake Management when John started managing me. Apparently, there had been a separate action made by Mrs Collins against me, but that had been dropped, and now the case hinged on whether John had acted secretly and dishonestly and whether Mrs Collins had a right to claim that SHOWBIZ TYCOON 'PINCHED MY ARTFUL DODGER' as the *Daily Mirror* shouted.

We had several meetings with the solicitors Harbottle and Lewis in London to discuss what was going on, and I suppose that was all slowly getting to me. As soon as we were given a date for the proceedings, me Mum was so worried about me (because I was going to have to go in the witness box as I was a witness for John Daly) that she made me go to the doctors to see if he could give me something to calm me down coming up to the court case. I remember going, only really to shut me Mum up basically.

'My Mum thinks I should take something to stop me worrying about the court case, but I'm not worried,' I said.

He thought for a while.

'So how's your BMW?' the good doctor asked. He had the same one as me.

We talked about our cars for a while, and then he said, 'I'll give you a script for Valium.'

'Haven't you got anything less heavy duty?' I asked.

He gave me some two or five milligram Valium tablets, so I guess he didn't. Me Mum was pleased I'd got them, but I didn't take them. I didn't actually say that to Mum; I'd just got it in my mind that I weren't going to take them anyway. If I wanted to forget about the court case, I'd have a drink.

I didn't know enough about courts to get really worried about it; it was only when we started going that I then thought, Christ, this is serious! This is the High Court with men in funny wigs! It was just like it looked on TV and it was all so overwhelming. And the press were always outside.

I remember going there every day, with Mum and Dad, but not really understanding what was going on and being so bored. The longer it went on before I went in the witness box, the more pissed off I was getting. Naturally I would see June Collins and Barbara Speake every day, though I couldn't, didn't, speak to them. I would see my solicitors and John Daly every day. I would sit and listen to the other side stating their case and try to remember the things they'd said that I thought were completely wrong. If they said something happened and I thought it didn't, I would think, well, I must remember in the witness box to say that they'd got their facts wrong there, because *this* is what happened, and *that* didn't.

Everyone talked about what a valuable product I was and that John had systematically turned me against Mrs Collins; allegedly, from the moment I'd met John, he had been determined to 'acquire [my] services for himself'. The Prosecuting QC went on to say that Mrs Collins had had no experience in negotiating international contracts and had turned to Mr Daly for help. She had shown Mr Daly her contract with me and asked him to become my business manager, and from that moment the counsel stated Mr Daly had 'worked like a beaver and acted secretly and dishonestly behind her back and against her interests'.

It didn't seem like that to me; why were they making John out to look so bad?

The Prosecution went on. He said that: 'Mr Daly had told Mrs Collins to sign some documents which she was told were to do with tax, but after she signed them, they turned out to be an agreement between Jack Wild and the Hemdale company.'

'Why didn't she just bloody read them before she signed them?' I whispered to Dad.

'I dunno son. I just don't understand it,' me Dad said, not for the first time.

The court heard John had offered Mrs Collins £700 for her management contract. She'd refused, and after the Oscar ceremony he left her a message saying, 'You go back to your two-and-sixpenny dancing lessons – that is all you are fit for.'

'It's not nice, but it's not a hanging offence, is it Dad?' I asked.

'I dunno son. I just don't know.'

The Prosecution concluded that: '[Mr Daly] induced the young star to break his agreement with Mrs Collins and consistently and repeatedly worked to turn the boy against her.'

'That's not true, Dad, it weren't like that; John never said anything against Mrs Collins – it weren't like that, Dad,' I said.

Me Dad looked bemused and bewildered.

As I understood it, I'd been under contract to CSM for five years straight off, plus I think it was another minimum of five years to run on top of that. I'd broken it off before the end of the first term, in 1969, and this is now over three years later and I've earned a lot of money since then. Had I still been with them, they would've been getting twenty-five per cent, so they were in theory losing a lot of money during that three-year period. But I'd been told by one of the solicitors that this contract was illegal because you couldn't sign a minor up for that length of time. This didn't come out in the court case. I don't know why, I couldn't understand it.

After about a week of all this my solicitor tried to give me some idea of when he thought I'd be needed for the case and what I had to do then:

'I think probably on Wednesday or Thursday you'll be going into the witness box. We will talk to you first and then you'll be cross-examined by the other side. Now that's where you're going to have to keep your cool and not get excited or annoyed at what they're trying to do. They will try and catch you out, they will try and upset you to make you lose your rag and say something stupid, so you must be ready for that.'

I'd seen June Collins and Barbara Speake go in the dock and had listened to what they had to say. In my opinion, what they had said in their defence and allegations was not a hundred per cent correct, and I felt that it needed to be known what sort of people they were.

Mr Justice O'Connor was in the chair. I was panicking on the day and wore my purple velvet suit for comfort. I was to be in the witness box for about three hours and I've never been so frightened before in my life. I tried to remember what my counsel had said and not get riled. But they did rile me, and I did take the bait, and I did lose my rag, because they would try and get you to say something, not that you didn't want to say, but you'd say it in a way that, had you been calm, you would've explained it properly, and they couldn't twist it round to make it sound as though you were meaning something else.

They asked me questions about my relationship with Mrs Collins, what the school had taught me, and how the agency had helped me build a successful career. Then they tried to find out why I changed my mind. I tried to explain that, as much as I liked Mrs Collins as a person, I'd much prefer to be with a man than a lady. I didn't really have any bad feelings towards Mrs Collins at all, other than that she obviously didn't know enough about the business to earn me as much money as I was capable of earning at that time. For what I would've made with them for the ten years or so that this contract was for, I made in my first year with John Daly!

But they kept making John out to be a kidnapper, taking property that didn't belong to him, and me out to be a nasty person; and it seemed it was alright for them to delve into what character I was and what character John was, but nobody went into what sort of characters June Collins or Barbara Speake were, or what knowledge they had about the industry. Or what they knew about handling a supposed star who's known in every country that has a cinema.

And obviously my wages showed that they were blatantly way out of their depths. Not from any fault of their own: they could only learn by whatever experiences were thrown at them at the time. But that was no good for me! And that wasn't shown in the court at all! Plus the fact that the length of contract in question was totally illegal anyway!

I thought I ought to point some of this out, but I was so nervous, and then angry, that I'm not sure what I said. I think I said that John didn't try to kidnap me, but that I was growing up and wanted things to change. I also said I began to have doubts when, during an interview, I realised that Mrs Collins had kept future plans from me, and I'd learnt that Mrs Collins let me go out cheap if the producers would take some of her other kids as well.

'Well, that's no good for me, is it, yer honour?' I said. 'But John... Mr Daly... never said anything to turn me against Mrs Collins.'

I also said about the Oscar tickets fiasco, I remember saying that; and also how they'd rung me Mum in the middle of the night from Hollywood upsetting her, I said that an' all. I said how, when I lost me rag in LA, they wouldn't speak to me Dad, but got on the phone to me Mum and said, 'This is what your son's done!'

'They spoke to Mum on purpose knowing that she suffered from asthma, and winding her up, to get her upset, for her to speak to me, to try and get me to change my mind,' I said.

I was beginning to lose my cool and hung on to the witness stand for support.

I was fuming at the memory of how they'd upset me Mum and made her have an asthma attack which, in theory, could've killed her. And that wasn't the first time they'd done that. When I needed to get out of a *Junior Showtime*, they'd said to Mum, 'You get on the phone to Jess Yates and you explain, you lie to him and say Jack's not well and get a doctor's certificate!'

I thought I'd better point that out as it hadn't been mentioned in court; but when I tried to mention it, of course I blew a fuse and although I explained it and said what happened, I didn't say it in a necessarily nice way. I didn't swear or eff and blind or anything like that, but I certainly could've said it a lot better had I been calm. And that's what's annoying, 'cos they are so good with their words, these bloody lawyers.

I was shaking with anger when I came out of the witness box. I don't think I've ever been like that before, or after, or since.

The trial went on for a total of three weeks, but after I'd been in the witness box for that afternoon, I didn't go again. The truth hadn't been told, to my mind: well, not enough of it anyway. I think both sides made mistakes certainly. I don't think I was to blame, I don't think they were to blame, I don't think John Daly was to blame. It was just circumstances; and, looking across at Mrs Collins after we'd been so close, it all seemed so unnecessary.

I still saw John as a very positive move forward for me and my career. He'd said from day one that he'd earn me so much more money, and he had. Although with hindsight now, I think he was perhaps just a bigger rogue to be dealing with. Years later, when I tried to work the figures out from my time with Hemdale, I was pretty certain that, although John had made me a lot more money, some of it went missing. But if I hadn't joined with Hemdale I wouldn't have been able to buy a house, I wouldn't have been able to buy cars, I certainly wouldn't have had the *Pufnstuf* contract that I did. Perhaps I earned more and lost more.

As soon as Hemdale found out that we were being taken to court, which they must have known by late '69, they'd said we should keep back twenty-five per cent of all my earnings in a separate account in case the ruling went against us. John had guaranteed me the losses wouldn't be over a certain amount if I would be a witness for him.

'But let's hope we don't lose, mate,' he'd said.

We lost. The judge ruled that John had to pay the costs of the twenty-day case, which were about £25,000; and John was also ordered to account to Mrs Collins the lost commission which was about six grand, but *that* money came out of *my* account so I don't quite know how that was worked out. I remember when we first met John I was determined not to pay two lots of commission and here I was, paying two lots of commission. But worst of all, in his ruling the judge said that I had 'deliberately concocted evidence'. I couldn't believe it: how could he say that I was lying!

They had called me at home with the ruling, where me and Gay were planning a holiday with some friends to go to Ibiza as soon as the case finished.

'We've lost, Gay; they bloody said that I was lying!'

I couldn't believe it; we'd lost the case but I was more annoyed by the fact that this judge had said that I was lying.

'How much is it gonna cost you, Jack?' me mate asked. But I didn't really care about the money.

'If I drop down dead now,' I said, 'I told it as I saw it and remembered it! *I did not lie whatsoever!*'

The next day the papers were full of it.

'The man who "stole" a child star's loyalty came to grief in court yesterday. Mr Daly, managing director of the Hemdale group of Mayfair, had acted in bad faith, the judge said. The judge also lashed Jack Wild, 20, for "deliberately concocting evidence"…'

There it was again! Now *everyone* will think I lied. I was about to throw down the paper when I noticed the date, Friday 13th April 1973. *Friday the 13th!* Bloody perfect, I thought!

When the court case was over, they put a restriction order on me preventing John working for me as he had done: a legal ruling limiting my career. It seemed insane! *And* I was paying lost commission for three years on an illegal contract. I didn't go in for the ruling; I wish I had've done even for my own piece of mind, but I'm sure I'd have blown a fuse!

So, professionally at least, I was on my own. Of course I would get another agent, but it seemed like all of a sudden I had to become an adult with all the responsibility that entailed. Some might say, not before time: after all, it was a business; it may have been a game to me, but it wasn't to them, any of them. I was just a commodity. I didn't really understand that then.

I didn't see Mrs Collins for years after that, but when I did she was as nice as pie. I don't think she, or I, would like to think that she ever actually hated me. Years after *that*, I was doing a daytime telly with Jenny Agutter, and Miss Speake and Mrs Collins were in the audience. Mrs Collins said where I'd gone wrong was not staying under her management, and some other unflattering things. I could've reacted, but I didn't. I was also sad to lose contact with Phil, though if he'd taken *my* Mum to court, I wouldn't have forgiven him either. I stayed in contact with Carole, Phil's sister, and she managed me later; and at social functions Mrs Collins is always very nice. She'd been like a second Mum to me and I suppose that is a complex relationship with ups and downs. I'd like to think we were friends now.

Within the week we went out to Ibiza with Robert Barrett and his future wife Linda to get away from it all. But the 'all' went with us. We arrived at the hotel and the reporters and photographers were there waiting for us. We'd had plenty of photographs taken of me and Gay during the court case: you know, me and Gay going to court, me and Gay leaving court, with shouts of 'How's it going Jack?' and all that bloody crap. The majority of the seriousness of going to court and a lot of the terminology being used went way above my head, so I wasn't really sure how it was 'going'. The only thing I knew and was really interested in was whether or not the truth was told, and if it was then I'd be happy for someone to give an opinion; so I said that.

It had been a horrible, horrible, experience; but I never said that.

And here they all were again, on holiday with us, wanting to take our photographs.

'What are we going to do, Jack?' Gay said as they closed in with their cries of 'Hi Jack, how are you feeling now?' And they sound like they really care and that they're friends, but they don't and they're not.

'What are we going to do, Jack?' Gay asked again.

'Well, we'll have our photographs taken,' I said, but I'd been told not to talk about the trial in case of getting done for libel! So when they asked me about the case I said, 'I'm sorry, I've got no comment to make!' And boy, did I wanna go to town about the judge! But there you are.

After the holiday, we came home to a drizzly day in London, but it was nice to be home.

'Did yer have a good holiday, Jackie?' me Mum asked. She was obviously worried about me.

'We had an alright holiday, Mum, you know; no, it was a good holiday actually,' I said as I tried to remember. I remembered I'd had plenty to drink.

We stayed in the north of the island at Portinaix, a place surrounded by pine forests. We spent a couple of days on the beach and then we'd found these stables that would take you out on horseback into the countryside away from the seaside for a day. You went to a tavern for lunch and trotted back home in the evening. The others were keen to go, I was less so.

'I don't like horse riding,' I said, stating my case clearly.

'Oh, but it will be great fun,' they all said.

'It's alright you lot saying that,' I said, 'but I'm terrified of horses. Alright,' I sighed, 'I'll tell you what, let me have a good drink beforehand and then I'll go. Make sure you only book it for an hour though!' I added.

So I had a good few Bacardi and Cokes, then I got on this horse and I enjoyed it so much I thought I was John Wayne. I didn't have any fear at all. At the end of the hour, I hadn't been kicked and everything was great; so I said, ''Ere, this is a piece of cake, this is. Why don't we book it again, but let's book it for the whole day and we'll go in the country?'

'There you are, mate,' Robert said, 'and you said you couldn't ride!'

'I didn't say I couldn't ride; I know how to ride, I'm just frightened of 'em that's all,' I countered.

So we booked the horses for the following day, which, as I had to have my drinks before we started, meant having Barcardi and Cokes very early in the morning to make sure I was in the right state of mind in time.

The next day we galloped and jumped, and flew over these ditches the size of the Grand Canyon. I was really going for it and didn't fall off once. The only casualty was an expensive Dunhill lighter that I noticed I'd lost at the end of the day. It must've fallen out of my pocket somewhere. I made everyone get off their horses and go back and look for it; and blow me, we found it.

The other thing I remembered was that we hired a car to tour the island. It was a little two-door Fiat, even smaller than a Mini, and we drove it onto the beach and got it stuck. We pushed it and pulled it, but couldn't get it to budge off the bloody beach. Robert was going bananas and we were crying with laughter.

Yeah, it had been a good holiday.

I didn't really talk to John about the court case when I got back, and as I could no longer be represented by Hemdale, John put me in touch with Denis Selinger at Creative Management Associates (later ICM). It was strange to sever connections with Hemdale; David and John were such a big influence on me. I did keep in contact with Melanie who still ran my fan club from their offices. She was great: 'I'll carry on running it for you, Jack, I don't mind,' she'd said.

Still, signing with Denis did seem to be a step up in my career. He'd been in the business donkey's years, was very knowledgeable and looked after everybody who was anybody. He had people like Michael Caine and Peter Sellers on his books and was probably the biggest agent at that time: not only was he known in England, but internationally as well. He was a very jovial man, tubby, and seemed quite old to me; well, he just had so much experience. He had a moustache and a deep velvet voice; he was lovely, and never changed over the years. I introduced Suzi Quatro to him when she wanted an agent; this was after I'd been with Denis, left him, and gone on, but he always remained very, very nice to me.

While I was with him he gave me a script called *Ghost in the Noonday Sun* which was a pirate film that Peter Sellers was doing. I read the script and loved it, but I didn't end up doing it. I found out years later that Peter Sellers said, 'I don't want him in it!' Someone said he didn't want any kind of competition in his film, but I can't imagine he felt that. I'd wanted to do it, but apparently when it was made it sat on the shelf for years and then flopped, so I didn't really miss out.

Although Hemdale weren't acting for me any more I still had work commitments with David, and so in July 1973 me and David went to the Berlin Film Festival where *The 14* was up for an award. We flew from Heathrow to West Berlin and on the flight he introduced me to these Rotring ink pens that I think are used for mapping. They're not really for writing letters, they're more for drawing, and they go from very thin ones to very thick ones. He had a whole set in his attaché case and I said, 'I've gotta have some of those!' I'm not entirely sure why, but within a week I'd got meself a set. In David's company I tried to keep up with him in any way I could. I even tried to match his drinking, so if he had a drink, I'd have one. I'd try to drink for as long as he did, at any sitting; on the plane, waiting for the plane, getting off the plane... but I did try to curb it at home.

At these film festivals they expect you to go for a certain number of days and attend all the showings of these different films. Lots of them either had subtitles or were in a language that I didn't understand so I had no interest in seeing them. You're photographed and interviewed about your latest movie, and if the showing was *your* movie, you get up on stage afterwards and answer questions and all that. David was awarded a Silver Bear for 'outstanding direction of child actors in *The 14*' but was a bit bored in Berlin and said, 'Jack, have you ever been to East Berlin?'

'No, why?' I asked. 'What is there to see, like?'

'Well, I don't know, but it's a Communist country and you can go over there for a day and you don't need a visa or anything. You've just got to take your passport and they'll stamp it and we can go and see how the Communists live!' he said.

I'm game for a laugh so I said, 'Yeah, alright then!'

This was in the days where it was very popular to have velvet suits, and at the time I had three. I had a cherry red velvet suit, a purple velvet suit and a brown velvet suit and they were all handmade by Dougie-the-Stitch. I thought, what should I wear to East Berlin? The purple one had already had an outing at the court case; and, as I didn't know anything about Communist countries, I plumped for the bright red one.

We got a taxi and went through the Wall that divided Berlin at 'Checkpoint Charlie'. The geezer checking the passports gave me a funny look and I thought, what's his game? I didn't say anything as there were soldiers with sub-machine guns. We asked the taxi driver to show us what he thought was interesting and where we were allowed to go, but apparently taxis could only go on one route in East Berlin, so that's where we went.

We were taken first to this big sort of commemorative cemetery for all the Russian soldiers that had died in the war. It was out of the city and there was no one there. It just had loads of gravestones and everyone had the same type of headstone for the grave. It was all in German or Russian or something. I couldn't understand it anyway, apart from the dates.

David said, 'We'll just ask the taxi driver to take us to a bar so we can have a drink.'

'Alright,' I said, and he took us to this bar in some grey street in the city somewhere. I got out of the car and I could see a lot of people and they obviously weren't tourists. It looked like everybody I could see was looking at me. And I looked back at them: a sea of charcoal grey. It was only then that I realised that in comparison I must look like bloody Father Christmas! I'm sure nobody had seen clothes *that bright* before in East Berlin and I felt such a fool, but by then it was too late. There weren't anything I could do. David was wearing just a normal sort of dark-coloured suit and blended in far better than I did.

'I think they're laughing at me 'cos of the colour of me suit!' I said quietly to him.

He grinned at me. 'Do you still want to go into the bar for a drink?' he asked.

'Yeah, well we're here now aren't we,' I said, 'and we aren't not gonna, are we?'

Whether he knew what the outcome of me wearing a red velvet suit would be, I don't know. We went in for a drink and the locals just couldn't believe their eyes.

But to see the actual Wall and what people had to do to escape meant much more to me later when I went to another film festival in Greece and met up with the actress Ingrid Pitt. She was Polish and escaped to the West while the Wall was still up. She told me she went for a walk one night by the River Spree after a performance and when she was challenged by the guards, she dived into the river and swam across to the West. I'd seen the area where she'd had to do it and seen soldiers with sub-machine guns and I thought she was amazing. I said to her, 'Blimey, I saw what the Wall was like and I wouldn't fancy trying to do that in a month of Sundays.'

When David and me got back to West Berlin the easy way, I went out on my own one afternoon and tried to buy a replica gun. I saw lots of guns I liked but I couldn't understand the legality of bringing them home and ended up not getting one as I was too frightened to bring one back. Apart from all that, I must admit I was very bored in Berlin really. I was glad to go home.

David and I stayed in touch and we met occasionally at showbiz parties and went to each other's premieres and that. Work commitments would also bring us together and of course we'd had the premiere of *The 14* in London. It was held at the ABC cinema in Shaftesbury Avenue and for some reason it was decided to release the film in the same week as the new Bond film, *Live and Let Die*. That's suicide for a movie because everybody wants to see the Bond film, but despite the bad planning it got fair reviews. One critic called it 'sincere and well-meaning', another said the family were 'about as endearing as *The Dirty Dozen*'. It played there for a couple of weeks and was never heard of again, although I thought it was a bloody good film because it's a true story. I found out afterwards that police had kept watch at the cinema in case the real-life Reg turned up there. He was wanted by the police for failing to turn up in court to answer charges about a car theft.

At the premiere, aside from me Mum and Dad, there was me Gran and Grandad, Arf, and Gay's mum, grandmother, and sister Lynne. It was the first time I was being photographed with all me new teeth and I felt as though my mouth was an elephant's graveyard; it didn't feel right whatsoever, but it was a lovely night.

Soon after that me, my teeth and Gay went to Hollywood. Marty Krofft wanted me to appear in a concert at the Hollywood Bowl, which I was pleased about, and to do a spot as Dodger, which I wasn't. Marty also asked whether I would like to do an episode of *Sigmund and the Sea Monsters* with Johnny Whitaker.

'Yeah, sure,' I said. 'Will it be alright if I bring my fiancée with me?'

'Yeah, sure,' Marty said, offering us his house.

Christa offered us slightly more when we got to Studio City. She grabbed me to one side and said, 'I hope I've done the right thing here, but I've put you both in the same bedroom.'

'That's fine,' I said.

Well, I was nearly twenty-one.

The next morning I had a meeting with Si Rose, one of the writers of *Sigmund*. The idea for the show had apparently come to Sid Krofft when he was hanging out at the beach one day with Si. Sid saw a clump of seaweed, and said to Si, 'Hey, that looks like it can talk,' and then with a creatively explosive flight of fancy that only Sid seemed capable of, *Sigmund and the Sea Monsters* was born.

I already knew Si from *Pufnstuf* and we sat down and went through the scenes that he'd written for me. He seemed anxious for me to be happy about them, maybe because I was playing myself for the first time and not just a character.

'Is that alright then, Jack?' he asked. I gave him a few suggestions which he readily accepted, which was mad really as this tall, grey-haired man was so very experienced in telly and knew the business inside out: he'd worked with Bob Hope for goodness' sake, so I don't know why he was asking me.

There was one line in the script about a 'lobster thermidor' and I didn't know what that was. So I said to Si, 'What's a thermidor?'

'Oh Jack, that's really funny,' he said, laughing. 'We'll put that in!' I think he thought I was trying to be funny and put in a gag when really I was just being serious. But for whatever reason he thought it was hysterical and he put it in and we shot it.

A lot of the puppeteers from *Pufnstuf* did *Sigmund* as well, and back with Sid and Marty, it was like home from home. It was four years after the *Pufnstuf* series and they were now shooting on video rather than film. That is a completely different ball game as there is more and cheaper stock so it's much less pressurised.

I introduced Gay to everybody that I knew on the set including Johnny Whitaker and we had photographs taken on the set as well. Billy Barty, Joy Campbell, Mario, Felix, Andy, Johnny Silver, Sharon, almost everyone from *Pufnstuf* was working on it. It was great!

As soon as we arrived at Marty's house in Studio City he'd said, 'While you're here, you can use Christa's old Ford Mustang to save you hiring a car.' As this was Gay's first time in America, I wanted to show her as much as possible. So I took her to Disneyland which she enjoyed immensely and, because I was earning a fair amount of money while I was there, I decided to take her to Las Vegas as well. We found out that Elvis was playing that month in the Hilton and I thought it'd be great, because I'd never been to Vegas either, if we went there and saw him live. Marty had asked me and Gay to go with him and Christa for a weekend up at Big Bear, and as it is half way to Vegas we decided to combine the two trips.

Big Bear was the place where we shot the opening sequences of the *Pufnstuf* series and the film. It is about eight thousand feet up in the mountains and it's a beautiful place with a massive lake and surrounded by forests. We went in two cars: Marty took his Roller and we followed them in the red Mustang.

We set off and it was great to be driving this big old American car, although it did break down half way up a mountain and in the middle of nowhere. I remember the road leaving the valley area to start the climb was a very bendy road with a sheer drop on one side. It was quite a scary drive, and half way up it I realised I was losing power. I thought, it's gonna cut out any minute on this hill; I started flashing Marty, but he carried on going. At some point though, he did realise that we weren't following and came back to rescue us, and eventually we arrived at this lovely log cabin Marty had hired in the middle of the woods.

We stayed a couple of nights and showed Gay where we shot the *Pufnstuf* thing, went for meals in the nearby town, and smoked some Hawaiian grass that Marty had brought. He told me it was the best on the market.

'This is the smoothest joint ever! I haven't got a sore throat or feel sick or anything. It's like the smoothest joint ever!' I said, several times.

We'd had marijuana before at Marty's place, and I remember one night we'd all had a few joints and were ravenous. Me and Marty went into the kitchen to start making something to eat and were preparing cheese and tomato sandwiches. I said to Marty, 'Is that tomato going anywhere?' and Marty thought this was hysterical. I've never seen him laugh as much as that.

He went back in to Christa and said, 'Did you hear what he just said to me? He started talking to this tomato and me and said, is it going anywhere? And the tomato is just sat there on its own doing nothing, and he said, is it going anywhere? Where's it gonna go to?'

I was just laughing and I was hungry as well and I was trying to explain to Marty: 'I didn't mean that. I meant, are you using it? Can I use it to make my sandwich with or are you using it?' That's what I meant, but I couldn't stop laughing long enough to speak.

I might have smoked a joint maybe half a dozen times a year if that. I had it really for special occasions, but not something to be used like alcohol was. I was always very wary about it because it was illegal. I thought if I got caught and done, it would go on my record and that'd mean I'd have trouble getting into America, and the Far East, and these were places where I couldn't afford not to be able to get in. But up in the mountains and with friends it didn't seem so bad and it was 'the smoothest joint ever'! I remember the log cabin and warnings of wild animals outside, but the rest is all rather vague.

When we left Big Bear, Marty and Christa went back to Studio City, and me, Gay and the Mustang headed off down the mountain, onto the desert and along into Vegas. Not ever having been to Vegas before, we thought, we don't know what to expect, so we'd better dress up nicely for when we arrive there because we've booked a lovely room. So I'd put on one of my velvet suits to drive the three-hundred-odd miles to Vegas. I must've lost three stone in sweat!

On the way we pulled in at a garage to refuel as the Mustang wasn't feeling so clever either. The temperature gauge was a bit high and when the guy came to fill her up and asked, 'Can I check your car over for you, sir?' I said, 'Can you just check the radiator? It's running a bit hot.'

We left him to it and went and got some cold drinks. We'd already got a couple of bottles of spirits in a carrier bag that Marty had got for us so that we could have drinks whenever we wanted as I was three or four months off my twenty-first. After we've come out of the shop I said, 'Was there anything wrong? Did you fix it?'

And he said, 'Yessir! No problem. A loose pipe, but it's all done. You take care now.'

So I paid him with a tip and off we goes.

When we arrived in Vegas I looked like a drowned rat. Still, on the Strip, everyone was all dressed up heading off to shows or whatever, and so we felt we were dressed right to arrive there in the early evening. We checked in, had a huge meal and then went to see Elvis.

The gig was an amazing spectacle! It was massive and his band was just phenomenal! There must've been fifty members in the band at least. He was phenomenal in the sense that, when he was singing, everything he did was perfection. There was just magic oozing out of him, and you were sent to such a high when he was singing that you didn't want to come down again. After twenty years in the business he knew how to work his audience: how to tease them, bring them up, bring them down, excite them. He knew his job.

But unfortunately, I felt that all that went down the drain when he started to talk. He lacked that charisma when he spoke to the audience. When he started singing again you went back to that high immediately, but he wasn't very good at talking to audiences at all. Then again, I suppose if he'd have been as good at talking to audiences as he was at singing, his name would've been God, not Elvis.

We headed back to LA, and it was so hot in the desert it was ridiculous. The Mustang didn't have any air-conditioning so we had the fan on cold air and the windows up. The windows down made it worse as there was just no air at all going through the desert: it was so, so, dry. We, at least, had shorts on this time, but the Mustang was struggling. We pulled into a gas station, and the mechanic opened the bonnet and found three spanners that the last geezer had forgotten to take out. He removed the extra spanners, checked the car over and we got some more cold drinks.

I noticed there was an ice machine and I said to Gay, 'Should we get some ice to put in our drinks to keep them cool?'

'Alright,' she said.

I put the money in, and I must've pressed the wrong button because just one two-foot cube of ice came out! I thought it was a joke. It was the last thing I expected to come out of this machine, just one giant cube! What good is that to anyone in the middle of the desert? Gay put her feet on it all the way back and at least it kept her cool.

Before we'd left LA, when I'd told Marty we were going to see Elvis, Marty had said, 'Well, we'll arrange for you to meet him, Jack!'

'No thanks,' I'd said, 'I don't want any of that! I'm not interested, thanks.'

I don't know what stopped me from wanting to meet him: professional jealousy, or shy of meeting him; I don't think it was that, but it could have been. Or maybe I couldn't be bothered with the rigmarole; I just don't know. Of course I should have done – it was insane not to – but there you are. We didn't even keep the tickets or the programme, I've no idea why.

Back in LA we started rehearsing for the Hollywood Bowl show, which took about ten days, and they wanted me to do a ten or fifteen-minute spot. At first they said, 'We want you coming on singing "Consider Yourself",' and I thought, I've been there and done that! I was going through a stage in my life where I thought it was a bit naff to sing that five years after *Oliver!* and I said, 'I would really like to try and get away from that.'

In the end they convinced me to just do a bit of it: 'The public would want that if they saw you live on stage. At least one verse and one chorus if nothing else.'

So I was persuaded. I came out dressed as Jimmy with Dr Blinky and the rest for the *Pufnstuf* sequence, and then Pufnstuf gave me a tatty coat and top hat to do my bit as the Dodger singing that song.

Just before going on for the finale I was told that the audience would be coming up on stage at the end; and that really kind of spooked me, because of the amount of people that were there. There were I don't know how many kids at the gig, which was a late afternoon show, but there must have been thousands there. So I thought, well, although this is being filmed for TV, what I'll do is after I've changed into my tux for the finale I'll wander on and just watch out, and if too many people start clambering up on stage and I feel a bit worried I will quietly disappear… which is what I did because it freaked me out. There were so many people there who would have taken care of me, but at the time I was really spooked. It had been a highlight for me, seeing my name outside the Hollywood Bowl: you know, APPEARING TONIGHT – JACK WILD! and here I was slinking off the stage to avoid the crowds.

The show was a success and the next day Marty said, 'You know, you should stay over here, Jack. You shouldn't go back to England, you should stay here!'

'I'd drive you bananas, Marty,' I said.

'I don't mean stay with *me*, but stay here in LA; you would have a big career over here. Think about it, Jack.'

But I didn't even contemplate it, not in the least, because I missed my friends and family. As much as I was enjoying myself, I wouldn't even think about it. I wouldn't entertain it.

'Nah, not interested, thanks mate,' I said.

*

When we got back to England, several papers announced our engagement; and we did a photographic session in Holland Park, in these lovely Victorian gardens. I did interviews as well, of course, but all they really wanted to talk about was *Oliver!* as if this was the only thing I'd ever done. So off I went again…

'I wasn't aware of the importance of the film or the huge impact it would have on my career and my life, and still continues to do so. So I think a lot of parts of his character are my natural, I mean… do you want your wallet back?' I said, pretending to feel for his wallet in my jacket. I don't know when I started doing this in interviews, but it always went down well.

'No, apart from the stealing,' I continued, 'I was very much like him; and for an actor, I mean, how the hell do you first be lucky enough to be cast to play such an incredible character, and how the hell do you keep that standard up? It's impossible! It really is! I mean, time has proven that. But having said all that, I'm not complaining because I have been so, so lucky throughout my life. It was amazing because overall, from the start of the auditions to when we actually finished the movie, it took a whole year and that is something you don't forget easily because of the length of time involved.

'The other thing was, it was relatively compact in comparison with, say, Universal Studios where we did the *Pufnstuf* movie…' I said, vainly trying to move on to something else I'd done.

217

October brought another film festival. This one was the Thessaloniki Film Festival in northern Greece and that's where I met up with Ingrid Pitt who'd just done *The Wicker Man*. She was a big buxom lady, had a great sense of humour, was probably mid-thirties and behaved like a teenager. She was a gas and I liked her enormously. Gay had come out with me and we all got on so well together. We had lots of meals together and kept in contact with Ingrid when we got home; she lived really close in south-west London.

She was one of the main women turning up at the film festival along with Jane Seymour who was there for *Live and Let Die*. I think there was a bit of rivalry between Jane and Ingrid. I thought Jane was a bit of a snob and had the impression she looked down on me at first, or was it just that I looked up to her? After all, she was a Bond girl. It seemed like she couldn't believe her luck in the success she received from the movie. If anything, she seemed embarrassed by it. And she was very skinny.

But we all got on well. Jane brought a girlfriend with her and she was saying to Gay, 'Look how cheap all the furs are here!' and she was going round buying jackets and skirts and waistcoats and everything in fur.

Gay said to me, 'I'm sure that fur isn't good fur at all. I think it could be rabbit. It certainly isn't fox or anything good!' So we didn't buy any fur, but I bought some tiger's-eye worry beads on a sterling silver chain instead.

Fiona Fullerton was also there because she'd just done a film, *Alice in Wonderland*. I don't remember ever speaking to her apart from swearing at her whilst being drunk and throwing dinner plates at her. We'd all gone to this Greek restaurant for a meal and everybody was throwing dinner plates onto the dance floor and I guess mine just got a bit closer to her than the rest.

I think if anything I thought she was showing off dancing and maybe I was jealous of the attention she was getting. She had a protective mother with her who checked any unwanted advances: she checked that the right questions were asked, the right photographs taken and the right caps were doffed. I threw plates at her daughter, but I don't think this unorthodox advance was noted either by the mother or by Fiona herself.

I didn't actually see many films while I was there and it was mainly due to two things: they weren't in English, or weren't interesting enough to get me away from the Metaxa. I'd got quite into drinking brandy after a meal in Greece, and I went out for quite a few meals! Metaxa was a seven-star brandy and really strong. It would've taken a blockbuster to get me away from that!

Chapter 16

SOMEWHERE AROUND 1974 IT STARTED TO COOL DOWN quite a bit work-wise. There were occasional TVs, but the films were only happening once in a blue moon. Up until now, I'd been fortunate enough to always be working and I hadn't really had a lean period for nearly ten years. Not that it was *that* bad: I was still working and earning a living. It was just that, as I was involved with Gay and engaged to her at this stage, I was that much more conscious of trying to get work; I didn't really care what it was, as long as I got it.

Slowly, over the last few years, a whole group of my friends had left the business, or at least weren't getting much work. Bob Bartlett was now working for Avis Rent-A-Car, and my brother was there as well. They led the pilgrimage, and Gay, Tony and Arthur's girlfriend all ended up working there, at some time or other. I think my brother's work had started drying up in 1971. By the time me and him went on the US radio tour he was as near as damn it not doing anything.

At the time I did whatever I could for him. He signed up with Hemdale because of me (which might have been a mixed blessing), and I don't think he'd have got a recording contract if I hadn't already got one. Irrespective of the fact that he had a better singing voice than me, I don't think Arthur would've got one off his own back because he didn't have a unique style to his singing. He sounded very normal whereas I sounded ridiculous; I sang straight from the mush.

He had done quite a lot of work. He did *Z Cars* twice, and each time he did it, in real life he was in trouble with the police: once for not paying on the tube and the other for the motorbike incident. Other tellies were *First Lady*,

Inheritance, City '68 and I think he did six episodes of *Coronation Street*. He played Ronnie Lawson – a new family on the street. *The Last Bus* for the BBC was quite a long job, I remember. He did one show with David Tomlinson called *The Impossible Years*. It toured, then came into London. I remember being very proud of him because it was the first West End show he'd got after having done *Oliver!*. On his last night in London, Grandad Wild died.

I did see *The Impossible Years*, but I didn't see him when he did *Peter Pan* with Wendy Craig on tour. He played one of the kids that flies in it. He used to tell me how painful it was. I think he did a couple of TV ads as well, along with the compulsory ritual humiliation of modelling kids' clothes. I don't know how he felt about having to go into other work outside the business; I never really asked him. I imagine if he'd have been given the choice, he would've preferred to stay in the business, but we never talked about it. Seeing all my friends going out of the business didn't make me think that would happen to me; not at all, not in a month of Sundays I didn't think that.

1974 was also the year that I played football for Dennis Waterman's showbiz team. He was a good friend of Gay's manager, John Foster, and that's how I met him originally. Then a friend of a friend who knew him said that he was short of team members, and so I was invited to go and meet him and then have a game. He used to go to a pub just over Kew Bridge going towards Richmond, and that's where we met for this one match.

Our opponents were the police in Hampton Court; they took their football seriously and Christ, they were dirty bastards. It was a tough game and I didn't actually get on that well with Dennis either. I don't know why. We had sort of similar backgrounds: he'd been successful as a child and then came back with *The Sweeney* as an adult, but I think he drank a lot and so did I. I also think I was starting to use alcohol for something other than socialising – not that I knew that at the time, but when that happens, you have a problem.

I didn't play for him again after that first game.

The next morning, I limped in to Shepperton Studios, mostly from aching muscles more than anything else.

'Good game?' Bob asked as I cautiously lowered myself into the first available chair.

'You should see the state of them,' I replied.

Bob had come up with this idea for what he hoped would be a TV series called *The Studio Kids* with a friend of his called George McKindoe. They had got offices at Shepperton Studios and asked me for my opinion on what they'd written. I think it was initially to see if I knew anyone who might be interested in making this sort of a vehicle. I read it and liked it and said I'd like to be involved in helping to get it going. So I started writing with Bob and George, a Scottish, eccentric, hippy-like guy, with long brown hair with Celtic touches.

We came up with the not so original idea of writing jobs for ourselves and moulding three of the characters into parts for me, Bob and Gay, along with an idea of getting my mate Tony Carpenter involved as the fourth member of the gang. Eventually we got Gay's father Glynne involved as well on the creative side of it and we'd often go down to our offices and throw ideas about.

There was only Bob in the office today.

'I thought you were going skiing soon,' Bob said.

'I am, in Austria,' I replied.

'Well, how are you going to do that when you can't even walk round Shepperton!'

'Oh, don't worry about *these* legs,' I said. 'I'm just wearing these ones in for a friend,' I laughed.

It was fun to be working with Bob again.

The offices at Shepperton were the old production offices of Romulus Films, which was really amazing because during *Oliver!* we'd only ever go there to be given our call sheet for the following day. Now we were running *our* project from these offices. I felt on top of everything now. We'd have lovely lunches in the restaurant where all the superstars had gone for their lunch. When we were doing *Oliver!* we'd go and have our double egg and chips in the commissary, but now we'd gone up in the world. We're in the actual restaurant having a nice fillet steak and a bottle of wine. That was really good – it was great. I really enjoyed the time that we spent there. We must've spent a good four or five months there on and off. We had such big ideas for it all.

We busied ourselves writing and looking for locations of where we could shoot this thing. We'd go here and there, taking Polaroids and saying, 'Oh, that'll look nice!' It seemed that in all the TV series and sitcoms that were on at the time, it was very popular to have an out-of-the-ordinary motor vehicle; and we thought, what can we have for our gang of teenagers? What could they drive about in that'd be different? We'd all agreed that it really needed to be a one-off type car, so everyone had been keeping a lookout.

I'd been driving back from Esher one day, came a completely different way than usual, and I just happened out of the corner of my eye to see a car that was on this garage forecourt for sale. I pulled in and had a look and it was a 1950s *Cadillac hearse!* It was full of chrome at the front, big wings on the back, what looked like oil lamps at the four top corners of the roof and it just looked amazing. They only wanted about a thousand quid for it and I thought, this'll be ideal.

I took the gang to see it and they went just as crazy about it as I did, saying how 'unusual' and 'different' it'd be. I'd wanted to buy it straight away, but Bob was more cautious.

'Well, how close do we think we are to getting the project sold?' he asked.

'But we don't want them to sell the car to someone else,' I said. 'Let's put a deposit down on it and see how we go from there.' We put a hundred quid down and felt very pleased indeed. We also found a lovely cemetery on the A3 down from Roehampton. It was massive and we set a few scenes in there in the first episode. We were hoping to get the money to shoot the first episode, and then sell it to a TV company.

I was enjoying the project so much that I almost didn't want to break off from it to go skiing, but it was all planned and so me and Gay headed off to Seefeld in Austria via the Christmas sales at Lillywhites on Regent Street.

We were going with another couple, Christine (who was a friend of Gay's) and her Turkish boyfriend, Eric. The four of us used to meet a good half a dozen times a year or so, and go to the cinema or out for a meal. We'd often go over to Eric's place to eat as he was a great cook and made lovely lamb kebabs. He was charismatic, always had a smile on his face and always seemed to be more concerned about other people's welfare as opposed to himself. Sadly, we had to be wary when they came over to us as my monkeys couldn't stand him. Billy even attacked him once; but Eric didn't seem to take it seriously at all, and his smile barely dimmed.

We arrived at Seefeld in the afternoon and it was such a picturesque little village, half way up a mountain, that looked almost Tudor in style with its half-timbered houses. The first thing we had to do at the resort was collect our skiing equipment from the local office which was about a quarter of a mile from our hotel. The walk there was alright, but it was a helluva trek on the way back carrying our boots and skis and sticks and all that. We had to be back in town the next day by 9.30 to start our lessons. So the following morning we got all togged up, me in my red and black outfit and Gay in red and yellow, and headed off into the winter wonderland weighed down by all the gear. I don't remember bothering to have a practice in the gear beforehand, and it was a right performance now as we all struggled to stay upright.

When we got to a T-junction where the road to town looped back on itself, I came up with a great idea: 'Look, what's the point of walking a mile along that road, to then go left and then come back on ourselves, when we can actually see the town from here and there's just an open space of snow? Let's walk across and it'll save a helluva lot of time and effort getting to where we wanna go!'

Everyone agreed and we started walking across this gap, but because the snow was very soft, we were disappearing at least a foot into it with every step we took. We'd only got about ten or twenty yards when this woman comes out shouting and screaming. We found out through her broken English that apparently we were in her garden; and it wasn't as though you could say 'silly old cow' and escape quickly, because we were stuck. So we made our apologies and tried to make her understand that we were sorry and that it was a mistake. I think Eric's smile won her over, but we didn't go that way again.

We arrived in town and were then put into classes. None of us had skied before so we were all put into Beginners. Very soon I was face down in the snow, having fallen with the insides of my feet facing the ground and my skis crossed over each other, incapable of moving. I felt so stupid, burst out laughing and couldn't stop. A young girl in the class felt sorry for me and was first to get to me to try and help me get up, but she tried to turn me around as though I was only wearing shoes. 'I can't turn,' I said, 'me legs will snap... Me skis!' I said, between gulps of laughter.

It was an energetic and frustrating day because it seemed that no sooner had you got moving than you were falling over again. At one point, we saw some medics flying down the mountain face, pulling a stretcher, which was amazing as I couldn't even stand up on the flat. But it was very, very enjoyable.

On the second day, at the breakfast table, we met up with a couple from Pontypridd in Wales called Mavis and Derek. Mavis was a very big, lovely lady, and her husband Derek was like six foot six tall and five foot wide. A large, ebullient man who looked like he should run a market stall; and in fact, he did.

We were given a list of all the outings and events that we could attend for the week, and at breakfast we all picked over the events and the croissants and decided what we wanted to do. There might be one event that we hadn't cottoned on to and we'd say, 'Oh, that looks interesting. If you're going, we'll come along as well.'

Our first event was a Toboggan Run. All six of us met at the hotel and a coach sped us away to Tobogganing mountain. We had a jolly time singing along in the coach, and when we got there the guide pointed a couple of thousand feet up and said: 'You see the lights up there? That is where we go to take our toboggans from and then we will be tobogganing all the way down.'

We took the ski-lift to the top of the mountain where they prepared you with instructions and a glass of glühwein. 'The track's been lit by torches all the way down the path you need to take that'll be safe for everybody; just follow the torches and we'll meet you down at the bottom, to get in the coach and go back to Seefeld.'

'That sounds simple enough, doesn't it?' I said. 'Come on Gay!' The first two lads in the party headed off on their separate toboggans, but as me and Gay were quite tiny, we could fit on one and headed off together.

All was well until about a quarter of the way down, where inexplicably all the torches guiding you down had gone out. We drew to a stop to consider what to do. You could actually see where you wanted to go to, but how the hell you got there was down to anyone's guess.

'We could be forever more in this forest, halfway up a bloody mountain,' Derek said.

And me, bright spark, said, 'Look, there it is. That's where we wanna go. Let's just… We've got toboggans, we'll just go down the hill and we'll be there.'

And I think Eric said, 'Yeah, but don't forget what happened the other day in the gardens!'

'It won't be anyone's bloody garden,' I said. 'There aren't any houses up here or anything, it's open land!' I don't think that was quite what he meant, but not wanting to let common sense get in my way I headed off.

'But I can see the torches even though they're not lit, it will be easy to follow the trail,' he protested. 'And the moon is shining on the snow… it's almost like it's not dark at all,' he reasoned.

'Follow me,' I called back as I headed off on our alpine adventure, aiming directly for the lights at the bottom of the mountain.

I was sat at the front, using my feet for steering and braking, and Gay was sat at the back hanging on to me. After a slow start to get the toboggan moving again, we were now hurtling down this hill on our short cut; and I'm thinking, bloody hell! This is getting a bit scary! I've gotta slow it down! And the next minute we hit a dip and we came to a stop, without me doing anything.

'Thank goodness for that!' I said, turning round to Gay to make sure she was alright, but she wasn't there. She'd got off before me and I could see this red and yellow Lillywhites suit walking towards me.

I looked back at our toboggan just in time to see it go. It had been on a slight slope, and flew off on its own down the mountain. All you would see every now and then was where it'd hit a bit of soft snow and loads of snow would fly up in the air, but we never saw where it landed.

We had to walk the rest of the way down the mountain. We could see the coach waiting for us, which was just as well as we wouldn't have known where the hell we were otherwise.

When we got to the bottom we made it out as though we hadn't lost our toboggan at all, and we decided if anyone was going to question us, we'd have said, 'We put it with the rest of them!'

As soon as we got down to the bottom, we went and had a drink at the bar and waited for the rest of the party. I think there were about three or four tobogganers that decided on the short cut with us, and we weren't the only ones that lost our toboggan and had to walk the mile and a half back. 'That's bloody nice, innit?' I said to the assembled company. 'You're a foreigner in their country, they get you pissed, stick you on a toboggan and push you down a bloody mountain!' We all thought it was a great joke.

On the way back to our pretty Tyrolean village, everyone was saying, 'What must've happened to all those torches?' Some people were seriously moaning, but the majority were just laughing about it and saying, 'Well, it's just one of those things. The oil must've run out.'

When we got back to the hotel the two lads who had headed off first owned up to it. They were two guys from London on a lads' holiday, and not blokes you'd want to pick a fight with. I think they recognised me, and one of the lads, Malcolm, said to me, 'We didn't mean any harm by it, mate; how did you go on?'

'Oh, we were fine, mate,' I said. 'We decided to take a short cut!'

Malcolm was quite a case; soon after we'd got back, he bought a baby lion and kept it in a three-bedroom house in north London. But they were lovely geezers and we all got friendly, and Malcolm and his mate joined our holiday gang.

Another night we went to another village, played bowls, drank glühwein and had a contest wearing silly hats. I think I drank rather a lot. I was recognised quite a bit, mainly by the English or maybe a few Germans as well, but it was just part of everyday life. I wasn't being as careful about drinking in public as I would have been at home, but glühwein didn't seem like real drinking: it was just hot wine with a tea bag in it, and anyway I was on holiday. We had a great time.

Back home I threw myself back into work. Apart from *Studio Kids*, the other project that me and Gay's dad had been working on was *Caterpillar Taxis*. Glynne was so good at so many things. He was a singer and musician, he composed and painted and, as I found out, had written a short story about these pixies at the bottom of the garden. He often worked at 'Panah', the family home. It was a lovely house and very big, which was just as well as it still housed my monkeys. I'd gone up to see him in the attic above the music room one day, when he'd told me about this idea he was working on. Not only had he written a story, but he had also painted pictures of the various characters. I thought it was great, and as we talked about it some more I said we should try and do something with it.

'I'll see if we can get finance from John Daly,' I said. 'Let's put something together so we can take these paintings up and let's write a short synopsis to show him as well.'

Glynne agreed, and I called John straight away.

'Is it worth me bringing up all the information for you to have a look at and then you can decide whether you want to get involved or not?' I said.

'Yeah, you do that. Make it next week sometime and arrange a time with Melanie,' John replied. 'How are you keeping, Jack?'

'Yeah, great, thanks mate,' I said.

'Busy?'

'Oh yeah, so so,' I said.

I did think the project was a good one, but I also think one of the main reasons for getting involved was the fact that there wasn't a lot going on for me workwise. I was looking for anything to occupy my mind, I suppose. I knew John's association with Isleworth Studios which was just around the corner from me in The Grove. I thought it could all work out perfectly.

Meanwhile Gay's mum Jean had got friendly with a couple of gay guys, Andrew and John, who were friends of a friend who'd come over on holiday from South Africa. They were in the business over there; one was a cameraman and the other an Assistant Director, so we roped them in to use their expertise. Me and Glynne got the basis of this synopsis together and we thought, well, if we're trying to make a programme, we might as well as give me a part in it. So we roped me in as well.

The film starts with me writing the story of *Caterpillar Taxis*, and we shot it as though it really could exist or might just be going on in my head. We tried to shoot it first of all on Super 8 film, but it was nowhere near good enough to show John Daly; it just gave us ideas about colours. Glynne had built a little set in the loft above the music room, had made the puppets and done the artwork in watercolours, so we took the pictures, puppets and synopsis to John.

'Yeah, I could finance that and it shouldn't cost a lot. You get a budget sorted out and send it to me and I'll arrange for you to shoot it at Isleworth Studios. You can also use a room there for all your sets and the lighting equipment.'

We were well pleased with the result and immediately got onto getting a budget sorted out to send to him. I think we got it to him within a week of the original meeting. He called us and said, 'We'll give you the two and a half grand to shoot a 16mm colour film with sound, between twelve and fifteen minutes long in total.'

We couldn't believe it and thought we'd hit the jackpot. We started a company called Red Plum Productions Limited with me and Glynne as directors of it, and I think Andrew and John had small shares in the company as well.

In high spirits me and Glynne headed off to Isleworth Studios. The studios were built in an old cinema and were used for commercials, photographic sessions, movie interiors and now for *Caterpillar Taxis*! We got to work straight away and made the sets out of plaster, wood, clay and all sorts really. Glynne did most of the painting himself and was very much a perfectionist with that. I helped him make some of the models, and we worked happily alongside of each other.

One time, when I was using an electric saw, our harmony was tested as I went straight through a cable and blacked out part of the building. I did feel a shock, but it wasn't anything too major.

'Jack, you've got to be careful there,' Glynne said. 'You've got to take more time with this. You know you nearly killed yourself there.'

'Sorry about that,' I said.

'Why don't we take a break,' he said.

'Okay mate,' I said, and we stopped to have a pipe in the darkness. Although Glynne smoked cigarettes he also enjoyed smoking a pipe; and because I'd got so friendly with Glynne, I started smoking a pipe as well.

I'd always loved the smell of pipe tobacco because me Grandad Boardman used to smoke a pipe. He smoked the old-fashioned way and cut up his 'twist' tobacco from a block. He'd died at The Grove in 1974 and I missed the smell of his pipe.

As well as working on the sets and models, we had to decide who could do the voices. We were lucky enough to get an actor called John Bird to do the taxi firm owner and Willie Rushton to do practically everyone else. He was so talented he could come up with almost any voice that you wanted. I did a couple of voices, and for the voice of my mother I got me Mum in to shout in a genuine Lancashire accent, 'C'mon Jack, your dinner's ready!' We recorded all the voices at Theatre Projects in Covent Garden and me Mum did her bit really well.

The film begins with me in the lounge at Panah with the inglenook fireplace, thinking and writing the story, then beginning to narrate it as we go into the animation. The story is set in a place called 'Pixie-Beyond-Tweesville'. The pixies live in mushrooms, and an elf called Y. B. Stranded runs the taxi firm. Hot-Rod and Dodger (!) are the caterpillars that will take you wherever you want to go; and Squiggles is a baby caterpillar, born inside a giant water-lily with aspirations of becoming a taxi. Y. B. is henpecked by his wife, his cabbages keep disappearing, and Mr Patch the cabbage seller has a cart pulled by ladybirds. There is a crazy professor who lives in a converted watering-can and is trying to make a rocket; a couple of mad ants; and Boris the Beetle is the villain. He is good at sabotaging everything and just wants to take over the whole world. I thought it was a very cute show.

We did a lot of single-frame shooting. Normal film is shot at twenty-four frames per second; anything below twenty-four would be very quick movements and anything above twenty-four would be in slow motion. The models were made of wood and they weren't that flexible: today, if you were doing single-frame shooting, you'd have them made out of plasticine or something which can bend or be moulded easily. It was very hard to do: twenty-four frames a second, keeping the lighting exactly the same, and just moving the character a little bit each time. It did work out and looked fantastic, but it took so long to do that we tried to cheat by having close-ups of the characters where we just moved them slightly for real. Of course Glynne wrote all the music for the show as well, and we were very pleased with the overall thing. We just didn't get it sold at all.

I think really John was just humouring me, and two grand to him at the time was petty cash. I'm sure he could easily use it as a tax loss and I think he was just helping to keep my mind occupied. Whatever happened nobody was sufficiently interested in it to commission a proper series of it, but it was a nice exercise and a good learning experience.

My other project, *Studio Kids*, was also turning into a learning experience! George McKindoe disappeared one day, and gradually it all seemed to fall apart. It would've been a lovely idea, but we never got anyone to invest any serious money into it. I don't actually think we ever got past the hurdle of getting a finished script, and obviously that would have been a help. But it was such a lot of fun and perhaps just dreaming of impossible things. There was still that hundred quid down on the Cadillac, but we never went back for it. The project just sort of petered out, and by that time nobody was really bothered about the hundred quid, so we left it.

Around March 1975, I was still at The Grove, the house that I'd bought for the whole family to live in together. Since my Grandad had died, it was Gran, Mum and Dad, and Arf who lived with me. All my money was due to come back from Jersey after the five years and I would soon be able to pay off my mortgage. It had been a couple of years since me and Gay had got engaged, and we were starting to talk about getting married and looking round for somewhere to live together.

So I started having talks with me Mum and Dad. I wanted them to find somewhere else to live; I would sell The Grove and buy somewhere to start married life with Gay. There were lots of talks and discussions about it and it caused a lot of upset.

'But we haven't got any money to buy a house with, Jackie,' me Mum said.

Although I'd bought The Grove, they hadn't got much money from the sale of their house when they moved in with me, because it was heavily mortgaged. They'd spent money on furniture and moving costs, because we had so little furniture in the old house anyway and The Grove was a five-bedroom property. They were lucky if they had three or four grand from the sale of their house. Although they were both working, the bottom line was, they were no good at managing money, not large amounts of it anyway. They hadn't taken care of the last few years of good luck and had got used to me looking after them and hadn't saved any money for a rainy day. They were as near as damn it broke and certainly couldn't afford a three-bedroom semi in Hounslow.

I must admit I was surprised they got upset about it, especially after the way I'd shared my money with them and I'd bought everybody cars, looked after Gran and Grandad, and now…

'We're going to need a bit of help, Jackie, because we can't afford it,' me Mum said, cutting across my thoughts.

'I'll have to go and do some figures and come back to you and let you know how much I can give you towards a good deposit for a new house,' I said. 'Don't worry, Mum, we'll get it sorted.'

I had to work out how much I was expecting to come back from Jersey, and how much I owed on the mortgage, and also how much the move to a new house would cost. It took me about a month to gather all the figures, and during that time the atmosphere in the house certainly wasn't as friendly or nice as what it had been. It got to the point where the talking would be down to an absolute minimum.

Within a month I went back to them and said, 'I'm sorry, but this is the maximum amount of money I can give you, seven and a half grand.' This represented half the cost of their new house. They weren't pleased, because inflation in the five years that they'd lived with me meant they now had to more than double the mortgage they'd had, to go back to living in the same sort of house. The atmosphere in The Grove didn't improve. You see, it not only affected me Mum and Dad and Arthur, but it also affected me Gran as well.

And that was the other argument that came about. I wanted everybody to move out and just have it that and me and Gay would live there until it was sold and we'd found a place where we wanted to live. Me Mum had other views. She was always concerned about what the neighbours would think, and what the family would think, so she said, 'Please, will you let Arthur stay with you then, so it won't look as bad if you're having Gay living with you? Arthur was working as a warehouseman at Isleworth Studios, but he wasn't paying his own way. Me Dad said I should take money off him for food, but me Mum didn't think that was right.

I spoke to Gay. 'Look, this is my predicament; I hope you don't mind but, for now, Arthur is gonna live with us.' It wasn't that I minded supporting Arf: I'd supported the whole family since I'd been successful, and it was only going to be until me and Gay got married, I reasoned; but it was for me Mum's sake that I let him stay.

Mum and Dad started looking for a house and soon moved to 704 Hanworth Road with me Gran and the relationship did get easier then. As I'd reluctantly agreed to let Arthur stay, I thought I might as well say to Bob, who worked at the airport nearby, that he could have a bedroom there if he wanted. I then said to Gay, when she agreed to move in, that we might as well bring the monkeys to The Grove because we've got plenty of bedrooms so I'll just give them a bedroom too. I knocked up a makeshift run outside for when it was nice and just left it on the patio to use. So me and Gay moved into the master bedroom, Arthur was in his usual bedroom which was the first one on the left, the monkeys were in the second one, and the third became Bob's.

With not having my parents about, I'd have quite a few parties, quite often. The music would always be loud, it'd all be drink-orientated and The Grove was a great place in which to have a party. As you came into the house you walked into a big oak-panelled hall and four rooms led directly off there. I'd keep all these doors permanently open so people could circulate round the rooms getting what they needed. The L-shaped lounge had the hi-fi and a modest supply of drinks in the globe minibar. The kitchen had the majority of the booze and there was a hatchway into the dining room if you needed drinks in there. If people wanted to play music, or play an instrument, they'd go in the front room because that's where my piano was. If Tony Carp was coming, I'd always tell him to bring his guitar along, so that we could have a sing-song half way through the evening. And parlour games were in the lounge.

One of our favourite games was, if we knew a lot of upper-class people were coming, we'd behave very hippyish and pretend to smoke dope. We'd wait until everyone was three-quarters pissed and the party was in full swing, and then me and Bob would sit in the middle of the lounge on the floor rolling what looked like joints. We'd actually be rolling Old Holborn, but handed them round like joints so people thought they were getting stoned. You'd have all these upper-class idiots losing their posh accents and starting to talk like hippies, saying, 'Hey man, this is really out of sight!' It just sounded ridiculous and me and Bob thought it was hysterical.

Whenever it came time that I'd had enough and wanted to go to bed, which was when I was very drunk, I'd tell everyone, 'You can all piss off now! I'm tired and I want to go to bed!' If they didn't go home quick enough, I'd go and get my Winchester BB rifle and start firing at them. I thought it was just a laugh. I'd fire it at them just to frighten them and get them to go; only in their arms or legs, and it didn't hurt them that much as everyone was so well anaesthetised. I suppose if someone had of complained about it the next day, I'd have felt bad about it; but nobody did, so I didn't.

On this one occasion Tony just wouldn't go home. He was standing by his car and he was still talking in the drive. 'Fuck off! Go home and let me go to bed!' I said, and he just wouldn't. So I fired at him and hit the guitar in his hand. It was a fabulous Eko guitar that I'd actually sold him months earlier. There's still the mark on it even to this day. He was a bit taken aback at first, but he did go home.

He has laughed it off many, many times since and always makes a joke about it, saying, 'Don't get Jack annoyed, because he'll get the guns out and you'd better start running then!'

Another one of our parlour games was the Ouija board; it was very popular in the early seventies. There were loads of people trying to ban them being sold because they thought it was promoting witchcraft, but we were well into that; and, knowing how frightened of the dark Tony is, we decided one weekend that we'd have a séance down in Esher. We chose Glynne's house because it was the oldest and most atmospheric, and we spent the whole day rigging up the room where we were going to have the séance. We planned to have it on the round coffee table right by the inglenook and had written the letters of the alphabet to go all around the outside. In the middle, we'd got 'yes' and 'no' signs and the compulsory crystal wine glass.

We attached fishing line to some dried flowers, placed them in a big vase and stood them in the inglenook fireplace, feeding the wire back to the table. We also rigged up an ornament on the dining room table. We attached wire to the ornament's neck, that led up to the chandelier directly above it, then went along the ceiling to a pulley, and then down from this pulley to one of us below.

We bought bangers and broke them open to get out the gunpowder. We then dug out a candle, filled it with the gunpowder and dripped hot wax back onto it again so that it looked normal. Then we'd have this candle lit and, some time during the night, the candle would explode.

I phoned Chris up and asked, 'Do you think it's going over the top?' We didn't want to upset her, or Tony for that matter. We just wanted to have a bit of fun.

'No, he'll be up for it! He'll like the attention anyway,' she said.

So we spent the whole day setting this room up, and of course we couldn't wait to get him down there.

We got some wine out, some music on, and when it was dark one of us said: 'Right, let's all have a séance!' as though it's a spontaneous sort of thing. As soon as we'd said it, you could see from Tony's body language that he didn't think this was a good idea at all.

'No, no, no,' he said, 'I don't want to get involved in all of that!'

But after about five minutes – 'Oh, don't be a baby! It's just a bit of fun. We're only having a bit of a laugh. It's only like a glorified Ouija board! It's just a lot of nonsense really!' – we convinced him to join in.

So we all sat down, rested our fingers lightly on the crystal glass and began.

'Is anybody there?'

'Is anybody there?'

'If there's somebody there, give us a sign!'

I did most of the talking.

It'd been arranged that I'd be pulling one string and Bob would be pulling another one and Gay would be pulling another, all at different times. We tried to work out a plan of who would do their bit first and then who would follow that and so on.

We were all looking at the centre of the table with our fingers on the wine glass... 'Is there anybody there?'

All of a sudden, Bob pulled his line; there was this rustling of flowers right by where Tony was sat, and he saw it immediately.

'That moved!' he shouted.

'What are you talking about? "*That moved!*" Don't be so silly,' I said. 'Let's get back to it!'

And so I continued: 'Is there anybody there?'

Bob pulled the line again and Tony screamed, 'I'm telling ya, that thing is moving! There's something moving over there!'

The lights were really low and we'd got candles lit. It had been decided that the next thing we wanted to happen was this ornament to float up off the dining table and hover in mid-air.

Tony was very uncomfortable by now and so we were expecting him to move his eyes away from what was happening on the table, look around and just catch this thing out of the corner of his eye that's floating in mid-air. We were all concentrating and I was asking the 'spirit' questions, and the next minute Tony jumps up and shouts 'Fuck me!'

'What's the matter, Toe?' I said.

'Look at that!' he said, pointing at the dining room table where the ornament was in mid-air. 'I don't fucking like this! I don't like this at all,' he said, backing away; but as he gave it a second look, he saw the piece of wire and twigged.

'You bastards!' he said. 'It's a bloody wind-up, isn't it?'

We had a good laugh and a few more drinks and then said, 'We've had our joke now, but being as we've got it out, let's see if this really works or not. Let's have a serious attempt at it.'

'No, I've had enough now! I'm not getting involved in it any more now,' Tony protested. 'I'll just sit and watch you lot do it.'

Tony sat out of it while we tried to get a spirit in the glass.

'If there's anybody there, give us a sign,' I said.

And the candle blew up within three seconds of me saying that. We couldn't have timed it better if we'd have had a button. Because none of us knew when the candle would explode, everybody jumped up frightened. And Tony, I've never seen him as white before. He was obviously terrified and we spent the rest of the night trying to explain it all. When he smelt the gun-powder in the candle he eventually realised it was part of the set-up and that we hadn't been visited by the other world, but his reaction was priceless and it was well worth all the preparation.

Now because terrifying Tony worked so well, we decided that we should terrify him again in The Grove. So we had Tony and Chris come and stay over for the weekend in the bedroom above the garage, which used to be my room when we first moved in. We spent all day doing up their room with wires and concealed laughing bags, but the main event was this fluorescent puppet that I'd brought back from Hollywood when I was doing the *Pufnstuf* movie out there. We rigged that up to start moving and making funny noises.

I can't remember whether we told Chris or not, but I had to tell Arthur because his room was next to theirs and he was a miserable bugger during this time and would come home and want to go to bed. It just saved a lot of aggro if I told him not to take any notice of it. We weren't getting on so well at this time and he only seemed interested in himself and Roberta. Perhaps he was jealous of my success, especially as he had pretty much left the business whereas I was still in it. And he was living in my house. I guess it must have been hard for him, but at the time I just thought he was a miserable git who wouldn't join in the fun.

'You're so bloody childish,' Arf said, and slammed his bedroom door.

'Suit yerself,' I said to myself as I headed downstairs.

We had lots of drinks, played music, laughed a lot and eventually we decided to go to bed. I turned off all the lights and waited almost patiently for Chris and Tony to fall asleep. I then came quietly out of my bedroom and crawled down the corridor to where the wires were at the top of the stairs. The wires went all the way around the landing in a full circle. I started pulling the wires and I could hear Tony in the bedroom waking Chris up.

'Chris! What was that?'

'What are you talking about?' a tired Chris enquired.

'I heard a noise, there's somebody in the house!'

Chris sighed.

For the last hour before we went to bed, we'd started talking about ghost stories so everybody's mind was thinking about that. I told Tony how I could still hear my Grandad, after he had died, shuffling along the corridor: '... and some nights I hear doors opening and closing after I've gone to bed!'

This was actually true. I never went to bed without locking every door downstairs so that if anyone broke in they wouldn't be able to get upstairs. The only way would be if they broke in through the front door and that would make a great noise which would wake me up. If you ever went down to check all of the doors in the middle of the night, and I did this a few times, every time they were locked; and yet if I'd heard a door open and close once, I'd heard it a dozen times.

'Chris, I know I heard something; you don't think its Jack's Grandad coming to speak to me or something, do ya?'

Chris sighed again, and I giggled. Tony must have heard me and came out onto the landing.

'You bastards! Why do you always have to do it to me? You know I don't like the dark!'

We never really tired of terrifying Tony, but he was a busy actor both in London and on tour with *Pump Boys and Dinettes* and *Mutiny*, and then in Canada playing Noah Claypole in *Oliver!*, so there were enforced breaks in our campaign.

Me and Gay were still looking for somewhere to live. I had found one house that I liked and I'd got John Daly to come and have a look at it with me. It was a bungalow in Surbiton, and John advised me what to offer on it and not to go over that figure. I was still with the Midland Bank at the time, but because I hadn't got my money back from Jersey yet, I had to ask for a bridging loan. The bank refused even though they knew I had thirty-or-forty-odd thousand pounds coming back from Jersey within a matter of months. I showed them proof of all that and they still refused to give me the loan.

'Well then, I'd like to close my account please, and I'll go and join another bank!' and I took all my money out, walked round the corner and deposited it into another bank straight away.

The vendors didn't agree to my offer for the bungalow; and because I knew that John knew what he was talking about when it came to business I said, 'Well, bugger it. We'll find somewhere else.'

We did find another house that we liked, a bungalow in a private estate in Kingston Hill, Surrey: a proper 'Millionaires Row'. I'll never forget it. The area of land was about an acre and it was completely walled. The building and walls were Mexican-style and all painted salmon pink. I know that sounds awful-looking, but it was intermingled with black wrought-iron fitments and looked very picturesque.

We imagined ourselves living there and having barbecue parties, and me and Gay would go every week to try and get a better look inside the grounds. We never really succeeded because it was so well hidden away and secure and impossible to get a good view of it. Eventually we thought, it's probably out of our price bracket anyway, and we gave it up as an impossible dream.

'Still, if Carlo gets me a well-paid film...' I said.

'Maybe,' Gay replied.

I wasn't that serious about Carlo getting me a film. I can't remember where I'd met him, but he'd given me his card that said CARLO PONNAMPALAM – FILM DISTRIBUTOR. I think he was originally from Ceylon and had offices in Wardour Street, London which was the heart of the film industry in England.

I think he cottoned on to the fact of how popular I was in the Far East and we came up with the idea of a spoof of James Bond, with me as 003½. The working title was *The Man from D.A.F.T.* To sell the idea, Carlo said he needed to get some photographs of me dressed as the character. It was around the time of the Bond film *The Man with the Golden Gun*, and so we hoped to replicate that style with me trying to look like James Bond in a suit with a Beretta pistol. I think Bob took the photographs for us with my camera and we shot them in the woods of Gay's parents' house in Claygate.

Carlo went round all the film festivals and had meetings with producers and he did try for a long while to get someone interested. When I first went to his offices for a meeting, however, they turned out to be much smaller than I expected and certainly not like a successful film distributor's office should be. I guess I should have known from that meeting about the chances of success, but he still seemed so confident. Perhaps predictably, we never got anyone interested enough to put money into furthering the project and getting a script written. The relationship with Carlo did span well over a year, if not two, of him trying to get me a film. He never did.

Me and Gay had still not found anywhere to live by the summer and so we decided to go on holiday to a campsite at Hurley, near Henley-on-Thames. We went there most summers and often with a crowd of friends. After the second or third time that we'd been there, we found out that there was so much history attached to the place with battles and so on. Apparently, the field right opposite the campsite was the scene of a big battle back in the Civil War or something where hundreds of people had died. We'd also found this lovely pub called 'The Dewdrop Inn' about three or four miles from the campsite, which was an old haunt of Dick Turpin's. I loved all that history.

We'd often go to the pub and this one particular night we were on our way back to the campsite in two cars. I was driving my BMW with Gay, Chris and Tony, and the others were in the car behind me. It was a dark, single-track road with hedges either side; and, as we were coming to this bend a few hundred yards from the entrance to the campsite, we all saw, maybe fifty yards in front, this headless figure walk across the road. I pulled over.

'Did you just see what I just saw?' I said.

'But he looked like he didn't have a head?' Tony said.

'Come on, we've gotta get out and have a look!' I said.

It was pitch black and Tony wouldn't get out of the car. So me, Gay and Chris got out and left Tony in the car. The others got out from the car behind, but it was gone.

The following day in the campsite, this was obviously the topic of conversation; and for the rest of the holiday, each night when we were coming back from the pub, it'd be dark and we'd be slowly creeping through this area to see if we could see this ghost. I was very spooked by it, I must admit.

'I'm glad you lot are so frightened by this,' Tony said.

'Aren't you then?' I said incredulously.

'Course I am, I'm bloody terrified; it just makes a change not to be the only one.'

Every year when we went back we always looked for it, but we never saw it again. Tony remained convinced: 'I know it's haunted round here; I can smell it, a real ghost smell.'

Chapter 17

B ACK AT HOME WE CARRIED ON trying to sell The Grove. It was made that much more difficult to sell if the people coming round weren't that keen on pets. I would double-check that they were into animals, and if they weren't I would leave them in the lounge while I went and got the monkeys out of their bedroom, opened all the windows to try and get the smell out and then get the monkeys in their makeshift run in the garden. I could then take the prospective buyer to show them that particular bedroom, explaining that it would obviously be redecorated fully so that 'you know, it will be all humanly liveable in and decent'.

My Auntie Elsie, love her, had made knickers for the monkeys, with press studs either side and a hole for the tail. But the thing is with monkeys, you can't housetrain them and they really do pee when they feel like it; you'd be changing their nappies every five minutes. So we gave up on the knickers, and instead I put a whole roll of linoleum down covering the carpet in their bedroom. In theory, then, all I needed to do was throw the linoleum out the window into the garden which'd get rid of most of the crap, and then it was only like the stains on the wallpaper. I had a large children's climbing frame in there as well to keep the monkeys entertained.

Some buyers found it hard to see past it all.

At the beginning of the year, I'd been sent a film script for a comedy called *Can You Keep It Up Downstairs?*. They told me they'd got Diana Dors interested, she was discussing it and was probably going to do it and would I like to do it?

I thought it would be lovely to work with Diana again as I'd got to know her and her husband, Alan Lake, quite well on *The Pied Piper*. I read the script

237

and thought it was quite funny, very much like a *Carry On* movie, so I said, 'Yeah! I'm game for that!'

They said they'd like me to grow a moustache for the part. I said, 'If you'd like to delay your movie for twelve months, I might be able to help you there, but other than that I can't, you know.' So they gave me one of those stick-on jobs which was bloody itchy and drove me mad!

We did the main shoot at Knebworth House in Hertfordshire, a gorgeous old place, and some of the interiors afterwards at Elstree. The story was set in a Victorian mansion with all sorts going on between the rich owners, the guests and the servants. Lord Cockshute (pronounced 'Co-Shoot'!) was the head of the household; and I played his son Peregrine, who was looking for an application for his new invention of rubber. There was also Hampton the butler (rhyming slang, 'Hampton Wick'), Lady Bottomley, Rogers the footman and Mellons the gamekeeper. My character was an innocent, shy inventor who doesn't understand that his stepmother is trying to seduce him.

It was about a sixty-mile drive to Knebworth House from The Grove and the thing was, I was really into drinking red wine. I'd started drinking red wine with Peter Bartlett when I was doing *The 14*, and for some crazy reason I now drank gallons of it. Whatever I'd been doing the night before, I never turned up on the film not being able to work, but getting there was a problem. Thankfully I never got stopped because I'd have been well over the limit.

From what I can remember, I tried to be that much more careful not to make illegal moves or go over the speed limit or anything of that nature. Of course you only need one drink to affect your judgement. That millimetre of a second longer to make a decision and it could be the difference between life and death; so in that sense, I was like a human being in a killing machine! Thank God I didn't.

So you see, I remember so little about the filming and what I do remember is all a bit vague.

One thing I puzzled over was this woman who would always be on the set in a dressing gown. She'd go up to the director, Robert Young, and start to take her dressing gown off, without a stitch on underneath, saying, 'Is this the bit? Is this the scene?'

And he kept saying, 'Put your clothes on, love. I'll let you know when we're ready to shoot it!'

And if I saw this once, I saw it a thousand times. I didn't know what this young lady was trying to do, whether she was making a career move or what, but all the time all she was going on about was, 'When can I take my clothes off? Can I take them off now?'

I didn't remember seeing any nude scenes in the script, so I suppose in many ways it should have been an indication to me of what the finished thing would look like; but I was too drunk to put two and two together.

Come the last day of shooting, I'd done my bits by lunchtime, and they said, 'That's it, you're finished now! Are you going to stay for the party?'

I thought it would be madness to go home and then come back at six, so I said, 'Yeah! I might as well stay in the bar!'

I rang home to say I was staying and spoke to Bob.

'Everything all right with you, mate?' I asked.

'Ahhh, you won't believe it,' he said.

Apparently, it had been a nice sunny day and so he'd decided to put the monkeys in the run on the patio. When he was trying to put them back inside, however, Billy took a liking to the drainpipe, jumped on it and started climbing up the building, ending up sat on the top of the roof, on the chimney pot.

Bob said he was going mad and panicking because he didn't know what to do. 'I would've loved to have been a fly on the wall, mate,' I said. I've never, ever, I don't think I've ever, even to this day, seen Bob panic.

'You should have got hold of Bluebell…' I said helpfully after the event, '… 'cos Billy will normally come if you've got hold of her.'

He had grabbed Bluebell, and he'd grabbed some mealworms to try and entice Billy back. Mealworms are live, maggot-type things that you could get in a pet shop. I'd go and buy these things maybe once a week as a treat for the monkeys. I did go into how to breed them myself because they weren't cheap to buy, but it seemed so complicated; plus the fact that I'm not really into little insecty, crawly things. Anyway, with the heady combination of Bluebell and mealworms, Bob eventually managed to coax Billy back down.

I put the phone down and headed off to the bar, still smiling at the thought of Bob panicking. I had lunch to start with, and then carried on drinking.

By mid-afternoon, however, someone was sent to get me: 'We forgot about this one particular close-up that we need from you. Can you go and get dressed and made up so we can shoot it?'

So off I went, got dressed, got the moustache stuck on again and all that business so at least I looked right, but I was well and truly out of it. They wanted a reaction shot to one of the lady servants who had gone underneath the dinner table and started interfering with some of the men. At the time we didn't see what they shot going on underneath, which might have made me suspicious if I'd stopped to think about it. I was meant to be a bit merry in the scene anyway and I certainly do look drunk. They kept the shot in the movie and my eyes are so bloodshot: no acting required.

When it came to the first private screening, we were all having pre-movie drinks in the foyer of this preview theatre, and the producer came up to me and Diana and said, 'We've written the sequel and we'll be sending the scripts out soon, and we'd like you both to consider doing it.'

Well, of course, we said, 'Yeah! No problem! Send us the scripts, we'd love to!'

After they'd moved on, Diana said to me that surely I didn't need to work again with the amount of money I would have got from *Pufnstuf.*

'That was a huge show, wasn't it Jack?' she asked.

'We only actually made seventeen episodes,' I said, 'but I think it's on TV somewhere almost constantly.'

She again expressed surprise that I hadn't been set up for life with the residual payments. I said something like: 'It didn't quite work out that way.'

I was also delighted and surprised to see Willie Rushton at the screening. 'Nice to see you, mate, what are you doing here?' I asked.

I was surprised to learn he was in the film and even more surprised to learn that we had had a scene together. Admittedly, there were other people in the scene as well, but I don't remember seeing him on the set or anything. I don't remember him at all. I don't know what the hell my mind was going through, but I must have been well out of it.

We were eventually led into the screening and were expecting to sit down and have a good laugh watching the film we'd spent three months making. I'd taken Gay and her mother; but, as we watched it, it didn't seem to be the film we'd made at all. It was just not funny and much more fruity than I was expecting it to be. In two hours, nobody laughed at all. It was so, so embarrassing and, at the end, I just wanted to disappear.

We found out later that while we were shooting all the dialogue scenes in and around Knebworth House, there was a second unit based in a flat in Earls Court in London shooting all the extra sexy bits, which they'd presumably pre-sold to Scandinavian countries or to whoever wanted fruity bits! They then slotted these scenes in, which made it look as though all of us had actually taken our clothes off, and all sorts of crazy things were going on. I thought, I hope to God me Mum doesn't see this 'cos I'll be well in trouble.

My agents had been fooled the same as me. We did say we were going to have a word with the union, Equity, but they didn't come up with anything satisfactory. So it was left at that. Needless to say, we never made the sequel. I still feel ashamed of it, even now.

Eventually, I sold The Grove. It had taken about eight months and so now we all had to move out. Gay and the monkeys went back to Esher, Arf went to

Mum and Dad's and I ended up going to live with Bob in Wimbledon, while I looked for the marital home.

Work seemed to be picking up, and as soon as I'd finished the film, I went to see a director at the BBC, Peter Hammond, to talk about playing the part of Charley Hexam in Dickens' *Our Mutual Friend*. I don't remember too much of the first audition, but the second time I went to see him was when I first met Lesley Dunlop and, if I remember correctly, we both read together. She'd gone up to play my sister, we both had similar eyes, and we thought that had a lot to do with it; and there is something in my mind about Peter Hammond saying, 'Do you think you can play brother and sister together?' and I'm sure I said, 'You won't get anyone better.'

The series was seven fifty-minute episodes, so it was a lot of drama and everybody who was any good at acting was in it. Leo McKern and Kathleen Harrison were Mr and Mrs Boffin, Alfie Bass was Silas Wegg (with a wooden leg), Polly James was Jenny Wren, Jane Seymour was Bella, Warren Clarke was a fantastic and powerful Bradley Headstone, John McEnery was John Rokesmith, Ron Lacey was Mr Venus, Andrew Ray was Mortimer Lightwood, Nicholas Jones was Eugene Wrayburn. The list of names went on and on. John Savident, Richard Stilgoe, Brian Wilde, John Collin, Sean Clarke, Patricia Lawrence, Debbie Ash, Ray Mort, and those are only the ones I remember. It was an incredible cast to put it mildly.

I'll never forget seeing David Troughton playing Sloppy in it and sending shivers down my spine; he was incredible! So, so, believable. I could go on but you'll get bored.

We used to rehearse at the old North Acton rehearsal rooms and I'd often bump into Lulu, because she'd be rehearsing for her TV series there, and Dudley Moore, who was a regular guest. We'd stop and say 'hi' so it was all very friendly. We'd all use the same cafeteria at the top of the building, or the local pub that was a hundred yards away on the corner of the one-way system.

During the first few days, when I was rehearsing one scene with the other actors sitting around the sides, the director turned round to everyone and said (and how I didn't strangle him to start with God only knows), 'He's been away from the TV screens for a long while and it'll take him a while to get back into it all!'

I couldn't believe he'd said that about me, *and* that he'd said it in front of everyone *and* that the 'everyone' had been such a distinguished set of great actors. Maybe he thought I'd been cheeky at the audition and I needed to be brought down a peg or two. I wanted to walk out, but I didn't. It did affect our relationship, though, and it did put a damper on things.

Still, being as I'd just finished *Keep It Up*, I'd got a few bob in the bank; and, as I was now doing this TV series that was four months' work with good money, I thought that now would be a good time to get married. So we decided to get married on Valentine's Day 1976.

And, as I had a few bob in the bank, I went to the Motor Show at Earls Court. I'd seen the new Jensen GT and I really fancied it, so I ordered a new one. They only actually made 510 of them; this was from Guy Salmon in Kingston, and I put my BMW in part exchange for it. I couldn't wait to get hold of it. It was the first dark car that I ever bought and it had the opposite way for the gears – it was very odd. It was black with black leather seats and electric windows and a wooden dashboard and it had all the gubbins.

Gay had the hump because I was spending money on a car as opposed to looking for somewhere to live, and that gave me the hump. And really, I thought, what right did she have to tell me how to spend my money? But anyhow, I only had it a month, because no sooner had we gone out in it than we'd break down. We never went on any long trips, only to see the vicar or go to the church to arrange having the banns read, and every time we used this car it'd cut out. I had to get the AA out each time, and we kept taking it back to Guy Salmon, and each time they kept giving me brand-new cars to drive while they tried to sort it out. This happened about two or three times, and in the end I got fed up with it.

'This is ridiculous,' I said. 'It's all very well this "Buy British!", don't buy foreign stuff campaign; I mean, that was one of the main reasons why I decided to buy a Jensen, 'cos it was English. It is a beautiful car, but it just doesn't go enough.'

The last time they had it in the garage, after about three weeks they phoned me up and said, 'We've fixed it now and you can have it back.' They'd found out that it was an automatic switch-off for when you had a crash. So any jolt and the fuel would stop; I was going over a bump in the road and it was thinking it was an accident and cutting the bloody fuel off.

'Nah, I don't want it,' I said. 'I just want my BMW back!' But it was a beautiful, beautiful car.

Once we'd organised the church and the reception in spite of the Jensen, I put a notice up on the board in the rehearsal room saying that I was getting married and everyone was invited to the wedding.

'Congratulations! Down the pub for lunch then,' Warren Clarke said.

We'd rehearse each episode of *Our Mutual Friend* for about two or three weeks and then we'd spend two or three days in the BBC Centre for final rehearsals and to film it. It weren't like a movie where you rehearse and film, rehearse and film; we'd rehearse for two days in the studio and then on the third day, in the evening, we'd film it as though it was live. Straight through, all the way, and you'd have to wait to the end to see if it all worked. It was quite stressful when you were filming it and very rarely were there any retakes.

For each episode there would be anything from six to ten different sets in the studio, of interiors and occasionally exteriors as well, and this one week there was a set for Mr Venus's shop: a preserver of anatomical specimens. The set was right opposite the set I was on and so, when I was rehearsing my scenes, I could look straight across and I'd see all these pickled arms and legs, heads, feet, hands, and animals as well, all pickled. They all looked like genuine articles from medical laboratories. On the first day we got in there to start rehearsing, I said to Warren, 'Look at that, look at that head over there! It's looking at me!' It was a pickled head of this geezer, and one eye was open and one eye was closed; and it seemed I could go to any part of my set and this one eye was still looking at me! It didn't matter where I was, and that just tickled my fancy something rotten! I had to avoid looking in that direction at all costs, because I couldn't keep a straight face. Me and Warren thought that was very funny. Back on our set, I had to say to Warren, 'She's a pert, crooked, little chit!' which was hard to say, especially after a dozen glasses of white wine, and we found that very funny as well.

There was another lovely actor called John Collin who played the part of Riderhood; and, at the time, he was having problems and was hitting the bottle very hard. It was arranged between everyone that he shouldn't be left alone while at work and we took it in turns to sit with him and make sure he wasn't having a crafty snifter while nobody was looking. I thought, poor bugger, he must be feeling really desperate to let himself get like that. I like a drink, sure, but I'll never, ever get like that! It was the most difficult when we got into the BBC TV Centre, trying to keep him out of the Club Bar. I think we succeeded, at least while we were working with him anyway.

Around this time, me and Bob started going to a Cowboy Club. I was always well into cowboys and I think I'd seen this club featured on *Blue Peter* or something. 'Cor, I'd love to go and have a go at that,' I said to Bob. So we went in Bob's car, although it was a helluva long drive, down near Gatwick Airport.

It was held in this field that must've been about five or six acres, and one of these enthusiasts was the farmer who owned the land. He was called John Truder and he just apportioned part of this field with an old shed, and we'd go to sit in there in all weathers. The shed was done up to look like an 1850s building, and we dressed as nineteenth-century cowboys to match. You weren't allowed to wear wristwatches, only pocket watches; no zips, because they hadn't been invented then; and, if you smoked, no filter-tipped cigarettes. We even bought American hand-rolling tobacco that came in a two- or four-ounce cloth bag. I couldn't roll my own cigarettes at the time. I could only roll joints, and those badly, so I had to use a tin machine to make mine, much to the disgust of all the other men.

We'd sit and chat and talk about cowboys and Indians, and play cowboys and Indians (not so much Indians but mainly cowboys) and have quick-draw contests. It was great.

Often we would talk about films and TV with regard to the way cowboys were portrayed and who we thought were the best cowboys ever. I was very proud to say that I actually met John Wayne, the daddy of them all.

There weren't any ladies in the club then, whereas now they do have lady members as well, I gather. We used to eat a lot of bangers and beans along with strong coffee, and I do remember using my bowie knife to open cans of beans. But after eight or nine hours of roughing it, it was nice to come home to the luxuries of the twentieth century.

The great thing I got out of going there was getting rid of stress. I could forget everything that was going on for the time that I was there. It was really amazing how much stress you got rid of by firing a few blanks from a 9mm Colt 45 in a quick-draw firing contest. The power you felt was really very frightening! We also learnt about the real life of cowboys herding cattle from one state to another, and the plight of the American Indians. In lots of ways I learnt quite a bit from my time there and thoroughly enjoyed playing the part.

We once had a professional photographer come and take photographs of us; we were all unshaven and a bit dirty and the guy took a brilliant photograph of us and had it made in sepia. And honest to God you would swear blind that this was a photograph from the 1860s.

Occasionally they would do charity shows and, after I joined, they planned to do a re-enactment of the O.K. Corral at a mental hospital somewhere near Brands Hatch out in the country. Because I was an actor, they said, 'How can we best work this out?'

'All you need to know is two things,' I said. 'One, who is the person that's gonna die before you, 'cos you've gotta keep watching them because you're next; and two, who is the person that's gonna shoot you. So that's quite simple for all individuals just to learn that.'

Or it sounded as though that was the simplest thing; but of course, putting that into practice with a group of men who are hell bent on being 'John Wayne' was a different matter.

I had a blank-firing Winchester that fired 2.2 blanks and an under-lever Greener twelve-bore shotgun, but for the show I was allowed to borrow a Colt 45 (four-and-three-quarter-inch barrel) to put in my holster. I'd had this holster handmade especially for me, because in them days, when your life depended on how quick you were at drawing your gun, you had to make sure that it fitted all your individual requirements. I felt the real deal wearing this, I really, really did. It still fits me now.

So I was allowed to use this Colt 45 but, of course, after you've fired six shots, you've then got to reload it, and if you're reloading, you can't be watching who's been shot. I hadn't taken that into account. And you only need one person to be reloading his gun and not looking for the person who's dying before him, and then it just cocks up everything!

Well, it all went up the creek! Somebody, and we never found out who, didn't die at the right time which buggered everybody up. Then everybody was looking at everybody else saying, well, who's gonna die next? at the same time as firing their guns as though there's no tomorrow and trying to kill everyone. The audience wouldn't have known what the hell was going on! They must've been saying to themselves, is this really what happened at the O.K. Corral, because it's not what it says in the history books at all!

The actual battle in real life only lasted maybe ninety seconds. Our version went on for about twenty minutes. At the end, everybody was moaning and complaining because they'd used up so much ammunition, and in them days blank ammunition cost a fortune. Everyone had blown their week's wages on getting so into this 'oh, he's not dead yet!' *bang! bang! bang!* business. It was a total cock-up and I got the blame: 'You and your bright ideas! Keep 'em to yourself in future!' We never did another one while I was there, but Christ, it wasn't half a lot of fun! And it's amazing the amount of adrenalin that goes and you just lose all track of time. I was just trying to kill everybody with my Colt 45. I lost count of the number of times I had to reload. I must've blown about thirty quid on the ammunition. It was funny, though. It was worth a thousand quid just to be involved in the fiasco!

The other big event I was organising was the upcoming wedding day, or perhaps more accurately Bob was organising. Originally I was going to have either Bob or Tony as my best man, but me Mum felt I should ask Arthur; so to please me Mum, Arf was best man and Bob was head usher. So Bob ended up being responsible for everything, sorting out the reception, the flowers, the band, transport to and from the church, everything really.

Bob also came with me to sort out the suit hire, and he hired his from the same place as well. I don't know where Arthur hired his from, but he did it himself. Arf didn't get on that well with Bob; he never did. I think all that was down to the fact that in lots of ways I treated Bob more like a brother than I did Arthur. I don't know when that started. Anyway, me and Bob went up to the Strand in London to Moss Brothers and as we got kitted out in all the regalia, I said to Bob, 'I'm gonna nick my top hat!' and I did. Actually I just didn't take it back. I said it had been stolen at the reception and they didn't charge me for it.

As soon as I'd had my schedule from the start of doing *Mutual Friend* I checked to see whether or not we could have a honeymoon; and, as it turned out, I could only have a couple of days which was the Saturday, Sunday and Monday. So we planned to have a couple of days in Paris, leaving after the reception on the Saturday and coming back on the Monday.

On the morning of the wedding, I arranged to go and have my hair cut, although I couldn't have a drastic one because of *Mutual Friend*. Bob drove me up to High Street Ken where Jeff, my hairdresser, worked in 'Crimpers'. Jeff had been doing my hair for a good five or six years, and when we got there we all had champagne at ten o'clock in the morning. We'd had quite a bit of champagne the night before as well as I'd had some friends round at Bob's house. There might've been about half a dozen of us and we just had a lot to drink and played poker.

'Come on then, let's get a bit more for the fans,' Jeff joked.

Jeff had told me somewhere along the line that, because I'd done an interview for either *Fab 208* or *Mirabelle* and mentioned that I had my hair done with Jeff at 'Crimpers' in High Street Ken (or Baker Street where it was originally), fans would phone up or write in to the shop and say, 'Could I have some of Jack Wild's hair?' It was one of the trendiest hairdressers around London and very busy, and because they had so many people asking and never enough of my hair, they'd just sweep up anyone's hair as long as it was the same colour as mine and send it off.

'As long as it was dark brown hair, off it went,' Jeff said. 'We used to have a right laugh and say, should we send them some blonde hair and say he had a quick change of mind this weekend and had a blonde rinse!'

Bob picked me up after my appointment to take me back to Mum and Dad's where I'd arranged to meet Arf. 'Thanks mate, see you at the reception,' I called to Jeff as we left. He couldn't come to the actual wedding as he was working. Bob dropped me off and then went on to do whatever jobs he had to do, and me and Arf had a couple of drinks before heading off to the church. Arthur drove me to the church in his car, a red Riley 1300cc four-door, because mine had been parked at the reception place the day before.

As we approached the church I had this mad idea and said to Arf, 'When you drive around, I'm gonna lean out the window and shout out, "I've changed my mind!" and as soon as I've done that, you put your foot down and we'll drive off and leave them for ten or fifteen minutes to let them panic!'

Which is what we did; and at the time, there was Bob, Tony, Robert Barrett and the rest, a good six or eight young men all dressed in Ascot top hats and tails, and because it was a sunny day, they all had their sunglasses on and looked like 'The Jack Wild Mafia'.

It was funny seeing everyone's faces when I shouted out, 'I've changed my mind!' and we went to the next pub for a drink and a couple of fags and then went back. Bob didn't panic and assumed I was just having a laugh, but apparently some of the relations started whispering concerns to each other.

We'd arranged for my favourite photographer, Ron Howard, to take all the photographs for us. He was a balding lovely nutcase whom I'd first met when he took my photos at stage school. Subsequently I'd often bump into him at TV Centre as he used to do the photos for *Top of the Pops*. He was the type of bloke that everyone wanted as their favourite uncle. So whenever I wanted new photographs, I'd call him for a session, and he'd always tell me laddish stories about what he'd been up to and I'd always believe him.

The reception was in Upper Court, a massive mansion in its own grounds with large Georgian pillars at the front. I'd got shares in two restaurants in London, and I'd got the band that used to play in the private club to play for us at the reception. It was a three-piece band, piano, bass and drums, and was very jazz-orientated. As well as the musicians, there was also a discotheque and dancing and speeches, and the reception seemed to fly by.

Glynne said, 'I had Gay, and Lynne and Edwina, and now I have Jack; it's increasing not diminishing, and I'm a bloody big brother to them all, sorry to swear but that's the truth of it. I don't wish them happiness, I *know* they're going to have happiness. Pure and simple as that.'

Me Dad's thoughts were a little less poetic, but I think nonetheless heartfelt. 'I'd like to wish you all the very best, and I hope you have as much happiness as we have, and I hope you come back on Monday and you've enjoyed yourselves.'

We left the reception early and went to get changed because we were leaving at six o'clock to get to Heathrow to catch a 7.30 flight to Charles De Gaulle airport. The venue was like a palace with a garden to match; and, when we came to leave, they'd dug up a rhododendron bush and put it right in the centre of the bonnet of my BMW. They'd also covered it up with tin cans and you name it and it just looked ridiculous.

'Look at it,' I said laughing, 'I only bloody washed it yesterday!'

We said our goodbyes and I looked for me Mum to say goodbye to. She looked worried. 'Are you okay, Mum?' I said.

'Course I am love. Now have a nice weekend, have a nice honeymoon and forget all your worries.' I looked puzzled – what worries did she mean? – but she carried on, 'Have a safe journey, love,' and she kissed me goodbye.

We headed off, as everyone else headed back in to the party. Me and Gay didn't want to overdo being newly-weds – if anything, we were trying to keep it quiet really – but I didn't bother taking the stuff off the car, as we were in a rush to get to the airport and not miss the flight. So I drove it all the way to the airport like that with this bloody rhododendron bush on the front of the car. And of course everyone coming the other way was flashing their lights and horns and pointing.

When we got to the airport I realised what else had been done. If I went to take my passport out, a ton of confetti would fall out. I'd go to take my airline tickets out, and they were full of confetti. If I accidentally dropped the suitcase, confetti goes flying everywhere. Whatever I did, a sea of confetti followed and told everyone I'd just got married. The check-in people were saying, 'Oh, congratulations!' and they'd look at the tickets and say, 'Oh, Paris! You couldn't have picked a better choice for a lovely romantic place!' And me and Gay were going bright red. I was cursing Bob because I didn't expect him to do that, although when I got back I found out that he'd got his mum and dad to nobble my suitcase and my going-away outfits. Mad it was!

At Charles De Gaulle we went to the Avis Rent-A-Car place to pick up a Ford Granada. I'd asked for a big car on purpose, because I knew how mad they drove in Paris. The first time I'd been to Paris for the *Oliver!* premiere, Ron's car had been involved in a smash-up in front of us on the way to a TV interview. I could not believe how they drove and I wanted to be ready.

The one thing I forgot was the whereabouts of the hotel, but we had the name and address so I said to Gay, 'I've got a good idea. We'll hail a cab and tell them that this is the address where we want to go to and we'll follow it and we'll pay him when we get there.'

So of course, in broken English, this French taxi driver says, 'I don't trust you. Woman come with me, you follow me and then you pay me!'

It was dark by now and I thought, if that's the only way, that's what we've gotta do, but I can't lose this guy because I've given the address to Gay and I can't speak French!

So I was going through red lights and all sorts following this geezer because I was terrified of losing him, but I just thought I was driving the same way as they were so it wouldn't really make that much difference.

We made it; and had a lovely weekend. We had a meal up the Eiffel Tower on the Sunday, did a bit of shopping and went to a McDonald's. We couldn't believe there was a McDonald's in Paris. At the time, I'd just recently got an American Express card; and, because I hadn't used it yet, I was being flash and used it for everything while we were there, buying furniture and lamps and all sorts for when we got our own place.

We didn't really see any of the sights there, but I couldn't get over their driving, so I kept saying to Gay, 'C'mon, we'll go out in the car again.' I kept wanting to go around the Arc de Triomphe because it was just like a racetrack. Oh, I was enjoying that, treating it like a go-kart. I had a great time doing that. So that was good and then we came home and I went back to rehearsals.

After the wedding I stopped living at Bob's, and lived in a mixture of Claygate, Esher and Holland Park until we'd found somewhere to live. Holland Park was Gay's mum and dad's business property, a grocer's shop called Holland Dairy. Eventually in May 1976 me and Gay saw a house in Chiswick that we both really liked and made an offer.

The house had a self-contained flat, with a separate entrance on the second floor, which was one of the reasons why I liked the property as I thought it would be great for a regular income. Our part of the house had three bedrooms and two bathrooms which meant we'd have a spare bedroom so Bob would always have his room, and we'd also have a guest bedroom for friends if they stayed. I think the owner wanted £40-41,000 for it and I think we ended up agreeing to £38,500, putting three quarters down and mortgaged the rest for ten grand. I thought the flat rental would pay for that as near as damn it.

As soon as we moved in I wanted to build a massive outdoor run for the monkeys. The walled garden had two sheds at the bottom on either side, and I thought we'd keep one as a normal garden shed and the other one would be for the monkeys. I'd insulate it, get electricity down there and put in a radiator to heat it for them. I got all that organised and planned to build the run onto that. The run ended up being about twelve or fourteen foot square and about twelve foot high. Bob and me built it, cementing in the posts, choosing the best wire to use (chicken wire wasn't strong enough), planting trees, bushes and seeding it with grass. It must've taken a good few months to get that done, but as soon as I could, I brought the monkeys home and that was all lovely.

In the meantime, if ever I saw a book or an article about primates or monkeys as pets, I'd always read them to see if I could learn anything that I didn't already know. This one particular time, I read that because monkeys in captivity get bored quickly, they need something to occupy their minds, especially if they haven't got humans permanently in contact. So they suggested that you buy them a pet! So I thought, okay, fine. What can I get them that is relatively easy to look after? And I thought, I know, I'll buy them a tortoise! I didn't know anything about tortoises, but I went down the pet shop, bought one, took it into the run and they were completely terrified of it. Apparently monkeys get really spooked by tortoises, snakes and anything reptilian. So that was no good, so I put it in the garden.

Then some bright spark suggested getting them a rabbit. That's a good idea, I thought, and I went and bought a hutch and put it in the monkey run next to the shed. I thought, it doesn't matter what breed so I'll just get any one. And again, I didn't know anything about rabbits; and I looked at all the different breeds and saw this Argentinian floppy-eared one, which had ears that dragged on the floor. It just looked an hysterical animal which is why I felt, I want one of them! It turned out to be a female. We introduced it to the monkeys and they thought it was a giggle and would grab hold of its ears, sit on its back and sort of ride it like you would a horse: the ears would be like the reins for a piggyback ride. I don't think the rabbit was over the moon about the idea, but I think on the odd occasion it did sort of join in with the fun as it were.

After about a week of this, I thought, poor bugger! It's on its own! With the monkeys, I bought two for that reason so that one wouldn't be lonely, so I went back to the same shop with my mate McNeil. The pet shop was in the old Shepherd's Bush Market and a friend of McNeil's worked there.

We said to the geezer, 'Look, we don't care what breed it is, we really don't care, but you must make sure it's a female.'

'Okay,' he said, 'I'll show you all the females and you can take your pick and you'll be sorted.'

I saw what I considered to be a normal-looking rabbit with ears that stick up. It was in actual fact an Old English breed, a light charcoal grey, almost silver in colour.

'You're sure this is female, though, ain't ya?'

'Oh, yeah!' he said. 'All them that I pointed out to you now are all female!'

'Okay, we'll take this one then,' I said.

So, that was a bloody mistake because we took it home to introduce it to the other rabbit and to the monkeys, and it all seemed to be going reasonably well until three weeks later we have another eight rabbits! Female indeed! And it just went on from there. I started taking them to pet shops in return for animal food. The worst I ever had at any one time was just under thirty rabbits all in the run with the monkeys. I then had to catch them all to bring them in to the house. I bought a baby's playpen, turned it upside down and had it in my lounge with these rabbits, awaiting their trip to the pet shops. I didn't have anywhere else to put them. It was a mad house. I had piranhas and two dogs as well then.

I do remember one rabbit that we couldn't give to the pet shop. He looked a right sight. He looked exactly like his dad apart from the fact that he had one eye that worked and one eye that didn't, one ear hanging on the ground and the other stuck up in the air. With these looks he wasn't exactly the pick of the bunch, but what he lacked in looks he had in character in abundance. We kept him and called him 'Deadeye'. He lived a short while before being killed by a fox.

Occasionally we would take the monkeys away for the weekend: once to Wales, and another time to see friends in Brighton. We'd take the baby playpen with us in the car; and because you couldn't put a lead on a monkey, only a belt around their stomachs, I'd tie their belts to a stage weight that would normally sit on the back of scenery. Then they could sit in the back window of the car or on the passenger seats, but couldn't come in the front. Not surprisingly, they were always pleased to get back to their run and their increasing number of pets.

Eventually, after about eighteen months, the female rabbit dug her way out and left with her last litter. I'm sure having babies every three weeks can't be a lot of fun. I think she decided, I've had enough of this for a laugh! This is getting outrageous! And she buggered off with her little ones and left the old man behind. He was too stupid to find the hole before I found it and filled it in and he stayed behind as the monkeys' sole pet.

About four months later, we got a letter posted through the letter box, and then another, and another and another, all saying, 'Have you lost a rabbit?' They implied that there were lots of mixed-breed rabbits running around Chiswick, with their ears not hanging on the floor and not stuck up in the air, but somewhere in the middle. It was obvious our lot had gone round breeding and going bananas.

'If you know of anyone who's lost a rabbit that looks similar to this, please contact this number.'

I said to Gay, 'No! We don't answer it! We know nothing!'

*

A couple of months after finishing *Our Mutual Friend* I started on another classic serial, *The Government Inspector*. It was three half-hour episodes chronicling Gogol's story and was produced and directed by Ronald Smedley. Ron had produced and directed loads of things that me and Arf had done over the years including an early telly I did with Bob called *Bonjour Françoise* in 1965.

Ron's version of *The Government Inspector* took Gogol's Russian setting and moved it all to Wales. Robin Nedwell played the man everyone thinks is the Inspector and I played his servant, Osip. Before this, I'd never heard of Nikolai Gogol. I did find out afterwards that Danny Kaye had done a film of it called *Inspector General*. He played all of my part and most of Robin's, but you don't really need two whole actors when you've got Danny Kaye.

I did think Robin was great in our version, and I think we had good chemistry between us. We played the two outsiders who arrive into all this Welsh madness. The wonderful Welsh contingent was headed up by the fantastic Freddie Jones, who played the Mayor. Then Talfryn Thomas was Griffiths the Post, John Clive was Lewis the School and David Pugh was Owen Bowen. The show was so well cast and I thought the interpretation that everybody was doing for their character was fabulous.

We rehearsed it up at the North Acton BBC Rehearsal Rooms where I'd worked on *Our Mutual Friend*, and all the variety shows I'd done over the years. We'd rehearse there for one episode and then spend two days at the BBC Centre: one day for blocking it all, doing like the tech run with the cameras, and then the second day shooting it. Then we'd go back to North Acton to rehearse the next episode, and so on. It took a good six or seven weeks to do it.

At lunchtime, we'd often go to the pub and everybody would be together on the one table. There'd be Nedwell, Freddie Jones with his pint of Guinness, me, all of us would be there; it was such a great company. One lunchtime I was talking to that mad Welsh actor Talfryn Thomas and he was saying about how he had, over the years, got to play very good cameo roles and how this wasn't any different for him. He said, 'Whenever you've got a small part, Jack, you can always steal the scene by reacting to whatever is going on, so always continue acting until you're told otherwise!'

After that, I'd sit and study him in the rehearsals, and I got so much from watching him reacting like mad whether he had dialogue or not. If *I* was doing it before, I did it nowhere near as much as I did after. Before, I was doing it unconsciously, whereas now I knew what I was doing. That was something great to learn at the time; although, blimey, I'd been in the business twelve years by then, but there you are.

During the rehearsals, there'd be contests to see who could do the most absurd Welsh accent! It was hysterical. I think the Welsh accent is probably the worst of my accents, so I didn't try to compete with them, but just cried with laughter as their pitches soared to greater and more death-defying levels.

It was a laugh from day one and such good fun, although I did find my monologue in the first episode difficult. My character, Osip, is laid on his bed moaning about his master, and complaining that he is so hungry, his stomach thinks his throat's been cut. It was the longest spiel I ever had to learn for TV and it took a lot of work getting it right. In *Inspector General*, Danny Kaye did it with a routine involving a horse, a dog and some goldfish!

After the village has mistakenly treated mine and Nedwell's characters as dignitaries, the real Government Inspector and sidekick appear at the end of the show. For these two characters they hired Stratford Johns and Frank Windsor. They were both huge on British TV for playing the detectives Barlow and Watt in the original *Z Cars* so everyone would get the joke. I'd worked with them in a very early episode. They were friends of the producer, Ron Smedley, and they came in just on the last technical rehearsal before we went into the studio. Frank Windsor just had one line to say and Stratford Johns just had to stay very glum. Anyone could have played these parts, but with those two actors, they brought an added weight and class to the final scene.

I was very proud of our *Government Inspector* when it came out and wanted to build upon that. But alongside all this reputable stuff, I kept being sent these sex film scripts that wanted me to take my clothes off. I didn't want to do them, especially after *Keep it Up*, and I felt it went against my image. So in complete contrast, I accepted an offer for a *Jackanory Playhouse*, a kids' show. The BBC used to do a storytelling show for children called *Jackanory* and every month they used to do a 'playhouse' which was a little half-hour drama with a storyline involving kids. I had a lot of time for *Jackanory* because I did one of my first telly jobs for them when I was thirteen.

This current one was called 'Michael' and was about a lad who's having trouble coping with separated parents, a father who's disabled, and is playing truant from school. I was married and twenty-three years old, but still playing a schoolkid. When I was eighteen and still being asked to play children, I was a bit fed up with it. By now, I'd got to the point where I thought, at the end of the day, I'm just an actor; I entertain people by pretending to be someone other than myself. So therefore you shouldn't take it personally, all of this work you're being offered. It's what's available at that particular time and they obviously think that you would be suitable for it. I think what helped a lot was being brought back down to earth by Bing Crosby; I still thought about that time.

The guy who played my dad in it was a bloody good character actor called Michael Robbins. He was lovely and great to work with. He'd had success himself with *On the Buses*, which was one of the most popular sitcoms at the time, but there weren't any of that 'I'm a celebrity' rubbish. I felt like I'd got over all that sort of nonsense by then, too.

My character, Michael, struggled to stay in school, but when he was there, biology and science were his favourite subjects. Mine had been maths, spelling and tap, which may have been why I struggled to remember some of the lines for this one scene set in a biology class. I had to name all of these different frogs and toads in English and Latin. I thought, I'll never be able to learn this! Although, strangely enough, I still remember the natterjack toad now: it somehow stuck in my brain.

I was going over my lines under my breath as I left the house.

'Talking to yourself again, are you Jack?' my neighbour called. His name was Pat Chamberlain; he was a builder, a Jehovah's Witness and had six kids. He was, in fact, the guy who'd sold us our house. He'd then bought next door to rip it all out, redo the inside and then move on to somewhere else, because that's how he made his money.

Equipment for the house would often arrive bright and early at the front, and in the summer, with the windows open, I'd hear Pat shouting for me to get up. 'Jack, I need some help 'ere! Aren't you up yet?' I think he thought, I'm up, everybody should be up! They were a mad family and lots of fun. I'd often argue with him about Jehovah's Witnesses, he'd always be ready to argue back and we both enjoyed it tremendously. We became great mates, and me and Bob started playing squash with him every week.

He also gave us advice on renting out the flat: 'I always used to rent it to nurses from the West Middlesex; you should do the same. I didn't have any trouble with them. As long as you make the contract under a three-month let, you'll be fine,' he added. He gave us copies of contracts that he'd used and all the information he had to make sure that I didn't come unstuck with it. That's the kind of bloke he was.

'So no real work today then, Jack?' he called, indicating the cement mixer.

'Not today mate!' I called back.

I'd been given a certain amount of scenes yesterday to learn for today's location filming. I didn't learn them now as quickly as I did when I was a kid. I gave Pat a wave and went back to naming toads.

We did the location filming for about two weeks and then the studio work. In the studios we did it like a normal telly where we'd learn all the interiors as a show, then record it putting in all the location filming as we went. So in theory, when you recorded it in the studio, it'd be very much like a one-off performance; although you could, at the end, if things went drastically wrong, go back and redo it, because it's not as though you had an audience watching it.

It took the rest of the summer to do and I was reasonably proud of it. I thought it was a good little thing to do for children's telly, and at least me Mum would be able to watch this one.

*

'I always know when the mother-in-law's coming to visit: the mice throw themselves on the traps!' We were having supper with Les Dawson at my private club and I was helpless with laughter. It wasn't actually my club, but I had shares in it.

When I'd had a recording contract with John Velasco, he'd put me in contact with a friend of his who was a top showbiz accountant, Neville Shulman of Shulman and Co in London. Neville advised me that there were shares being sold in these two restaurants and it would be good for my tax purposes to invest. One was a very popular restaurant just off Wigmore Street called 'La Petite Montmartre' and, based on the success of that restaurant, the owners had bought this other place and turned it into a private club called 'Quince'. It was just around the corner from the BBC at Portland Place and Terry Wogan had some shares in it. He used it a lot because it was so close to where he broadcast his BBC radio show from.

Before I put my money in, they showed me around. It was a fabulous place. In the bar, the drinks tables were all backgammon tables and that's where I first learnt to play backgammon. In the kitchens, they had tanks for live trout, crabs and lobsters, and the only time I'd ever seen that before was in the States in places like Boston and Philadelphia, except they had separate tanks for different sorts of lobsters whereas ours were all in together. I invested five grand in the two restaurants and spent a lot of time at the club. I went to La Petite Montmartre a couple of times and the food was fabulous, but I went to the club a lot more. I'd go down there quite often for meetings with John V. There was a three-piece band there that played at our wedding, and I'd go there at least three or four times a month. I attended record launches at the club, and I think one launch might even have been for one of my singles.

One night when I was there with Gay's manager, John Foster, he mentioned that he was very friendly with Les Dawson who was doing a TV series for Thames at Teddington. I'd always been a great fan of his and I said to John, 'Tell him I'll take him out to dinner the next time he's in London 'cos I'd love to meet him.'

The night was arranged and me, Gay, John Foster and Gay's mother went to pick him up from Teddington, where he was staying at a friend's penthouse flat. From the moment I picked him up in the car to drive him to London, it was hysterical. I'm not kidding. I don't know how many times I nearly crashed the car because I was laughing all the way until we got to the restaurant. And I laughed all the time in the restaurant and I laughed all the way back to Teddington. Nearly five hours in all. That may sound as being way over the top, but you just couldn't get enough of him.

We had a lovely meal at Quince and he was so, so, friendly and so down to earth, and at the same time absolutely hysterical. He was just so dry and, without smiling, he'd just say these terrible things about the mother-in-law or whatever it was and I was crying with laughter. I paid for the meal, and it weren't cheap, but it was well worth it because being in his company was just so memorable.

When it came to about 11.30, the restaurant was as near as damn it empty and the band had just finished their last set. They left all their equipment in the middle of the restaurant because they'd be back on the Sunday; we only had live music there at the weekends. We were all on the brandies and coffees, and during the conversation John told Les that Gay was looking for songs to record for a new contract. Les said, 'I started out as a pianist in the clubs, you know. They were hard to please there. I remember one night I finished a set and didn't get any applause, except from a bald bloke over in the corner. "Thanks for clapping, mate," I said. "I wasn't clapping," he said, "I was slapping me head to keep warm." But seriously,' Les went on to Gay, 'I think I've got a song for you that would be ideal. Come over to the piano and I'll play it for you.'

He took her over there and it was a picture. He started playing 'My Way' the way that he did, where he'd play it all out of tune. Gay hadn't twigged at all. She was really into her career and was listening carefully, hoping this was going to be a number one song for her written by the famous Les Dawson... and then he played that! It was priceless it was!

We took him home back to Teddington and he was flirting, but not seriously, with the mother-in-law, and of course she loved all that and it was just great. His timing was amazing. I'll never forget that night. It was incredible really.

I was telling Tony about it the next day. 'When he started playing "My Way", honest to God, Toe, I was crying...' We were up in the flat writing songs. We'd decided we should start writing songs to try and earn some money, and were using the flat before renting it out. We'd always taken guitars to each other's houses to mess about with songs, but this time it was serious. As we were going into the music business, I decided we really needed a music room and planned to create one just off the bar area in the lounge. When I'd first moved into Chiswick I'd said I'd wanted to build my own bar, and with Glynne's design and Bob's help I'd done it. Now it was time for a music room.

The first thing I installed was the piano that I'd bought when I first moved into The Grove. It was very ancient now, but then it was new and had a rhythm box for different drum beats. I'd gone mad when I first moved into The Grove, and bought all this expensive hi-fi for my bedroom, and a Revox two-track professional model tape machine. It was the best reel-to-reel, quarter-inch tape recording machine on the market. I set up the music room with all this kit with microphones, stands, speakers, the whole lot and when it was done, I was so pleased. I said to Toe, 'Now, you can come over to my place and I've got plenty of room and we can be left on our own to record and create songs.'

I weren't that good at learning how to use machines; and the first time we used the room, I don't know how it came about, but as we were recording, we'd got sound coming out of these big speakers in the room and we needed to get a level on this two-track machine. Tony said into the mike, 'one two, one two,' and his voice echoed out of these big speakers like he was talking from Cheddar Gorge; it sounded like he was in a bloody cave three miles deep! When he heard it, he started laughing, which then got me laughing, and the first five minutes on tape was the sound of us both on the floor, crying with laughter.

Once we got going, we found a great way of working together. I'd come up with chord sequences that were interesting, and then I'd leave it to Toe to get a tune from it. I'd never ever come up with the tune. We'd then get together to write the words and do it fifty-fifty. The words were the weakest point of it all really. They were bloody rubbish! And that's putting it very mildly.

One thing that used to annoy me, although I never admitted it, was that Gay would always come up with beautiful tunes. She wouldn't know what the chords were necessarily, but the tunes would be beautiful and her lyrics I thought were so, so, clever. Far cleverer than what me and Tony ever came up with. And so, once or twice, we got her to do some things as well.

On the odd occasion I'd write a song with Gay because I'd play a chord sequence to her and leave her to do the rest and then we'd come out with what I consider to be a classic, but nobody else did. We would record them at home and then take them to publishers. 'Look, this is our latest, what do you think?'

And because, more often than not, it'd either be just a piano and a voice, or guitars and a voice, or on the very, very odd occasion it'd be piano, guitar and a voice, but there wouldn't be any backing vocals on it or anything… so, in answer to our question, the publishers didn't think a lot.

Me and Toe planned to write about a dozen songs and keep attacking the publishers. We went to as many publishers as would allow us time to talk to them (I suppose, at the time, I was still reasonably well known for my acting which maybe helped), and we set up a meeting with Jonathan King, a very well-established producer and entrepreneur. He'd originally been a singer and I'd met him years ago with John Daly. He had his own record label and offices in Denmark Street which was where all the publishers from the sixties were. It's where you'd go to get new songs, and I went there many a time when I had recording deals to listen to new songs with Brian Lane.

'Right mate, how are we gonna play this?' I'd said to Tony before we'd gone in, and we'd worked out what we wanted to get from the meeting and who was going to say what. We were shown into his office by his secretary and I went in and shook his sweaty hand. He had curly brown hair, was medium height, wore big glasses, and was about ten or fifteen years older than me.

'This is Tony Carpenter, my co-writer,' I said, and they shook hands and we sat down. No sooner had I taken a breath to start my selling pitch than Jonathan started talking. And that was it for about seventy-five minutes. Me and Tony didn't get a word in edgeways. We tried many a time but all he was doing was talking, and talking about himself! Our carefully laid plans went out the window. I don't even think we left any songs for him to listen to; the meeting was that much of a joke.

When we got out of the office, Tony just looked at me and burst into laughter. He said, 'I don't bloody believe that!'

'Well, one down, ten to go!' I said and off we went to another meeting.

We'd started writing in June '76 and, come September, we'd written enough songs to arrange to go into Magritte Studios in West Drayton: the first time me and Tony had gone into a recording studio together. By this time Gay had been working with the producer Denis Taylor and we asked Den if he'd produce it for us.

'Yeah, sure, that's great,' he said, 'I'd love to, man,' and he didn't charge us for doing it.

I think Gay and Chris came along with us, and we had a drummer, a bass player, a trumpeter and about six hours to put down three tracks with backing tracks and everything.

Tony has always been a McCartney fanatic and we'd both seen the Bond film *Live and Let Die* and loved the theme tune. I mainly loved it because it had that reggae bit in the middle. We wanted to write a song like that and we did ours as an instrumental. It was insane. It was such a second-hand version of a 007 theme tune, with only a handful of us instead of a sixty-piece orchestra. Tony was playing two different sorts of guitars and I was playing the guitar and piano. After we'd done the instrumental and got Den to mix it, we didn't like the end result. We decided to try and put words to it which made it even worse. It was dreadful.

The second track was called 'I Can See It In Your Eyes'. We thought this was me and Tony's best song that just me and him had written. There was an Australian guy called Jeff Brownrigg who was working doing some demos for Den, and he really liked the song too. He was tall, skinny, blondish and about the same age as us and we all got on well. When he went back to Australia he called Den and asked if he could record it. We'd given the publishing rights to Den in order to get our first release on vinyl. We said we'd allow him to record it as long as he sent us a copy. I'm sure we thought we were Lennon and McCartney! Jeff recorded it as an A-side single in Australia and it was released by Jefferson Records. We thought we'd made it then! He sent us a copy of his version and me and Toe thought ours was better, but we were chuffed that we'd got one of our songs on vinyl at last. I'm sure we weren't ripped off, but we didn't get any money for the record; it could've been Number One for all we knew.

The third was one that Gay was involved in writing called 'Little Girl', which meant we had a ballad, an instrumental and a very pop, danceable song.

With the tapes from this session, me and Tony set about trying to get a publishing deal, and in the autumn of '76 we had a meeting with Chappell. We played them a couple of songs and, amazingly, they not only showed an interest, but they also offered us use of their facilities. They had a room with a piano and a Revox and said we could use it to work on our demos.

We were over the moon. We thought, they must definitely want to sign us up if they're allowing us to use their equipment!

We came out of that meeting into New Bond Street and both looked at each other and said, 'That's it mate! We're millionaires now! We've got a publishing deal!' We were hugging each other, grinning like Cheshire cats and saying, 'Come on, let's go into Chappell now and decide what we're gonna spend our money on!'

Right next door was the Chappell Music Shop and it was massive. It sold top-class instruments and music. I was going to buy a special American bicentenary edition of an Ovation guitar; it was close on a thousand pounds, and Tony was going to buy another Gibson, I think.

As we were about to go in, Tony said, 'That's Wayne Fontana over there!' I knew the name but I couldn't automatically think what any of his hits were, so I said, 'Oh, right, okay.' I think I was more interested in the fact that we were close to getting a publishing deal, and close to buying my Ovation guitar. I thought I could also get a four-track Revox and we could build our own recording studio in my flat in Chiswick now everything's go.

I remember being so much happier about that than I was about the *Pufnstuf* deal or the Capitol record deal or anything. I don't know why but I just thought, yes, this is it! I'm a songwriter now!

So for a few weeks we went into Chappell and worked on demos; and I think it was about the third time we went in when they said, 'Look, you do realise that we're not going to sign you up until you come up with the goods? Because, as of yet, you haven't come up with something that is substantial or good!'

We were a bit deflated.

'Oh, bugger this! Who needs this?' I said to Toe. I thought, why keep travelling up to London to go to work when we could do all this at home. We'd got a piano, and we'd got a Revox two-track machine which is all they were allowing us to use in their offices. So after that we just stopped going in there and just went looking at other ways of trying to get records done. And that was that.

We found out later that, at the same time as we were trying to get a publishing deal with Chappell, Wayne Fontana and Mark Knopfler from Dire Straits had gone there for a publishing deal as well. All three of us were refused. 'So we weren't in bad company if nothing else!' Tony said.

We carried on writing, together and with Gay; and one song that all three of us wrote was 'Love That Rules'. We had it as a B-side on Gay's next single, 'Blue Guitar' which was written by her father, Glynne. It went out on the President Label in the UK. Gay's singles got quite a lot of radio play, if not always sales. A few years back she'd done a cover of 'Da Doo Ron Ron'; it hadn't charted, but we had high hopes of 'Blue Guitar' and 'Love That Rules'.

And that really was our height, I suppose, of being songwriters. Our recording career had spluttered into first gear and then petered out, but we loved every minute of it.

*

Around this time, Elizabeth Taylor and Richard Burton were always in the papers or on telly, and me and Gay had seen Elizabeth photographed with a Lhasa apso under her arm. We'd never seen these dogs before and so we decided that we wanted one. We phoned up the Kennel Club and found out where all the breeders were and ended up going down to somewhere the other side of Brighton to get 'Papillon', and she was cute!

The following year, we decided we should allow her to have one litter. I wanted a second dog, one that I could call my own, and Gay's sister Lynne liked Papillon and wanted one too. So I arranged to take Papillon down and pay a stud fee for a dog to get her pregnant. I got Arthur to come with me; and, on a lovely sunny day, we headed off down the M3 to the south coast, somewhere near Portsmouth, with Papillon.

We got down there a little bit early, so of course me and Arf went to a pub and had something to eat and a few pints. After lunch we went to the breeder's and this woman took us into her lounge, brought a fold-up table into the middle of the room and put a plastic sheet over the top.

'I'll just go and get my dog now. If you want to put Papillon on the table, I'll be right back,' she said. I don't know whether Arthur twigged as to what was about to happen, but he sat down and grabbed hold of a newspaper and started reading it.

I stood by the table with Papillon and the woman comes back in with this gorgeous-looking dog, and she explained what a good pedigree this dog had and that it had won Crufts. As she went to pick her dog up to put it on the table with Papillon she said to me, 'You'll have to excuse me, but I'll have to help my dog!' and I thought, what the hell is she talking about?

I heard a rustling sound and saw out of the corner of my eye Arf concealed by a paper, shaking with laughter.

And of course, she was giving it a rub to get it excited to get it going. I'm not sure Papillon necessarily knew what was going on, but she wasn't particularly pleased about it. It seemed worse to me because a lady was doing it. I was stood within three foot of her, holding Papillon, the dog was on top, and the woman was facing me with her hand underneath rubbing away like hell. I've never been as embarrassed as that, I don't think, ever.

I thought, I can't look while this is going on. If she looks at me, I'm just gonna die! And I'm doing this to a dog that I love. I don't know whether I like this or not. I didn't know what the hell to do. Then I thought, well, you know, we've gotta go through it if we want some more.

After however long it took, I was bright red and must've looked like a plum tomato. I was so pleased when it was finished and she grabbed hold of her dog after it had dismounted and she'd put it on the floor. Arthur had obviously realised that it had finished and I looked at him. I nearly collapsed because there were tears! I'd never ever seen Arthur in tears of laughter before. Even to this day, that was the only time I ever saw him like that. He was bright red as well, but there were tears rolling out of his eyes through laughing and not knowing what to do.

We paid the stud fee which was £75 and she said, 'If it hasn't taken, bring Papillon back down again and we'll give you a second go free!' And I thought, bugger that! I hope it does take 'cos I don't wanna go through that again 'cos that is so bloody embarrassing.

On the way home the car broke down on the M3 about twenty miles from home. The engine just cut out and the fuel gauge was empty. 'But I don't understand that, Arf, 'cos I filled up just before?' We could smell petrol inside the car which wasn't too clever as me and Arf had been smoking constantly. We called Dad and he came out with a gallon of petrol. We put it in the tank and then watched it pour out of the engine while it was stationary. So I put my fag out and called the AA. They fixed the fuel leak and replaced the offending part and we got home a good three or four hours later.

Papillon didn't get pregnant. I think Gay wanted to go back down for a second time. 'Well you can take her,' I said. 'I'm not going through that again.' To avoid entering into further discussions, I headed off down the pub for a swift half with Arf.

Arthur was living not far away in a flat with his girlfriend, Roberta. She used to live in the same estate of these private flats with her mum and dad, until she bought one with Arf. Her father was an actor as well, called George Tovey.

With Arthur having got to know the area first, he'd already got his local – 'The Hole in the Wall' – so it seemed obvious to use that as our local as well, because in theory I could easily walk to it, as it was only maybe a quarter of a mile from the house. I'd always take the car.

It was Tommy Cooper's local as well and that's where I first met him and his wife Gwen, his son Tom and daughter Vicky; and from then on, we used to see a lot of him. Tommy was bloody hysterical. I've only ever seen three people in my life who you'd only need to look at and they'd make you smile and that was Les Dawson, Tommy Cooper and John Cleese. I never met John Cleese, but I saw him riding a bicycle once in Holland Park and I was crying: his legs were the length of the M1.

Tommy was a very shy man really, I think, but he thoroughly enjoyed two hundred per cent entertaining people and would do anything to make people laugh. He'd be in the pub most days if he wasn't working. I'd get him a drink, he'd get me one and we'd chat, just like normal drinking friends. We'd talk about the business or about what was in the press at the moment, and we got quite close, I think. I could sit and listen to him all day. Not only was he funny, but he'd always have magic tricks on him that he'd do.

One day he turned up at the pub with a fiver on a piece of fishing line. There was no one in but us, and he placed the fiver in the middle of the floor and came and sat down. He carried on talking and waited for someone to come in and see it on the floor. Then, as they went to pick it up, whilst looking around to make sure no one was watching, Tommy pressed this button on the line and the five-pound note flew back to his hand. The guy was left in the middle of the pub, kneeling down, trying to find a fiver that wasn't there.

Another time he said to the bloke sitting near us, 'Are these your cigarettes, can I borrow them?' Tommy picked up the pack and opened it. 'Right,' he said, putting the packet of fags on the table and taking out a pack of cards. He gave them a quick shuffle and then said to the guy, 'Give them a shuffle.'

As he did so Tommy said, 'Now do you think it's possible for me to know where any one particular card could be in that pack?'

'Well, no, I don't think so,' said the fall guy, 'but I'll shuffle it again and make sure.'

He then handed the cards back to Tommy and Tommy said, 'Now, pick a card out of the pack, have a look at it and show all the rest but then put it back anywhere in the pack and let me see you do all that.'

So he did that and Tom puts the cards back in the box and into his inside pocket. Then he grabs the packet of cigarettes.

'You're not going to believe this, but the card that you've chosen is in one of these cigarettes in this pack.'

And everyone was aghast with this, because it's amazing: 'How the hell has he done that?'

So Tommy says, 'I want you to tell me what the card was.'

'The six of spades.'

'Right, you've got eighteen cigarettes left in there. I want you to choose just one cigarette because I've already put the card that you've chosen in the cigarette that you are going to pick out.'

So the guy pulls one out and Tommy says, 'Right, I want you to rip the cigarette all the way from the tip to the end. I want you to rip it up very carefully because it's very thin and you will find your card in there.'

'This is amazing,' says the guy and rips up his cigarette. But there's nothing there.

'Well, it worked at home. I can't understand that,' Tommy said. 'Let me pick one!'

So Tommy rips one up in exactly the same way the guy has just done and there's not one in his either. 'That's odd,' Tommy said; 'pick another one!' He did: and when they'd ripped up fifteen of the guy's fags, the guy finally realised that *'It's not a trick at all!'* The ashtray was just full of ripped-up fags! The culprit realised he'd been done completely and he thought it was hysterical. Not many people could do that to someone and be loved for it, but that's what Tommy was like.

He enjoyed a tipple and, at throwing-out time, somebody would always offer to take him home. This one time he said, 'Are you staying until it closes, Jack?'

'Yeah, probably,' I said.

'Well, if you want to come back to my place for something to eat, you can do!' So I drove him home at closing time, no more sober than he was. His wife Gwen had made loads of sandwiches for him, as if she was expecting a dozen people to turn up after the pub. She was always so hospitable whenever I went there, and I was often there.

Over time he got to know how into magic I was, and I'd always be asking him to show me a trick. I could talk to him for evermore about magic and the principles of it all. If you saw him on telly you might think he was bloody useless; but the thing was, he really was an ace magician, at close-up magic as well. He was a big guy with large hands, so for sleight of hand he had plenty of area where he could conceal things, whereas my hands are so small, I couldn't hide an ant let alone anything else.

After sandwiches he showed me his famous ball-and-three-cups routine.

'Ball, cup, cup, ball,' he said as he put one of the cups over the ball. 'Right Jack, watch closely as I move the cups. You can see where the ball is now, and you've got to tell me where it is when I stop.'

I watched closely until he stopped.

'Right, there! It's there!' I said, pointing to the middle cup.

He lifted it up and it weren't there. He lifted up the cup to the right of it and said, 'Here it is,' and put the cup back down.

'Now, watch again and tell me where it is.'

So he did the same again.

'Where is it now?'

I pointed to the left one, he lifted it up and there was nothing there. He lifted the one on the far right and there it was.

'I'll do it slower for you this time.'

This time I was sure there was no way that I could've got it wrong, it was that bloody slow! After about three minutes he said, 'Right, now where is it?' and I knew I was going to be right because it was that slow, I could not have missed it. I pointed and said, 'It's in the middle!'

He lifted it up. 'It's not!' he said, and it weren't! Now I would've sworn on anyone's life that that's where it was.

'Where do you think it is now?' he asked.

So now, I've got a fifty-fifty chance of being right and I said, 'Well, I've got no idea, but I'll take the right one!'

He lifted that up. Nothing!

'It's obvious where it is now, isn't it Jack?'

'Well, yeah,' I said, 'it's under the one on the left!'

Would you believe, he lifted the one on the left and instead of a ball, there was a bloody grapefruit that shouldn't have fitted under the cup in the first place! How the hell did he do that? I was three foot away from him watching closely, and he even cut the grapefruit up to prove that it was real. And that's how good he was! An amazing guy he was!

On 15th April 1984 Tommy Cooper died and I was so, so, gutted. He collapsed on stage doing a live show on telly. We recorded it because we were going out that night, and it weren't until the following morning when we read it in the papers that I thought, I've got it on bloody video. He'd had a heart attack, but apparently at first the audience thought he was just acting.

Me, Arf and little Johnny, the barman from the pub, turned up late to Tommy's funeral. We'd arranged to meet Johnny down the pub: it seemed fitting really. 'Jack, Arthur,' he said as we came in, his habitual smile gone. He looked like an ex-jockey gone to seed. He had small features, enjoyed his booze and was well liked. It was a dreadful day and the sky was black. The ceremony was about 3.30 or a quarter to four in the afternoon, and we stayed in the pub till closing time at 3.00. By the time we left, it must've been quarter past.

We drove to Mortlake and it was pouring: coming down in sheets, it was that bad. None of us had any coats and we had to park such a long way away, we'd have been drenched if we'd have gone. So we just stayed hunched up in the car.

'Well, at least we're here, and he knows we're here, and he'll be laughing because we don't want to get soaked!' someone said.

We should've left earlier, but we thought we had plenty of time. We wanted to get in as much booze as we could, and each time we thought of leaving someone said, 'Let's just have another one.' It was 1984, and the drink was more important.

Chapter 18

WORK WAS STILL COMING IN AND, at the start of 1978, I had two great jobs that ran on from each other and kept me working all year. Alongside my established acting career, I also ran my new fledgling drinking career, although I was hardly aware of its inception as everyone around me seemed to be doing the same. Both careers seemed to be going well: I was certainly enjoying them both.

For the first job, I went up and had a meeting with Bill Kenwright. I thought he was a lovely guy. I'd never met him before but was told that he was an actor originally, and that he appeared in *Coronation Street* for quite a while. He was an ex-actor now and obviously had had a hard life as he wasn't that much older than me but had completely grey hair. He wanted me to do this new rock musical set to tour all over England, called *Big Sin City*, and to play the part of Slic.

It was written by the Heather Brothers and at the time they weren't well known at all. I read the script and thought the part was fabulous. My only concern was that my character was the narrator as well, and after each scene had a big monologue. It might only have been ten lines but it was more than enough for me as I was well into my drinking. But I loved the character, very much a streetwise guy from the East End of London, always ducking and diving; so I said, 'Yeah, I'd love to do it!'

At the first day's rehearsals I met everybody and they were all young. At twenty-five, I think I was one of the eldest in it, apart from this crazy girl called Su Pollard who was a couple of years older than me I think. We got on so, so well but she was insane. She was mad, bubbly, over the top and a real extrovert in everything that she did. She'd got a heart of gold, but her dress sense was hysterical to put it mildly. When I met her she wore sparkly stretch Lycra and a pair of 'Queen Elizabeth II Silver Jubilee' ankle socks; she just looked outrageous.

Deena Payne played 'Dolores', the love interest in it. The plot was a typical scenario of 'boy meets girl, falls in love, loses girl'. Girl gets kidnapped by criminals, boy decides to rescue her, she gets shot, he's heartbroken and we seek revenge and that's it. Deena was ideal in the role. She was bubbly and eager and very well endowed. All the fellas just gawped at them all the time.

'She's not going to drown, is she?' one of the lads said to me. I didn't like to look.

The other male lead was a guy called Michael Price, who was very gentle and shy. He'd started in the business as a singer, but had no experience in acting. He was a very nervous performer, but when he started to sing you saw his professional abilities soar to the surface. He had such a fabulous, powerful voice. He played the part of 'Al', and me and him were the only ones in the cast playing just one part. The others all had great little cameo roles in it.

We also had a fantastic band. There were five of them and they were so, so together. John Heather was the MD of the show, playing piano. He was very tall and quite shy really, but he was a great leader; he was always serious about his music and laid back about everything else. Keith Hayman was the joker of the band and an amazing guitarist. Within a few days of starting rehearsals we all were great mates and it was a great laugh from the start to the finish of that show.

In the last week of rehearsals we were given *Big Sin City* T-shirts to wear for publicity. We all had a group photograph done outside this pub where we rehearsed on the Marylebone Road: the Green Man, I think it was called. I've got a copy of the photo somewhere, and we had another one done inside the pub for the back of the album. The Heather Brothers must've spent a long while setting it all up because they'd already arranged the record deal for a cast album before they'd even cast the show. So, during the month's rehearsals, we also had to record the album. We were rehearsing and recording, and all had a collective sore throat by the time we were ready to open, at the Ashcroft Theatre in Croydon. But it was all tremendous fun.

In the first week, we had a few technical problems: wobbly steps that ran up either side of the stage, six recalcitrant, hand-held mikes and foot-grabbing wires. We'd spent a huge amount of time arranging where the mikes would be at any given time, which works well when you're stood still singing and not so well when you're singing *and* dancing. The mikes and wires refused to remember what they'd rehearsed and tripped us up constantly.

I think we'd also all been drinking a great deal because, on about the third or fourth night after opening, Kenwright came backstage and said to all of us: 'This drinking has got to stop. The quality of the show is going down!' And so we all cut down on our drinking a lot. I found Bill to be kind, bubbly, quietly spoken and bullying – he was all those things when he needed to be. He knew what he wanted and went for it and was as tough and as loveable as old boots. He had a twinkle in his eye that drew you to him, so we fell in line, as much as we could. He was definitely one of the lads and was boyish and cheeky after work, but in work he was everything he needed to be.

And so with firmer steps, obedient mikes and a little less alcohol, we headed off on tour.

I don't really know how much the alcohol was affecting my performance, but the character I was playing allowed me a helluva lot of scope for ad-lib. Not so much within a scene, but when I was talking to the audience: it was like pantomime where as long as you keep to the storyline, anything goes – almost.

After each scene I'd be at one side of the stage for these bits in a spotlight. Quite often you'd go in a new theatre where whoever was on the follow-spots maybe wasn't one hundred per cent on the ball. If I ended up sat there in the dark, I'd wait a few seconds and it'd be obvious that the guy didn't know where I was, so I'd start shouting, 'I'm over here, to your right!' And that would make the audience laugh. Then as soon as he'd get to me, I'd say, 'Right, just follow me yeah?' and go back to the script. That happened quite often really.

Each new theatre brought a new challenge for Mike as well. He had dark, curly hair, was a few inches taller than me and used to wear glasses. He'd take his glasses off for the show, however, and then couldn't see more than a couple of feet in front of him. I'd push and pull him around the stage in every new theatre we played.

But it really was a bloody great show to do, a fantastic show to do. In fact, I'd love to do that again, even in the same way. If we did it exactly as it was then, it'd be great!

Each new theatre would also bring a new set of complimentary tickets for that week's performances. You'd have to check on the first day at the new venue what the comps situation was, and then you could go shopping. If I saw something like a piece of jewellery – an antique gold pendant, say – and they wanted sixty quid for it, I'd say to the shopkeeper, 'I'll tell you what, I'll give you thirty quid, and half a dozen tickets for the show, how about that?'

Whatever towns we were playing, I'd always be asked to do the local TV news programmes. And before this particular one, somewhere down south, we'd all been to a joke shop; we were always playing jokes on each other in the show. We got on so well that we'd often go about together exploring each new town. Anyhow, this one day, we'd been to a joke shop and I'd bought this flower that squirted water. I was really into wearing waistcoats and I'd cover them in badges and all sorts. So I stuck this flower onto my waistcoat and went off to the interview.

The news programme was going fine, but the guy who was interviewing me, I'm sure he was lovely, but he seemed a bit sort of serious and a bit too boring so I thought, I'm gonna squirt him during the interview with my flower! And I did. He seemed very shocked, but obviously knew it was a joke and had to take it all in good part. I didn't actually get to speak to him afterwards, because it was a live show, but I thought it was hysterical. Now, I think that's totally wrong for one professional to do that to another. There's a time and a place for that and live TV isn't one of them. But at the time I thought I was being hysterically funny and, of course, all the cast thought it was great. But if I could go back and change it, I would.

I wasn't really quite together. I'd be drinking most of the day. I wouldn't start until lunchtime, but then we'd stay in the pub for a couple of hours. I wouldn't then drink between that and getting to the theatre, but as soon as I got there I'd have a pint, and I might get someone to get me another for the interval. Then I'd have another couple before we left the theatre to go back to the digs. I'd also take a litre of white wine to the theatre to keep in the dressing room 'in case I have visitors coming to see me afterwards'. It got finished whether I had visitors or not.

I shared a dressing room with Mike, whose wife and kids toured with him in his old Rover 3.5 saloon. I think I got on his wife's nerves because, when I was drinking, I wanted to make sure that everyone else was happy too.

'Go on! Have a drink with us, it won't do you any harm!' I'd say, trying to push people into drinking the same amounts as I was.

'Are you gonna have a drink with us?' I insisted. I imagine I could become quite obnoxious, but you don't see that at the time.

Touring is a funny business. Most of us were away from our friends and family with nothing to do during the day; sharing digs and dressing rooms, days and nights, in more intimate ways than you perhaps would want to, with people you've only just met. It was very different to when I was a kid, when I had people I knew there with me all the time.

As the tour went on, all the girls in the show learnt that I'd get very embarrassed if they started changing costumes in front of me. I would go bright red and wouldn't know where to look. Quite often Su Pollard would call down the corridor, 'Jack, can I just have a word with you about that first scene?' And I'd walk in there and one minute they'd all be fully dressed, and the next they'd whip their tops off to wind me up. I'd go bright red and they'd laugh. I used to swear and scream at Pollard for doing that to me.

She'd often do things like that, and after about the first three weeks I got to know her quite well and would always be wary of her. Once or twice I'd forget and I'd end up in a chemist's shop with her, and she'd start saying loud enough for everyone to hear, 'What sort of Durex should we try tonight darling? Should we try the ribbed ones? They sound great!' And I'd go bright red and wouldn't know what to say for the best.

Or other times she'd shout out to me, 'Will you get me some extra large sanitary towels, darling?' She'd stand there grinning at me, each item of her clothing fighting with the others for attention. And bright red I'd go again. She was a bugger, she was; and, I thought, she was a lovely breath of fresh air. And somehow, in spite of the mad collection of clothes, the overall combination was just delightful.

We'd constantly stay in the same pro digs and, more often than not, we'd stay in pubs because they were the cheapest places, aside from enjoying the booze. We'd have a few drinks at the theatre before going back to our digs and make sure we were back in time for last orders. At one pub in Leeds the landlady would always have sandwiches for us when we'd get back, which was nice, although we were more interested in the drink. One night when I got back, I'd had far too much to drink and went straight off to bed. I was sharing a room with a guy called Roy, who was the ASM; and he had a soft spot for Su. I was asleep in bed, but woke up to a commotion in the room. It was Roy and Su who had finished their drinking and were coming up to bed. Su came in saying she was bursting for the loo and didn't think she'd make it. I opened one eye at this alarming statement and saw her heading for our sink. Oh she can't be, I thought, closing my eye again, wishing I could stop listening as well. Oh she is, I heard: she is. She is weeing in the sink. She is actually weeing in the sink! I pretended to be asleep. But she weren't happy with me being asleep and came and dived on me to wake me up.

'What the hell is going on?' I asked.

'Oooo sorry darling, did I wake you?' she giggled.

One of the other guys in it was a fantastic actor called Nicolas Chagrin. He was a bit of a Romeo, with dark features and dark brown hypnotic eyes. He loved a drink like me, but took his acting seriously; one hundred and ten per cent went into his performance. His brother Julian was a well-known mime artist, and I remember Nick showing me what his brother would do in his act; and he was tremendous, incredible.

We must have been playing in London when I had a party at home in Chiswick. I got drunk and pressured Nick into performing.

'Go on, do it. Show them what your brother used to do!'

And of course when you get asked to do something, and you're socialising, it's the last thing you want to do. And I kept pushing and pushing; and I can't remember actually whether he did it or not, but I do remember getting up the next morning feeling so, so, embarrassed that I'd pushed him into doing that. I can't remember whether I actually apologised to him or not. I hope I did because I really liked Nick, but I'm just not sure.

The alcohol shields you from seeing all these things at the time, then sobriety removes that protection and wants to show you all your indiscretions all at once. A collection of things you wish you hadn't done: well, who wants to see that? So bit by bit, over time, sobriety became a harder and harder thing to do.

The Heather Brothers were constantly trying to write better songs to put them in the show as we were doing it. Towards the end of the run when we were playing the Roundhouse in Camden, we'd got a new choreographer in and we'd got this new song in the show that none of us liked. We had a big sort of hoo-ha about it. Kenwright came with his girlfriend, Anoushka Hempel, an actress/property-tycoon lady, to sort it out. We said, 'This is outrageous, asking us to learn a new song in a matter of forty-eight hours and then just bang it in, especially when we're playing so close to London. It's another thing if we're playing in Scarborough or somewhere where nobody is gonna see it and we can work it in.'

He listened, but we still ended up doing it; and eventually, after not very long, it got taken out again.

He then collared us at the end of the week at the Roundhouse and said, 'Look, we've lost so much money on the tour so far, we're going to have to give you two weeks' notice for this; but we do have other dates for later on in the year. You can either have two weeks' notice now, or we can continue doing it and, when the money runs out, that'll be the end of it. We'll just have to pack up. Which would you prefer to do?'

I thought that was very fair. I've never experienced that before or since.

So we all thought, we might as well as do our best for two weeks and then call it a day, and hope we can all get back together to finish the tour whenever. And that's what we did: we played for two weeks and then stopped; and it did start up again, but by then I was filming for the BBC so I couldn't do it. Everyone else went back in it, and I did go and see the show a couple of times with the new guy in it who'd taken over from me. He was from the TV series *The Fenn Street Gang* and played it completely different from the way I did it.

When I went to see it in Birmingham, I took Arthur, Roberta and Gay with me and we drove up in Bob's old Triumph 2000 automatic. I still thought it was a great show and it was lovely to see everyone again. On our way home, I got pulled in by the police on the M1: not for the way I was driving, but for a spot check because it was an old car. We were drinking a bottle of wine in the car; and I don't know what the laws are over here, but in the States it's illegal to have an open bottle of alcohol in your car if you're driving. So I was panicking and said to everybody, 'Hide the glasses and the bottle of wine!'

The policeman asked a few questions, and I think he might have recognised me. I guess he didn't smell any alcohol on my breath because he waved us on our way and I got away with it.

I'd decided to get rid of my BMW because I'd had a crash at the Ashcroft Theatre at the start of the tour. This woman pulled straight out onto the roundabout and I'd just nudged her. I thought, I ain't done any damage and I can't be bothered to stop, and had carried on. After we'd finished the week at Croydon, we then went off touring and Kenwright hired a coach to take us from one venue to the next, so of course I'd left my car at Chiswick. Anyhow, the other driver had obviously got my numberplate and reported it to the police because I didn't stop to exchange particulars. I got done and got two endorsements on me licence for failing to stop. Because of that, and because I'd got the TV show, I thought it's time to change my car now.

I remembered, in the States, Pat Davis had had two cars: a Buick Riviera which was fabulous, and also a Datsun 260Z sports car. He took me driving in the Datsun when he used to take me go-karting, and I'd said to him, 'When I can drive, I'm definitely gonna have one of these cars!' And so I finally got one. It was a fantastic car, really nice. A big, long bonnet and a two-seater hatchback: fantastic!

I drove it to work on the first day of rehearsals for the BBC's *Everyday Maths*. Stopping as I got out to admire the big Wolfrace wheels, I caught sight of myself in the car window. My hair was quite long now. I had a flat cap on, dark sunglasses, jeans, a white jacket and saddle bags that I carried my script in, slung over my shoulder. When I got to the rehearsal rooms, I was introduced to Arthur English who was wearing a greyish two-piece suit, a shirt and a tie. We were quite a contrast. He told me later, 'I took one look at you and I thought, blimey, I've got a right one here;' but strangely we clicked from the word go.

Arthur was playing my grandfather, Sam Lucas, a man who has 'retired' himself early, with various 'illnesses' which only materialise when anyone suggests work. My character, Mike, hasn't had a regular job since leaving school, and both men rely on Gwen, Mike's mum/Sam's daughter. It was a schools programme which followed these two men when they are left on their own as they negotiate for the first time the world of shopping, rents, measurement, timetables, percentages – the world of 'Everyday Maths'!

'Can she leave the two laziest men in Watford to fend for themselves?' the *Radio Times* asked. We spent fourteen episodes finding out.

Andrew Morgan, the director, had the creative idea of me and Arthur behaving like Laurel and Hardy with Arthur as Oliver and me as Stan. I loved the idea as I thought they were hysterical. Arthur had started in the business as a stand-up comedian in variety and was brilliant at that comedic, physical style of acting. I thought he was a wonderful man, really, really great. He was one of the old school and I learnt a helluva lot of comedy timing from him; his timing I thought was perfect. I remember in one scene he indicated to the television to hold on while he answered the door. He was so funny and was always throwing things in like that.

The producer, David Roseveare, was an ex-headmaster of a proper school. He knew all about the School Authority and was concerned to make sure we got everything right. It was not long after decimalisation in Britain and he explained that there'd be lots of over-the-shoulder shots showing us adding up or taking away and so on. I used to naturally write a figure four going straight up, diagonally down to the left, then come across the original vertical line. David said, 'Oh no! You can't do it like that! The way the English teach people to do it is, you go down first then across to your right and then go down and through the line you've just written. That's how you do a figure four!'

I remember when I went to the secondary modern school for a week, my brother told me I would have to do algebra. That terrified me. I couldn't see the point of adding letters and numbers. How was that going to work out? Now it would appear I couldn't even write a four!

Because it was a schools programme, whatever was written in the text you had to stick to. You couldn't paraphrase it at all. Lines to do with reading a train timetable or a map were so awkward to remember, but you had to say it perfectly. We did laugh about it because it was so hard to actually do.

And because it was a schools programme, it was a guaranteed showing of either two or three times a week each episode, so therefore it was like doing three different TV series all at the same time; so financially speaking it was very good. I didn't need algebra to help me work that out!

We did about three weeks of location shooting in Watford, then we spent the next seven or eight weeks rehearsing and then filming at the BBC Centre. A lot of the time we'd rehearse in Chiswick, and there was a fantastic delicatessen at Turnham Green Terrace called Durbin and Allwright's. They sold about seventy different cheeses and fifty different cold meats, and we'd have lovely lunches with wine and cheese; it was the first time I was introduced to French cheese. I got quite tubby and went up to about ten stone, but I didn't half enjoy those lunches.

After lunch I would always remind Arthur to take his tablets. He was such a lovely man and I just wanted to look out for him. We became so friendly we'd occasionally go over to Arthur's house in Aldershot to have a meal with him and his wife, Teresa, or quite often Gay would come up to the BBC Centre for us all to meet in the BBC Club afterwards. You could only join the Club for the time you were working at the BBC unless you were employed directly on a permanent level.

Arthur told us about his variety days, doing vaudeville, singing, dancing and stand-up comedy. His gimmick had been a large kipper tie about three foot wide and five foot long. It was very brightly coloured and his first wife Ivy had made it for him.

Once, when we were having a drink, I admired a cross that he wore with a diamond in it. He said that Ivy had given it to him. She'd died just before their thirty-fourth wedding anniversary and he'd obviously been devoted to her. I learnt such a lot from him and we got on oh so well together; it really was a very memorable time and experience. On the way home I said to Gay, 'I'm gonna get one of them crosses whenever I get some more money. I've never seen one like that before.' I did get one made finally and it's never left my neck since.

One of the early episodes they did in the first shooting block had me as a Watford Football Club supporter, and they wanted to do some location filming at the club during a league match. So, with a club scarf and hat, I was sent in with the local supporters. They hid the cameras as much as possible, so that they could capture me in the crowd reacting to whatever was going on on the pitch.

It was a cold day and we were all jammed into the terraces. I couldn't see much because I'm not that tall, but I could hear a bunch of hooligans who had obviously recognised me and were starting to have a go. It did get a little bit scary, but I thought, if I've heard it, the crew would've heard it as well and they'd make sure that it doesn't go any further than general abuse.

I could hear the hooligans swearing and shouting and saying what they were gonna do to me and I was very wary, constantly looking around my back because I was worried that one might get close enough to get me. I think we had people from the club around me making sure none of these hooligans got near me, but it's very hard to control a crowd. I kept thinking, you only need one lunatic who is hell-bent on injuring you, and he will. Trapped in the terraces, the crowd was constantly moving; and each time I was pushed or shoved, I thought, here we go! I couldn't wait to get out of there. I was well relieved after we'd finished shooting that particular sequence.

Earlier in the day, one of the crew owned up to crashing into my beloved Datsun 260z whilst parking his car near mine. Perhaps it was karma for the car I wrecked in *Danny the Dragon*! It was only a small dent but at the time I was fuming! To make matters worse, although he said he'd give me the details of his insurance at the end of the day, we both forgot about it totally. I guess the day's filming and my drinking would've had something to do with my forgetting the incident. Later that day I bought an old acoustic guitar from a junk shop. It was a twenty-year-old Eko six-string and I only paid thirty quid for it. What I've saved on buying that, I reasoned, will cover the cost of fixing my Datsun, so it hadn't been a bad day after all.

Each episode we'd have these really well-known good character actors to do cameo roles: Sam Kydd, who seemed to have been in every British film ever made, did two or three. In one of the last episodes Brian Peck was guesting and playing Reg Smart. Brian had directed *Big Sin City*. By then in the storyline, me and Arthur were doing a bit of painting and decorating to earn a few bob and Brian's character was selling dodgy second-hand cars. It's funny, but he seemed to be a totally different person to how I remembered him in *Big Sin City*. I guess it's because now he was an actor in my TV series as opposed to my director. I much preferred him as an actor, and he was very much a thinking actor; not that he wasn't a good director, but maybe he was just far less stressed as an actor.

Another summer's day we were filming with John Rapley and Nan Munro playing a henpecked husband and his wife. We were shooting a car chase, the comedic rather than nail-biting variety, with the battleaxe wife driving an old Rover 90 and we were in a banana-yellow Austin 1300.

I was in the passenger seat and there was a camera attached to my door which meant that if I wanted to get out of the car, I had to climb over to the driver's side to get out. Arthur was sat in the back as a passenger and the husband was driving. Well, just as they were setting up the camera, a wasp flies in to my side of the car and it's the size of a bloody jumbo jet! Well, panic? You never saw anything like it. I screamed so loud, they must've heard me on Venus!

'Kill the bastard!'

I really don't like wasps and this must have been fitted out in a suit, it was that big. On hearing this commotion, a crew member who'd been annoying everybody on the set shouted so that everyone would hear him, 'Leave it to me Jack, I'll get it!'

And with his thumb and first finger he squashed it to smithereens! It looked so impressive, but as he walked away, with his back to everyone, it was obvious that he'd stung himself in the process and his face was a picture. All screwed up with the agony of it all. He was so embarrassed; he didn't say a word for the rest of the day.

We were working on quite a tight schedule, but it was a helluva lot of fun working on the show and everyone, including all the camera guys and the make-up ladies, everyone was lovely. Anyway, after the car chase we had to shoot this scene where I'm pushing a handcart around a roundabout and they decided to shoot this about 4.30 in the afternoon. They couldn't stop the traffic because it was a main road and they had to get the shot done that day because of the schedule being so tight. So that was a bit dangerous to do.

They wanted me to run on to the roundabout and take the third exit, pushing my cart full of bloody paint and all sorts, trying to do hand signals to let whoever is behind me know where I'm going: '… and make it as funny as you can, Jack…!'

'Well, I'm game for a laugh,' I said, thinking this may be an opportunity to restate my manly credentials after the wasp incident earlier. I did it without causing any real accidents and I was much calmer than with the big ball of fluff from earlier; and, perhaps because of this, I received a proposal.

Somebody on our film unit said that their partner was working on this new series for ITV called *Star Games* and would I be interested in doing one of them? It was a competition between three different teams of TV presenters, musicians, and actors, battling it out at swimming, five-a-side football, relay race, tug of war and other sporting activities. All the teams were raising money for charity. It sounded a laugh so I said, 'Yeah, okay, I'll do one!' And it worked out that they were happy to have me, and so I finished rehearsals on the Friday late afternoon and drove up to Cambridge that night.

By the time I'd been home and changed, it was about 9.30pm when I got to the hotel where there was a big dinner dance for everyone to get together and say hello and all that before filming on the Saturday. I found my table with my name on it with the Drama team. It was nice to see the familiar face of Roy Kinnear beaming at me whom I knew from *Melody* and *Pied Piper*. There were other faces I recognised too, like Julie Dawn Cole who'd done telly like *Angels* and *Poldark* and Christopher Biggins, who'd been in *The Rocky Horror Picture Show*. Jack Hedley was to be our team captain. He'd played British officers in *Colditz* and *Who Pays the Ferryman?* so a perfect choice, if a little over-qualified.

After the meal, at about 11.30pm, we had to go to someone's room to pick up our tracksuits and sneakers; and some bright spark says, 'They've got an indoor swimming pool here, should we go and do a bit of practice for tomorrow?' With everyone having had a few drinks, we were all very happy to do so. Well, bugger me, I didn't get to bed till about 4.30 in the morning and we had to be up again at seven to get to the reception and then be driven to the location to start filming. In the cold light of day I said, 'Well I'm definitely not going in the pool outside. I'll do anything but I'm not swimming. It'll be too cold. I'll do everything else!'

As it turned out, there were so many events in the swimming pool that I had to go and do one of them, so I settled for rowing in a blow-up dinghy. And, as it turned out, I ended up in the water as I had to jump out of the boat to let someone else jump in before pushing it off. Still, we all got pretty wet as it was raining, but at least we won the event.

Other pool races followed, and by the time we broke for lunch we were doing so well that some of us went down the pub to have a few to celebrate. The Obstacle Course was in the afternoon; and, as it hadn't been decided who was going to do it, I suggested: 'Why don't we go over there before we start filming again and time everybody and see who's the quickest, and whoever is the quickest can do the event!'

As it worked out I was one of the fastest of the boys so I did it for our side. We got through to the final and I was up against Robin Sarstedt from the Music team. He was a hip solo artist, with long hair, and was bloody fast. He had a hit with 'My Resistance is Low' so I hoped that was a good sign. I was in the lead until the rope ladder when he caught me up and jumped over the wall ahead of me. I landed second but I got to the next bit before he did – the rope swing over the water. I saw my chance and steamed through to win. It was all filmed in one take, with no retakes, and as I'm running up to the compere, Michael Aspel, it was quite slippery underfoot because of the rain, and I went arse over tit. I landed right on my backside as Michael was coming up to me to say, 'Well done, how do you feel?'

I *felt* an idiot because I was sitting on the ground in the wet, but at least I'd won so it made up for it! And I was so chuffed because I found out later that nobody had done it any quicker than me and I held the record for the whole series, 17.3 seconds!

What I didn't know was that if your team won their round on Saturday, you had to stay overnight to do the next round on Sunday; but because a lot of the actors thought it was such hard work on the Saturday, the majority of them didn't want to win and have to do it again the following day. When it came to the final round, the result depended on the Tug of War, and weight-wise we should've walked it in our sleep: but, very suspiciously to my mind, we lost. I was fuming, but what can you say? If I'm competing in anything, I want to win, otherwise what's the point in competing; but we didn't, so there you are.

Thinking about it as I drove home, I could've quite easily broken me leg or done something and not been able to go back to work on Monday. I hadn't even thought about that. The *TV Times* had suggested it could have been called Scar Games, as in a previous show the soccer put one actor out of action 'and many others limped home with bruises, aches and pains...'; and this was for Thames TV, so I doubt the BBC would have been too impressed. Still, we didn't win and I came back in one piece to shoot another aquatic adventure, for *Everyday Maths*.

The scene was where me and Arthur both fall into a swimming pool, fully clothed, after being chased by a Great Dane. We shot it after lunch and they spent a lot of time setting it up as they wanted to get it right first time. I checked Arthur had taken his tablets, braced myself and hoped we'd get it in one take. Thank goodness we did, as the water wasn't heated and was absolutely freezing! I also had to kiss Julie Peasgood in this episode and we were both very shy about it. It was a toss-up who was more embarrassed. I really hoped to shoot this in one take as well.

About half way through the shooting of the series, it became obvious to everyone that the chemistry between me and Arthur was magic. Lots of people on the show were remarking, 'This would make a great sitcom for telly!' and, 'Someone should send it to the Head of Programming!'

I do remember the director, the producer and John Tully, the writer, discussing which episode they should send, but I don't remember whether it was actually sent to the Programming department. Nothing more was ever mentioned about its prospects; personally, I think it would've transferred really well into a sitcom, but there you are.

Things were going well. I'd loved being on tour in *Big Sin City*, but you couldn't live like that all the time. Now, I was back at home, eating well and working with Arthur, and I was very proud of *Everyday Maths*. I wasn't always that happy with my telly stuff, but I was pleased with the chemistry between me and Arthur. I think the chemistry between me and Robin Nedwell in *The Government Inspector* worked well too; so maybe twenty-five per cent of what I've done I'm proud of and the other seventy-five per cent I think is rubbish!

It's so hard to tell what the end result will be like when you're doing something, but you do get a feeling. For me, it's something to do with whether or not I'm happy when I'm actually doing the job. I'd been very happy doing *Big Sin City*, and thought it was a great show, irrespective of the fact I was pissed a lot of the time. And I was very happy now. Things were so much more settled, and working with Arthur was a big part of that; alright, I was still drinking more than was good for me, but it was under control. After all, I couldn't be that bad: I'd run the fastest Obstacle Course Race! I was very, *very* proud of that.

Chapter 19

'WHY DON'T YOU COME AND JOIN US 'cos they'd love to have you. They're screaming out for celebrities to play!'

I'd been telling Tony about *Star Games* and he'd been telling me about the Showbiz XI football team. He'd been playing with them, and thought I should too.

It was a great privilege to be asked to play for it in the first place because it certainly was the biggest and probably the best showbiz team to play for. Partly because it'd been going for so long – they'd started playing when I was five – and partly because they'd raised so much money for charity. On the odd occasion, I did play for other Showbiz teams, but Showbiz XI was the premier league.

'Yeah, why not!' I said. The only exercise I used to do then was play squash once a week with Bob at the Richmond Squash Club. So I agreed to play; and, within four matches, I realised that not only did I really enjoy the football side of it, but also the other major element, which was drinking. And if you were single, so much the better because there were lots of girls around too. I obviously weren't going for that; I was going for the soccer and the booze, possibly in that order.

The team varied from week to week because of work commitments of the celebrities involved. The radio DJ David Hamilton was the honorary president and played a lot, and Jess Conrad was the team manager who rang round to organise the team each week. Jess was always so well turned out and looked like he'd got make-up on from the moment he got on the coach. He was just outrageous. He played in goal; because, he said, he wasn't much good on the field and would dive completely the wrong way if there was a camera around.

Then there was Tony Osoba, a very tall thin guy from *Porridge*, and a young actor called Nigel Rathbone who was in a very popular television show called *The Gentle Touch*. He was a Beatles fan and played the guitar like me, and we became quite close over the time we played together. He had dark hair, was always smiling and, if you didn't know better, you would swear he was up to something. There was also Rocky Taylor, a James Bond stuntman, and Graham Dene from Capital Radio.

There were also a lot of people from the music industry who would come and play as well. Aside from musicians like Denny Laine who used to play with Paul McCartney and Wings, you had record producers who would come and play. There was also Paul King from Mungo Jerry, the singer Ronnie Carroll, Tom and Dave Farmer from the group Blackfoot Sue, some of the Dooleys band, and Rudi Grant, Eddie's brother, who was a real cool guy and a lot of fun.

One week Gary Glitter came to play a match. He just looked like Gary Glitter without the make-up really, and was just a bit shy. I think he was going through a difficult period of his life with bankruptcy and all that.

He'd done his getting to the top of the music industry and now he told me he wanted to get into acting. He didn't really seem that confident about himself as a person and was asking me for advice about getting an agent.

'I'll give you names of three or four agents who I think are great and would be good for you, and then see how you get on,' I'd said.

He came across as a lovely guy, and I had a photograph taken with him. I couldn't believe it when I read about him years later. I was completely gob-smacked.

Along with the players, you had the tallest man in England, Chris Greener. He was seven foot six, wore size 17 shoes and he would sign autographs and pretend to be our coach. If ever we were playing any physically strong-looking teams, he would go up and have a word with them for the crowd's benefit and say, 'Now behave yourself, or you've gotta deal with me!'

And we had this other guy, Derek Bird, who was a professional lookalike of Michael Crawford's character Frank Spencer from *Some Mothers Do 'Ave 'Em*! He had the beret and the raincoat and was bloody mad, this geezer. He would do all the sort of cock-up type things that Frank Spencer did on his TV show. During the match he'd be on the touchline, doing crazy things to try and put off the goalkeepers; he'd run along the touchline with a flan or custard pie flanning anyone from the opposite side, including the referee and linesmen as well. Occasionally Derek and Chris would start fighting between themselves and there'd be custard pies everywhere!

The madness spread and, if ever one of our forwards had beaten everybody else and only had the goalkeeper to beat, the goalie would go way over the top and jump on him to stop him from scoring. And because it was such an outrageous incident, our whole team would go and attack the goalkeeper and all hell would break loose. It really was very much a complete show.

The fun actually started before we got to the ground, as more often than not they'd put on a coach for us that'd pick everyone up. From when we got on the coach, there was booze; and a lot of us would be tanked up before we got to the ground. By the time we'd met everybody at the ground and had a few more drinks and then got changed, we're well on the way to being happy, and then of course afterwards we'd continue drinking again.

When I first started, Tony 'Banger' Walsh was playing quite often. He was a wrestler and used to be a tag partner for Giant Haystacks. We became really great mates; and on the odd occasion where we'd go for a game, say, in Scotland, it'd take too long to drive, so we'd fly up there, stay overnight, and me and Banger would share a room. Everybody would be enjoying having a good old drink but he'd always make sure that I was okay and keep his eye on me.

This one particular weekend when we were up in Scotland, something happened in the bar the night before and Banger went to sort it out. I don't remember a great deal about it because I was that drunk, but this Scots geezer was just giving it so much mouth and wouldn't listen to Banger, so Banger ended up whacking him one.

Another lookalike that we had was Tony Williams, a dead ringer for the actor Trevor Eve, and he used to do a running commentary of the matches, with terrible jokes. The next morning he was describing over the tannoy what was going on on the field and I heard him say, 'Tony "Banger" Walsh has just done a good tackle there and he's knocked it up to Nigel who's on the left wing, and I'd just like you to know that Banger next week is appearing in a new TV series called Crack-a-Jock.'

I nearly collapsed on the pitch in laughter and consequently lost the ball. We won quite a lot, I'd say, but there was never any desperation like with professional football where you want to win at all odds. It was, after all, about raising money for good causes. Still, we wanted to give a good game and I always wanted to win if possible, so I steamed down the pitch, still smiling, to get my ball back.

I played every week more often than not, and over the years we supported just about every charity going. One time, I did arrange a match for Suzi Quatro and her charity. Gay had become a backing singer for Suzi and we would go and have weekends with Suzi and her husband Lenny at their manor house in

Great Waltham. We met there for dinner once with her gynaecologist. Suzi was trying to have kids with Lenny and, during the course of the evening, they said that they were trying to raise funds for some scanner unit at a hospital in Romford. I said, 'Well, I'm sure I could arrange a football match to raise some money for you if you wanted.' We did, and Suzi kicked off for us about six or seven months pregnant.

It was a good day, and hopefully not only were we raising money for the scanner, but we were also entertaining the public; that's always been so important to me. As I was signing autographs and having my photograph taken and all that, I was thinking about when I was a kid and had been taken to a Showbiz XI match. It was before I'd started in the business when we'd first moved up from Manchester to Hounslow. Bernie Winters was playing and I'd stood in the pouring rain for two hours just to get his autograph. I was well into comedians like Morecambe and Wise, Pete and Dud, and Mike and Bernie Winters; and when I'd seen Bernie playing, I had to have his autograph. I was like a drenched rat when I met him, but he was lovely and I was so, so, pleased I'd got it.

I said goodbye to Suzi and we all got back on the coach and had a round of drinks. We had a great coach: a double decker just like professional footballers use, with a bedroom on the ground floor with a double bed in it. On one trip, on the way there or on the way back, one of the guys had got a girl in there and we'd been trying to stop him from getting up to anything serious. We ended up letting a smoke bomb off: we lit it, threw it in the bedroom and ran back up to the top of the coach. None of us bothered to think about what the driver would think; we thought there'd be just a little bit of smoke, but bloody hell, smoke started pouring out. Anyone would've thought we'd dropped an atomic bomb. There was smoke everywhere, people coughing and spluttering and the driver pulled over, afraid that the coach was on fire!

It was the one and only time I argued with Chris Greener, because he was shouting and screaming that we shouldn't have done it; and although he was right, I just didn't like the way in which he said it.

'Oh, shut up and pass us a leaky handbag,' I said.

For that season we were being sponsored by Grants of St James's who made two-litre cartons of wine with a tap on them. If you took them out of the boxes you just had a bag and a tap. We'd throw them at each other during our drinking sessions, and of course we'd puncture them and they'd be leaking all over the place which caused havoc. They sponsored us for one season and of course, when they sponsor you, you've just got gallons and gallons of wine; another season we had Carlsberg Lager as sponsors and so then there were gallons of that everywhere.

Chris wouldn't chuck me a leaky handbag and he wouldn't let it go. I ended up saying to him, 'Shut up, you lanky bastard. Just 'cos you ain't got any oxygen up there, there's no need to take it out on us down here, is there?'

This guy was three times the size of me, but I was too small for him to bend down and grab hold of me.

The thing was, nobody would own up to whose idea it was, and I couldn't remember. I thought the best way out of that was, we know it was wrong, let's all admit it and get it over and done with; so I said, 'There weren't any one of us who decided to do it. We all agreed, all at the same time, that we're gonna do it for a laugh; so you either blame the lot of us or none of us!'

They blamed the lot of us. Well, Chris Greener, Tony Williams, the driver, Jess Conrad, all the serious ones basically blamed all of us stupid ones.

It was great fun. It was like being on tour again: the coach, somewhere new each week, the camaraderie, the drink. I did actually love football as well and was a lifelong supporter of Man United. I'd first met George Best when I was sixteen years old in 1968. I've still got the programme signed by Sir Matt Busby and all the team and I've got it framed with George's signature on it. The father of one of my fans had a box at Old Trafford where United were playing a European match. I was invited to see the game and then go to the bar afterwards to meet the players. I was speechless. I was totally in awe of the whole team. They were a team of heroes to me.

The thing I enjoyed as much again about Showbiz XI was getting to meet all the professional footballers. One year we actually played with Gordon Banks. He was the England goalkeeper when we won the World Cup in 1966. After that unfortunately he had a car accident where he lost one eye, and obviously that affected his game and he had to give up.

Anyway, he was great and asked me, 'Do you play golf, Jack? Because we do lots of charity work through golf tournaments and we'd love to have you play with us.'

'No, sorry mate, I can't,' I said. 'I'd love to and I enjoy it, but I'm bloody useless.'

In the match Nigel Rathbone was on the left wing and Gordon was marking him. Gordon was incredibly fit and flew round the pitch and Nigel. At half-time, we were sat in the dressing room and Nigel said to me, 'Bugger me, I'm never gonna live this down: he's only got one eye, he's old enough to be my dad, and he's running rings around me!' I laughed and handed him a drink. We always had drinks at half-time. I remember once when Jim Davidson played, he brought his own half-bottle of spirits with him for his dressing-room interval refreshment.

One time we played at the Sheffield Wednesday ground with the ex-Leeds Eleven. Their team included Billy Bremner, John Charles, Gary Sprake their old goalkeeper, Jackie Charlton and Peter Lorimer. In his day Lorimer used to have the fastest shot of all the divisions, ninety miles an hour. Jess Conrad was worried about playing in goal, in case the ball hit him in the face.

'I'm not going in goal if he's playing for them! If I'm hit in the face and disfigured, that would be the end of my career!' The trouble was, Jess wouldn't ever play on the pitch either because he was too frightened of getting injured.

We all teased him, of course, but he did have a point. We weren't covered if we were injured; and if we couldn't go back to work on the Monday morning, and were contracted to work, we'd be sued! They said they didn't have the funds to insure us.

'Well, that's not very good for our health, is it?' I'd said with another drink in my hand.

In the end Jess stayed on the sideline and geed the audience up instead. It was a great game and I've still got the match ball because it was the only time I scored a hat-trick. I was always a forward, and I scored three goals; and in any pro game, anyone who scores a hat-trick gets given the ball afterwards. So I was given it and I got everyone to sign it.

A large part of our success was due to Charlie Williams who was playing with us that day. He was a black comedian whom I admired so much. He had grey hair, the broadest Yorkshire accent and the funniest one-liners.

He was bloody great, he was. I didn't know, but he'd been a professional footballer for Doncaster Rovers before he was successful on the TV show *The Comedians*. He was full of charisma and had respect for everyone. If ever God was black, it was him.

The whole time that I was with Showbiz XI, it was one laugh from the moment you got on the coach until you were going home. I was drinking myself silly, and Gay did nag me, but I couldn't be too bad. As I said to her, the other week I'd done a charity walk round the White City dogs stadium which was fifteen laps, only I had to run it because I was playing Showbiz XI in the afternoon. If I could do all that, there couldn't be too much wrong with me, could there?

My other passion, occupation, distraction, call it what you will, was animals. I was mad about them; animals and fish. I had two fish tanks made especially for me at The Grove and they were made to look like an old pirate treasure chest, with these funny shapes around the outside of the tank in wood and glass that you could see through all the way around apart from the back. The lid had what looked like lead straps going over with padlocks on. It was a lovely ornament: a piece of furniture. The first one I had made was two foot long and I thought that was really lovely, so I got them to make me a four-foot one as well.

The local fish shop, Paul's Aquatics, made them for me. It was at the corner of Staines Road and Wellington Road North and opposite the pub where me Mum and Dad used to go, where they first met June Collins. I would go there twice or three times a week to look at the fish and talk about them. There was this one kid, he could've only been seven or eight years old. He used to come in every Saturday morning to buy a fish to put in the piranha tank to watch it get eaten in the shop and I thought, you cruel little bastard! The shopkeeper would put a guppy in the tank with the two piranhas and they'd attack it from either end. Then they'd just twist, and the guppy would be snapped in half and that's it, goodnight! This kid used to come there every weekend when he got his pocket money to see this; and of course the fish shop loved it because it saved them feeding the bloody things.

I used to feed my piranhas dog food, and sometimes raw pig's liver or kidney. They used to go bloody mad for that. When I first bought them, they had an argument as soon as I put them in the tank. Although they were all in the same tank in the shop, when I got them home (and after I'd let them get used to the water temperature, then let them out), literally within five minutes, two of them were in bits! I thought, bugger me! What have I bought 'ere? They were obviously very hungry, so I stuck a tin of dog food in there.

Over time I got used to them, and I knew they wouldn't attack anything bigger than themselves unless they were in a massive shoal, of hundreds or thousands of them; and I'd only bought six. When we had parties I'd dare people to feed them and hold their hands in the water with raw lumps of liver or kidney. Nothing would really happen because they'd just go for the bit where the blood was. You had to be reasonably careful: if you just dangled your hand in there willy-nilly with blood pouring out of this lump of meat, there was a possibility of you getting a nibble, and you didn't know if they'd got any diseases; but I was never, ever bitten.

You'd get the odd drunk who'd say, 'Come 'ere, I'll do that, I'll feed em!' But I was always there watching so that if anything did go amiss, I could stop anything drastic happening.

There'd be times where I'd go in the fish shop and I'd think, oh, I've never seen them fish before; and I'd say, 'Right, I'll have some of them, they look nice!' At one time I had two community tanks which meant you could put loads of different species of fish in together and they'd live quite happily. I bought some once that looked lovely and I didn't know at the time that they were live bearers as opposed to laying eggs. I went to bed one night and got up the next morning and I'd got bloody hundreds of them. I was so pleased.

I bought another one and this was a big fish. I can't remember what sort it was: I don't know whether it was called an oscar or we called it Oscar, but we had him a really long while. He was about a foot long and quite a big fish for the size of tank that I had. One night the heater got jammed and it boiled! I was gutted because I'd had the fish about three and a half, four years.

There was a fantastic fish shop in Shepherds Bush where I used to go, and he used to supply fish to the BBC. He had a fantastic choice of tropical fish, and that's where I'd go and find out about piranhas because he had a couple of big piranhas in one of his tanks. I used to spend a lot of money on them.

I also found this aquarium shop out by Heathrow Airport which was called Sea Life Aquatics and it sold marine fish and coral reef fish and sea anemones, and I thought, oh, that'll be nice! I'll have some of them, and some clownfish that live in the sea anemones and all that business.

I spent a fortune on them, but they were diabolical to keep because you had to get the chemical content right in the water, your pH and your salt. But the brightness of the fish: it was just like the Beatles' 'Yellow Submarine' with all these beautiful psychedelic-coloured fish.

I remember buying one that was called a pufferfish. In the wild, if ever it got attacked or wanted to defend itself, it would always emit a poison that'd kill everything within six foot of it. And one of the fish in my tank started having a go at this pufferfish and so it killed everything in the tank, everything, apart from a red coral shrimp. Killed about two hundred quid's worth of fish! It was a right ugly bastard, this fish was, and I only bought it because it was ugly and I felt sorry for it. I thought, no one will buy you because you really are ugly! And then it goes and does that to me!

But I used to love them all, and seahorses, though they never lasted long ever. The only thing I had that really lasted and was well worth it was this red coral shrimp. It was bright red-and-white striped with two big pincers; and it was like a snake where, every so often, it'd shed the whole of its skin. You'd get up one morning and you'd think, bugger me! There's two of 'em in there! It lasted a good three or four years, that one. The average time would be about three or four months.

Bob was round one day, and I was showing him my latest acquisition. I was telling him that I'd wanted to buy an Australian stonefish. 'But then I thought, if you went to rearrange the fish tank, right, and picked up the wrong stone, and got the venom from that, within a matter of minutes you're dead if you haven't got the anti-venom shot to take!' I said. 'Now that ain't funny, is it?'

He agreed it wasn't funny.

'That's getting a bit serious, that is,' I added.

Just then Gay called out to me, 'Jack, I think she's started.'

She'd been chatting with some friends when she'd noticed Papillon getting agitated. After my thwarted attempts to get Papillon mated in Portsmouth, I'd been true to my word and not gone down there again; but, as it happened, she'd got pregnant quite by accident.

Gay's mother had been moving to Chiswick, and there'd been a convoy of cars taking furniture from Esher up to Chiswick. Lynne had given up waiting for Papillon to get pregnant and had bought a Lhasa apso from another breeder. With the doors kept open for everybody to bring furniture in and out, we'd shut the two dogs in a room and closed the door. I was on a furniture trip so I didn't witness it myself, but apparently there were yelps of pain, and the two dogs were stuck together and only released with a bucket of water.

The birth seemed to be no less dramatic. For days and days and days we'd been expecting Papillon to drop her litter any minute, and she'd obviously decided to have them now at eleven o'clock. It was an awful night. We'd all had quite a bit to drink: well, I had, and my mate McNeil had, and we stayed up most of the night with Papillon. I had a drink in one hand and the phone to the vet in the other.

The second one had got stuck and it was in a breech position. It was about 11.30 at night.

'The body is so long – it's massive in comparison to the first one that was born,' I said. 'It's been stuck for three minutes; what can I do to, like, help?'

'You've got to do it very quickly because otherwise the puppy won't have enough oxygen and will suffocate. Get some Vaseline and try and slowly pull it out, but do it now or it will be born dead!'

Eventually we got it out, but he weren't breathing. I got a bit of brandy and water with one of them eye-drop things and, after I'd blown in its mouth to get all the mucus out and massaged its chest, I just gave it a drop of that; it sort of coughed and spluttered and came to life. I was so relieved, I was in bits.

Although she had five, two of them died, and I remember it like it was yesterday. Each time one of these puppies died, I was crying, pleading with it not to die, but I mean it was just too weak. By the time we'd gone to bed, she'd had four, but only three that survived. One died before we eventually went to bed; I tried but I couldn't make it recover. Papillon had a fifth one during the night on her own, but that died the following day. It was like the runt of the litter and just not strong enough. But, oh my God, I broke my bloody heart when that happened.

We felt that a dog in the right circumstances should be allowed to have one litter and then at least they've experienced being a mother; and we kept all her pups within the family. Glynne ended up having the breech puppy. He called him Caesar and he grew up to be a bloody mad dog, lovely, but very hyperactive; maybe it was the brandy. The next one that came, I had and I called him Chopin (he kept doing symphonies all over the place!), and the only female that survived the birth was the one that we gave to Gay's grandmother.

Later that day I buried the tiny little pair in the garden, and as I weren't working I spent the rest of the day with Papillon and the pups. I think Gay had to go out to a gig or something, but maybe Bob came round.

Gay sang with the Tony Evans Showband who were the resident band at the Hammersmith Palais. It was about a twelve-piece orchestra and they were bloody good, I thought. Occasionally they would do cruises on the QE2 and other gigs as well, and I think she did a good couple of years with them. She also sang with the Ray McVay Band, one of the three or four different show-bands that did top gigs up and down the country.

Noel McNeil, an Irish singer, was already singing with the band when Gay auditioned for it. She became very friendly with him and he really was quite a character. One of my first memories of him is when he came over to a dinner party where we were having fondue for the first time. He brought his mate who was another Irish geezer and an ex-monk. When they saw the raw meat for the fondue, the monk turned to McNeil and said, 'They've forgotten to cook it!'

'Well, it's sure to be an experience,' he replied.

I thought that was hysterical.

Macca was a very good-looking guy who'd come from a rough area and had a dreadful upbringing. Dark-haired and baby-faced, he'd become famous in Dublin as a youngster singing in big showbands. He always got a lot of press in Southern Ireland and was one of the funniest guys with an incredible sense of humour. But what came with that was that he was lethal once he was drunk, and became psychopathic and paranoid. He couldn't control his temper and would often end up in fights; he was something like one below a black belt in karate and he really could handle himself.

At the Palais you'd have lots of women after him because he was so charismatic, but he wasn't interested. Then the boyfriends of the girls would get pissed off and want to start having a fight with Macca, and of course he'd defend himself. The only times he ever got batterings was when more than one person was fighting him. I never, ever knew him to get beaten up by just one guy because he was that good of a fighter.

Occasionally we'd go to gay clubs with him and have a laugh, and he used to wear contact lenses which we thought was very avant-garde; but you always had to be wary when you were with him because he was capable of causing absolute merry hell. He loved his drugs, would always smoke dope, and occasionally go for the more serious stuff as well.

He played in a band with Tony Carpenter at one stage, touring Germany, and I heard the police were called to a hotel one night. McNeil was arguing with somebody, or about to start a fight, and there was a siege-type situation with Tony locked in a room with Macca who was drunk and going apeshit. It doesn't take a lot to make Tony panic: and when he'd done what he could to try and calm Macca down, he climbed out of the window and sat on the roof of the hotel until it was all over and safe to come back in. McNeil was a helluva lot of fun, but a rough diamond one minute and fool's gold the next!

One weekend we decided to take him down to Devon with us to see some friends. We'd met Mavis and Derek on the Austrian skiing holiday. They had a successful market business and about half a dozen stalls in Pontypridd selling fruit and veg. They'd bought a house in North Devon and frequently invited us down. They knew McNeil, so all three of us headed off in my two-seater Datsun 260z to the pretty village of Dunster.

On the Saturday night we went out for a lovely meal, then back to their big, big, house where they also had some relations staying. Of course we'd all had plenty to drink, and eventually everyone said 'Goodnight!' and 'See you in the morning!' and we went up to bed. McNeil was sleeping downstairs in the lounge as the house was full.

Next thing we knew, Derek, who's six foot six and five foot wide, wakes us up saying, 'Can you come and sort McNeil out because he's throwing a blue fit downstairs?'

Gay got up first of all to go down to speak to him and see what the problem was. By the time I'd woken up and come down the stairs to see what all this noise is about, McNeil has grabbed hold of Gay and pulled her into the lounge, closed the door and started shouting and screaming. Derek didn't know quite how to deal with the situation and equally, I didn't know what was going on at all; I thought perhaps he was hallucinating. I thought the only thing to do was to try and talk to him, get him to calm down, so that we can see what the situation is. So I started talking to him through the door, and I could hear furniture breaking and glass or pottery being smashed and all sorts and I'm thinking, what the fuck is going on? What's he doing to Gay?

I said to him, 'C'mon McNeil, open the door, I wanna talk to you; it's only me.' He was shouting and screaming that the police were going to get him. I just kept talking to him and somehow, thank God, I convinced him to open the door. I said to Derek, 'You just try and stand further away so he don't feel threatened by you.'

'Okay, but I'm ready in case!' he said. I was sure Derek could handle himself, but I also knew how lethal McNeil could be as well when he wanted to go.

As McNeil opened the door, I held my hand out while I was talking to him; and, not taking my eyes off him, I said, 'You let Gay come to me now, and tell me what the problem is.'

And at first he wouldn't let go of her; and I said, 'C'mon Mac, Gay wants to go to bed. Let her go to bed and me and you can sort this out.'

He finally let go of her and I grabbed hold of Gay, pushed her behind me and said to her, 'You go back to bed now and it'll all be alright.'

As soon as I knew she was behind me and Derek was stood somewhere near me ready to pounce if need be, we carried on talking; but probably for no more than thirty seconds. Then McNeil decided that he'd had enough and didn't want to talk any more and he slammed the door shut.

We heard sounds that gave us the impression that he was barricading himself in that room. So as soon as he'd closed the door, Derek said, 'We can't leave him like this with us in the house. He could come up and try to kill the lot of us. I suggest that we all get in one room and stay together and one of us should get out of the house and go to the police station and get some help.'

They had a phone, but it must've been in the lounge, so we decamped upstairs into one room and started talking about who could escape out of the window and climb down the drainpipe. Derek and Mavis were both a bit too large, the other three guests were a bit too old and obviously I didn't want Gay to go, so it was down to me. But in Dunster all the street lighting went off at night, it was pitch black outside and I had no idea how to find the police station. So we decided that we'd all stay in the one room together and hopefully he would go to sleep, and the chances were he wouldn't remember anything about it in the morning anyway.

The shouting and screaming downstairs went on for maybe ten or fifteen minutes more, then it died down; but I don't think any of us slept that night.

Gay told me that while McNeil had her in the room, he'd smashed one of these big decorative brandy glasses, grabbed hold of one of these pieces and said to Gay, 'We're not going to let them get us! We'll do ourselves in before they get us!'

Derek looked worried.

'Don't worry,' I said, 'if he's still there and alive in the morning, we'll send him back to London on the train.'

The next morning, McNeil remembered very little about the night before. 'I'm so sorry...' he said. There was quite a bit of damage, but Derek said he was just pleased that no one had been hurt. Me and Gay felt dreadful, and determined that we certainly couldn't allow it to ever happen again.

We took Mac to the station with Derek, and sent him back to London, but our relationship was so strained with Mavis and Derek that we lost contact with them after that. Me and Gay were both so embarrassed about what Macca had done; and I can't remember what was said, but I don't remember ever seeing them again.

McNeil eventually killed himself in the early 1990s; he was in his early forties. He'd tried to commit suicide loads of times before but it was always a cry for help. A desperate cry for help. He would take tablets or whatever he had, phone people up and say, 'This is what I've done!' and people would come and save him. Me and Bob rescued him once in a flat in Fulham. I had to climb up a drainpipe and get in the first-floor window which thankfully was open, wake him up, and get him to stay conscious. When he did die, he'd done the usual and was expecting his partner to arrive at a certain time, see him unconscious, call an ambulance and then he'd be alright. For some reason, the guy was delayed and when he arrived at this hotel somewhere in Wales, McNeil was already dead.

He was in and out of our life for about twenty years, and even though he was totally screwed up, he was a lovely guy, a great singer, so, so funny and a loyal friend to the end. It's just the more drink he'd have, or the more drugs he'd take, the more paranoid he'd become, which more often than not would cause problems for him. A sad old case but certainly a one-off; I just had the feeling he was always looking for his crock of gold.

*

I'd finished *Everyday Maths* in October '78 and started work on a new children's television series for Southern TV in January the following year. I was contracted to do *The Ravelled Thread* which was set in the 1860s down on the south coast of England. It was about a plot to smuggle weapons and troops from England to the Southern States during the American Civil War.

In the book of *The Ravelled Thread*, my character, Gegor, is described as an 'undersized, twisted, palsied thirteen-year-old'. I was actually twenty-six and thought I looked alright really.

I was playing a young thief (!) and 'Gegor' was the slang for 'beggar'. The script had loads of Victorian slang in it and when I read it I thought, well, this is a children's TV series and they won't be able to understand what we're talking about. It had lines like 'he's not prigging our push' which meant 'he's not stealing our money'.

I had long discussions with the producer about this, but he wouldn't have any of what I said at all. I'd bought a book called *The Victorian Underworld* by Kellow Chesney because it had all the slang from those times. I think it was the only time I ever checked out and did any research into anything that I've ever done. And I was so disgruntled with no one taking me seriously, I thought, I'm not gonna bother researching again. So I never did.

The main hero, 'Sedgwick', was played by the heart-throb of the time called Steven Grives. He was a bit older than me and drove an old Volvo sports car like Roger Moore in *The Saint*. He'd just done a series called *Flambards*, an adult drama where he played a Casanova-type character and all these women were throwing themselves at him. Steven is the sort of actor who laughs with his eyes. You only needed to look in his eyes and you knew he was laughing which made it very hard to do serious drama stuff with him. He was a lot of fun.

We shared digs when we were filming on location, stayed in a farmhouse and had champagne breakfasts. I remember the landlady was all over Steven like a rash. I've not drunk in the morning before, I idly thought, as the landlady fluttered around Steven. Not that Buck's Fizz was really drinking, certainly not like the drinking we used to do at night.

There was another guy in it who was a very well-known character actor called John Junkin, and he played 'Dobbs'. He had big, big eyes and had done loads of comedy as a supporting actor. John used to drink large vodka and tonics and, at that time, I was drinking large vodka and lemonades. I tried sometimes to keep up with him but I couldn't seem to get anywhere near his capacity at all. One night in particular we were in Dartmouth, all in the same hotel, and as we sat in the bar I thought, I wonder how much he *can* drink? I wonder if I can keep up with him? We were having double measures of spirits and I think after about ten or eleven that was me done. I couldn't drink any more and I knew I was only just capable of walking let alone anything else.

'I've had enough, I'm going to bed,' I said, and crawled up the stairs on my hands and knees. I seemed to remember doing that somewhere before.

It took about three months in all to finish the shooting, which was a mix-ture of studio work and location filming. I saw it all through an increasingly familiar and happy haze of alcohol. I didn't let it affect my work and I didn't *have* to have it, I just enjoyed it. I was back working with people my own age and they were all enjoying themselves, and I did too. We all had so much fun making it and we laughed so much.

I remember doing one scene in a rowing boat with Steven and a young lad just out of drama school called Mark Wingett. Mark was well into all these different tablets that he carried around in a see-through plastic bag. He played Billyboy, one of the tearaways, and was great fun. His character was described as 'a rugged, fifteen-year-old lad with a mop of unruly, auburn hair which, like the rest of him, needed a wash'.

We were on the River Dart in Devon and were supposed to be rowing out to a big old two-masted schooner, climb aboard, discover the chests of muskets and get into a fight. Apparently the Dart is known for having one of the strongest tides for a river that goes into the sea; and, in all our nineteenth-century clothes, if any of us had fallen in with this tide, we'd have drowned definitely!

Me and Mark were rowing the boat with Steven shouting encouragements; and, because of the tide, the idea was to go past the schooner, then come back inland, go alongside and climb on board, all without safety gear or doubles.

So we started rowing out for the first time; but bugger me, because the tide was going out, as we got alongside the ship, no sooner had we stood up and put the oars in to climb on board than the tide had taken us, and we were about fifty yards away from the ship. They sent out a motorboat to drag us back so we could try again. We had to time it very, very carefully so that as soon as we got close to the boat, we could have the oars in and we'd try to get on board while holding on to the side of the schooner to stop us from being swept out to sea again. If we did this once, we must've done it about a half a dozen times. We'd had plenty of booze the night before, it was a windy day with quite choppy conditions, and we were all various shades of green.

The next time we were rowing along, we were now laughing at anything and nothing because nothing seemed to be going right this morning. I looked in the water where my oar was hitting the waves and I saw a dead sheep floating past. I turned round to Mark and said, 'Oh look Mark, there's a dead sheep!' And his eyes just screamed with laughter. I mean, it weren't funny at all, but he was crying. And me seeing him crying got me going and then we were just useless for the rest of the bloody shoot. It just finished us off. We did get it eventually, but they only used a few seconds in the final cut.

We also had an awful lot of trouble with the guns in one scene, where the troops were training, with muskets firing and explosions going off. The muskets were the old type where you had to put the ball and powder in separately, and they were having so much trouble with them, getting them to fire when they were meant to – obviously without ball bearings in them.

Steven and I were supposed to be watching this battle scene unfold, but with the guns not working it was making us giggle and the valiant director was talking over the filming, saying, 'Now, roll the film and I want you all to look to your left… now!' There was lots of smoke for the cannons that was wafting past us and we could barely keep a straight face as we were choking with laughter and smoke. Looking back at it now, it still makes me smile.

We did quite a lot of night shooting on it, and one particular evening we were out at this beautiful old Grade II listed building. We had to do one scene where we are all trapped in the manor and my character has to climb up a chimney, onto the roof, down the drainpipe and break into the house to get the rest of them out of captivity.

It was to be shot on the rooftops of the mansion and the stuntman was going to do it because it was so high up, but something had gone wrong because they couldn't locate Derek and we were on a tight schedule. Derek Ware was the fight arranger, played a few small parts in the series, and doubled for me as my stuntman. He was beaten up in nearly every episode, thrown down steps, pushed into the sea and had to wear a wig if he was doubling for me.

I'd been down the pub at the break with everyone else, and when we came back we were kept hanging about; and they said, 'Well, you're not going to be used for a couple of hours – go down the pub again if you like and we'll come and get you when we want you.' It was only a couple of hundred yards down the road so we all headed back. We came back a few hours later, and it must be about eleven o'clock now and they're still filming; and we gets there and for some reason they still couldn't get hold of Derek, and they were moaning saying, 'We're behind schedule!' and all this.

And I said, 'It's alright, I'll do that, don't worry about it!'

'Are you sure, Jack? It's about fifty foot up in the air,' they said.

'Yeah, no problem,' I said.

'Just because Sally is watching,' someone said.

Sally Stewart was the PA that all the guys had a soft spot for, but that's not why I volunteered. At stage school Barbara Speake had drummed into us that whatever you are asked to do – you can do it. So maybe it was latent memory, or maybe it was just the alcohol, or maybe I just wanted to be helpful when they were running behind schedule. Whatever the reason, I did it. They filmed me coming out of the chimney, black from the soot, although to look at the colour of me, you'd think the make-up lady had had one too many too.

Later that night, as I was being me, being Derek, I thought it would be exceedingly funny if I nicked Derek's wig to do the next bit of me running up to the mansion and breaking in. So I stuck it on my head, went to get inside, couldn't open the door, threw off the wig, tried again and went in.

It was in the early days of *It'll Be Alright on the Night* and we thought, if we do a few of these cock-ups throughout this job, we might get on one of the shows! We didn't, although someone compiled all the mishaps like the pistols not firing, horses not behaving, the rowing boat and the wig incident for an end-of-filming party at the Southern TV studios. My belly hurt from laughing.

Chapter 20

SOMEWHERE BETWEEN JULY AND AUGUST OF 1979 I had a phone call from John Daly who said, 'I'm involved in this film which is a musical very loosely based on Lewis Carroll's *Alice in Wonderland*. Would you like to do it, playing the part of Mock Turtle?' My agency by now were Plant and Froggatt, but John had always stayed in touch.

'Yeah, great,' I said. I hadn't done a film for a while so I jumped at the chance. I couldn't actually think who Mock Turtle was so I went and got a video of *Alice in Wonderland* to find out. I was a bit disappointed as it didn't look that interesting, but when they sent the script through, there was a completely different take on the story and it was now in a contemporary setting with not an animal in sight. Alice, a suicidal divorcee, meets the Rabbit, a businessman, while he's jogging in a park, and the Queen of Hearts is a rich lady who sends a couple of assassins after him. My character works with Alice in a television factory, wears full leathers and rides a motorbike! My vision then changed from a cute costumed cameo role to seeing myself as Steve McQueen flying over a barbed wire fence: the coolest of the cool.

The less glamorous part of the role was that my character carried around a book of knowledge, *The World's Almanac*. He continually quotes from this book to his disinterested friends.

'Do you know that duelling in Uruguay is legal as long as both parties are registered blood donors?'

He speaks in *non sequiturs*, hiding behind these useless bits of information as if there was some universal truth to be found in these disconnected facts.

Mock Turtle: 'I'm going away next week to start a new life.'

Gryphon: 'As what?'

Mock Turtle: 'I don't know. Joseph Conrad couldn't write a word of English until he was forty-seven.'

Gryphon: 'You're going to be a writer?'

Mock Turtle: 'No.'

Perhaps it was deeply significant, some cryptic code to be cracked. I'll be damned if I know. Still, least I would get to ride a cool bike.

I was told that Lulu was doing the music and had already recorded songs for it. I was told that Susannah York was going to be the Queen, a French guy called Jean-Pierre Cassel was playing the Rabbit, Sophie Barjac was Alice, and Paul Nicholas the Cheshire Cat. A young actor called Dominic Guard was to play my friend the Gryphon in it, and I'd also get to see Tracy Hyde from *Melody* because she'd got a little part in it as well. It all sounded quite a good gig. They sent me a copy of the soundtrack, and that really sold the film to me as I thought the music was absolutely fantastic.

It was to be shot in Poland, and I first met up with Dominic Guard at Heathrow Airport on our way out to Warsaw. We were a similar age, with the same agents, and he came over as being a lovely guy. He was very introvert as opposed to me being extrovert, which I thought was great casting to have the two opposites, although I don't think that dynamic came over in the finished film.

We had a good chat on the plane and got on from day one. We exchanged things like 'have you ever been to Poland?' – neither of us had. 'Are you looking forward to riding a motorbike?' – we both were. 'What are you expecting it to be like in the Eastern Bloc?' – we thought it would be interesting.

'The only other Communist country I've been to was East Berlin,' I said, 'which was a big giggle. Oh, and I also refuelled in Moscow which was a big giggle, so I expect this to be…'

'… a giggle as well,' we both said.

'And don't forget the Russian rocket fuel,' I said.

'Polish,' Dom said and we both laughed. This was going to be fun.

It also came out in conversation that I knew his brother Christopher Guard who'd been Lesley Dunlop's boyfriend at the time we did *Our Mutual Friend*.

It was a Belgian/English/Polish production with a few Americans thrown in for good measure, so there was an eclectic mix of nationalities involved. There were two Polish directors, Jerzy Gruza and Jacek Bromski, who couldn't speak a word of English and all the direction went through interpreters.

When we arrived, a young girl student introduced herself and said she would be our interpreter and look after me and Dom. I forget what her name was, but she was very butch and ever so nice. She had short brown hair and she looked like a guy really, but she was so helpful; and what with having these two bloody directors who couldn't speak a word of English, in this crazy city, she was invaluable.

Before we'd even left home, we'd been told to be wary of exchanging English money on the black market. I was told that for a Polish person to get out of the country, they had to have foreign currency in their bank, as the Polish zloty wasn't worth a penny outside Poland. I was also told they would buy things off you and would go mad if you had a pair of Levi's on. They'd want to buy them because they couldn't buy them normally as there weren't shops that sold that sort of stuff then or anything Western really.

We had to be careful because not only were people trying to encourage foreigners to deal on the black market where they'd get ten times the amount of money for their exchange as they would if they did it legally, there were also double agents working for the Polish government trying to catch foreign tourists doing just that. They'd come up to you in the street and say, 'Have you got any English currency or US dollars that we can buy off you? We'll give you a good exchange rate.'

I took it all with a pinch of salt. I thought, this is all a laugh this is! It's like movie time, like James Bond and spies and all that! I thought it was all a wind-up to start with – until it started happening to me in the streets.

One of the Polish guys in the film who played an assassin apparently had lots of dealings in these matters. He was a very thickset guy and looked like either a boxer or a wrestler. Somebody said, 'Speak to him because he'll tell you all the do's and don'ts if someone comes up to you and wants to buy your Levi's.'

And he just said: 'You must be very careful, because, who you're dealing with, it is hard for you people to be certain, yes? And many men here can do you harm. So, anything like that you are wanting to do, you talk to me and so I make very certain that you will not be coming to any danger, okay?'

'Okay.'

We were actually given quite a lot of money for expenses in Polish currency anyway, so it's not as though money was that important to us. And it's not as though in Communist Poland there was anything good to buy in the shops because there wasn't, but we thought if we get that desperate for money, we'll go to the assassin.

The one thing that did seem worth buying were these religious artifacts of one sort or another. There were paintings and religious antiques and they really were beautiful. I wasn't religious whatsoever so it didn't mean much to me but they were incredible to look at. The whole city was amazingly atmospheric: the buildings, the culture, the people. It was autumn while we were there, so it went dark quite early in the afternoon, and walking through the big cobbled square of the old town was so interesting and unnerving. It felt like you were a very long way from home. Years ago when I was in Greece, I was in a car with Jane Seymour and we were being followed. I can't remember much about it now, but I remembered this feeling of unease, the same feeling I had here. I felt I needed to be on the ball all the time otherwise you could get into so much trouble without even doing anything.

I went for a costume fitting one day at the Warsaw Opera House. Some of the background people in the film were from there and we also used a lot of their costumes which of course, being opera, were really incredible. I remember there was a very short, black jacket with sparkling beading, like a Spanish bullfighter's tuxedo. I wanted to nick it but I thought if I got caught, they'd just put me in prison, throw away the key and you wouldn't have had sight or sound of me ever again. That frightened me into not trying to nick it, but it was beautiful. If I'd have been in England, I'd have definitely nicked it, or in any other Western country, I'd have nicked it.

One of the first scenes we shot in Warsaw was set in a TV factory. We could only use the factory after they'd stopped the production line which was about ten o'clock at night. So the factory scenes were all night shoots from 10pm to five or six o'clock in the morning. The scene was a musical number where me, Dominic and Sophie are on a forklift truck. Dominic was quite taken by Sophie and I was quite taken by the forklift truck. I really wanted to drive it, but both of the directors wanted Dominic to drive it instead so that pissed me off.

What I hadn't realised was that, when they played the tracks to me to give me an idea of how it would sound, that that *was* the music for the film. I had assumed that we would record our own songs, but instead we were expected to lip-sync to these voices. Still, apparently Susannah York didn't even know it was a musical until she had flown in and started shooting. At least I knew what songs I'd be involved in. What I didn't have was a lyric sheet to see what lines I'd be singing until the night before, when I was given a tape and told that's the line I'll have to sing. I'd never been overdubbed for a film before, and my prospective voice was just so deep it didn't feel or look at all natural – it sounded like me miming to Barry White.

'Please let us re-record it when we get back to London. It'll only take five minutes and it'll be so much better.'

They said no. They weren't interested in spending any more time or money on it. Still, Sophie even had her dialogue overdubbed; at least I got to keep my own speaking voice. I'd hoped we'd be able to convince them not to overdub all the singing and that when they saw the final edit they would realise their mistake. But, in truth, the music stood out in the final cut. It was like an ill-fitting but stylish jacket. Without the music it probably would never have been made. Having seen it several times, I've still got no idea what it's all about, but the music is toe-tappingly good.

We filmed in a variety of locations in Poland, and wherever we went we'd take over at least one hotel, sometimes two, with all the cast and crew. It was a lovely company. Everybody I spoke to for the whole time that I was there, from extras to lighting people, could only speak very broken English, and it was really very hard to understand them, but their attitude was so great. It really was an incredible experience.

When we all moved up to Stettin to film they booked us on internal flights, and me, Dominic and Tracy all sat together. It was one of these old propeller planes where the back opens up and you just walk in. As we got on I thought, bloody hell! I'm glad I've had a few, I don't like this!

The pilot obviously wasn't that keen either, as when we saw him get on, he had a bottle of vodka sticking out of his pocket. That's it, I thought, we're not gonna land! We'll land in hell if he's driving! It's one thing if you try and hide the booze, but this was sticking out of his pocket!

It weren't that long of a flight but the turbulence was horrendous, and it was a bumpy landing, but I was so thankful when the wheels touched the ground because I really did think that we weren't going to arrive there safely.

As soon as we landed I said, 'Right, when do we go back to Warsaw?'

'Oh, in five days' time or six maybe,' they replied.

'Right,' I said. 'Well, I'm not flying! Get me a car, get me a train, get me a donkey! Anything, but I ain't flying! Bollocks to that! I ain't doing that again!'

Dominic and Tracy said they felt the same, so they said they'd arrange for us to go back to Warsaw on a train.

The following day me and Dom were recovering in the hotel bar. We went and sat there while everybody was working on the set, and had vodka and Cokes or whatever it was. The barman didn't give you a pub measure, but poured it manually, so more often than not it was a double; and the vodka was twice as strong as normal vodka. We had four or five and then just sat there eating pretzels from the bar. To be honest that's all I really ate. I did try lots of food because they had location caterers while we were filming but it all tasted the same. It's like they'd only got one pan and they had to cook everything in it. If you had fish, it tasted like meat. If you had meat, it tasted like fish and everything tasted the same. A lot of the time it was stews that we had and the food was bloody awful! We did find out that they'd recently opened up a fish-

and-chip shop in Warsaw that was the nearest thing to Westernised food, so one night we went there. Thank goodness for that, I thought, 'cos I'm bloody starving! But it tasted the same: it tasted like the meat-fish we'd already been eating.

The hotel in Stettin had a big glass frontage to the street, and me and Dom were sat at the bar situated towards the back. All of a sudden, we hear this screeching of car tyres and we looked around and saw a Mercedes screech to a halt outside. A guy leapt out, came into the hotel lobby, had a good look around and makes a beeline over to us at the bar. He tapped us on the shoulder and said, 'You want buy zloty?'

We weren't sure whether we'd heard him right or whether it was a *Candid Camera* set-up.

'Sorry, pardon?' we managed.

'You want buy zloty?' he repeated.

'Well, I'll have some!' Dominic said, recovering first. I think to be honest I was too frightened to say anything. I'd had some experience of the black market – when I joined the Cubs, I bribed my way to get enough badges to become a 'sixer' – but this was clearly a different league.

'How much you want?' the guy asked.

'Oh, I'll take forty quid's worth of zlotys, please,' Dominic said as if he were just exchanging traveller's cheques. 'I'll go and get the cash from my hotel room.'

'Alright. Meet me in toilets over there, five minutes,' he said, indicating the gents' which was about thirty yards away, immediately off the reception area.

The guy went back to his Mercedes where his driver was waiting.

'Do you realise what you are doing here?' I said to Dom. 'If he's a double agent, you could be put in prison and they'll throw away the key and that'll be the end of it!'

'No, it'll be alright,' he said. 'They wouldn't come in here if they weren't legit. Don't worry about it,' and headed off to his room.

I sat there drinking my vodka and thinking, sod this for a game of soldiers!

When Dominic came back with the money he said, 'I'll be back in a sec now. I'm just going in the loo to get the zlotys.'

'Okay then, I'll keep an eye out for you,' I said, thinking, it's a bullet in me head any minute now.

So he goes in and I'm sat there looking for the geezer to come back from the car with the money, and I saw him come back, and I saw him walk in the men's toilets. He'll be out in a minute, I thought. I continued with my vodka and a couple of minutes went past and I thought, this is going on a bit long isn't it? I looked at my watch and thought, bloody hell! They've been in there ten minutes and none of 'em's come out yet! What if he's killed him and left him in the cubicle or something? And I thought, what should I do? Should I go in? What if the guy's still in there and he's murdered him? He'll murder me now! What the hell do I do?

Well, I can't bloody sit here and do nothing, I thought; I've gotta do something even if it's phone the police. I know, I'll slowly make my way over to the loo and please God they'll come out before I get there, 'cos otherwise I'll feel dreadful if something has happened!

So I took the longest thirty-yard walk in history and tried to make it last as long as possible; and of course, the closer I was getting to the door, the more the sweat was rolling off me and I was thinking, this is it, I'm gonna die now!

Just as I get to the door and I'm summoning that last amount of courage to push the door open and go in, the Polish guy comes flying out of the gents' and runs to his Mercedes which drives off, tyres screeching.

Something's gone amiss here. Something ain't right! I thought, just as Dominic comes out with a grin as big as a Cheshire cat!

'Look at that wad of notes I've got!' he cried. It looked like he'd got a fistful of the biggest notes in Poland. 'Let me buy you a drink!' We headed back to the bar and he waved the notes at me. '*Look at that!*'

'Bloody hell!' I said. 'What are ya gonna do with it? There's nothing to buy in the shops!'

As we were walking back to the bar I said, 'How much did he give ya?'

'Well, I don't know, but we've got plenty here to last us till kingdom come!'

We sat back down at the bar and his face was a picture: you'd think he had won the lottery. He began to count his money and the outside notes started promisingly enough, but the denominations went quickly and disappointingly down; the majority of notes were just ones. When he added it all up, he'd lost out well and truly. He'd got less than what he'd have got if he'd have done it legitimately. We could not believe it after all that palaver.

'That'll teach us, dealing with the Polish Mafia.'

'Where's the assassin when you need him?'

'We'll send him to sort that geezer out,' we joked.

The filming in Stettin was less eventful, although we were shooting on one location and we got lost and ended up in an ex-prisoner-of-war camp. It was in the middle of the country and really spooky because there weren't any birds singing or anything. It just felt so eerie.

After a few days we headed back to Warsaw. We went back by train, but they'd decided to book us on the equivalent of a bank holiday train. I don't think it was punishment, but we couldn't get a seat and had to stand up for six hours. We ended up sitting in the corridors of the train; it was horrendous, but I much preferred it to Polish flying.

When we got back, me and Tracy decided to try and find something good to eat at the modern hotel where some of the others were staying. Me, Dom, Tracy, Sophie, Jean-Pierre and a few of the others were staying in an old Gothic hotel. It was very elegant and regal inside although it was suggested that you should not drink the water from the taps; it certainly did come out a very funny colour. Susannah York and Paul Nicholas among others were in the modern hotel, so we decided to go and see how the other half lived.

It was nice to see Tracy again. Face-wise, she hadn't changed at all since *Melody*; we just weren't kids any more. We arrived at the hotel and tried to get a table, but they wouldn't let us in. We couldn't understand it, or them, but eventually all became clear. They wouldn't let us in because they thought I'd picked Tracy up and that she was a hooker! We thought it was hysterical. After a lot of aggravation of trying to prove Tracy wasn't a hooker, we called some-one up from the film in the hotel to vouch for us because there were lots of people from the film at the hotel.

After supper, which tasted like fish-meat, I left Tracy there because she met up with someone that she knew; I think she was seeing someone on the film. So then I headed back to my hotel. My hotel was in the centre of Warsaw and could've only been maybe three or four miles down the road, but it was cold. One night in Warsaw, it had been minus twenty-eight degrees or something outrageous like that and I've never known cold like that. It wasn't like a damp cold. It was a very, very, dry coldness. It was horrible, so I hailed a cab.

'I'll take you, but you give me foreign money or I charge you many zloty.'

They'd told us to beware of getting cabs in Warsaw, because if you didn't have any foreign currency the taxi drivers would charge you ten times the normal amount they'd charge a Polish person. We'd been told on average how much to expect to pay, going from one hotel to any of the six destinations we could be going, and not to pay more than that. And I thought, I'm not being ripped off! So I said, 'No thanks mate,' and walked on. I stopped about three or four cabs in all, but because they wanted what I thought was extortionate amounts of money, I said, 'Bollocks! I'm not paying that!' and walked on.

I'd spent my foreign currency in the shop in the hotel. It was like a duty-free shop where you could buy cartons of Western cigarettes, alcohol and chocolate, and it made you realise that home wasn't really that far away.

I had loads of zlotys and it looked like they were giving us lots of money; but the thing was, there was nothing to buy in the shops outside the hotel. They were the most minimalistic shops I've ever, ever seen in my life. If there was a clothes shop, there might be five mannequins in the shop window of which only three would be clothed, and they'd be clothed in things you wouldn't really want to wear and no bright colours at all.

One day, we saw fresh tomatoes for sale and there was a queue about two miles long, all the way around the block. You were only allowed to buy the equivalent in weight of a pound of tomatoes and the queue wasn't just formed of one behind the other, it was like six abreast, so there must've been four or five hundred people. If you went into any food shop, there'd be very little food for sale. It was like somebody had burgled the entire city and nothing was left.

I was told that the Communist government at the time wouldn't accept that there was an alcohol problem in Warsaw, and yet you couldn't walk down the street and not see nine hundred drunks. They were the sort of drunks that, if they bumped into you in the street, they may not be able to speak a word of English but they'd be so apologetic. I didn't meet one aggressive Polish person the whole time I was there. I don't know where the government walked, but as I walked back to my hotel there were tramps everywhere, in minus twenty-eight degrees. I was freezing, but having so much Polish vodka in me kept the chill out; and when I got back, I warmed up with a few more.

When I was first approached to do the film they said to me, 'You can ride a motorbike, can't you?'

'Yeah, course I can!' I said. 'I did on a TV show last year!'

In *Everyday Maths* I'd had to ride a motorbike. I wouldn't say I got to any great speed on it, but I did change gear and get up to fourth. I could've spent the whole series doing that if I'd had my way. I'd really enjoyed riding this 125cc motorbike so I thought, yeah, course I can ride a motorbike. No problem! But bugger me, when I got there, it's a bloody 750 or 900cc or something outrageous like that. Ride it? The reality was I couldn't even hold the damn bike up. Everyone was always trying to find somewhere with good food and not really succeeding, so I wasn't a hundred per cent fit anyway from not eating; and certainly the Polish vodka had taken its toll.

I certainly wasn't in a fit state to ride it safely, so I had the shock of my life when we got on the set and they're expecting me to take charge of this bike.

'It's too heavy for me. I can't do it!' I said, and Dom looked none too impressed either. They got round it by having stuntmen for both me and Dom, to help us out; but we did manage to sit on them a lot, and act the part of bikers.

Our last scene in the film was shot on location on the main motorway into Warsaw. It was a chase sequence with me, Dom and our stuntmen on our motorbikes chasing Jean-Pierre Cassel in his car. They didn't have a closed set for this scene: just one brave policeman, no cones, and only a small lollipop sign with an optimistic NO ENTRY to try and stop the traffic.

We were to corner Jean-Pierre into pulling over; Jean-Pierre screeches to a halt, leaps out and whacks the both of us, thinking we're a couple of hit-men. The first director came up to us and through his interpreter said: 'This is your last scene in the movie so we want it to be spectacular. It must be very dramatic! So after you've been knocked to the ground, we want it to be very dramatic. Okay?'

So that's how we shot it. 'Cut'. The second director came up and through his interpreter said, 'Don't you realise, guys, this is your last scene in the movie? You've got to play it for laughs. We want it to be funny! Yes?'

And so it was from one extreme to another.

'Okay, here's what we do,' suggested Dom. 'We'll end up having a fight amongst ourselves about the fact that we've allowed ourselves to be hit by this toerag and see how that goes down.' We shot it again and both directors seemed to be happy, but it was hard to tell. In the final edit you only see us just starting to fight and then they cut.

I wasn't eating, I was just drinking this Polish vodka, and I was becoming iller and iller; and this one morning, it was quite a late start, about 9.30 or ten. I was getting ready to go to the set, when I became aware of a pain in my stomach. By the time I got into make-up it felt like I was being repeatedly stabbed in the stomach. We'd often go to the Polish TV studios to get made up, and an old friend, Patrick Newell, was doing *Sherlock Holmes* there. I'd wanted to go and see him today, but all I could think of was the pain. I didn't even notice the make-up artist's more and more desperate attempts to keep the make-up on my face. It kept sliding off me in the rivers of sweat.

Tracy's voice faded in and out. 'You don't look well, darlin'.'

I could only sit there and manage half a smile, but I was inclined to agree with her. And the pain grew. Then concerned voices, a doctor called, someone laid me on the floor, which for a moment cooled the fire. More concerned voices and a car to the hospital.

As we pulled up at this grey, uninviting building I wondered where they had brought me. They half-carried, half-dragged me in. Then someone was wrapping me in what seemed to be a super-thin sheet and putting me in a wheelchair: the pain and fear grew in equal measures. We seemed to glide around the hospital for hours and hours, and by now the fire within me had been replaced by an all-consuming freeze. I was so cold that I couldn't ever imagine being warm again. With the slightest touch I was sure I should snap and shatter into nine hundred million pieces. It didn't look like a real hospital at all. It looked like they found an empty building and thought, oh, let's put a few beds in and make it *look* like a hospital. All the beds were different sizes: some were long, some short, some high, some low, but Goldilocks was nowhere in sight. The curtains hung apologetically around the beds, limply held together with a safety pin, an orange stain clinging to their hems. The colour stood out strongly against the relentless sea of gray.

And then I remember waking up to find myself tied to the bed. My arms and legs were shackled to each side. Panic rose up through me. I fought and struggled but I was tethered and caught. I strained to see a familiar face, someone who spoke English, someone to make sense of… My moment of clarity slipped away.

Later, much later I think, I woke to find my interpreter from the film with Tracy and Dominic talking in hushed tones around my bedside.

'What have they done to him?'

'He has been hallucinating, you see… for his own safety… they think he is a drug addict…'

My interpreter could only come when she wasn't on the set with Dominic, but she did manage to come at least once a day. The man in the bed next to me had had a leg amputated just above the knee. I'd been watching him all day. He sat there cloaked in misery and bewilderment gazing at his oozing stump. A man cut down and abandoned. And I had no idea – my interpreter spoke to him and found out that it was the other leg that was damaged and they'd cut off the wrong one.

And no sooner do I find that out, than an hour later my doctor comes and says, 'We've found out what is wrong with you, yes? And we're going to operate on you in the morning.'

Then there were lots of phone calls saying, 'Jack's in hospital!' and they're phoning Hemdale to say, 'We've got to change the schedule for filming because Jack's in hospital.' And they phoned Gay to say, 'Your husband is in hospital but he's okay and it's all under control. They're going to operate on him now.' Then twenty-four hours later she'd get another phone call saying, 'No, they've decided to fly him to Switzerland to be operated on!'

And then another twenty-four hours later… 'No, we've decided we're going to fly him to Paris now!'

And another twenty-four hours, another phone call saying, 'We're going to fly him back to England!'

I remember constantly being given injections, constantly: of what, I had no idea. I remember Jean-Pierre Cassel coming to see me with his girlfriend. And I remember the pain of it all. And most of all – I just wanted to go home.

'I've been to your room and packed all your clothes, darlin', so don't worry about a thing,' Tracy reassured me.

'Because of your condition, a doctor will have to fly with you.'

They ripped out three rows of seats to put a stretcher on the floor with a doctor by my side on the flight back to Heathrow. We arrived at Heathrow early morning and an ambulance was on the tarmac, flanked by Bob. I was taken to Charing Cross Hospital, and as we pulled into the hospital we crossed through a group of people holding banners and placards. I thought, the last time I was here I was doing *The 14* seven years before.

I was taken into Casualty where they confirmed the Polish diagnosis of acute pancreatitis. 'Twenty-five years ago we would have operated on you as well, but it's good that you came back because we can now deal with that with tablets and treatment.'

It was good to be home.

'The only problem is, I am afraid we can't admit you as we are on strike.'

There is no place like home.

They gave me a letter to take to my GP which I accepted, and some advice which I didn't. 'If you carry on drinking, you will die.'

'Yeah, yeah, okay,' I said with complete indifference.

'You'd be better off being run over by a double-decker bus – it will be less painful than dying from drinking,' the doctor persisted.

It was like vodka off an alcoholic's back. I refused to believe I had to stop drinking completely; and maybe, somewhere in the back of my mind, I knew I couldn't. But I decided to make one concession to my illness.

When I got home I told Gay that they had advised me to cut back on spirits and stick to just beer and wine, until I was feeling better. So I poured a glass of wine to help me on the road to recovery. I can't have had a drink for a few days, but had been too ill to notice; now I was home I could put that right.

I was still hallucinating and I remember vividly phoning Arthur English on several occasions, at various stages in the night. I was convinced that I had seen him in the reception of the hotel in Poland, but couldn't speak to him for some reason, so I was calling him to apologise for not speaking to him.

I'd kept in contact with Arthur since *Everyday Maths*, but I was so embarrassed about phoning him through the night, we lost touch after that.

The office kept calling to see when I could go back to finish filming. I found it all very confusing, and in the night I kept going into one of the two spare rooms on the same floor as our bedroom because I felt sure there was a door in there that went back into my hotel room in Poland. I knew I had to continue filming this movie.

I'd already missed the scene right at the end where Rabbit rescues Alice from being beheaded as they couldn't rearrange that. It was a huge scene apparently, shot on the Sherlock Holmes set, but shot without me as I was too ill.

After about a week, when Hemdale called again, I said, 'I'm okay, I'm ready to go now, I'll go back now.' And obviously I wasn't well enough at all, but within a week of arriving in England I was back on a plane to Marseilles to continue filming. I remember getting on the flight at Heathrow on my own and I thought, well, you know, lots of the doctors have said 'Stop drinking!' so how about if I stay off the Polish vodka and just drink beer and wine and just have that?

So I thought, if I do that I'll be alright; so when I was on the plane, as opposed to having spirits, I had some beer and wine.

When I got to Marseilles, with my tickets and information it said, 'Because the flight arrives late, get yourself a cab from the airport to the hotel in Marseilles and we'll reimburse you the cost of the cab.' It was about an hour and a half to Marseilles and the fare cost me nearly fifty quid, so of course by the time I get to the hotel, it's midnight and there's no one about. I paid the cab and I was well pissed off because I'd now run out of cash and I wouldn't get any more money until I was paid my expenses and to top it all off, the bar was closed!

There was a minibar in my room but it didn't have any beer or wine in it, only spirits. I thought, I'm going to have to have something. I'll have to have a brandy! And so I had a couple of doubles of brandy before I went to bed.

The next day I told everyone on the film set, 'The doctors said I had to stay off any spirits and I can only drink either wine or beer, nothing more!' It was beginning to sound like the truth, I'd said it so often. I certainly believed that I was strong enough to have beer and wine and it not to affect my body. I believed I was stronger. I believed I was in ultimate control. I was feeling alright now, as you only need one drink when you've had a binge the night before to make you feel okay.

We went out for a meal that night and were told that a lot of Marseilles was run by Mafia-type gangs. 'Me and Dominic will be alright,' I said, 'we've dealt with the Polish Mafia and survived!' Everyone laughed. It felt good to be back at work.

I hadn't really got back into eating because I was still recovering. I'd lost my appetite and hardly ate anything that night, which was a shame because the food did look good, but I was feeling so much better than in Warsaw.

The next day I went along the seafront which was beautiful. I was still having twinges in my stomach, but nothing I couldn't deal with, so I headed into work. We were shooting the scene where Sophie is singing a song and we run round the city with her, larking about. At one stage she had to throw tomatoes at us and they were doing it where one of them hits me on the head. We did it a few times, because from what I remember Sophie wasn't that good of a shot. One time when she did hit me, by now I'm a bit bored so I thought I'd make it funnier and fall over. Well, after I did that the first time, the directors said through their interpreters, 'Oh, that is great! Keep it in and we'll use that!'

I was glad my bit of artistic interpretation was accepted. The last few weeks had been a horrendous experience for me, but apart from that, the filming was very enjoyable; I'd survived it all and was getting back on form.

While I was being treated in London, they had to rearrange the shooting schedule, so after we finished in Marseilles we then went back to Warsaw again to finish off filming, and from there, home.

Chapter 21

'**H**OW MUCH HAVE YOU HAD TO DRINK?'
'I'm just relaxing,' I protested.
'Well, make sure you're ready to go, because I won't be here to sort you out.'

'Yeah, yeah,' I said, 'it's all under control.'

Gay had got a job with a female dance group called 'Love Machine' and was getting ready to go on tour. They'd got a month's work over Christmas and New Year, with two weeks in Singapore and two weeks in Bangkok. Love Machine was actually a rip-off from a black American girl group. They hadn't copyrighted the name worldwide and so Gay's band used it in England, Europe and the Far East. And, because I'd been ill, I decided that I'd go out with them for a holiday.

I couldn't actually get on the same flight as Gay, because she'd been booked along with the band months before, and I was a late addition. So I planned to go out a few days later to join them before their opening gig; and besides, I had some business to attend to in London.

The club I'd invested in wasn't doing so well and I needed my money back. Four years ago I'd bought five thousand pounds' worth of shares, but they didn't seem to be doing any good really and I was trying to get out of it. I had a meeting with the manager and said I wanted to get my shares out. He tried to talk me out of it but I said, 'Well, I don't see what good this is doing for me!'

He said the only way I could sell them was to sell them back to him, and because the business wasn't doing that well and the club had lost so much money, the prices had gone way down.

'Well, I will buy them off you, but the maximum I can give you is the going rate now and that would be a thousand pounds,' he said.

It was either that or I wouldn't get anything, so that's what I did. I sold the shares, losing £4,250 in the process. Still, at least I had nearly a grand in my pocket.

For the first two weeks at home, as I weren't supposed to be drinking, I'd been trying to stick to beer and wine as much as I could. Although I was still arguing with Gay about my drinking, I was trying to keep it more under control. On the flight out there, however, I did drink spirits as I was on my own, and I do remember that I was well tanked up by the time I'd got to Singapore; but as soon as I got off the plane, I didn't drink any spirits at all while I was there.

We were all staying in a top five-star hotel where the band was playing in the hotel's nightclub. We were given food vouchers to go into any of the hotel restaurants and eat anything we wanted. I liked this coffee-bar-type place where I used to eat a fillet steak every day; I stuck to wine or beer and I didn't get drunk once.

I felt physically fine. In comparison to what I'd gone through a few weeks back, I *was* fine. This was my first holiday where I wasn't doing any work whatsoever since skiing four years ago and I was going to enjoy it. I was eating well, and I'd bought a Hitachi cassette/radio/colour TV that I'd wanted because Bob had just bought one in England; *and* I'd got it cheaper. I was also having a good time going about Singapore with this geezer called Dieter. He was the tour manager for the band: a German guy, six foot two with blonde hair, and he'd been all over the place touring with loads of different bands.

He told me about this place in Singapore called Boogie Street where there were a lot of sleazy strip joints, sex shows, prostitutes and drugs: all the nasty things in life, I suppose. Dieter also said there were a lot of guys there who'd had sex changes, but it was so hard to tell and you'd swear blind that they were ladies as opposed to men.

He took us all there one night after a gig and this must've been about one or two o'clock in the morning. It was something like what I remember the old Portobello Road to be like, where it was very busy and everywhere you looked there were deals being made, whether it was for legitimate merchandise, or whether it was for illegal substances; the atmosphere was electric. It was all lit up, and we sat outside this bar drinking beer.

Dieter was pointing out these amazingly beautiful girls to me and saying, 'This bird, walking towards us now, is a bloke!'

'How do you know?' I asked.

'You take it from me, because I know!' he said, rather puzzlingly. This particular one that he pointed at, I would've swore on my life or anyone's life that it was a woman because she was just too beautiful. I must've been looking at this guy with my mouth hanging on the floor and, as he passed, he pulled the strap of his dress down and lifted out one of his tits and said in a sort of very unreal American accent, 'These are real, honey!'

I just couldn't believe this!

We must've stayed there a good couple of hours drinking and talking.

'As you know, Jack,' Dieter said, 'with Singapore being a naval base for the United States, it is well known for prostitutes to be found murdered.' I wasn't sure how these two facts were connected.

'How do you mean mate?' I asked.

Apparently, I found out, a lot of these sailors would come off the ships and want to sow their oats for having been on the sea for so long. They'd pick up what they thought was a prostitute and then, when it got down to the basics, they'd find out that she'd got a dick, go absolutely bananas and kill her.

This was a whole new world to me.

We met one prostitute who was, I'm presuming, homeless. She had with her a young kid and this kid was so adorable, I wanted to bring her home with me. It was a little girl, a dark-haired little girl, and what a picture. An absolute angel, and to think of her having the lifestyle that she had there: it was just a waste, and presumably the mother would've been hooked on heroin or something horrendous like that. It was awful. An experience and a half to see how other people lived.

On Boxing Day Dieter said, 'One of my mates is playing in another hotel and he's invited me down for drinks, do you want to come?'

It was strange being in that sort of climate for Christmas. It just didn't feel right for it not to be freezing cold outside, and it didn't feel right to be eating turkey when it's eighty degrees outside. Stranger still to be going for drinks by the pool with Gerry Marsden from Gerry and the Pacemakers. Gerry and the band all knew Dieter from way back. I'd bought their records as a youngster so it was great to meet them. I'm sure I did tell them that. He was lovely, a really nice, normal geezer: a typical one of the lads, and so were all of his band. We talked about our careers and he said that he enjoyed me in *Oliver!* and blah, blah, blah. As we sat there talking, a rainstorm came and the rain came down in buckets. It felt so warm, you didn't feel bothered that you were sat getting soaked.

After a few drinks at the poolside, Gerry suggested a game of golf. 'Are you any good at this?' he said. 'I'm trying to learn and get a good handicap!'

The golf course was within the grounds of the hotel. When it came to my go, I grabbed a wood because I'd seen everyone else using one. I'll have a go with one of them, I thought, and hopefully it'll go a fair distance.

I hit the golf ball and I thought, yeeesssss! That's a good whack!

About two hundred yards away, there was a man sat on a drivable lawn-mower doing the greens. And bugger me! The ball flew straight towards him. It was so close to killing this geezer on the lawnmower, I bet I didn't miss him by two foot. It looked like inches!

I really panicked, thinking that I'd come close to killing him. I knew how strict they were in Singapore. You never saw litter in the streets; if you were caught spitting on the street, you'd be fined or put in prison.

The drummer of the band with Love Machine had already been in trouble, just over his hair. The authorities were very fussy about anyone who appeared on stage, or in front of an audience of any kind, even on telly, or in films for that matter. They had to look respectable, and the drummer had hair down to his shoulders. He looked like a hippy beatnik and at the airport they said, 'You can only appear on stage if you have your hair cut!' He was going mad about this, but he had to do it otherwise he'd have been on the next plane back to London. Goodness knows what they would have done to me if I had killed a geezer.

I really enjoyed that day with Gerry and the Pacemakers. Apparently, at Gay's gig that night, Barry Manilow came and saw the girls perform, so they had had a good day too. I think he was performing himself somewhere in Singapore.

We then flew from Singapore to Bangkok which seemed to be a much more chaotic sort of place; you were putting your life at risk just crossing the road. We were met at the airport by the agents for this gig, and they took us to meet the owner of the nightclub where the band was playing. It didn't seem to be such a good venue as in Singapore, and the owner seemed to be a bit dodgy, but we didn't stay there long. From the nightclub we were taken to our hotel on the outskirts of the city.

It wasn't as palatial as Singapore, but it was still nice, and I was still on holiday. All the rooms were around the hotel's swimming pool; at breakfast I'd eat freshly prepared fruit there, and at nights we'd have a couple of drinks there after the gig. We all soon set into a pattern: we wouldn't get up till lunchtime, then we'd have a kip mid-afternoon before having something to eat, and then go and do the next performance.

One day, there was a wedding reception in the hotel and they fenced off the whole of the swimming pool area, which threw our pattern straight away. Then, the wedding party had an organist with microphones playing live music at afternoon kip time. Of course everyone was trying to sleep and we couldn't. We met in the corridors and said, 'What are we gonna do about this music then?'

We decided to try and find out how we could stop all this music ourselves. So we went hunting around in the hotel, found the electricity source, switched it off and went back to our rooms. It took them close on an hour to find out the cause and switch it back on again. Dieter then tried the more conventional approach and asked them to turn it down because we were working nights.

After a few days, the owner of the nightclub invited me into his office and Dieter came with me. I wasn't sure what it was about at first as he was telling us that he was very close to the Head of Police in Bangkok and about the difficulties of running a nightclub. Anyway, apparently he'd recognised me early on and he said to me, 'Next week, you can be the compere for the show!'

I suppose he was thinking that this would get him more punters in the club.

'Yeah, but how much are you gonna pay me?' I said.

'Oh no, I'm not going to pay you. You can do it as a favour!'

'Oh no, I ain't doing it! Not as a favour I ain't!'

He pulled out a gun from his desk and started playing with it; and I thought, I've been here before. He didn't point it at me, but I think that was because Dieter was there; if he hadn't have been I'm sure he would've become threatening. So I joked with him and said, 'Thanks but no, I've come here for a holiday and if you don't mind, I want to relax!' And not for the first time I talked my way out of it.

After that incident, I think he wanted to at least show us off to his friends, so he took us all to another nightclub on the group's night off. It was a very popular place at that time in Bangkok and it was his police mate who ran it, and Christ it looked such a dodgy place. I was even frightened to go to the loo on me own so I said to Dieter, 'Look mate, I wanna go to the loo. Will you come with me 'cos I don't like it in here?' He came with me and you could see people in there with guns sticking out of their pockets. We went back out and had several drinks, but even that didn't help and I couldn't wait to get out of that place.

I wouldn't start drinking until lunchtime, but I did get drunk in Bangkok and broke my 'no spirits unless it can't be helped' rule. We'd been to a TV station to do some publicity for the nightclub. The band had gone on and been interviewed about their gig in Bangkok and the station gave them a case of brandy. That night, when we had drinks by the pool, we had a case of brandy to get rid of. Some of us swam and some of us drank. I do remember getting particularly drunk that night and I vaguely remember the Scottish, short-haired, drummer being flash with his diving and trying to teach me; somehow neither of us drowned.

From time to time, the bloke and young woman who were the agents for this gig would pop in and see that everything was going AOK. One afternoon they came to the hotel and said to Gay, 'We've been in contact with a guy who is doing a TV ad and he'd like to have you in it.'

Gay had said, 'Well, you'll have to speak to Jack. He'll sort it out with you.'

So they came over to me and said, 'It will take a day to shoot it and it'll be done at Bangkok Airport. We want Gay to play the part of an airline stewardess serving drinks on the aeroplane.'

'Okay. How much are you talking about paying?'

'Oh, we'll give you seventy-five US dollars and we'll pick her up from the hotel, and we'll get her back into the hotel by no later than 6.30 in the evening because we know she has a show to do.'

'That is outrageous!' I said. 'Seventy-five US dollars? You add a nought on the figures and you've got yourself a deal! She is a member of British Equity and the minimum she'll do it for is 750 US dollars and it'll have to be cash in the hand.'

The girl said, 'Seventy-five dollars, and you can have my younger sister for the night.'

'No, I'm not interested in your sister,' I said. 'I'm happily married, thank you. I'm not into that.'

Then the guy said, 'Alright then, seventy-five US dollars and you can have my sixteen-year-old brother for the night.'

'No, I've told you, I'm not interested. I've told you what the deal is; it's either that or nothing!'

The two of them walked away, had a quick chat and came back and said, 'Okay. We'll agree to that then.'

Gay did do it and I went with her.

On one particularly humid day we went sightseeing to the Royal Palace in the centre of Bangkok. Dieter told me as we were walking into the Palace that the King of Thailand was a really hip guy because he could play the saxophone. At the time I thought he was winding me up, but apparently it was true. Me and Dieter had become great mates. During the live shows, while he was adjusting the sound levels after each song, I would make sure he had a drink at all times, even though I rationed myself to only one small bottle of beer per show. For that and that alone, I thought my drinking was totally under control – irrespective of the fact that, as soon as the show was over, I'd be back to drinking as normal. That was the downside of the not-drinking-spirits rule: you had to drink so much wine and beer to get you to the same level that the spirits would.

A group of us went on this trip to the Palace; there was me and Gay, Dieter, Teresa and John the bass player. We decided to have a look at the market first of all which was right opposite this magnificent Royal Palace. They advertised the market as 'you can buy anything in here!' It was massive and maybe a mile square, full of stalls, selling everything from live animals to aphrodisiacs. You could drink warm snake's blood, cut from the snake in front of you and poured into a glass; I don't know what that was for. They were selling day-old chickens that'd been dyed fluorescent colours. They were like pink, blue, green, yellow, and they had monkeys painted like that as well. It was horrendous.

Because it was so hot and airless, I'd decided to go there in jeans and a denim waistcoat, with a black and white embroidered eagle on the back of it, left open. Apparently, I wasn't dressed properly and they wouldn't let me into the Palace. Fortunately, the market that sells everything even sold things you wanted, so I went in and bought a T-shirt so that I would be allowed in.

And the Palace was amazing. I didn't know that in the Buddhist religion you had to go and buy gold leaf to give as an offering to a statue of Buddha, and you could see all this gold leaf flying everywhere. I said to Dieter, 'Let's go and get a hoover! We can make a fortune here with this lot!' I couldn't understand why all these people who were so poor were giving gold away to these statues. I found that very hard to understand.

On another day we hired an air-conditioned limo because we wanted to go and see the bridge on the River Kwai. Gay's uncle Ossie had been out in Malaya during the Second World War but never got to the bridge, so we told him, 'If we go there, we'll bring you back a bottle of water from the river!' I don't think he was actually an uncle but a family friend who came up from the valleys with them; I think they'd kind of adopted him into their family, and so he was adopted into mine.

It was about an hour and a half's drive from Bangkok up north and it was amazing to actually get out of the city and just see the countryside. As soon as we arrived I said, 'The first thing we gotta do is go and get this water from the river, right!'

It was quite high up, and to get down to the river was about a 150-foot dash. I didn't want to get bitten by a snake, or spiders, or tigers, or crocodiles, or I don't know what, so I flew down there, got to the riverside, got the water in a shampoo bottle and flew back up the hill. I was happy then and went and bought a few pieces of Burmese jade to bring back. I think he was pleased with the water when we gave it to him, but it didn't really look any different to anything else. We could've given him water from the Thames, and he wouldn't have known any difference.

I wished I'd looked on a map to see where I actually was because I was so near Hong Kong, so near Australia, so near Borneo, and I would love to have seen orangutans. If I'd known where I was, I would've said to Gay, 'Let's have another month after you've finished and we can go and do that tour as well before going home!'

But with me being pissed, it didn't happen.

Still, at least in Thailand I had my photograph taken with crocodiles and baby lions, tigers, cheetahs, leopards, black panthers, monkeys, gibbons and all sorts. Then I saw a chimp and I said to Gay, 'I've gotta have my photograph taken with this chimp!'

I went up to where this chimp was and I said to the handler, 'Can I have my photograph taken with your chimp please?'

And he said in broken English, 'You take him to bar and buy drink, he sit with you and have drink!'

I grabbed hold of the chimp's hand and he came with me over to the bar.

'What does he want?' I called back to the handler.

'Coke, no ice,' he called back.

I got a Coke for the chimp, myself a beer and I gave Gay the camera. 'Please take a load of pictures of us together, as many as you want.'

I gave the chimp his bottle, he grabbed hold of my hand and led me to sit underneath a table; and there we sat, under the table, drinking together. After a couple of minutes he took me to sit on a low wall, and by now I wanted to have a cigarette.

I pulled one out and went to get my lighter out of my pocket, but no sooner had I gone for it than this chimp pulls out a Zippo lighter, lifts the top, flicks the wheel, gets a flame, and offers me a light! And Gay clicked just at the right time. Amazing, absolutely fantastic! I really did enjoy that. On the way back we were walking along the high street towards the city centre and we saw a bloke on an elephant. What a great place!

*

I came home in the January of 1980 and got back to my serious drinking. I wasn't working, so I filled in the time with drinking; it'd be drinking, playing squash, drinking, playing Showbiz XI and drinking. And that was mostly it for 1980.

At some time in the late seventies, I think, I'd become preoccupied with drink. It always seemed to be on my mind, all the time. I seemed to become obsessed with drink and started to make sure I had a good supply and choice at home. Living in London made things easier; if the off-licences were closed (and very early on, I got to know their opening and closing times, half days etc.), there were always shops open till about midnight within walking distance from the house.

Many times Gay would say, 'Why do we need to have all this drink in the house?'

I'd always find an excuse. The one I used to use a lot was, 'Well, what happens if so-and-so turns up unexpectedly?' and name someone I knew in the business, or whoever I was working with at the time. I guess I was in a fortunate position having some money behind me, so that I always had a large supply and always made sure it was on hand twenty-four hours a day.

At some stage I also started to hide booze all over the house, so much so that I'd often forget where I'd hidden it half the time. It became so frustrating, knowing that it was there somewhere, but I couldn't find it. If friends, or my parents, or Gay's family came round, I'd either not drink until they'd gone, or, if I had a drink when they arrived, I'd make it last until they'd gone. Unless, of course, they'd come for a meal or to watch a film. That being the case, they'd normally bring a bottle with them. If they ever stayed a long time, I'd be gasping and I'd make an excuse and go to my bar-room whilst they were in the lounge. I'd have a quick slug, pour myself another and leave it behind the bar, so I could come back a bit later on and already have one there poured out.

When I went to work, I'd always have some in the boot of my car, especially if we were on location filming miles away from anywhere. Almost a hundred per cent of the time, there was some drink in the boot in case I went to friends' houses and they didn't have any. Booze came before anything, or anyone for that matter, including Gay.

'I thought you were going to stop drinking,' she'd say. It was so annoying being constantly nagged by Gay about the booze.

'They said to cut down, and I have,' I'd reply. I don't think anyone ever said just cut down: they said stop completely, but I didn't tell anyone that. Well, what did the doctors know? With the constant nagging, in lots of ways I was glad whenever she went away working because then I could drink myself silly without being nagged, and think that I could get away with it.

If Gay was working at the Hammersmith Palais or for one of the show-bands, quite often I'd pick her up at two o'clock in the morning from the other side of London. And quite often, I'd have fallen asleep at home through being drunk, and she'd phone me up.

'Where the hell are you?'

'I'm sorry, I fell asleep. I'm getting in the car now and I'll be with you as quick as I can.' It happened many a time, and the journey home would be the same.

'How many did you have?'

'Only a couple,' I'd reply, which would be sort of true, except that they were bottles and not glasses.

It would've probably been about March time when Tony told me that Chris had fallen pregnant and said they wanted me and Gay to be godparents. I said to Tony, 'Look Toe, I don't care what time it happens when Chris has to be taken to hospital, with it being her first, give me a call and I'll be there with ya!'

That winter, Tony did call me in the early hours of the morning and said, 'I'm on the way to the hospital with Chris. Her waters have broke!'

'What hospital are you going to?'

'Hammersmith.'

'I'll meet you there mate!'

I got up, drove up there and sat with him, clutching a bottle of champagne. We saw Chris going to have a last bath before the birth and she just sort of waved to us from the bottom of the corridor. I stayed there until Holly was born, and then of course we drank the bottle of champagne. That was on 25th November 1980.

And that's all I've got in my diary for the whole year so I must've been well and truly pissed. The doctors warned that my drinking would lead to blackouts where I might lose parts of the day. I was losing whole parts of the year.

Around this time Gay was doing gigs with Suzi Quatro. Suzi told me she wanted to get into acting again so I introduced her to my old agent, Denis Sellinger from ICM. I'd left ICM many years before. They had offices in all the capitals throughout the world, and Denis had said to me, 'Next time you're in LA or New York, call in the office and say hi, or give them a bell and say you're in town.'

So I did; I was finally put through to someone who said in so many words, 'I didn't realise that we represented you!' and I thought, great! I've got supposedly the best agent on the planet and they don't know that I'm on their books! What bloody good is that? I always liked Denis and thought he was a wonderful man, but when I came back to England I started looking to change agents. That was a long time ago.

Denis took Suzi on and we started talking about an idea for a series we could do together, like Bonnie and Clyde only she would be the leader of the gang and I would be the sort of stooge. That was the idea behind *The Foxes* and we decided to put some money up to try and get it off the ground. I can't remember much about it. I think the idea was, Suzi had come over to England to do some robberies, needed somebody English who could help her out with it, and collared me.

I was very keen to work. It had all been so much easier when I was a child. Work was just there. Now I was twenty-eight and I *had* to work; but I was a commodity, in a ruthless business, that no one wanted to buy.

Suzi talked to Denis about *The Foxes* and he said that he'd got someone who could write it for us but they'd want three or four grand. I didn't have the money spare so I asked me Dad if he'd lend it to me and he did. We paid the guy, but I didn't think it was a good synopsis of it. I wasn't happy with the amount it had cost and what came out of it. We did some publicity shots for it and got some interest in the press in the autumn but, to cut a long story short, it didn't go any further than that. We thought of it as a telly series originally, but we wouldn't have minded if it'd have been a film; in the end it was just a waste of money.

In September 1981, quite out of the blue, Bluebell died. I don't know what happened; she hadn't been ill or anything. I just went down to the cage one morning to feed them and she was dead. I'd built them a platform in the run that had a bucket in the middle of it for them to drink water out of. Whenever it rained it would be full of water and I'd only have to fill it up occasionally. They would have a drink, or play, or lay up there and she actually looked as though she was sunbathing with her arms and legs outstretched, lying by this bucket of drinking water. But she was dead.

I don't know when she actually died but I was absolutely gutted, totally gutted. I went in and Billy looked as bewildered as me and impossibly sad. We were both so shocked, but he slowly came over to me and I could almost see him crying. He was just so totally human. He came and sat on my shoulder as they both used to do and curled his tail over his body as though he wanted to go to sleep and not face this reality – I knew that feeling. I don't know how long we stayed like that, but at some point I went to get some booze. I was probably pissed already, but just in case I had some more.

I put Bluebell where I put all the animals that died in Chiswick: in this stone mausoleum, half way down the garden. It was like a tomb I'd made with paving slabs. Billy was very moody after Bluebell died, and the spring in his feet disappeared completely. I'll swear he just lost the will to carry on.

To be honest, the eighties was mostly a blur and only odd events stand out. I remember I'd got annoyed with Bob; I can't remember for what, but this one evening I'd gone to bed early because I'd been pissed, and I can't remember who was in the house but Bob was there and I think Glynne and Gay were there. I just remember coming downstairs with my shotgun. Although I did have real shells for it, I knew the difference between a blank cartridge and a real cartridge because a blank one is half as long and there's no way you can mistake them.

I came down the stairs, turned around to face him and he was in the middle room between the lounge and the kitchen. I flipped the lever down, put the cartridge in and pulled the lever back up so that it was ready to fire.

'Either go home or I'll fucking kill ya!' I said.

He looked shocked, obviously. I didn't fire it. I drunkenly went back up to bed. When I sobered up I was totally disgusted with myself. You cannot mistake the cartridges, but drink can do crazy things to you. I could've quite easily put a real cartridge in, thinking that it was a blank, and then decided to try and frighten him and fire it at him. I could've killed him.

After that I thought I should really get rid of this gun because if I'm capable of behaving like that with it, then it's serious. I didn't think about not drinking. Within nine months I got rid of it because I just kept thinking it could have happened again with the way my lifestyle was and the way I was drinking; it was better in the long run not to have it around so then I couldn't get hold of it. That was just being responsible.

I didn't see Bob for a long while after that. I say a long while, but at this stage I'd see him at least four or five times a week because he'd always be over, but it was probably seven to ten days before we spoke. I can't remember who made the first move to get things back to normal but it was soon forgotten about, I think; because of my own mess, it was hard to know what was going on for other people.

The shotgun was actually the climax of the incident. I think I'd argued with Bob upstairs in my bedroom. I'd grabbed him, got me Bowie knife out and shoved him against the wall.

'Don't push it!' I'd said, or some bloody rubbish because I was pissed off with him. Presumably that wasn't enough for me and I got out the gun. I didn't ever think about getting rid of the knife.

And still I kept drinking.

*

I'd never ever thought of doing pantomime before, but the work was just not happening now. I'd had the whole of 1980 where I hadn't done anything. Not that I was capable anyway – I was on planet Smirnoff – but I was desperate for work and I was offered a pantomime in Hereford at the Nell Gwynne Theatre for 1981/2. We opened with *Cinderella* on Boxing Day. I played Buttons, Peter Vaughan Clarke was Prince Charming and Bruce Trent was Baron Hardup; he was a well-known singer from way back. It was directed by Aubrey Phillips and we did that twice daily, six days a week in Hereford.

It was the first time I'd met PVC and he was an old friend of Mark Lester's. He was well known from being in the children's sci-fi series *The Tomorrow People* and he was great fun. We rented a cottage together about five miles outside the town, and arranged to travel up there together in my Datsun 260z.

Because this was my first panto, I was a little bit naïve as to what went on in pantomime, but Aubrey Phillips was a great help to me with the songsheet and all the panto biz that I hadn't been used to doing. I was drinking for England at this stage. I'd be in the pub at lunchtime and I'd have three or four pints at least and then, depending on what I was doing, would determine whether or not it carried on in the afternoon; and if it didn't, I'd be continuing after I'd finished work.

In one scene I was to be cut in half with a Black and Decker jigsaw. I remembered through a haze that I'd been cut in two before. It had been someone's birthday at Paramount studios, I think, on the set of Witchiepoo's Castle. I remember one of the puppeteers – Scutter, that was it – and a box, and being egged on to have a go. I remember the steel plates, and Scutter, and my stomach ending up to my right, with my legs sitting somewhere sort of below my head and a gap where my stomach should have been. I felt a bit like that now. But at the time I had no idea how he did it. We were all amazed and I didn't feel a thing.

But that was Hollywood and a very long time ago, and this was Hereford and I knew how this worked. Just as the saw is about to go through the body, the blade disengages. You go across the body as though you're going through the stomach, and another blade clips on at the other side when the person goes to lift the saw up to show that the blade is still going. Except this was Hereford, and one night just before the second blade attaches, one of the table legs broke and it all collapsed on the floor. I was drunk and just laughed it off, and suddenly remembered a trick that Scutter taught me with two sticks and tassles or something. I don't know.

It was freezing that winter, and one night I'd parked the car outside the cottage after a night out and it'd snowed so much that, when I got up the following morning, I couldn't see the car at all. The Datsun was very low to the ground, and with so much snow it had completely disappeared. As we were on a farm, I said to Peter, 'Well, we'd better get all the snow off it so the farmer don't drive over it in his tractor!'

'Where is it?' Peter asked.

'I don't know,' I said.

'Well, where did you leave it?'

'I can't remember,' I said. 'I don't even remember driving home.'

Peter sighed as he looked at the sink. On one of the first nights staying there, we'd had baked beans with grated cheese on top. I thought that was fantastic and had never had that before. We used to eat that a lot at the cottage, but you could tell how cold it was because we'd put the washing up in the bowl in the sink, filled it up with water and, in the morning, it was solid with ice!

Peter sighed again. 'Well, I can't wash up and we need to get to work,' he said, so we set about finding my Datsun.

We did find it, but eventually we arranged with two members of the band to pick us up. They had digs a couple of miles further on at another farm and as they had to pass us, and because the weather was so bad, they gave us lifts and I left my car at the cottage.

Me and Peter had open fires in this cottage and I thought one bag of coal was the same as the next, but we'd obviously bought the cheapest and it was like burning paper; a bag of coal would only last maybe an hour and a half and that's it. So we thought, it's gonna cost us a fortune keeping warm!

Then we remembered the scenery dock at the theatre. It was a massive place where they'd store stuff. When we saw this scenery not being used we thought, we'll use it, save it going to waste! So we started chopping up the scenery, filling the car with it and taking it home to burn.

The backstage crew didn't seem to mind: in fact they helped us. They were on another planet as they were smoking dope, and I was on another planet as I was pissed; we didn't even seem to be on the same planet.

Boxing Day, me Mum and Dad came down to see me for the opening and so did Gay. She came down on Christmas Eve with her mum and they stayed in the proper hotel in Hereford. I stayed there too, just for a couple of nights. We had the traditional Christmas meal, it all went well and then everyone went home.

Come the New Year, the whole cast had decided to go to this nightclub in town to have a meal. We'd hired a taxi to get to the club so that we could have a good drink; and I thought, being as I'm the star of the show, I'll buy them three or four bottles of champagne to put on the table. That sort of thing is expected of the 'name'. Anyway, we had a good meal, but when I got the bill for the champagne at the end, I thought it was a bit steep and wondered how I could get my money's worth for having been ripped off for the cost of this champagne. So, as I was leaving, I stole this silver soup ladle and slipped it into my coat pocket.

As we were driving back to our cottage in the taxi about two o'clock in the morning on New Year's Day, I was telling Peter about what I'd done. I said to him, 'They might've ripped me off with the cost of the champagne, but I've got my money's worth because look what I've got!' I pulled the ladle out of my pocket, brandishing it with a flourish.

The taxi driver must've been listening to what me and Peter were talking about and he said, 'Do you know who I am?'

As I'm pissed as a fart, I thought, he's taking the piss he is, so I said, 'Do you know who *I* am?'

'No seriously,' he said, 'do you know who I am?'

I thought, this is getting ridiculous.

'The club that you've just come out of belongs to my brother! He owns it!'

The ladle drooped in my hand and I felt so stupid. I looked lamely at Peter and was getting ready to offer to give it him back and say, 'ere you are, have it back, we were only having a laugh like, when he said, 'Don't worry about it. It happens all the time, that; but if you thought that was silver, it ain't!'

The next day at work, the company manager said that, if we wanted to, we could train with the local football club. The club was right opposite the theatre and I said, 'Oh, I'd love to do that!' Then on second thoughts I said, 'Actually, the weather is too awful. I can't be bothered!'

'Or,' he said, 'Hereford is near where the barracks are for the SAS and they said we could go canoeing at Ross-on-Wye. Apparently it is the best canoeing in England.' I had my second thoughts first and said no to that as well. I wanted to, but the weather was just against it all.

We went off to the local instead where the bitter was really nice tasting: lovely and strong. After at least half a gallon, we came home and I was so drunk that I remember falling in the snow and almost completely disappearing because it was that deep. I could not stop laughing. I must've been on the floor about ten minutes because I just couldn't get up.

The ASM eventually helped me up and we went in and lit a fire. We had a spare room so the ASM was staying with us. She was lovely: very butch, would do anything for you if you needed your props fixing or whatever, and we treated her like a sister. She didn't have anywhere to stay for a few nights so she came and stayed with us in the cottage.

One Sunday, we invited the two guys from the band and the ASM to the cottage for lunch. Of course, me and Peter got up late on the Sunday morning, started preparing the food and then decided to go to the local for a few drinks and meet the others while it was cooking. After a while Peter said, 'I've got to go back and check the dinner.'

I said, 'I'll be over in about an hour to help you. The others can come back when the pub closes.' I had another game of darts and another couple of pints and then went back to the cottage to help Peter.

When I got there, I tried to get in but Peter had been smoking dope and he'd locked all the doors and windows and wouldn't let me in. He was just laughing his head off on the first floor. I shouted up to him, 'Open the door!'

And he shouted down to me, 'No, I'm not letting you in!'

By this time I was cold as well as pissed so I yelled, 'If you don't open this fucking door now, I'm gonna break it down!'

He was crying with laughter.

'You bastard!' I said. 'If you don't get down here now, I'll bloody break a window,' thinking that actually might be more manageable than the door.

He was still laughing so I said, 'Right, you bastard! I'm gonna do it now!' and I went and found something to smash the window with so that I didn't cut myself; and just as I was about to smash it, he opened the door.

We got the dinner ready, the three of them came back from the pub and we had a lovely Sunday lunch.

At the last show, I remember being told that, as I was the star of it, I had to thank the front-of-house and the bar staff; and I forgot about it. I thanked everybody on stage and forgot about everybody in the theatre. Afterwards, when we'd all got dressed and everyone was going in the bar for a last drink, I apologised.

'I'm sorry, I forgot to thank everybody who made our stay here so great; but I'd like to thank you now, and I'm sorry I didn't say it in front of the audience. I forgot,' and I slipped off into a comforting vodka.

That night, or it could have been another night, me and Peter ended up at this drunken party doing cabaret. We got dressed up as women and did a Diana Ross and the Supremes song. I remember high heels, suspenders, bras and all sorts. I was totally out of it.

And that was the first pantomime that I did.

The run finished at the end of January and I came back to wedding plans. Arthur was due to be married. He had left the business by now, was doing bits and pieces of work and drinking too much than was good for him. He'd long since split up with Roberta and had gone into hospital because of the booze. There he met Julie, a consultant nurse, and they got married on 13th February 1982 at St Mark's Parish Church, Regent's Park.

I was pleased for Arf and I hoped life was beginning to work out for him. Perhaps it had been difficult for him. I didn't see it at the time, but really from after the *Oliver!* film came out, he was treated as Jack Wild's brother. With no disrespect to Arf, I think he resented that. For a very short time I was in the same position when he was playing Oliver in the West End and I was playing Charlie Bates. It was a much, much, smaller part than playing Oliver, so I was second fiddle to him. Except that I never really ever *felt* second fiddle to him, or anyone for that matter; I was a cocky little bugger then and was always confident about my own capabilities. But the film changed everything for all of us really. I never felt then that there was any competition with the work that we were getting… I see it now.

I don't think he felt directly jealous ('Oh, you bastard, you're being more successful than me!'). I think in Arthur's case it was, why can't people treat me as an individual? I am Arthur Wild. Alright, yes, I am Jack's elder brother, but I'm not Jack Wild's brother first and then Arthur Wild second; which is fair. I'm sure I would've felt exactly the same if the roles were reversed. He wanted to be known as Arthur Wild for himself and then, in brackets after that, Jack Wild's brother. That would've been fine for him, but that wasn't the case.

Even though my career had now gone a bit quiet, I don't think that ever left him. Whenever people saw him in the local pub, or out and about in Hounslow, they would always say, 'Hello Arf! How's Jack?' So he'd always be reminded of me, and I can understand that was hard. You can't take anything away from Arf for feeling like that. It's just it seemed to me in lots of ways it's understandable being like that when you're a teenager and you're growing up, but surely to God you should be able to accept that when you're an adult. I don't think it affected how I felt about him, but I do think it affected his view of me and ultimately our relationship.

I'd like to think that he would be defensive of me in my absence as long as I was sober; he would never stand up for me when I'd had a few drinks. But at least we were companionable in our drinking careers, because I never really wanted to drink on my own. It would be okay to drink on my own if no one else could see me, if I was in my bedroom or in my own home or something like that. But I could never go and sit in a pub on me own and drink. I found out years later Arthur would get at my vodka or gin and fill it up with water to hide what he'd had. He admitted that, years down the line. I'd been drinking watered-down measures; no wonder I had to have so much!

Coming home that night from Arf's wedding, it must've been about two o'clock in the morning and I was driving down Chiswick High Street and I saw this thing, I couldn't see what, running across the road and I swerved to miss it. I thought, whatever it was, it was still alive, so I pulled in to see whether or not I injured it.

It was a hedgehog, so I said to Gay, 'We can't leave it here in the middle of the High Street; what should we do?'

'Oh, let's take it home,' she said. 'We'll put it in the garden and take it out into the woods tomorrow!'

I put it in the boot of the car because they're full of fleas, and took it home. I put all the garden lights on when we got in and carried it into the garden. I thought, I'll just put it on the lawn. I can't put it on the patio because if a cat came, it could torment it and it wouldn't have anywhere to hide. I thought if I put it in the garden it can't get out because I've got walls all the way around. But in the morning, could I find the bugger? I had Bob over looking for it. I had everybody I knew over looking for it. I never saw it again! And that was that. I don't know where the hell it went.

With no prospect of work on the horizon and mad ideas never followed through, I set to organising a party: I was good at that.

I decided on a fancy-dress party down at Gay's parents' house in Esher and invited lots of people: there must've been a good hundred to a hundred and fifty people who turned up in fancy dress. I can't remember what Gay went as, so that shows how drunk I was. I went as Merlin, and Bob went as the cast-away character who introduced the old Monty Python TV show. He had a big sort of flowered Hawaiian shirt on and a grey fluffy wig, and he just looked hilarious. Arthur came as a Prince with this bird that he'd picked up in a pub. Mark came as either the Queen or King of Hearts, Peter Vaughan Clarke was there, and of course there was no party without McNeil.

It took a long while to organise, prepare the house and everything and it turned out to be by far the best party we ever had. It was so much fun. Everyone was in fancy dress; including Gay's gran, Charlotte! Whenever we had parties at Panah, Glynne would always arrive home late around 11.30 or twelve o'clock when the party would be in full swing. He'd join in, getting straight on the grand piano for everyone to have a sing-song. This night Glynne was dressed as an aborigine with a grass skirt and a massive plastic bum. It was so, so funny but he sat down and played, his plastic bum notwithstanding!

I was responsible for cooking food on the barbecue outside in the landscaped garden. The barbecue was by this massive pond that had big koi carp in it and a concrete bridge crossing it; so I was out there, Bob was in the kitchen cooking his fabulous spare ribs and Gary Osbourne, a singer from the Palais, was looking after the bar in the garage. The party was held in this massive music room above the garage, with the room next to it for, firstly, everyone to put their coats in, and secondly for me and Gay to sleep in at the end of the night.

I was cooking away (and, because I'm pissed as a fart, I'm burning most of it) when I heard this commotion. Not surprisingly it involved McNeil, so I put my burning to one side for a minute to go and see what was happening. Macca was on the outside of the house, trying to get up this ladder and into one of the bedrooms.

''Ere, what are you doing?' I said.

'I've gotta get something out of my jacket!'

'What?'

'I've got to get something out of my jacket.'

'But that ladder isn't a real ladder. It's one that's used for walking on roofs.'

'Don't worry Jack, I'm not going on the roof.'

'I mean it isn't strong enough to hold your weight! Anyway, why don't you go through the house?'

'I can't find the way.'

'I know the way mate, come down and I'll show you.'

He stopped half way up, as though considering this; then with a huge grin on his face he said, 'I'm half way there now; I might as well carry on.'

He was stoned and I was pissed and I thought I would just have to go up the ladder with him. At this point, Gary came over and said, 'Leave it Jack, I'll sort him out.' As I walked away I could hear Macca explaining again, as if we were all very stupid, that he just needed to get something from his jacket.

It was about eleven o'clock and I'd done all the cooking on the barbecue, but nobody wanted any of it because it was burnt to a cinder. They were waiting for Bob's food from the kitchen, so I thought, sod this, I'm not standing out here. I'm missing half the fun! I went inside, drinking and saying hello to everybody; and quite early for me I thought, I can't drink any more! I'm just going to fall over. I'll be better if I go and have a kip for a bit.

I went into the bedroom next to the party room; took off my big long wig and clothes, so I'd only got my T-shirt, knickers and make-up left on, and went to sleep with the coats.

The next minute, I'm woken up because Bob's knocked himself out and they are trying to put him on the bed with me and my coats.

'What the hell's going on?' I said. 'I'm trying to sleep here!'

Various people explained that Bob had been busy in the kitchen, cooking away, and then came running along the corridor to the music room where there were three steps that went down into the room. He thought he was going to jump the three steps and land in the room and tell everybody that the food was ready. But he'd forgotten about the steps, took a jump, nutted the ceiling, and knocked himself out.

'Let's get him onto a bed quickly,' someone had said. 'I think he's about to swallow his tongue.' By the time I'd realised the seriousness of the situation, he was conscious, but he'd got a big cut on his head and it was pouring with blood.

Everyone was talking at once:

'We should send him to hospital.'

'He might have concussion.'

'Let's him get checked out.'

'I'll phone for an ambulance.'

'I'll go with him.'

'*I'm* going with him. *I'll* sort it out,' I said. I was up by now and dressed in normal clothes again, but had forgotten about my make-up. I knew there was no way I could drive so I called a cab to take us to Kingston Hospital.

It was about one o'clock in the morning and Casualty was completely empty so they saw to him straight away. He disappeared from view while they examined him and then one of the nurses came out and said to me, 'We're going to put a couple of stitches in his head wound to stop the bleeding. He'll be out in ten or fifteen minutes.'

I waited, bored as hell, pacing up and down. I was slowly sobering up and walked around looking at the magazines and in the fish tank to see what was in it. As I was gazing in, I saw my reflection in the glass. It looked familiar and I was trying to work out who it was when a police car arrived and two policemen brought in this geezer who must've been six foot six at least. I wouldn't say he was that stocky, but I wouldn't want to have to deal with him by myself, I thought.

I overheard them saying that he'd escaped from an asylum or something, that they couldn't take care of him, so the hospital would have to look after him. The policemen sat this geezer down and said, 'You wait here and they're going to have a look at you and make sure you're alright.'

They left him sat down, walked back to their car and drove off. So now there was just me, him, and the nurse behind her desk who couldn't have been much older than me and certainly no bigger. Within three minutes of the police going, this geezer decides that he doesn't want to wait to be looked at, but wants to go, and he gets up and starts walking out of the glass double doors.

The nurse flew round to stop him, saying, 'Come along, you've got to stay here until you are seen by the doctor!'

I thought, I can't stand here and not help her because that's going to look bloody awful. So I flew up too, but the guy was twice the size of both of us. As we tried to convince him to come back inside and sit down, I caught sight of that reflection again. This time, it was in the glass door; and I suddenly realised that it was me, in all the make-up left on from the party.

'Fucking prat,' I said to myself as I looked at the smudged sea of blues and greys all over my face.

'No, not you mate, I was talking to myself,' I said quickly to the geezer as he looked like he was going to lamp me one. Me and the nurse got him to sit down again and after that he seemed to be alright.

'You silly bugger! It's none of your business, you shouldn't get involved,' I said to myself as I sat back down. But the nurse thanked me and it was not long then till Bob came out.

We caught a cab home and, by the time we got back, the party was winding down: there might've only been twenty or thirty people left. They were all concerned about Bob and he said he was fine and just had a bit of a sore head like. I was ready for another drink and we sat and chatted into the night. It definitely was the most successful and funniest party we ever had. Having said that, I do remember a 'barn dance' party we had in the woods where Mark Lester impersonated Rod Stewart singing Maggie May; now that was hysterical!

Within ten months of Bluebell dying, Billy died in me arms. I'm sure he died of a broken heart because he didn't even last a year without Bluebell. He looked at me and I could see all the whites of his eyes; I just knew he weren't well. I'd taken my gallon of wine into the run with me, I was cuddling him, and he died. Gay was working part-time at IBM in reception, just around the corner from our house by Gunnersbury tube station. I phoned her up and told her about Billy dying. I was totally gutted!

I wasn't very together, or very well, but perhaps somewhat surprisingly I still continued to work. I was offered the part of Bob Cratchit in *A Christmas Carol*. It was a UK tour from August through till December; but it wasn't a musical, and turned out to be such a depressing show for me to do. It felt awkward and hard work and I felt totally depressed all the time.

In each place we played, we had different local children to rehearse into the play, with Tiny Tim being one of them. For the whole tour, I don't think I ever met one Tiny Tim who wasn't my size or bigger than me. I had to do this one scene where we were supposed to be walking home, and Tiny Tim was supposed to be on my shoulders and bloody hell, some of those kids were heavy.

It's not like I was weak from not eating. For some reason my appetite had got much better. Up until this time, I wouldn't eat at all during the day and just have a meal in the evening. Now, I was eating breakfast, I was having something for lunch and I was having an evening meal as well. My drinking had increased too, both the amount and the desire. I would look for any excuse to have a drink, although I remember very little about any social events during the run of the show at all. It was all getting very difficult.

There was one scene where I had to get very upset about Tiny Tim and I'd go through the speech immediately before going on stage. I don't think I ever got it right once throughout the whole run. And it terrified me. Bryan Johnson was directing it and also playing Scrooge brilliantly. He was fantastic and most of my scenes were with him; but with him being the director, *and* on stage with you, it was very hard work. I always used to meet him in the pub because he used to enjoy his pints of Guinness like I used to enjoy my bitters, followed by a few brandies. I remember there was one party scene at the Fezziwigs and I actually missed it one night. I'd fallen asleep in my dressing room through the drink. At the end of the show, after the curtain calls and before we left the stage to go to our dressing rooms, he said to me, 'What happened to you in Fezziwig's party?'

'I'm sorry, Bryan,' I said, 'I fell asleep and by the time I woke up, the show had already gone past that bit, so I couldn't do anything about it. I'm ever so sorry.'

'Well, don't let it happen again!'

I didn't let it happen again.

When we played Wythenshawe near Oldham, I received a note at the stage door before the afternoon show from Davy Jones of the Monkees. That was a nice surprise. It said that he was coming to see the show and would like to meet me for a drink afterwards.

I think he'd played Dodger on Broadway; I'd definitely bought his albums. We'd met briefly in the early '70s when I was invited to a private screening of a movie for something. I vaguely remember him doing a moonie at the audience.

After the show it was pouring with rain so we went to the nearest pub to have a few pints and a chat. We had a great talk about lots of things, mainly showbiz stuff, but also the fact that he was into racehorses. At the end of the drinking session we agreed that I would visit him at his home before I moved on to the next town; and as we left the pub, I stopped to wave goodbye. I wanted to see what car he was driving, and I couldn't believe it when he got into an old vicar's car, a Morris 1000 saloon. I thought he'd at least have a Jaguar or a Roller; but I suppose they are very hip motors, I thought.

It was nice to get away from the play, and a few days later I popped over to his place, which was a very large Spanish or Mexican-style bungalow. He showed me pictures of all of his horses, and talked about trying to be a jockey when he was younger and that he'd like to have a go at it sometime soon. After a great chat (and this time a lot of coffee) we said goodbye and swopped numbers and said, 'We must keep in contact!' The most famous showbiz sentence in existence; although we did actually speak on a couple of occasions after that, mainly to do with business propositions. He was a really nice guy, and another one who got screwed as badly as me.

When we played Stevenage, although it was close to London, I thought I'd have digs because I didn't want to drive back to Chiswick every night. A lot of that was to do with the fact that if I was at home and Gay was there, she'd have been nagging me about drinking. Much of the time she was working at night, so I'd have seen very little of her anyway, so I weren't really missing anything by being away from home.

In January 1983, when I'd finished doing *Christmas Carol*, I realised that I'd lost a lot of weight and couldn't really understand it. I hadn't even been playing football as we'd been touring all over the country. I just couldn't work out why I'd lost so much weight, particularly because I was actually eating that much more; it just didn't make sense. So I went to my doctor. He said I was smoking too much, thought I'd got a chest infection, and sent me for an X-ray.

The X-ray came back clear, and the good doctor was happy; but I wasn't, so Gay said, 'You should really get this checked out. Go and see my doctor in Holland Park and get a second opinion.'

The second doctor didn't know anything about my medical history, but took one look at me, and I hadn't even opened my mouth when she said, 'You are not well. You need to go into hospital immediately. You look dreadful.'

Me and Gay were in BUPA so we thought that it would all be paid for by health insurance, so I went into the Masonic Hospital in Hammersmith for checks and I was in there for about seven and a half weeks.

Being in hospital was just like a holiday for me. I had my own private room, I had a TV and it was the start of breakfast television so I had telly on tap; it was perfect for me. Everybody was coming to see me: Gay and me Mum and Dad. Gay brought in things from home for me, Mum brought food and me Dad brought anecdotes: 'I remember when me dad was bad, his ulcers had busted, me mum told me to run down to the doctor's and put his name on the slate at the window bottom; it was raining that much it went right over me shoe tops.' I think my Dad thought I was in somewhere more like a hotel than a hospital.

'You'll be alright son, I don't know what you're makin' such a bloody fuss about.'

'*Jack!*' me Mum said.

Despite Dad's cheery outlook, I knew there was something wrong with me. Personally, I thought it was some form of cancer because of smoking; and it's like the first thing you think of when you think you're seriously ill. I wasn't too worried though. The first week I was in there the alcohol left in my body kept me happy; and after that, it sounds bizarre, but I found it quite interesting because they were doing so many tests. And I've always been an optimist.

One morning they'd say to me, 'We're going to do a test now where we'll get you to drink this and then we'll take you down, a few hours later, and see where it's gone in your body.' And then they'd take me and show me all these gadgets and medical machines and I was fascinated by that aspect of it all.

Another morning I said to them, 'When you're doing these tests, can you check my eyes because I can't read when it's got captions on the telly?'

This was after about three or four weeks of tests and them not finding anything out. I was watching TV constantly, but couldn't read the teletext, so I wanted to get that sorted. They gave me an eye test and several more besides, and after about five weeks they told me I was diabetic.

Funnily enough when we'd played Wythenshawe on the *Christmas Carol* tour I actually stayed with a real diabetic, and the way he was describing diabetes was that it meant your life was over. According to him, you couldn't actually do anything any more now. You couldn't drive, you had to be with someone twenty-four hours a day; that frightened the living daylights out of me. The hospital reassured me that that wasn't the case and if I looked after myself I would be fine. They tried me first on tablets to see whether that would control it, but that was no good so they said, 'I'm sorry, but you are going to have to go on insulin injections and that will mean you having either one or two injections a day for the rest of your life!'

I was terrified of needles. I only needed to see one and I'd faint or run a mile.

'It's alright, you'll soon get used to injecting yourself because, after a while, it'll be just like how you feel in the mornings about cleaning your teeth. You get up, you do it and get on with life and that's how it'll be!'

I couldn't imagine for one minute that it would ever be like that. They gave me an orange and a glass syringe and said, 'You can practise on this for a day, and then tomorrow we'll let you inject yourself.'

They spent the next few days working out a regime: what'd be a good dose for me in the morning and what'd be a good dose for me in the evening. Then they gave me loads of pamphlets on diabetes and about learning the carbohydrates that are in different types of food, and had me join the British Diabetic Association.

'Okay Jack, today we're going to inject insulin directly into your bloodstream so you can then feel what it's like to have a hypo – that's when your blood sugar level is too low. You'll feel sweaty, you'll become confused; you will feel very similar to having had a few drinks.'

'Bring it on,' I thought.

After about a minute they said, 'How do you feel?'

'I'm alright. I feel fine,' I said.

After about two minutes I started to feel myself having sweaty palms and being very indecisive and they said, 'How do you feel now?'

'Well, I wouldn't like to drive in the condition I'm in now!' I said because I was feeling a bit drunk, although I'd actually driven feeling a lot worse.

'Well, now you know: if ever you feel like this in the future, you will need to get some sugar or glucose eaten very quickly.'

So that was it; and although I thought it wasn't costing me a penny because I was in BUPA, I was wrong. It ended up costing me nearly four grand to find out that I was diabetic and needed glasses to watch the telly.

The other change that happened was that I stopped playing for Showbiz XI. Not because of the diabetes, but because none of the lads came to visit me once. Tony Carpenter came, but we'd been mates for years. None of the others did. I thought, sod you lot. It's not that they didn't know, because Tony had told them. I'd played for them for about four or five years on and off and I didn't get a card or nothing. So I packed that in and didn't play for them ever again. It really hurt that they hadn't come. I thought they were friends. Maybe they were: maybe they were good-time friends, drinking friends, on-tour friends; whatever they were, they weren't here now.

Things were definitely changing.

When I came out of hospital I had to start a new life, and for about the first three or four months it was like a novelty. I did get used to injecting twice a day and I tried to take care of myself and not have a drink, but it soon became a drag and I soon got bored with it. They said I would have developed diabetes at some stage anyway, but that I'd damaged myself so much through drinking that I had brought it on early. I was thirty. If I've already done the damage, I reasoned, it couldn't hurt to have a drink or two now. I can't remember to be honest when I started again, but within a month of leaving hospital I was back to normal as far as my drinking was concerned. The alcohol sent my blood sugars all over the place very quickly, and it's hard to recognise an oncoming hypo when you're drunk in the first place.

It was very dangerous for me to live like that and soon I was back in hospital because of it. The combination of my drinking and bad control of diabetes meant that they put me in the psychiatric ward in West Middlesex Hospital to try and stabilise my condition. This meant drying out which was always a hard thing to go through. I was surrounded by people with mental problems. All sorts of nutters, either from the way they were brought up or from their addictions to whatever. I'd just got off to sleep one night when I woke to find this guy getting into bed with me. I shouted for the nurse and helped her get him back into his own bed. 'You must stay in your own bed,' she told him; apparently he kept getting out of his bed and into someone else's.

One morning I got it into my head that they weren't treating me properly regarding the diet I needed to stick to for my diabetes. They weren't giving me a snack in between each meal. Now, whether I was hallucinating at this time is anyone's guess, but I decided to get dressed and take a walk outside of the hospital grounds and along the road to get some snacks. Nobody challenged me as I walked out of the psychiatric ward fully dressed with my sunglasses covering my eyes. As I was walking back from the shop I realised I had to pass a pub so, like any respectable heavy drinker, I nipped in for a couple of quick large vodka and lemonades. As I was ordering my second one, I saw, out of the corner of my eye, a familiar face. I thought, I know you from somewhere but I can't put a name to your face.

No sooner had I thought that than he looked me straight in the eyes and said, 'We're both in the same ward, mate! But I won't tell anyone if you don't, okay?'

We both grinned at each other and nodded in agreement. I finished my drink and said, 'I'll see you back there, mate,' and left him at the bar. I walked back through the hospital grounds giving myself squirts of my mint Gold Spot spray (I always carried it everywhere with me in the hope of no doctors or nurses smelling what I'd been up to) and got back into bed. Within a matter of days I thought, I don't need to be here, and I signed myself out of the ward against my doctor's wishes.

I wanted to have a chance at getting my career back to what it was like in its heyday. I needed to work. There were long lunchtime meetings of three hours or more with various industry people, where tons of alcohol was consumed and, perhaps not surprisingly, no work came. I tried not drinking for three days before I had a meeting so that I would at least look reasonable and not smell of alcohol, but it got to the point in my drinking where I thought if I didn't drink I would die. I thought it was that that was keeping me going.

It may have been around this time that Gay, I think, organised a meeting with a guy called Tony Tune. He was a close friend of Rod Stewart's, and had contacts with the Mervyn Conn Organisation, a PR agency that promoted people and products, I think. Tony said he wanted to help me out and get me some good work, so we arranged to meet him one night at the Hippodrome nightclub in Leicester Square.

I always carried with me a small glass bottle of Lucozade in case I needed it for my sugar levels; and, halfway through the night, as we were just talking about the business in general, I whispered to Gay, 'I'm just gonna go to the loo and drink my Lucozade.' I think the reason for not drinking it in front of him was that I didn't want him to think it was some form of alcohol. If he was going to help me get some work I didn't want him to question my health at all, so I thought the safest way was to drink it in the loo. What I didn't realise was that this was the midweek gay night, and so all the cubicles in the gents' were being used.

I thought, well, I'll just stand in the corner and drink my bottle. There was a huddle of men in the other corner, and I didn't realise at first, but they were all taking cocaine. I didn't want to make it obvious that I'd seen them doing something illegal, so I tried to be as inconspicuous as I could be. I turned slightly away from them, pulled out me bottle and started drinking it. I didn't look at them, but I had the feeling that one of them was watching me. I turned around and all six of them were looking at me. It was almost as though they were thinking, hang on, has he got a new drug that's just come on the market that we don't know about? Should we go over and see if we can try some?

I don't like this, I thought, so I drank it as quickly as I could and flew out of the toilets.

The rest of the meeting went well, and Tony Tune said he would introduce me to lots of different people but, to cut a long story short, nothing ever came from any of those meetings.

There was no work, and gradually my friends disappeared. I just couldn't figure out where everything had gone wrong. I was also lying about my drinking and fooling myself into believing that no one knew about it. I'd even try and fool the guy who was selling me the drink. Instead of buying a big bottle of vodka, which was cheaper, I'd buy about eight miniatures and tell him I was using them for cooking. God knows what I'd be cooking with eight miniatures of vodka!

At some stage I sold my BMW and the fella who bought it telephoned me afterwards to tell me he'd found a bottle of vodka hidden in the spare tyre. 'Well, I've no idea how that got there,' I lied.

And the rows with Gay about drink got worse.

'You couldn't wait any longer, could you?'

'Well, it's coming up to lunchtime,' I said.

'It's 11.30!'

'Well I'm hungry!'

'Is that your second or third?'

'My first,' I lied.

'It isn't, is it? Well, I won't sit here and watch you kill yourself.'

'Well, you do it then!' I said and threw the syringe of insulin towards her.

She threw it back across the kitchen floor, smashing it, and walked out.

I think I'm a coward really: I could have given myself an overdose of insulin – instead I just nutted the concrete floor. I'm not sure what I was trying to do; I didn't kill myself, but I didn't half have a sore head.

At some time, although it's hard to say when, Gay nagged me into going to Accept. I think by now I knew I had a problem with my drinking, so to keep the peace I decided I would try the Accept course. But there was a problem: you had to take an Antabuse tablet each morning in front of counsellors, and you can't drink and take Antabuse. Antabuse produces an acute sensitivity to alcohol, and the symptoms include flushing of the skin, accelerated heart rate, shortness of breath, nausea, vomiting, throbbing headache, visual disturbance, mental confusion, postural fainting and circulatory collapse.

Knowing what the effects were, and knowing that I was still drinking and lying about it to them, I refused to take the tablet and therefore I was asked to leave. I didn't tell Gay.

Her mother was ill and had been diagnosed with breast cancer. They'd given her an operation and a course of radiotherapy. I'd drive her every day to Hammersmith hospital, right by Wormwood Scrubs prison, for her treatment. Despite the treatment the cancer carried on travelling in her body and eventually killed her. I was actually in Charing Cross Hospital through drinking by then, and I said to the doctors, 'My mother-in-law is dying and if she dies while I'm still in here, I'm gonna have to go out and organise the funeral.' When she died, I signed myself out and came home.

At some point, because I couldn't do Accept and because they'd just brought out the first non-alcoholic lager called 'Barbican', I tried to stay dry myself. I loved Barbican, so that was good, but I was drinking gallons of it, on a daily basis. I was sober, if not really together, but I thought at least I'd done something right for once. I was staying off drink and I stayed dry for nine months, but it wasn't a stable sobriety and couldn't last.

I went back to the real thing when I went out for lunch with Lionel Bart to discuss a work project he was involved with. I was so excited about the possibility of working with him again. Over lunch he came out with the famous line, 'Go on, mate, just have the one glass of wine. It won't do you any harm!' I honestly refused a drink three times during lunch, but eventually I succumbed. I probably had three or four glasses by the time the lunch was over. My resolve had gone.

Once I started again I couldn't think of not drinking, and I've got no real recollection of 1984 at all. I felt life would be impossible not drinking and that I couldn't function without a drink. I actually needed it constantly to stop me shaking; I thought I needed it to live.

So there was like about eighteen months of really heavy drinking. I have flashes of memory like being pissed and streaking for a dare, but nothing is clear and it's all very messy. I was told by Alex Jay (who became my agent years later) that in the eighties as a young actor he'd been contracted to do a movie called *State of Wonder* that was being directed by a guy called Martin Donovan. Alex was told that, originally, I had been cast for his role, but I had turned up for a meeting 'totally out of it!' and they decided that they'd get someone else. This doesn't ring a bell with me at all, and I don't know if there are any more jobs that I was too ill to do because I turned up pissed. This could be a one-off, or there could be loads of them. I've no idea.

It's frightening not to be able to remember whole parts of your life. Anybody could say I'd done anything, and I couldn't be sure whether I had or not. In reality I don't think I actually did very much at all.

I'd speak to my parents at least once or twice a week, and more often than not I'd see them, say, once a month; but I was very lonely. I was losing faith in myself, and only had a growing faith in drink.

Gay was working away a lot with either Suzi or the showbands. She played on the QE2 and travelled all over, to America, South Africa, Australia; my world had pretty much shrunk to the house and booze. I'd got to the point where I'd hide my drink all over the house. In cupboards in the kitchen, in the garden, under the bed, in the wardrobes, hems of curtains, in my jackets, in my guitar cases, inside furniture, absolutely anywhere I thought Gay wouldn't look. When I'd run out, I'd go looking for it. I'd often keep it hidden in the bedroom, so that if anyone was in the house and I was in bed, I wouldn't have to go downstairs to the bar to get a drink: I could have it in the bedroom without anyone knowing.

One day, I was looking for some vodka in one of Gay's drawers. I was taking the drawer out to see if there were any bottles underneath on the floor when I found some letters and thought, what the fuck are these?

I opened them up and read them, and they were from Gay's lover.

I knew the guy. He used to come to our house. He was married with kids, and I'd met the wife. The letters were to Gay when she was abroad somewhere. I was totally gutted. I saw red immediately. Gay was working somewhere up in the Midlands, and as soon as I found them I phoned her up, swore at her and said, 'You'd better get yourself a solicitor 'cos I'm divorcing you! I'm not having this! I told you if you had an affair I'd do it, and I will!'

'Come up and we'll talk about it,' she said.

'No, there's nothing to talk about. I'm going now and getting a solicitor from Chiswick and you'd better sort yourself one out because I'm starting divorce proceedings naming him if necessary as the co-respondent! Either that or you openly admit to adultery and then there's no need to mention any names! It's up to you 'cos I don't care!'

She tried to convince me to go up and see her but I wasn't having any of it. To me it was horrendous. I couldn't accept it and that was it. I thought, it doesn't matter what it costs, I'm divorcing her. I'm having nothing to do with her.

I put the phone down and went straight down the high street and into the first solicitor's I could find.

'I want to start divorce proceedings against my wife for adultery!' I said. They asked me if I had any proof and I said, 'Yeah, I've got her lover's letters proving it all and I've told her what I'm doing!'

They took the case and, as soon as I knew that that was all in motion, I headed back home. I had to pass the Chequered Flag sports-car shop right at the bottom of the road and went in to have a look. It was a fantastic shop and it was a toss-up between a white convertible Rolls Royce Corniche, or a Panther Lima that I was going to buy. I stood in the shop and was suddenly struck by the thought that perhaps I should be sensible and save money if I was getting divorced, and so ended up not buying either of them. I went home and got pissed.

Sometime later, I'd got so much anger in my head, not only against Gay but also against the guy, that I phoned him up. He answered the phone.

'It's Jack here. I just want you to know that, one, you're not welcome at my house any more; two, I know all about it and how long it's been going on; and three, if you didn't have children, you'd be dead!'

I put the phone down. I must admit I did think about having him done over, and I could've had that done easily with some of the people I knew; but because he had a wife and kids, that's what stopped me organising it.

Much as I wanted to carry on phoning him up every day and driving him mad, I didn't. I only ever did that once and I never saw him again.

When Gay eventually came home she did try to persuade me to stay and said, 'Let's work it out!' but my morals wouldn't allow that. I switched off immediately on finding those letters. I just couldn't accept it. I'm sure a part of me did say, 'I'm gonna lose so much', but at the same time as, 'I can't put up with this!'

We sat down and talked about how we were going to split the house. Then I had to tell the two different sides of the family what was happening. I just said, 'We're getting divorced 'cos things just haven't worked out and that's the end of it.' We didn't go into any further details. We just decided to leave it at that. I told Mum and Dad, then Glynne, who was by this time in our flat above with his partner, Pat.

Somewhere between the starting of the divorce proceedings in April 1985 and it becoming absolute in September, I got this job, a new play that was going to be on for two or three weeks in a small theatre in North London. There were about five or six people in it and my part was that of a very screwed-up guy who was trying to hide the fact that he'd murdered someone.

I'd drive to work taking small bottles or cartons of wine with me. I'd have a few of them and then, when we'd break for lunch and go to the local pub, I'd just have one drink and make that last me: irrespective of the fact that, outside of the pub, I was drinking like a fish.

The character I was trying to create was a psychopath. At one stage in the play, he pulls out a knife and starts behaving very aggressively with this dagger, not towards any individual but towards the furniture. I said to the director, 'He should have something in his hands all the time that he constantly plays with.' I got the idea from a film with Charles Bronson and Jan-Michael Vincent called *The Mechanic* where Bronson always had this squeezy ball thing in his hand. He played the part of an assassin and this is what kept him cool. I went and got some Potty Putty to play with and the director liked that. I tried to imagine how Cagney would've played it and that's how I tried to do it; but unfortunately, I wasn't well enough to carry it off.

The director was a very young guy in his early thirties and I think he'd written the play as well. I don't think I was learning my lines quick enough and it got to the point where there was about four days left before we opened. The producer and director had obviously been talking during the day; and, just before we finished, the producer came over to me and said, 'Can I have a word with you, Jack?'

We were rehearsing on the first floor of this Salvation Army place and he took me outside on the fire escape and said, 'Look, I'm sorry, but we don't think you are going to know this well enough for when we open. We're going to have to let you go because we're frightened that you won't be able to hack it. Is there anything we can do to help you with this? What is the problem?'

I blamed my impending divorce for me not having learnt it as quickly as I could've done. There was so much going on in my head about where I was going to live. In actual fact I think the reason I hadn't learnt it was, one, I hadn't put the work into it in the first place because my mind was elsewhere, and two, I was just too pissed when I got home.

He said, 'Well, we're going to have another talk and see what we can come up with.'

We left it at that and so I left the rehearsal rooms that day on the understanding that I'd be going in the next day to continue doing it.

About 9.30pm that evening the director phoned me up and said, 'I'm sorry Jack, but we're going to have to let you go on this one because it just hasn't worked out!'

I was just so gobsmacked. It was the only time that I had ever been sacked. I could not believe it. From what I remember, I must've been pissed when I took the phone call, but I don't remember getting aggressive about it at all. I was just very apologetic to them and said, 'I wish you all the success with the show and please give all my love to the cast and wish them all the best and I'm just really sorry.'

Gay was out working and, when she called me later that night, I went bananas on the phone to her, saying, 'They've sacked me! I can't believe it!'

From what I can remember, which isn't that good, I'm sure she said, 'The way you've been behaving recently, is it any wonder! You are going to have to pull yourself together because no one will employ you otherwise!'

But nothing changed and I just went back and carried on drinking. One half of me was saying, 'You silly bastard, it's your own fault for letting this happen!' and the other half was saying, 'But it's under control and it won't happen again, you'll be alright!' It was a very foggy existence for me.

Later that week, I received a card signed by all the cast saying, 'We hope things get better for you in the next six months.' They'd obviously been told about my divorce coming up, and it was ever so touching, and it was so reassuring that at least somebody was on my side and not everybody was against me; that was a nice feeling.

I'd agreed to move out when the divorce became absolute. I couldn't believe what was happening. I didn't want to let go of the house and its memories. Gay didn't want to leave the house either, and with the money that she'd been left when her mother died, she could afford to buy me out. I didn't have any money to buy her out. I'd put thirty grand down as a deposit nine years before and we'd both paid the running costs equally since then.

I had to move to Mum and Dad's house, which was awful, while I found somewhere to live. I felt I'd lost half of my investment – not just the house, but the flat that was supposed to bring in an income for when times were tough – plus the fact that I needed to now buy a new house.

Gay had a silver Mini with a Mercedes front on it and big oblong headlights, and I had an MGB GT sports car. I used to let Gay use the MG if she was working and I'd potter about in the Mini, and when we separated, I let her have the MG. She said I could leave the furniture that I was going to have at what was now her place, until I'd found a place and moved in. I'd been told that as soon as her cheque had arrived at my bank, I had twenty-four hours to go. The only time I cried was when I had to drive away in this bloody silly Mini leaving everything behind. Within a month of me moving from Chiswick to Mum and Dad's, I'd got rid of the Mini; and, because I was still looking for somewhere to move to, I didn't want to spend a lot of money on a car, so I only bought a cheap old VW Scirocco. I drove about in that until I got that much more pissed and then I started spending money willy-nilly.

I drove off from there having given her the keys; and as I was driving away I remember that being such a painful thing, because I was leaving something that I considered to be mine. I hadn't had any visions of ever leaving there.

I looked at the house and remembered my old neighbour, Pat Chamberlain. He had long since gone, and sold his house to some antique dealers. I think Gay was happier, but I thought they were right snobby bastards. Pat would never ever see you done wrong by anyone. He'd always be there as a first-class mate. I was leaving my home now, and that would be the end of an era of my life; that was awful. That was just as bad as finding out about those letters, in actual fact.

I think there's some kind of method in all that madness. Had I not been looking for hidden booze, I wouldn't have found the letters in a month of Sundays. If I hadn't had to leave and had gone any further downhill, I could've bloody died there and she'd have had the bloody lot.

I switched off from continuing a relationship with Gay immediately on finding the letters, though through the divorce proceedings from April to September we shared the same house and on a few occasions we did share the same bed, but there was no kissing goodnight and it was all quietly hostile; it was as much as I could do without raising my voice. It wasn't easy. Although I'd switched off from the relationship, I hadn't stopped loving her. To be honest, that feeling went on for a good two or three years after that.

I couldn't believe what was happening and I found it so hard to let go of that life. We kept a superficial relationship, but there was very little meaning left. During July and August I looked for houses in Chiswick, Kew, Richmond and in Twickenham. Gay did come and look at a few with me, which seems extraordinary now. I don't know why she did it, but for me, I just didn't want to be on my own. I wanted a companion; it wouldn't have made any difference who was with me, at least I wasn't alone. That's the way I looked at it. I didn't look at it any further than that. I just weren't used to being on my own at all, and at some point I'd grown to hate it. When I *had* to live on my own, I compensated by having noise going on, constantly.

I made an offer on a detached house in Twickenham, but something went wrong with the survey, and in the end I saw a bungalow in Waverley Avenue, just around the corner from my Mum and Dad's. It was right at the maximum amount of money that I had to spend. I only had I think it was sixty or sixty-five grand to spend and this was like seventy-five. I didn't want to have a large mortgage. I didn't want to be paying more than I was in Chiswick, and there we had a ten grand mortgage so I didn't want a bigger mortgage than that. This bungalow was just over that limit, but because I liked it so much, in comparison with everything else that I'd seen, I thought, oh sod it! I'll have that and have done with it! and finally moved in there in November 1985.

So I was divorced, living in the bungalow, and I went out and bought a six-hundred-quid guitar that I couldn't afford and played Eddie Grant's 'I Don't Wanna Dance' over and over again. I'd got my mortgage and thought, right, well that's being paid for, so I don't need to worry about that then. But there was no money coming in, so how could it be going out? I didn't trouble myself with this particular question or with its answer: but just began, slowly, for the first time in my life, to slip into debt.

'I don't wanna dance

Dance with my baby no more

I'll never do something to hurt you, though

Oh but the feeling is bad

The feeling is bad...'

I sang loudly and poured myself another drink. At least I had that to rely on.

Chapter 22

T HAT CHRISTMAS, I WAS CONTRACTED to do another pantomime which was *Cinderella* again, but this was in Canterbury with Sally Thomsett. I'd last worked with Sally twenty years before on *Danny the Dragon* and by now she was known for *The Railway Children* and the TV show *Man About the House*. I hadn't done a pantomime in four years so I was a bit nervous about doing the songsheet at the end, but at least it would make a change from singing Eddie Grant.

I thought, right, I'm well over Gay now and what I need is a new image. I'd bought my first Range Rover, which was black, and I decided on a new image of me as a country squire with Barbour jackets and a hunting dog in the back. Arthur's wife Julie came with me to get a dog which was a long-haired Weimaraner called Jaeger. She was about four months old and already responded to that name so there didn't seem any point in changing it. I liked it anyway and kept it. So when I drove down to Canterbury at the end of November to start rehearsals, I took Jaeger with me.

We stayed in the hotel right opposite the theatre, and I remember one night I went for a meal all on my own. I had my usual prawn cocktail, fillet steak, vodka and lemonade and some wine with my meal. It was very unusual for me to eat out on my own and I only did it once while I was there. It made me think it's quite a depressing life really: an actor out on his own.

The next day I bought a fantastic tracksuit in a sports shop. It was a black tennis suit and had a massive emblem on the back that was embroidered with the name of John McEnroe on it. I don't think I ever wore it.

I tried to cut down my drinking as much as possible, but I was still drinking far too much which obviously also sent my diabetes up the creek, and things were getting a little unclear. Despite this, rehearsals seemed to be going okay; and this one day in particular, we had to go to this publicity thing at lunchtime. So when we broke, me, Sally Thomsett and the director headed off to this special-needs school to say 'Hi' and 'Look forward to you coming to see the panto!' and all that.

I'd had a drink and, while we were there, my sugar levels must've gone haywire and I started hallucinating. This sounds awful, but when I was looking at these poor mentally handicapped children, that's not what I was seeing: I was just seeing monsters, and I was terrified of them.

I tried to hold myself together. I thought, look, I've got a job to do here, so just try and block out what you're seeing; but it was terrifying and I whispered to Sally, 'I can't stay here any more. I've got to get out, c'mon let's go!' I said, pulling her arm.

'We can't go, Jack,' Sally said. 'What's the matter with you?'

'*We've just gotta get out of here!*' I said with rising panic. I couldn't stay a moment longer as my heartbeat shook my whole body and I couldn't find a breath of air to breathe. I quite literally felt frightened to the point of death. And within a short space of time I'd made such a commotion that we left.

I went back to my hotel, but the hallucinations continued. I became convinced that some East End of London gangsters were coming down to assassinate me. It was obvious that I wasn't safe in the hotel and I'd have to get out. So I thought, what am I gonna do? I'd better phone the police and tell them to come and stop me getting murdered!

I remember phoning the police from the hotel reception. My Range Rover was parked in the drive of the hotel, but I couldn't remember whether Jaeger was in the car or in my room. The police arrived and they obviously either smelt booze on my breath or certainly thought, there's something amiss with this lunatic – we'd better get him to hospital to get him checked over.

I continued to hallucinate in the hospital and was convinced that these people were coming to kill me. I thought, how can I stop them 'cos I'm not safe here! I thought, oh, I know what I'll do, if I pretend that I'm crackers, then they'll commit me to an asylum and that'll be a much safer place for me. So, I'll do that!

I remember impersonating John Cleese when he did Monty Python's 'Ministry of Silly Walks'. I remember doing that, and I remember them saying to me, 'Open your eyes!'

'I can't!' I said, and I can see this like it was yesterday. Whenever I opened my eyes, everything was in 'cartoon land'. Everything was very brightly coloured and the doctors weren't real. It was all monsters. Everything was monsters and I said, 'I'm not opening my eyes 'cos I don't like it!'

The two doctors were convinced that I was insane, and on 9th December 1985 they committed me to this institution.

Two or three days later, or that's how long it seemed to me, they asked who was my next of kin and I said, 'Me Dad is!'

'Well, we're going to send your father a copy of your rights which explains you're being held under Section 2 of the Mental Health Act 1983.' In theory it meant that I was going to be held in hospital or a mental institution and could be kept there for up to twenty-eight days. I wasn't allowed to leave and, if I did, I'd be brought back immediately.

Oh bloody hell, I thought, me Dad's going to go crackers!

As soon as I started to come down with my sugar levels, and get back to near normal, I started to realise where I was and I thought, fuck me! I'm surrounded by nutters! Prior to this I hadn't any notion of where I was; and I was constantly with a nurse or guard and it was like a prison, so I said to myself, I wanna get out of here! I want to go home!

They said: 'You are allowed one phone call, but your nurse has got to be with you when you make the call.'

So I phoned me Dad up and told him I was in hospital. Then I whispered so that the nurse couldn't hear, 'Look Dad, I'm surrounded by nutters here! If I don't get out soon, I'll end up like them, so can you come and get me out of here, and bring Bob with you so we can bring my car back as well please?'

Dad and Bob duly came down on the train and all three of us went back to London in my Range Rover with Jaeger. It was a long journey. Me Dad was fuming. I stared out of the window.

We drove past Hounslow Heath and I could see shadows of my childhood. I remembered playing there as a kid. A fairground would come there every holiday and I remembered our gang and the fun. We'd follow the fairground hands as they took girls into the bushes; we'd be chased away of course, and I remember the pain in our stomachs from laughing so much.

That was a long time ago.

And suddenly, I could see me and Arf delivering milk to the army barracks on the Heath. It was covered in snow and the float skidded and slipped. Bert the milkman would let me and Arf drive and as we wrestled with the steering, he'd roll an Old Holborn. We'd then stop for tea with the old man and his mandolin. And the memories began to fly across my mind and through my soul. Hazy, warm memories… a camp between two rivers like on our own private island… a waterfall behind… and something about having to ride your bike across the river without getting your feet wet; I don't think it happened very often… and the sound of a police siren and a chase through the woods.

We hid our cigarettes and joined in the pursuit. We felt like we were in the middle of a gunfight with Al Capone and the FBI... that was an exciting weekend that was and...

'Watch what yer doing, Jack,' Dad snapped.

'Sorry Dad,' I barely said. I'd just lit a fag but my hands were shaking so much it had escaped, and lay forgotten, burning on the floor of the car.

I felt sick and I wanted a drink.

So the Christmas of 1985 and the New Year of 1986 was just a complete drunken mess basically. Everyone, as usual, was saying that I'm killing myself and to stop drinking. Then at some stage the conversation shifted to 'Why don't you go to this clinic to get help?' What had happened was, Gay had been talking to Suzi Quatro about me and the drinking, and Suzi had got in contact with Pete Townshend from The Who. He'd set up Double O, which was a charity to help drug addicts and alcoholics get into clinics to get clean. Suzi must've phoned Pete up and said, 'Can you help with a friend of mine?'

And he said, 'Yeah. We can get him into Broadreach Clinic down near Plymouth – if you can get him to go in there.'

I'm presuming that for a couple of weeks during January 1986 there were lots of phone calls between me Mum and Dad and Gay, and Gay and Suzi. Eventually one of them said, 'Look, we've arranged, if you want, to go into a drying-out clinic. You go in there for six weeks and you get clean and then hopefully you can stay clean.'

At first I said, 'No, it's all under control. There's no need for me to do that.' I really didn't think that it was a problem. I knew that I drank far too much for it to be good for my health, but I honestly thought I had it under control. I was constantly drinking in my bungalow and people would only nag me if they came round and saw me. Or they'd have a go if they spoke to me on the phone and I was slurring my words. So I thought I could control the drinking, or at least the effects of drinking, by doing it at home and alone.

At some stage Bob did come round with Gay and cut all my credit cards up so that I couldn't buy alcohol. I went fucking bananas! I was just mouthing off something rotten, shouting and screaming, 'How dare you do that? I'm gonna call the police and sue you!'

As my cards were gone, I was then forced to use whatever money I had available to buy my booze. I'd sign on for Unemployment Benefit and use that for drink while I'd apply for new credit cards. It wasn't long before the new cards arrived and then I could buy even more drink. I would constantly have an alcoholic drink within three foot of me so that I could be constantly unaware of what's going on around me. At the same time I was expecting a phone call from Spielberg saying, 'I want you to be in my next movie!' which was insane!

My TV would be permanently on. It was never switched off and I would be in bed most of the time watching videos. I wouldn't get up, I'd only go out of the house to get dog food or more beer, or to get my giro cheque if I was signing on. Since being divorced and not having any work or money I'd be claiming Housing Benefit, but instead of paying my mortgage with it, I needed it to live and put petrol in my car, so I used that to fuel my lifestyle which was just being pissed permanently.

I was getting through three or four bottles of vodka a week easily. On a typical day I'd consume half a bottle of vodka and a couple of bottles of wine. My blood sugar levels were all over the place. I did have the occasional hypo and pass out, but either somebody found me or I would just have enough sugar in me to wake up and do something about it. As well as having an alcoholic drink by me, I'd also have a Lucozade bottle as well in case I needed a quick injection of glucose. One time that I collapsed at home the ambulance came to pick me up and I was so ill they covered me in cooking foil to conserve my body heat.

Mum and Dad were only round the corner and quite often me Dad would come and take Jaeger for a walk in the park because I weren't capable of doing it. She couldn't always hold on for him and the house began to smell a bit. I'd have constant arguments with me Dad and he'd be saying, 'You've got to stop drinking!' and any booze he found, he'd pour down the sink. I'd just go and buy more. I remember one day me Dad had me up against the wall when I was drunk and he'd lost his patience with me. As he towered above me, I thought of all the stories of him in Manchester as a young man. How he would deal with problems full of the quiet aggressive confidence of youth: 'I'll get it sorted,' he'd say, and go off and explain with his fist.

Me Dad would then go and do exactly the same for Arthur, who was living a few minutes' drive away in Wellington Road South. He was still drinking maybe as much as me, although he was doing a driving job at the time, not that it made any difference to him.

Despite all this, I honestly believed I was in control. Drink stopped me thinking about my problems, so to me it seemed that I was remedying the situation *with* drink. But they all just kept pressuring and pressuring me to go to the clinic and eventually I thought, oh for fuck's sake! The only way I'm gonna shut them up is to go and do it. So eventually I agreed.

Me and Dad drove down in his car to Plymouth on 29th January 1986 to start my six weeks in the Broadreach clinic. I didn't know what to expect and wasn't happy to be given a list of things that I could and couldn't take in with me. I'd wanted to take my tape recorder, my TV, my radio and my guitar, but apparently they weren't allowed! They'd also stipulated that I had to be free of alcohol for twenty-four hours before arriving there; which I did, only just. Actually I don't think I did that. I didn't drink for that day that I went down, but I'd most likely celebrated the fact that I was going in there the night before. So I was probably drunk when we set off; but Plymouth was a long journey.

I wasn't worried about going in there and didn't think twice about not drinking for six weeks because, in the past, I'd stopped drinking for nine whole months. Then, I'd only drunk alcohol-free Barbican which was awful, but six weeks seemed a doddle in my eyes. Anyway, I've always been an optimist and the main reason for going in there was to stop people nagging me, and that had worked already. Still, things certainly hadn't been too clever in Canterbury: to go from an Oscar nomination to being sectioned under the Mental Health Act was quite a long way to fall. Perhaps I could do with cutting down a bit.

Most of what follows is from the diary I had to keep while I was in there. I've changed the names of the inmates.

The Broadreach Clinic

Wednesday 29th January 1986

I arrived at 3.30pm and was met by someone from the office who was very pleasant. I got up to my room and they searched absolutely everything. They even opened up my Lucozade bottles to smell if it had any alcohol in it. Then they took away most of my cash, credit cards, aftershave, gas for my lighter etc... It was quite unbelievable. The nurse was telling me that they have had people sniff gas, drink aftershave, and even eat those blocks that you stick down the loo.

'Well, *I'm* not going to drink my aftershave,' I said.

'Well, it's got alcohol in it, and it has been done before,' the nurse said as she swept it all away.

Maybe this was going to be more heavy duty than I thought. How had I got into this position? I remembered in Hollywood being told not to have a drink, *any* drink, in public because it wasn't good for my image. So the only time I could relax was at home, in private, away from the public eye and the *long* eye of the press. Maybe that's why I was sick, and got drunk in the privacy of my own sort of boozing space where nobody could take a photograph of me in a state. And what happened was I felt I needed to get tanked up quickly before I went out anywhere because I wouldn't be able to drink once I was out. So I got used to drinking a lot in a short space of time. I don't know.

They have a strict timetable here so I had an early night.

Day 1 Thursday 30/1/86

I noticed, this being my first full day here, that everyone is so willing to listen to your problems and give advice if they possibly can, including the patients, that it makes me feel there is light at the end of the tunnel. I must admit, though, that I didn't like being classed as an alcoholic; I'm a binge drinker really. Somehow, it made me feel really disgusted and angry with myself for getting into this position.

Until I came here, I really didn't think I could be an alcoholic, because that was asking me to compare myself to the people who sleep on park benches, have no homes, are dirty, and down-and-outs. No! I was none of these, so therefore I wasn't an alcoholic and I didn't have a drink problem. I certainly wasn't and couldn't be put in the same boat as a drug addict. Thinking in this way made me feel content, thinking that basically I was okay and therefore there was no reason to stop drinking. Just cut it down a bit! But, when it was explained to me, I reluctantly agreed that I am an alcoholic of sorts: that is to say, I am chemical-dependent.

This afternoon we sat and listened to a tape recording from a guy in the USA who seemed to be trying to sell God to us; he went completely over the top. Every sentence was 'Pray to God', 'Tell God you're sorry', 'Ask God to forgive you', 'Ask God this', 'Ask God that'. After about five minutes, I started to get really annoyed with this guy. When he had finished I was half expecting a plate to be handed around asking for donations for his church. He was very much a strong Evangelist. Don't get me wrong. I'm not a non-believer. I do believe that a superpower of a kind exists, but I can't explain what it actually is. I just didn't want it rammed into me!

In the evening, we had a thing called 'life story' in which a patient tells the group all about his other life from the beginning. I thoroughly enjoyed this. It was very interesting, eye-opening, educating and personal. It's very reassuring to know that you're not the only one in the world with your own personal problem. There are thousands just like you, and many that are much worse off than you. I'm really looking forward to tomorrow to learn some more.

Oh, one thing I forgot to tell you. This afternoon we did yoga. Towards the end, the teacher made us do different exercises and put a tape on with just a piano playing. She made us lie on the floor and told us to try and relax. I wouldn't say it made me relax but I fell asleep! A fellow patient had to wake me up. I apologised to the teacher and she said, 'Don't worry, you obviously did relax.' So far as I'm concerned, yoga is great! Can't be bad for the first day eh! Roll on tomorrow! Oh, by the way, they started me on Librium today. It's meant to help you with withdrawal symptoms. It's really good stuff!!!

Day 2 Friday 31/1/86

This Librium is doing me the world of good! I had a really great night's sleep which put me in a great mood for breakfast this morning.

After daily chores it was time for my first group therapy. One thing I've noticed is that, no matter what kind of addict you are, whether drugs or alcohol, you are basically selfish with no respect or consideration for fellow human beings, including parents, family, lovers and so on. With eleven blokes in the group and only three ladies, we were being a bit selfish here as well, with too much loud, filthy language. We all apologised and promised it wouldn't happen again. More lectures and another life story later, though I got the impression that this bloke was saying drugs weren't a bad thing to get into if you wanted to have a good time, and I thought that was completely and utterly wrong.

Day 3 Saturday 1/2/86

I slept really well again last night. After breakfast, everyone went off doing his or her allocated jobs. Within an hour, it was group therapy time again. I started it off by talking about the guy whom I thought was trying to glamorise the drug scene. I told him that if I had children, I wouldn't want someone who was using drugs at the time looking after my kids. Before I could go on, the counsellor asked me if I'd feel the same if it was an alcoholic?

After lunch, we watched another video from America. This time I really enjoyed it. The one thing that made me happy was that the presenter said, 'When AA mention the word God, what they really mean is, whatever God, Belief or Superpower that you yourself have faith in and look up to for help.' This was very comforting to me, because yesterday I thought that God from the Bible was being preached to me, whereas now it's a question of what I believe in and look up to. It surprised me very much because this was a preacher, a reformed alcoholic in the cloth saying this. We then had a short break for tea and coffee.

The next thing on the agenda was 'family group'. This was a patient talking openly with his or her family in front of our group. This was very emotional, very personal and made me feel very uneasy. I felt as though I shouldn't have been there. But when the group gave their feedback to the patient as to how he had changed over the six-week period, I saw that must be invaluable to him. I didn't say anything because of having only known him for two days. Just before we broke for dinner, my counsellor came up and told me to do my life story tomorrow. I can tell you now, I'm not looking forward to that and I'm very nervous about it. I hope they don't think I'm deliberately name-dropping or being flash.

We did have a bit of excitement tonight. The light fuses blew three times – once during the horror movie, so we decided to tell ghost stories until they came back on again.

Day 4 Sunday 2/2/86

The lecture this morning was from America again, and was something about a young boy who catches a caterpillar; I found it all a bit vague and boring.

After lunch, we had visitors' time, which took up all the afternoon, and being as I haven't been here for a week yet, I wasn't allowed any visitors. I decided to sit down and read my AA book. (No! not the one to work out a route back to London! the other AA book!) Then I filled in some more questionnaires. It was really nice to see the other patients' eyes light up when their visitors arrived. In a way I felt a bit envious, but at the same time happy for them. It's funny, I now class the group as my family and if I've got a particular problem, I can ask any of them to help or give me some advice. It's a very heartwarming and reassuring feeling, but this time next week I'll have visitors so I'm really looking forward to that. We had a buffet dinner and then came the crunch. 'Jack Wild, This Is Your Life!' I had to tell my life story, to the whole group.

I started telling the story I'd told a million times before: me and Phil playing football in the park; *Oliver!*... Hollywood... *Pufnstuf*... 'If I look at it even now I see their faces behind the masks – it was a happy, happy time.'

I didn't want to say it was all bad; it hadn't been all bad at all. I'd had a ball, so how had I ended up here? I struggled to remember when things had started to slip away. I think change creeps up on you silently and it isn't always what it appears to be. It was obvious my life was going to change the minute I started stage school and got paid for my first job, but it changed in ways I didn't see at the time.

'You see, I think money corrupts. Even the comparatively small amount of money I was earning then, began to affect my relationships with other people.'

I remembered my grandfather slipping me half a crown, but when I started earning my grandparents were no longer the source of extra treats and goodies as I could treat and spoil myself. And so something shifted.

'And later I bought the family home so my parents were living under my roof. And that messes things up, the balance of things. Not that I minded at the time, but you don't see it then.'

Each purchase, be it as small as sweets or as large as a house, took me further away from the relationships and structures that formed my life.

The group didn't seem to be getting it. I didn't know how to explain it.

'When children become stars in showbiz, it's almost like becoming an orphan. You are taken from your normal surroundings and put on thrones and made out to be superhuman, and there is just so much time and money to play with. It's a shame there aren't places to go to learn how to prepare yourself mentally, physically and financially for the life of a celebrity. But there ain't. And in the late sixties you were on your own and left to make the mistakes yourself having no experience of adult life whatsoever. I think today the child stars have a better chance but then...' I trailed off. Was I just making excuses?

You *had* to tell your life story and I was just trying to explain what my life was like. I didn't want to blame my drinking on being a child star, because I firmly believed that I'd have been a heavy drinker even if I'd been a footballer or a doctor. I wasn't trying to blame my drinking on my career; I was just trying to explain what my life was like, and if I'd have been a doctor I would've been explaining what that life was like.

'So I just wanted to forget about my career. I wanted to numb my body and forget about everything, but I needed more and more alcohol to do it: I needed to anaesthetise myself with another and yet another drink.'

I saw a few nods around the room. Maybe they did understand.

'At the beginning I would just drink beer or lager. Then it went on to beer and wine. If we were out having a meal or having some people over for dinner, occasionally I would have a spirit: say a brandy at the end, or (as an aperitif) vodka and lemonade. Towards the later stages of my drinking, I'd have both. I then went through a stage where I used to like dry cider. I suppose it was just a change of taste. Then at the end, say the last one or two years, I would drink anything I could, even if I didn't like the taste. It's only now that I realise, over the years, I had to drink more to get to the state that whenever I would lie down, i.e. going to bed, I would fall asleep very quickly. I felt I needed to drink to help me cope with the day-to-day problems of everyday life. I thought it made life easier.

'By 1985, I had become a recluse. I didn't want to go out, see anyone or do anything. I was divorced in September 1985 and moved into a new home in October 1985 living by myself. The days of the wooden box were getting closer! I began for the first time to get frightened about my health and especially my mistress, Mrs Booze! She'd been with me now since 1977. How could I kick her out of my life? Divorce her?

'At the time, I had two diseases, alcoholism and diabetes, and I thought I only had one. Then, in mid-January, I read an article about Pete Townshend that triggered me off. This is it! This is my last chance! For the first time in years, I got on with it and now I've seen the light at the end of the tunnel. I can now look forward to cancelling that wooden box some time in March!

'I've come here to live again, not die.'

Well, I talked for about thirty-five to forty minutes about my life and, to be honest, it wasn't half as bad as I expected it to be. They asked a few questions after I had finished and then it was all over. The only thing that worries me is whether or not I bored them or went on too long. Anyway, I'm sure I'll find out in group therapy tomorrow morning.

P.S. Since Friday, I've been sleeping better than as far back as I can remember. I'm now on Librium twice a day. That's four tablets in all, whereas I started on four times a day and that's eight tablets in all! It won't be long now before I'm off them completely. I had a walk around the garden today. It was great! I did ask if I could jog around the garden but the nurse thought it better if I waited until I was off Librium which would only be a couple of days now. I'm really looking forward to that.

P.P.S. One of the visitor's kids thought that I was another star. He said, "'Ere mate, you're the one with the funny specs and plays the piano, aren't you?'

I said, 'Who do you mean?'

He said, 'I know, you're Elton John!'

Day 5 Monday 3/2/86

I was given my daily chores to do this morning and this consisted, firstly, of hoovering the upstairs landing, the stairs and the reception area. Then, keeping the urn full of water at all times and making sure that there's always plenty of tea, coffee, sugar and milk available. Not forgetting to pull the telephone off the hook when we're doing lectures, group therapy, reading, life story or yoga. The same applies at meal times. I only forgot once to pull the phone off the hook during yoga. I was told off about it, but being as it was my first day, they left it at that and told me not to let it happen again which I promised it wouldn't.

We started to play Trivial Pursuit and then Gay called. She was great and it really bucked me up. It made me feel that she's behind me all the way. She said she didn't know when she'd be able to come down being as she's working for the next two weekends and that's the only time they allow visitors, but I'm hoping we'll be able to sort something out one way or another. I'm going to call her again tomorrow night so we'll see.

Day 6 Tuesday 4/2/86

Today in group therapy, Donald talked about his problems and I could relate to a lot of things he said about the way he drank. He did it in exactly the same way as I did i.e. not sipping but guzzling as quickly as possible to get as much drink drunk in the shortest possible time.

After lunch, the second lecture was about the effects of drinking alcohol and what it does to your body. I knew most of them except that you could have spasms which include cardiac arrests. That terrified me because I've already had two and they say the third one is the one that kills you. I went completely numb. That gives me the only alternatives: drink and die, or complete the programme and stay dry forever. I'm gonna take the latter!!!

Day 7 Wednesday 5/2/86

After breakfast, I did my cleaning and hoovering. Then we had our group therapy. This morning was absolutely electric. John, the one who yesterday was trying to avoid getting his family in for a group discussion by making excuses, finally saw the light. Over a period of one and a half hours, he agreed that what we were saying was right. It was an incredible experience. It took all my strength not to cry with him. I'm really pleased and very proud for John. He's a diamond guy. You can tell how electric it was. There were eighteen people in that room and you could hear a pin drop. I could see that it takes a lot of strength and guts to go through and admit what he did. I myself was completely drained but yet I had a feeling of great satisfaction; the fact that I was a member of the group that had helped John to see the light in the right perspective and overcome his difficulty. It was great stuff!

We had another good lunch and then I was told my new duties starting tomorrow, to serve lunch and supper and clear up afterwards. I was then told that, although I won't be detoxed until tonight, I could go on a walk this afternoon. We ended up walking about three miles. The sun was shining, it was pretty cold, but the fresh air felt great. I must admit I enjoyed the exercise, and tomorrow I'm going to start jogging with Donald before breakfast, around the garden half a dozen times.

After a cup of coffee, the group was split into two groups. I was in the one with John (the gay drug addict). He started to talk about harmful effects he'd had with his family. Within a couple of minutes, I'd sussed him out completely. He was acting and playing games. I'm sure he was trying to win an Oscar, but everyone in the group saw through him. I got very mad because he was wasting everyone's time and, aside from that, he was not helping everyone else in the group with their treatment. I told him in front of the group and the counsellors that I didn't want it to go on any more because it was a complete waste of time, and when you've only got six weeks to do your treatment, that is very, very selfish on his part. I feel sorry for him 'cos he's very screwed up. He thinks he can play games here and pull the wool over our eyes but, in a place like this, it is impossible! He's a nice guy and I hope he's got the strength to pull himself together.

After dinner, John asked if he could have a word with me, so I took my coffee up to his room to talk. In short, he'd reassessed his position and saw the right way to get over his hang-up. After this, he thanked me for giving him a verbal bashing. I told him I felt bad about it afterwards but I had to be truthful and tell him my feelings. By the way, everyone agreed with me and told me afterwards that, for a small guy, I'd got a lot of guts! It had nothing to do with guts, just being truthful and caring.

Day 8 Thursday 6/2/86

In group therapy Andrew was doing 'harmful consequences and resentments'. He came across as very insincere with no honesty or feelings. He seems to want to cling to this Jack-the-Lad image. He'd given four people fixes, they'd all overdosed and he showed no feeling towards that at all. He'd introduced people to drugs who had since died and not a bat of an eyelid. I was really fuming with him and told him what I thought over coffee. 'If you want to succeed in your treatment, you are going to have to be honest with yourself and drop your defences.' I liked him and really hoped he could get his act together for his own sake.

After lunch, it was yoga again. I enjoyed it as usual and it wasn't until the last exercise that I relaxed too much and dozed off, but that's the longest I've lasted. Now I'm detoxed, maybe on Monday I'll get through the whole lesson!

After coffee I went jogging and did about half a mile, which I thought was quite good to start with. We've worked it out that six times around the outside of the garden is a mile and I did three. I'll do four tomorrow.

Day 9 Friday 7/2/86

I had to see the doctor because my sugar was way up. He suggested taking some more Actrapid and not to jog today.

After a quick coffee, it was 'firing squad time' and I was the target! It was my turn to do 'harmful consequences and resentments'. I took a handkerchief with me in case I lost control, and I was hoping not to crack up. As it happened, it was just as well I did take it. First on my list was about my health.

'Through my drinking, my physical health is atrocious! My body is a wreck! It's almost a walking human scrapyard! It makes me so mad that I didn't stop drinking sooner. Anyway, back to my body. The first thing that happened was, I was flown home from Poland with pancreatitis; which, for those of you who haven't had it, it is very, very painful; but not painful enough to stop me drinking. My doctor told me that if I carried on drinking, I'd be dead in two years. The next thing that happened, I'd got cirrhosis of the liver and was told by another doctor I'd be dead in twelve months if I drank! Still, I carried on! Four years later, I'd then damaged myself enough to give me diabetes. The doctors said "no drink at all" because it would kill me, at any time, mixed with insulin! For a very short period, I didn't drink at all; but then it became, I'll just have the one. Well, the one became two, then three, etc., etc., etc. until I was back to square one. I suppose, for that short period, it was more of a forced stopping.'

After I'd finished, Barbara told me there was only one guy who has been here who was worse off physically than me, and his name was Sam. He went through the treatment successfully. Stayed dry but was dead within three months. That scared me shitless! What that story meant to me was, what I actually thought, but was trying to put at the back of my mind: I really am at death's door. At least if I live long enough to complete the treatment, I'll be happy because that's all I have to give back to my ex-wife Gay. And if I stay dry, maybe I'll get a second chance with her. I must also take my diabetes seriously.

The time that I cracked up was when I told the group how I'd ruined a diamond marriage. The pain I felt was the worst pain I've ever had in the world.

'I got married on Valentine's Day in 1976 and, for the first three or four years, everything seemed to be going okay – apart from the fact I had started to get drunk more and my drinking heavier. I did quite a lot of TV and films but the drinking was always at home. I kept promising Gay I wouldn't drink, but I couldn't stop; I was powerless when it came to alcohol.

'I would lie many a time to Gay, saying that I'd only had a couple of drinks when in fact it was a couple of bottles; if she found an empty bottle I'd say that Bob drank it. She used to work at night singing and would come home in the early hours to find me drunk watching a video: she never knew what she was coming home to.

'We'd often have to break promises to friends because I was too ill to travel. If we did go, I'd have two or three drinks at the most and then when we got home, no matter what time it was, I'd make up for it. If it was very late and Gay was tired I'd make an excuse: "I'm not tired, let's watch a film," so then I could make up for lost drinking time. When we had been married about a year, a close friend of ours was getting married. We'd promised we would be there; but, through my drinking the night before, we couldn't go. We've never seen or spoken to them to this day. The end of my marriage was the ultimate loss.

'I just hope I haven't "caught myself", for want of another word, "too late"! I really want to live and be a nice person again. Not like the one who swopped himself for booze! I want to be the genuine Jack Wild who is teetotal! Drink had screwed up my emotions to such an extent that I became very confused, and eventually reclusive.'

The group gave me a lot of feedback. Two told me afterwards they were even crying with me. I felt very humiliated but relieved it was all over.

After we had a coffee, I went for a walk with Simon, Andrew and James, which inevitably ended up in a snowball fight. It was pretty cold but good, clean fun. Especially with Simon on his crutches! One thing I would like to say and that is, until you experience it, the group is a hundred and ten per cent behind you when you're honest and sincere, and the hope and strength they gave me this afternoon is indescribable. No words can explain it!!!

Day 10 Saturday 8/2/86

Still plenty of snow about. After breakfast, group therapy was mainly about an argument between Andrew and Adrian that happened last night. At one stage I was asked to sit back-to-back with Adrian and pretend I was Andrew. After- wards Andrew came up to me and said I was spot on and how he wished he could open up and say exactly the same things. Later that day I asked A and A how they felt and they both said 'close to the group, relaxed and happy'. It just goes to show how much the group helps one another. I feel great! I'm part of that group!

Day 11 Sunday 9/2/86

More lectures, tests, peer evaluation and a 566-question questionnaire to fill in. After lunch Beth asked me to read a letter she was thinking of sending to her husband. Her problems are very similar to mine, except she's a lot healthier than me. I gave her my opinion; I hope I was some help to her.

Man United were playing Liverpool tonight. I put on my Man U shirt, and Simon and I were geeing each other up about who was going to win. I put a knotted handkerchief on my head (Monty Python 'Gumby'-style) and went to make coffee shouting 'U-N-I-T-E-D!' Ruth came out of the dining room and said, 'Do you mind, Jack, we're having a meeting in here.'

'I'm very sorry,' I said, and quietly sat down with my coffee and watched football with the boys. It was a draw.

Day 12 Monday 10/2/86

Today's group therapy was a disaster! Simon (who's still on probation) used the office telephone twice more last night after the permitted call he'd made to his mother: once to Dial-A-Disc (how stupid can you get?) and secondly to call his girlfriend. He was caught. Now, bearing in mind his probation was up for review today, to go and do something like this last night was totally crazy. The office telephone records all calls and the staff was able to check up whom he had called. After all this had come out in group, he was asked to go upstairs, pack and then leave. I was very angry and felt let down by him. The whole group was shocked, horrified and very angry.

Now, if that wasn't enough, after he'd left the room, John (the guy who taught me to roll my own fags) said that *he* was leaving this morning. This again had the group shocked. His excuse was that he thought he'd gone as far as he could with the programme. This made the group, including myself, feel let down yet again! This guy had been in treatment for four weeks already. What a stupid man! My impression of the group was of complete bewilderment.

I think Simon just didn't want to give up drugs. He didn't want to walk out, so the next easy way out was to be thrown out. Whereas with John, he either wanted to go back to drinking, or had a large amount of aggro from his girlfriend, or both. Either way, both of them made stupid mistakes.

After this, six of us read out our peer evaluation forms. Everyone was criticised for something or other. Me, well, I was criticised for joking about in the dining room and also that I don't have to entertain the group all the time, even though they all said the light relief was welcome most times, and to be myself. In other words, REAL! Well, after all the commotion this morning, everyone felt drained. By now it was time for lunch. After we'd eaten, it was coffee and then yoga. Today I'm determined *not* to fall asleep. And lo and behold, I didn't! 'Ere, I'm really getting into this yoga lark!

I sent four letters today: to Gay, to Gran, to Suzi and Lenny and to Mum and Dad. That's all folks!

Day 13 Tuesday 11/2/86

Before breakfast, Tim decided to walk out without even having the decency to say goodbye to the group. He left everyone in the house feeling angry and hurt.

After breakfast Barbara wanted to talk to me about my assignment. We'd been asked to pick a character from a fairy story and to explain their thoughts and feelings through the story. I'd chosen *Jack and the Beanstalk* and Barbara asked me what I thought it told her about me. I answered, 'A kid who lives in a fantasy world.' She agreed.

We talked for a while and it was interesting, but I was more concerned about what she would say about my confession. Four days ago I'd burnt a hole in the pillowcases and sheet whilst in bed doing the fairy story. I told her I knew I'd broken house rules and was frightened I'd be asked to leave which is why I hadn't said anything earlier. She told me I wouldn't be thrown out, and to bring it up in group, and go and tell Margaret in the office. After I did all that, I was so relieved. I'm sure I wouldn't have admitted to that before coming here, so I am changing, slowly but surely.

I watched Everton slaughter Man City and went back to the assignment. Tomorrow, I'll have been here two weeks. It really does get tougher as the days go on; still, keep slogging away!

Day 15 Thursday 13/2/86

It was my turn to act out different parts of my life finishing up to date. I wrote ten pages. I started out okay and it brought back happy memories of my past up until about 1979 when I was brought back from Poland. From then on, it became painful. Inside, I was angry with myself for letting me get into that position, with the final crunch being my divorce. I finished by telling the group that I didn't like the person I became when drinking. I hated *that* Jack Wild. I don't want to see him ever again. But now, the *real* Jack Wild is being reborn at this moment! It won't happen overnight, I know that. I also know that it won't be easy work, but hard work. It will also hurt and be painful at times. But I'm determined to score the goal that I want. As in 'One Day at a Time', I think it's sensible to think on the lines of 'one goal at a time' too. The feedback from the group on my life story was very much one of me being a very lonely person, which I think is true to a large extent, especially since '79. I think I learnt quite a lot about myself today.

After lunch it was yoga time again. I didn't fall asleep and I enjoyed it immensely. Then Ruth asked me to her office ('cos Barbara didn't come in today – she's ill) and gave me my First Step to do which really made my day! Now I really am making progress!

Each of the Twelve Steps in AA is designed to take you in stages through facing up to and overcoming your addiction, to the point where you can go out into the world and put it all into practice; helping others as well as yourself. Step One is defined as 'We admitted we were powerless over alcohol – that our lives had become unmanageable'.

The sheet of paper for my First Step said: 'It would be impossible to over-estimate the importance of the First Step because the chances of quitting drugs and being contented with yourself and your life are very poor until you accept the seriousness and totality of the illness. Each patient of this unit is encouraged to make a list of destructive behaviours caused by his powerlessness over mood-altering chemicals and unmanageable life.'

Right! Well, that required some thinking about.

After dinner and then coffee we had Miles's life story and, my God, talk about sad! That's the saddest story I've ever heard. He was so honest and sincere that, although he was crying, there was many in the group with tears in their eyes, including myself. The life this guy has had, it's no wonder he's here at Broadreach. To be honest it's a wonder he's not in a mental hospital, or committed suicide. My heart, and I'm sure everyone's in the group, went out to him. After he'd finished, I asked him if he was feeling better and he said he felt ten stone lighter.

Must start reading about my 'First Step' which I have to have ready in a week's time.

Day 16 Friday 14/2/86

After breakfast we had our usual group therapy with Ruth. It was more or less a general conversation, starting with, how were we feeling? Donald, who is normally quite quiet and reserved, started having a go about the hygiene in the bathroom and toilets. (That's his job this week. Me, I'm back on the tea and coffee urn; don't know what I've done to deserve that, it's the worst thera-peutic duty you can get!) Anyway, Donald said, 'They are filthy, and if a health inspector came, the place would be closed down.'

I thought he was just angry and over the top, but I got the feeling he was hiding something. He'd had a nightmare last night about 2.30 am. I woke up to find him trying to get inside my wardrobe! Then he went over to Adrian and started shaking him, saying, 'Adrian! Adrian! Come on, get up!' and when he woke up, very startled, Donald put the light on and said, 'Oh, sorry,' switched it off and went back to bed. When we asked him this morning if he remembered he said, 'Yes! That's the first nightmare I've had since I've been here! I was dreaming someone needed help.'

We all had a coffee, then sat down to watch a video lecture from the States. It was about 'Alcoholism, the Disease'. I thought it was fantastic! Apparently, the reason why some people become alcoholic and some not is that, in your family, you always find heavy drinkers or alcoholics in past generations and they pass on a chemical called THIQ. This goes to your brain and stays there forever, which means, if you have your first drink, it's only a matter of time before you become alcoholic. THIQ is very similar chemically to heroin. This really made me believe that *it is a disease!* I must admit, THIQ really frightened me!

Day 17 Saturday 15/2/86

After dinner, I spoke to Gay. Her flu is a lot better. She's singing with Sacha Distel tonight. I also gave Gran a ring to wish her a happy birthday.

After I'd spoken to Gran I found myself thinking about filming in Ireland. It's strange the things that come back to you. Gran and Grandad had said, 'When you're in Ireland, will you try and get us a four-leafed clover to help with the bingo, Jackie?' Me Gran used to love going to bingo.

So when we were on location, if I wasn't failing to catch fish, I'd look for four-leafed clovers. And Christ, if I found one, I must've found a good half a dozen of them. The first one I gave to me Gran, another to me Mum and one I gave to Gay before we got married; I think it broke.

Day 18 Sunday 16/2/86

I had a good breakfast of bacon and eggs and then did my therapeutic duties. I'm back on the tea urn, telephone, hoovering and cleaning the downstairs cloakroom floor and the front hall floor. This one is by far the worst job of all because it starts at 8am and doesn't finish until 11pm. Then we had a lecture entitled 'Addicted to the Addict' which was about the effect on the family. For example, when the addict becomes preoccupied with his chemical, the family and/or close friends become preoccupied with the addict. They are constantly thinking about the chemically dependent person. When they go to bed at night, they often think things like, is he in trouble with the police? Is he still alive? or, is he dead? It was a very interesting lecture, but the guy did ramble on too long. He could have come to the point in half the time.

After lunch most of the patients had visitors so I went upstairs to continue Step One. I was having difficulty with the category entitled 'Effects on Your Spiritual Life'. It was really beginning to give me grief. I finally ended up speaking to Adrian, Andrew, Donald and John. I was getting nearer, I felt, but still not there yet. I went looking for a counsellor. I collared Anna and later Ruth. Now, I thought I'd got it in my head. I went and found a Bible, but the way it was written wasn't very clear. Then Stewart (who left about two weeks ago) turned up for aftercare therapy and I asked him to explain it to me. After this, I came upstairs to continue writing. About an hour later, I finished this category, which was a great relief.

I spoke to Gay twice today. Her flu is a lot better. She did say she was looking forward to seeing me. The one thing I mustn't do is raise my hopes too high regarding Gay. I keep saying to myself, one goal at a time too. Yeah! Yeah!

Day 19 Monday 17/2/86

After breakfast and our daily duties, we had our peer evaluation group which is about your last week's progress, mistakes, what you need to work harder on, and how the group can help you with it. My feedback from the group was that I was great at helping other people, but that I should tell people how *I'm* feeling. If I'm worried about something or have a problem, however big or small, go and ask for help from someone or from the group as a whole. I think the reason for this is that I'm not used to going to people and asking for help. It's always been the other way around with me, them coming to me for help, and I don't know how to approach it. I suppose the only way of learning is to take a risk and just simply ASK. After all this came out, I felt confused. How was I going to get around this one?

After dinner, I got ready very quickly to go to my first AA meeting. I'd been looking forward to this for quite a while. A group of us went in two taxis from Broadreach into Plymouth. We arrived at the hall at 7.20 and there must have been about two dozen people there, most aged between twenty-eight and fifty. We were given cups of tea and at 7.30 the meeting began. About eight or nine people talked of their experiences. Then Andrew, on behalf of us all, got up and said that we'd all enjoyed the meeting and thanks etc.

I thought in some parts they were very condescending towards the group from Broadreach. Almost like a 'them and us' situation. Firstly, they said at the start of the meeting, 'Welcome, Beginners,' which didn't go down well; and the second-to-last speaker was very smug and aloof. He thought that just because he had eight years of sobriety behind him, he was the higher power HIMSELF! He said, 'I'm going to have my say and you' (looking at me and Michael) 'can have your say after!' My blood was boiling over, but I thought it best to keep quiet. But overall, I was pleasantly surprised that you could get a feeling of closeness outside of a controlled environment like Broadreach. I'm really looking forward to finishing my treatment and going to my local meeting in Twickenham.

Day 21 Wednesday 19/2/86

After breakfast and doing my duties, it was time for group therapy. First on the agenda was Jo. She said that she had discharged herself and was leaving! She had told a few of us before group that she had been put on probation for fraternising in the bedrooms with Ken and Andrew; and also her boyfriend Ted had been banned from visiting her because, apparently, he's married and still with his wife! The only way Broadreach works is in honesty. Everyone in the group was speechless! We were shocked and angry at being used by her. It was sheer selfishness on her part. She couldn't have cared less. It was written all over her face. She was leaving for one thing and one thing only: to drink!

After the commotion, it was my turn to do my Step One. I was really frightened at first, but within a couple of minutes I could feel the whole group behind me and I began to relax.

Frequency of Use

In the early days of drinking I would have a drink almost every day. Then I became more of a binge drinker. I'd binge for three or four days, then I'd be ill, I'd wait to recover, maybe have a week or two off, sometimes more, then I'd start again. I thought, I can't be an alcoholic because I don't drink every day like I used to.

Lying About Chemical Use

'No! I haven't been drinking!' If I've said that sentence once then I've said it a million times. I used to lie all the time about drinking to whoever questioned me about it. I always used to carry a breath freshener (minty spray) in my pocket to cover up any alcohol on my breath as well. I'd also lie about how many pints or glasses of wine I'd drunk. After becoming diabetic, whenever we were out while I was supposed to be dry (I was a secret drinker when no one was around) I'd often say to people when offered a drink, 'Who, me? Oh no! I don't drink at all!' and I'd have a Perrier with ice and lemon.

Destructive Behaviour

There was an argument at one of my parties. I can't actually remember what the argument was about; it must've been petty otherwise I would have remembered. Anyway being as I'm against violence, I went in the back garden and punched the shed door twice. That got rid of the anger and in return gave me the pain. On other occasions, I'd punch a hole in the downstairs toilet door. In the end, it had four or five holes in it.

I've got to do some more Step One tomorrow, and Barbara said she'd give me Steps Two and Three. She also commented on how well I controlled my anger this afternoon with John, so between that and hopefully getting Two and Three tomorrow, I think I'm beginning to make a little progress.

Day 22 Thursday 20/2/86

Beechy* was in the chair for my Step One. I was a bit nervous at the start but no sooner had I begun than I got the feeling from the group again! It's really hard to explain until you've experienced it; the feeling of togetherness and not being alone. Anyway, everything seemed to flow so smoothly and naturally I could hardly believe it.

Then we had coffee. I was sat in the lounge when Barbara came from behind and gave me my Steps Two and Three. (Step Two: 'Came to believe that a Power greater than ourselves could restore us to sanity'; Step Three: 'Made a decision to turn our will and our lives over to the care of God as we understand him.') It wasn't so much of a surprise but, God, it made me feel very happy and proud at accomplishing my First Step. I was on cloud nine!

Next Wednesday Gay's coming down! I'm on to Steps Two and Three tomorrow and my daily duty has been changed from the stinking tea urn to an easy job in the laundry room. Anything's better than the f....... tea urn!

Day 24 Saturday 22/2/86

Just before lunch, Barbara had me in her office and told me what she wanted me to do for my Steps Two and Three. First she wanted me to read a book called *Why I Am Afraid to Tell You Who I Am*, and afterwards do a collage about the different roles and games I played whilst I was drinking. After lunch we all watched a video from the States entitled *If You Loved Me*. It showed how we all play games and tell lies to our families, and also about hiding your chemical. I related to many things in it.

Day 25 Sunday 23/2/86

I got up this morning and outside was covered in about four inches of snow. Anyway, I had breakfast and set off with my therapeutics. Then I sat down for a coffee and to await the arrival of the papers. They didn't turn up. Everything outside was at a standstill. I took James up a coffee. He's doing his collage in my room because there's only one pair of scissors and one set of crayons. We got so much into our work we didn't realise what time it was and were late for dinner.

Then it was time for Phil's life story. Well, talk about laugh! This guy is dryer than the Sahara! Although it was a sad story in parts, the way he told it

---

* Beechy Colclough was one of the therapists, who now has his own clinic in London. He was a fabulous, very young guy of a similar age to me and he'd been a drug addict and alcoholic.

was like a situation comedy. He always saw the funny side of disasters, but I think he uses this as a defence. The best laugh of all is when he was in a mental institution and he was surrounded by nutters. One bloke who was sat next to him at the dinner table kept falling in his soup, while another came up to him and said, ''Ere, you borrowed a fag from me ten years ago! Give me one back!' That story was a killer.

I got a letter from me Mum; it read:

> Here's a few lines to let you know we are ok just now and we hope you are... The weather here is very cold, it isn't even warm in doors, I expect it's the same down there. We were pleased to hear you passed your first step, so keep the good work up, it will be all worth while in the end, it won't be long now before you are coming home.
>
> Arthur rang up tonight, he is settling in, but they can only use the phone once a day, and someone has to be with them at the phone, so we are hoping he gets sorted out too.
>
> Anyway Jack I think this is all for now so goodnight and God Bless and look after yourself. *

Day 26 Monday 24/2/86

Normally, two nurses stay overnight; but last night, because of the snow, only one could get in, and trust our luck, it was Avril. You've heard of the lady with the lamp? Well, she's the lady with the torch! She comes in during the night to your room and shines the torch in your face and wakes you up!

I don't sleep well at the best of times and Avril and her torch woke me up at ten past two in the morning! I didn't appreciate that! I thought it was seven and started getting dressed to make the coffee. In the commotion, Adrian woke up as well. We've all come to the conclusion that the woman is mad! She's the one who needs treatment!

Today at peer evaluation, I was told that I had made progress from last week in terms of sharing my feelings, but I still need to share more and relax more. Instead of helping others all the time, help myself! Let the real Jack

---

* Arthur was drying out at St Bernard's in Ealing Hospital. Reading the letter now she sounds amazingly stoical about her two boys in their respective drying-out clinics – it's as though it's the most normal thing in the world. But that was Mum. She always fought to hide how worried she was for us; and was hopeless at it. I can only imagine how desperately worried she was about us. I feel dreadful, totally dreadful about putting this tiny, generous, courageous spirit, this petite bundle of energy who loved dancing, people and her fags, this secret extrovert, through the worry and stress and desperation that I did. And the worst part – that she would never see either of her sons beat their addiction.

come out of his shell! I wasn't really surprised by this. Somehow, I seem to not want people getting too close to me. I'll just have to keep hammering away at this wall until it's completely demolished! Tom was also told that if he doesn't stop playing games and start sharing with the group, he's out!

I spoke to Mum, Dad, Arf, Julie and Gay today. Gay seemed okay and I can't wait to see her on Wednesday.

Day 27 Tuesday 25/2/86

Today when I got up and looked out the window, the sun was shining and it was great! After breakfast and duties we were told we were going 'walkies'. Everyone got wrapped up well and we left the house at 10am. It was very crisp outside, but not as cold as last week. We went the normal way until we got to the bottom of the hill; then, instead of turning the usual way, we went right and headed for the church at Bickleigh. It was very old, seventeenth century I think. After having a good look around, we headed back to the house as it was getting late. We got back just in time for lunch. I reckon we must have walked five or six miles easily.

After lunch, Barbara gave a lecture on 'Guilt and Shame and the Difference between the Two'. Then, after dinner, we had Brian's life story which was quite interesting, especially when he told us about getting out of the Foreign Legion. He'd signed up for five years, and when they were going to send him to Chad in Africa, he poured melted candle wax in his ear, went to the doctors and got a medical discharge for having a perforated eardrum!

After we had finished, I went to get a coffee and came upstairs to finish my collage. I'm doing it in group tomorrow morning. I finished it at 11pm, watched a bit of telly, had some more coffee, and then an early night. It's gonna be a heavy day tomorrow, starting with me boiling eggs for eighteen people. Goodnight.

P.S. I got something to look forward to tomorrow: Gay's coming to visit!

Day 28 Wednesday 26/2/86

I got up this morning not looking forward to cooking the eggs as they're very fussy about their three-minute eggs. As it turned out, they were like bullets! After breakfast, I did my therapeutic duties and started to get myself ready for my Step Two in the morning group. I felt really nervous. Somehow I thought there was something not quite right with it.

When I got in the lounge, there was a strange atmosphere as the group started. Apparently there had been some aggro between Brian and Angus about drug talk and also about smuggling drugs into the house. Both of them were put on probation. To get all of this sorted out took over an hour. I was fuming! I'd got all psyched up for Step Two for nothing! I knew that there were four people today supposed to be working in group, two in each session, so there was a possibility that I may not do my work! Anyway, with the upset supposedly over and done with, we had lunch; but immediately afterwards, there was another group to continue from this morning. Angus had decided to leave. All the group were angry and upset and tried to convince Angus that he was making a bad mistake, but he wouldn't have it. Something was said between Tom and Angus that a gang who used sawn-off shotguns in Exeter could very easily get involved. It was intimidating for all of us in the house.

After this we had a lecture from Tony the vicar about Step Five, and then eventually we split into two groups with me doing my Step Two in the lounge.

I certainly wasn't in the mood for this, but there was no way out of it. Well, to cut a long story short, the thing that I'd been dreading for years happened! I was in a corner (and that was putting it mildly) and had to face the facts! It was very, very painful and it *hurt*! Admitting and accepting that I was *not* God, I'm *not* indestructible, I'm no better than any human being: all of these are hard facts that I had to face up to. Afterwards, I was glad that it had happened. It had to for my treatment to go any further. I feel a helluva lot better for it!!!

Gay arrived, we both had coffee and then went into Barbara's office and Serena (the trainee counsellor) was present too. I started by trying to explain to Gay about all the things I had learnt about myself in the last month. Then came the hard bit! Telling Gay how I'd been a bastard to her in the way I treated her over nearly ten years of marriage. I'd literally wasted ten years of her life. That was extremely painful and the hurt I felt was unbearable! It was just dreadful!

At the same time, I was very surprised when Gay said that for the first two or three years I was the best husband anyone could wish for. I mustn't let it get to me! As in believing that it was me who did these terrible things. It was the DRINK that did it and I myself was powerless! What I must do now is, look forward to going home after my treatment is over and standing on my own two feet as a man, not a boy! And, most important of all, *be myself for myself!* Anything after that is a bonus!

Although today was painful, at least I know that, if the worst comes to the worst, I've still got Gay as my 'best mate'. She told me that in the meeting and I treasure that very much! I'm a very lucky guy in more ways than one and I'm thankful!

Day 29 Thursday 27/2/86

Listening today to Iris doing her 'harmful consequences', it was a sad state of affairs and I could really relate to the situation of being alone at home and the only friend you thought you had was your drink! I had a coffee and then Barbara asked to see me. I thought she was going to give me a new assignment for Step Three but instead she gave me Steps Four and Five; I nearly fell through the floor! I was so happy. I couldn't believe it. She said she wants to see me tomorrow, so I think I might get a leaving date then!

Serving lunch and dinner is my new therapeutic duty, and after dinner me and Adrian tried to get cleared up as quickly as possible so that we could watch *Top of the Pops*, one of the highlights of the week. We finished washing, drying and putting away eighteen place settings in eighteen minutes exactly, with twelve minutes to spare!

After *Top of the Pops* we had a talk from two people who've been through the treatment here. The main point that they kept insisting upon was to keep up the aftercare and go to AA meetings regularly. Without this you would be certain to go back to the old way of life.

Later I finally got to the phone to speak to Gay and tell her the good news. She was pleased for me too. I came upstairs for a bath and to wash my hair. I did borrow some gel off Andrew at lunchtime, but it didn't work! It only made my hair look dirtier! I'm not trying that again. Anyway, I've asked to have my hair cut and I'm waiting to be told when. Probably tomorrow I'll find out.

Day 30 Friday 28/2/86

Barbara mentioned about me changing my image again which quite threw me for a minute. She said maybe a sophisticated Scott Fitzgerald, a kind of Gatsby look. I'll have to take a long look at that one, mate!

Day 31 Saturday 1/3/86

We started group therapy early today and it was really a continuation of yesterday's discussion with Euen. He still hadn't changed his attitude at all about drinking. The way he was looking at things was through rose-coloured spectacles. I did at one time ask him if he wanted to borrow my blue specs to look at the situation he was in and how serious it really was. (This was when I'd got angry with him and was trying sarcasm!)

He was even blaming his wife, and couldn't see how close to death he was when he arrived here. As far as I'm concerned, until he accepts the truth he won't get any better. It was very tiring; I don't know how Barbara and Beechy do it.

After we broke, I had a coffee in the lounge and Barbara asked to see me. I knew what it was for. She told me that my Step Five was on 10th March at 9am and I could leave, all being well, on the 14th March (exactly three years to the day since being diagnosed diabetic, taking into consideration a leap year in 1984!). Barbara said she was sorry but she would be on holiday when I leave. She also told me to stop punishing people in feedback when I get angry. I knew exactly what she meant. When people don't listen to my feedback, I seem to jump in for the kill. I must be aware of this and stop it. She also gave me another assignment to do for Tuesday, to write about my change of image and what I will leave behind.

I spoke to Gay again and gave her the good news. She was very pleased for me. I've done another three pages on my Step Four ('Made a searching and fearless moral inventory of ourselves').

Day 32 Sunday 2/3/86

After lunch Bob arrived. It was really great to see him. I made him a coffee and we sat in the lounge to talk. He said that all was well at home, the dogs were fine, but he hadn't yet sold my Range Rover. He'd brought a load of clothes for me in his car (a Mercedes Estate!) which I took to my room. We had another coffee and then watched football.

Day 33 Monday 3/3/86

I had a coffee after breakfast and, before I knew it, it was time for peer evaluation group. I put down on my form that I thought I had accepted myself for what I am and that I'd been dethroned! I climbed down off my pedestal and if the group was to see me climbing back on, to push me off it again! I was very pleased with the feedback I got from the group. They for once had agreed with me. I put my goal for the week as 'find a balance'. It's just a question of me keeping my feet on the ground now.

Afterwards we had coffee and then it was Adrian's 'goodbye group'. Everyone was sad that he was leaving. I (as I'm sure everyone is) was so pleased and, in a funny way, proud of him finishing his treatment.

At the AA meeting in Davenport, the same bloke (Roger) that none of us liked from last week's session was there again, and he had a go at us again, saying very vindictively that if we didn't listen to what went on in the meetings, none of us would ever recover. John started to share and, in a very subtle way, proved that we were taking in everything. Then, Andrew shared and said much the same in a respectful way and then I (controlling my anger) decided to share. I said that it was so nice to be able to have so many true friends in the Fellowship and that true friends are hard to find in the outside world! Although Roger gave out a number of looks tonight, he didn't get a bite from Broadreach. I was pleased with myself for not blowing my top. I was in full control tonight!

I tried to call Gay tonight, but she was out. So I came upstairs and had a bath for tomorrow's 'change of image'. I'm dreading it!

We had a new patient arrive today. He's just come out of hospital for liver failure. He's a user and a dealer in London.

Day 34 Tuesday 4/3/86

After breakfast, I got ready for my new image. I felt a bit uneasy wearing my white silk suit (minus the waistcoat), silk shirt and boots. We had a good discussion about images and the feedback I got was favourable. Everyone seemed to agree with me that I need to change my dress so that I look like a thirty-three-year-old guy, not an elderly teenager.

Barbara told me today that some people go straight from here to a halfway house like in Weston-super-Mare, but she had arranged (if I liked) for me to stay with Charlie Watts' wife and help her in her stables in the country. I told Barbara it would drive me to drink 'cos I'm frightened of horses; she laughed. I thought that was very thoughtful of Barbara. She was saying it for me to be with showbiz people.

Day 35 Wednesday 5/3/86

After breakfast, I had a read of my Step Four; and after this, it was time for group therapy. John was asked to do his play about a conversation with his higher power. This is where I came in. We did it and John got some really good feedback from the group. I wasn't really surprised how quickly I got into my role because, when I came to Broadreach, I thought I was God; now, here I was *playing God!*

Afterwards, the trick cyclist asked if he could have a word and, for a minute, I thought, oh shit! I hadn't had the results of my IQ test and whether or not I had any brain damage, but he told me all was well. My IQ was above average, 113 in fact, which was between O and A level standards. He also said I was much too impulsive, I had an engineering mind and I was a social extrovert. Then I had my hair cut. It wasn't too bad for £2.

Today has been really hectic. About seven or eight people have asked for help or advice. I feel like a counsellor.

Day 36 Thursday 6/3/86

After breakfast, instead of group therapy we all went for a walk. It was a lovely day, the sun was shining and it wasn't too cold either. On the walk me and Tom chatted about our past and what we hoped would happen in the future. I said what I would really like to do is not to be in the limelight, but to be behind the scenes and produce and direct. It felt like I'd really hit the nail on the head.

Andrew did his assignment about his higher power, his self-will and himself. I thought it was really great! I did try to call Gay tonight but she was out.

Day 37 Friday 7/3/86

Today we watched *A Sensitive, Passionate Man* with David Janssen (himself an alcoholic) and Angie Dickinson. Well, talk about heavy duty. It was much too close to home for comfort! It was fabulous! It was like watching my life story almost (except for the kids). After it finished, there was a strange silence in the room. I think it really hit home to everyone: the seriousness of all our problems. I'm definitely gonna get a video copy of it. It was so powerful that I'm sure, when I'm outside, if ever I feel the urge to have a drink, I'll put that on and that'll stop it for sure. I tried to call Gay, but she was out again!

I came upstairs with a coffee and came to the conclusion that even more now do I believe that my higher power has been looking after me all along, and it was he who guided me to Broadreach. Without him I wouldn't be alive today.

Day 38 Saturday 8/3/86

In family group we had Charlotte and her lover Pam in the hot seat. They were both very honest with each other, and both stated how much they loved each other and how important it was for them to stay together. I was pleased for Charlotte, as we all knew how nervous she was about the outcome. But she needn't have been. It all turned out okay! It took a lot of guts for Charlotte to say and do what she did in group and she did it admirably!

Then, it was Ken's turn with his mum and dad. It was really great to see the three of them as a close family unit. Aside from being happy for Ken, I was also happy for his mum and dad. You could see their happiness in their faces. Really good stuff!

Now, we had a short coffee break before finishing up with John and his father. Here again, it was great stuff. To see the bond between father and son finally back was fabulous! I was pleased for both of them. We finally finished and Ruth and Beechy looked absolutely shattered! I don't know how they do it, I really don't. I must admit it's really a pleasure to help anyone working in the group. It really makes you feel good to be part of it.

Ken calls me 'Jack the Snack'. I weighed nine stone two pounds today. Broadreach statistics say nearly everyone puts on a minimum of one and a half stone during their treatment, so I've got six days to put on another twelve pounds; but with me being diabetic I think it'll be a lot less.

Day 39 Sunday 9/3/86

Gay called to say Theo, her grandfather, had been taken to hospital. I had a quick chat to Gran and told her I'd be there on Friday. I called Gran and Gay again later on and they said they were taking it day to day. I said I'd call Gay tomorrow night to see how things are.

Late this afternoon, we found out why Adrian hadn't come to aftercare. The day he left here, that night he went and used! He may have used the excuse of being in court on the Tuesday and he was worried about it; but Charles, Ken and myself spoke to him when he came out of court and he seemed fine. Anyway, he's now at Weston-super-Mare in the halfway house. But he's had to start from scratch again, starting with his life story before starting Step One again. It just goes to show how powerful drugs are and how easy it is to make a slip, or in his case he just simply wanted to use again. 'Just one more time': famous last words!

Day 40 Monday 10/3/86

I didn't sleep at all last night! I must've gone through Step Five ('Admitted to God, to ourselves, and to another human being, the exact nature of our wrongs') at least half a dozen times. Anyway, I had a really good breakfast and afterwards I quickly did the lounge with Ted. Then I came upstairs to get ready for my Step Five.

At just gone 9.30am, I went into Beechy's office with Ted, the vicar. I sat down with my cigarettes and coffee, he made me feel relaxed immediately and I began reading my Step Five to him. Every now and then, he compared his own experiences with what I was saying. Within no time at all, I'd finished and it was eleven o'clock! I couldn't believe how quickly I'd gone through it.

Ted said I'd done a thorough and well-written Step Five. I can tell you, I felt on top of the world walking out of that office! I felt as though all my past had been left behind in that office! What a relief, I'd actually done it! I said thanks and goodbye to Ted and he said he'd see me again before I left on Friday. Then, I took a coffee upstairs and laid on my bed feeling very proud of myself but at the same time, in a daze! I didn't know what to do next.

After lunch we had yoga, then a lecture; and then Ken told me that Ted was upset because his divorce had just come through. I knew from my own experience how painful that can be so I had a good talk with him.

I called Gay and she said that Theo was much the same. I think she was a bit upset, but I told her to be strong and I'd call again tomorrow.

I was really tired so I had an early night. I must admit, now that my treatment has finished and I've nothing much to do, I'll get bored quickly; but at least I can be of help to the other members of the group and that'll make me feel good! Mind you, I'm on a high anyway! I have been since lunchtime! Don't get me wrong, I'm no way complaining!

Day 41 Tuesday 11/3/86

Before breakfast I found out that Brian had decided to leave treatment this morning, so that wasn't a particularly good start to the day. I didn't feel angry because I had switched off from him a while ago. He seemed to be playing games with everyone. He wanted to carry on using. I just knew I was powerless so I let him go. After breakfast I did the lounge with Ted as usual. I was and still am on top of the world.

I spoke to Gay and Theo isn't any different. She sounded upset so I didn't ask too many questions. I told her to keep her chin up and I'd be back on Friday. I also said that I'd call her tomorrow night.

Day 42 Wednesday 12/3/86

At one o'clock, we all went for a walk and this time took a different route on a National Trust Walkway. We went through a forest and ended up by a river. It was really great! Very peaceful and tranquil. I had a good chat with Beechy about all sorts of things including the forty-kilometre walk on 11th August. We got back to the house at about two-ish. We'd walked about four miles and I was knackered. And there's me talking to Beechy about a twenty-six-mile hike! I must be mad!

Day 43 Thursday 13/3/86

I slept well again last night, and somehow I seem to be getting into a normal sleeping pattern, which I haven't had for about fifteen or sixteen years really. I can't believe how good I'm feeling after my Step Five. In the afternoon, I went in the second group of yoga, and yet again I relaxed too much and fell asleep! I think I've only been awake twice the whole time I've been here. But I really do enjoy it. I suppose that's another thing I'll miss when I leave!

Well, I'm going home tomorrow at lunchtime and Dad's coming to pick me up! Goodnight! xxx

A Plan For Living

1 Go home and live a life of sobriety.
2 Act responsibly like a thirty-three-year-old man.
3 Stand on my own two feet.
4 Work through the programme with the help of my higher power.
5 Attend AA meetings regularly.
6 Work towards getting back together with Gay, which I've already accepted that, if at all, it will take at least a year.
7 Lead a normal, happy life.
8 Try and get into the other side of the business i.e. producing, directing.
9 Strike up meaningful relationships with whomever I am in contact with.
10 Try and repay Broadreach for what they have given me: A New Life! i.e. do charity events!

I never thought I was an alcoholic; but, since being at Broadreach, my belief is totally different now. I accept the fact that I *am an alcoholic*, and I am so grateful now not to be drinking. The times I'd ended up in hospital through drinking, each time I immediately went into self-pity. It doesn't make sense, but I blamed it on others. 'Why didn't they help me and stop me from getting into this state? They can't love me to let me get into this state!'

This obviously wasn't the case. Everyone had tried without success to stop me. I just wouldn't listen to anybody but myself and all I was saying to myself was, I'm indestructible. Nothing can kill me! The doctors don't know what they're talking about! They're just trying to frighten me and it won't work! After coming out of hospital, I was soon back on the booze. It really makes me mad and angry to see how stupid I was. I was even trying to fool myself! I knew that I couldn't stop drinking by myself, but I wouldn't admit that I needed help from someone! I just couldn't admit I was powerless when it came to alcohol! I can now.

I now have the courage to leave Broadreach, to make sure that all the knowledge I have learnt here works for me, and to grab that sobriety and never let it go.

*

Within a week I was drinking again; I never attended AA meetings, and very soon I went back to my usual existence.

The day that I left Broadreach, I think me Mum and Dad came and picked me up. I remember going home feeling super-confident; I didn't feel nervous leaving there at all. I was looking forward to getting out and being free. What I didn't realise was what the pressures were going to be, because alcohol was everywhere.

I'd spent six weeks in a prison-type environment; learning about myself from the basics, and how to behave like a responsible human being as opposed to someone that's addicted to a substance. It became like school, but I was just looking forward to the day that I'd be free again (irrespective of the fact that I could've left whenever I wanted, but then I would've felt that I'd let everyone down and not gone through the whole procedure). So I couldn't really wait to come out. I suppose most of the time I thought, this will teach me how to behave in the real world, as opposed to a confined space, although obviously the test would be when it's all available for you and then you choose not to pick up the first bottle of vodka.

I wouldn't admit it if anyone would've asked me, but having done two thirds of the course, I secretly thought to myself, it's alright, I will be able to drink, but I will just have to keep it down to an absolute minimum. So, at any one time, not have more than two drinks; and when I say two drinks, I mean two single, pub-measure drinks. So if I was going out for an evening, that would have to last me all night. If I was going out at lunchtime, *that* would have to last me all that session as well. And try not to drink at home at all. The fact that I was thinking I could go back to a controlled way of drinking was a mistake in itself to start with.

Mum and Dad dropped me off at home and made sure that I had food in the house for me and Jaeger. They had taken care of her at my house while I'd been away.

'Are you alright now love?' Mum said as they left.

'Yes thanks,' I said, and meant it.

As soon as Mum and Dad had gone, I said to myself, I'll just nip down the off-licence and get a bottle of champagne, some orange juice and a packet of fags. I felt like I'd passed all my exams and I should celebrate; and how do you celebrate, but with a bottle of champagne. I felt having done the course, I was in complete control and the celebration would just be a one-off. But it tasted good and made me feel good. I thought I deserved it after what I'd been through, and had no feelings of guilt. Looking back at it now, it was obviously insane. I realised that everything I was criticising everyone else for – I was doing the same thing.

While I was at Broadreach I hadn't stopped smoking: I continued with that addiction. Their opinion was that it is hard enough trying to quit one addiction without trying to quit two at the same time, and by giving yourself too much pressure, it's easy to say, 'Oh sod it! I can't cope not having a drink *and* a smoke! Which one should I have?' and I would suggest in my case I would've reached for the drink immediately.

The shop was only eight hundred yards down the road, but I went in my car because I'm a lazy bugger. Well, after drinking that bottle of champagne I watched some videos and listened to some music as I'd been deprived of all this for the last six weeks; I was back in my own environment. I remember thinking so clearly that I was completely justified in celebrating the fact that I'd stopped drinking because I was only going to celebrate it once in my mind.

The following day I went round to see me Mum and Dad and I thought to myself, I'll get a bottle of wine in the fridge so that it's in there if I want one. But I'll try and make it last as long as I can.

It didn't last long at all, because once I'd got the taste again, it just lit up that addiction. I certainly had not got rid of it in the drying-out clinic. I might've physically got rid of it, but mentally I hadn't.

Literally within a week I was back to 'normal'. Mum, who was always sympathetic, would say to me, 'Look Jack, you were supposed to have gotten over all of this now. You were supposed to have stopped drinking for good.'

And all my excuse would be is: 'But it's only one, Mum! It's alright. I'm not getting drunk, so it's okay.'

When I'd left Broadreach I'd got my little medal and they said, 'We have an aftercare facility and we also suggest to everyone that they should continue their aftercare with their local meetings of AA as well. And do come back to visit us to let us know how you are doing.'

I didn't ever go to AA as I didn't feel I had a problem any more. I did think I might try to get into Buddhism. We'd talked a lot about it between ourselves at Broadreach; maybe the yoga and meditation had sparked it off. I bought a book and thought if I could get my legs into one of the positions I would build a zazen bench as it had the measurements in the book, but I could never get my legs to bend that way so I thought this Buddhism lark isn't for me and gave it up as a bad job.

After about two or three months, I bought some very powerful pellet guns that went with my 'country squire, Barbour jackets, gun dog' scenario. I remember inviting two of the guys who were in the clinic with me over to see me at the bungalow. I was obviously back to being pissed and so I couldn't work out whether they were using or not. I don't know whether they realised about me, but we had a bit of fun with my guns in the back garden one afternoon. I never ever saw them again and never found out whether they stayed clean.

I was back in my own world of waiting for the phone to ring with a top film director or producer saying, 'I want you in my next movie!' I honestly believed that that was going to happen. There would be phases where my body would say, 'I can't take any more!' It would get to the point where I'd be so ill from the amount of alcohol I was drinking, the only thing I could keep down was liquid. Because of my diabetes, I'd have to have glucose or something like Lucozade to try and combat my alcohol intake. I'd drink as much milk as I could as well, to give my stomach a lining which hopefully would then make me able to eat food, and actually keep it down, so that I could then drink more alcohol.

I don't remember anything about the rest of that year at all. It must've been a drunken mess, waiting in hope of a job. I didn't think anything about paying my mortgage or the running costs of the house or anything like that. As long as I had my credit cards, so I could go and buy my booze, my car, and my car insurance, everything was alright. The only thing that wasn't alright was that I wasn't working; but the drinking thing, that was alright in my mind. It wasn't a problem at all.

Even though I wasn't fit enough, I just wanted to work: not so much for the money, but just that that'd always been my life from the age of twelve. It was working and doing something that I enjoyed – entertaining! It had a lot to do with the high that you get when you get a reaction from your work. I don't think there's any substance on the planet that gives you a high that equals it at all, although a lot of people try and experiment with different things to try and get the equivalent, but it's impossible. It's very addictive; and with me having an addictive nature, it weren't easy.

Chapter 23

THE CHRISTMAS OF 1986 WOULD'VE BEEN VERY BORING. I was thirty-four, divorced, and it would've been just a typical drunken Christmas of planning how many films I was going to record on telly. It could've been around this time that store cards first came out for places like Dixons. I'd always been into my gadgets so I bought Nikon cameras with it, not thinking about how I was going to pay for it. I also bought a camcorder and I was so happy with it, but I was too pissed to read the manual to learn how to use it, so it stayed in the box for the next two years.

I also messed about with games computers that you plugged into your telly. I was always interested in anything that gave me enjoyment at home because I was spending so much time at home with not working.

And there was so much, too much, time to think. All the people who had been around when life was easy seemed now to have inexplicably disappeared. I was alone and lonely and drunk.

The phone rang.

'Hello, my name is Lisa Ward and I would like to come and interview you about the upcoming release of *Pufnstuf* on video?'

I thought, well at least it would be nice to have someone to talk to, so I said, 'Okay, yeah, fine; you come round to my place and we can do the interview here.'

It was February sometime and I think she got my number from Carole Collins, June's daughter, who was now my agent. I wasn't in touch with many people at this time; the only regular company, if you could call it that, I'd have would be occasionally seeing Arthur's wife Julie, and Mum and Dad. I'd see Bob occasionally, but not that often then. I'd speak to him a lot on the phone, but he wouldn't pop around much. Nobody really would be calling round and I'd very rarely go out in the car because I was always getting so drunk and I knew it was insane to tempt fate. I loved my car so much and always have done; I don't know what I'd have done if ever I'd have got banned. I must have been doing a lot of chatting on the phone, though, because my phone bill was always high.

When Lisa came around, I hadn't thought she'd be as young as what she was and, with me being lonely, it just went from there: 'I'd like to see you again.'

She was twenty, and I don't think she knew straight away that I was an alcoholic, but she would've certainly known that I drank too much. I don't think I was in a fit state to know what was going on in her head at the time, but looking back on it I think because she hadn't had a father, perhaps I stepped in to that father-figure role first of all.

I started seeing her; and then in June of '87 I received a phone call from Columbia saying, 'We want you to do a charity show in Beverly Hills at the Beverly Wilshire Hotel with Ron Moody and Shani Wallis. It will be one show for an invited audience which will commemorate the twenty years since the making of the film of *Oliver!*'

'Yes, I'd love to do it!'

I hadn't been to the States since I took Gay there in '73, so of course I wanted to do it. I think Lisa was jealous when I told her I was going there. She hadn't been anywhere like that, exotic like, so I said, 'It's only two and a half, three weeks and I'll be back, and I'll call you when I get home.'

I was well pleased to be going to Heathrow and flying first class in a jumbo jet. I hadn't done that in fifteen years since the trip to Japan. I'd forgotten how good it was. Ron was on the flight with me, but sat on the other side. I sat on my side drinking champagne for eleven hours or so: champagne and vodka which was lovely. I was eating for England as well because I loved my steak and seafood.

When we got Stateside there was a stretch limousine waiting to take us straight to the Beverly Wilshire which was my favourite hotel; I'd stayed there the first time for the *Pufnstuf* contract negotiations and the Oscar ceremony.

At the reception desk there was an envelope for me with my itinerary of what was going to be happening for the next two and a half weeks. We had about ten or twelve days' rehearsals and we did snippets from the film. I remember thinking, because it was an invited audience and there'd be lots of important people there, I mustn't have a lot to drink while I'm rehearsing it and also I mustn't drink a lot for the actual show either.

We did it in one of the big ballrooms that they had in the hotel and it was just like old times rehearsing with Ron and Shani again. I hadn't seen Shani since the premieres, eighteen years ago. It was really lovely seeing her and she hadn't changed. She still looked great. She was fabulous.

I phoned Marty when I got there to let him know that I was in town and that I was doing this show.

'Great,' he said. 'I'll arrange some tickets and we'll come and see you. And then you can come over to the house and see the kids.'

I rented a car and then I phoned Billie and Kay up and said, 'I'm in town and would love to see you both.'

I met them at Farmers Market; they are diamonds.

On the night of the performance I think I had a couple of beers in my suite before meeting Marty. In fact I could've had anything that was there, so I wouldn't like to say I only had beer – I probably had vodka and all sorts – but I thought, I'll meet Marty in the bar an hour before the show and I'll just have one drink in that bar.

From what I remember, I stuck to that. I just had the one drink and made that last, irrespective of the fact that I was probably well on the way from whatever I'd had during the day.

I wouldn't say I was drunk during the show and I hope the performance wasn't compromised by the drinking to any large degree, although if I'd have been driving during the show, I'd have been well over the limit! The only thing I remember was a loss of concentration right at the end. Me and Ron were doing a song, and at the end of the number I was supposed to go offstage. There had been a rumour going around that Michael Jackson was going to be coming to see it. And in my subconscious this sort of stuck in my mind and I found myself thinking, I wonder what he looks like? I must see if I can spot him.

At the end of the song I remember looking in the audience while the applause was going on to see if I can see him, and I must've outstayed my welcome because Ron turned to me and said, 'It's alright Dodger, you can go now!'

I then got back into the present and thought, oh shit!

'Alright Fagin,' I said, 'I'm off!' and left the stage.

By the time the show was finished, Michael had got so many bodyguards around him that I didn't see him; he certainly didn't hang about afterwards and was soon gone.

Still, it was all such an ego boost for me. It'd been so long since I'd been treated like that and had that response from a live audience. It made me want to have it even more. I didn't think I had a drink problem at all. I thought it was all under control, so really if anything the trip did more harm than good because it just prolonged my thoughts of, well, I'm fit enough and I'm here in Hollywood, I've just done a live show. There can't be that much wrong with me!

I don't remember much else about that trip other than obviously enjoying the first class treatment on the flight home. Being treated like a star again in my mind reinforced the thought of, well, this phone call is going to happen. Spielberg is going to be on the phone saying, I want you in my next movie! Or Marty's going to call because of all these people going bananas when I came on stage!

When I got back Lisa said that she wasn't happy living at home and she felt claustrophobic living with her family, so I said, 'Well, why don't you move in? I've got plenty of room here.'

She jumped at the chance and moved in in the September, but she moved out again by the beginning of November because we'd argued. I'm sure it would've been drink-related and I would've said, 'Well, I'm sorry you know, if you don't like it, you might as well go then.' In my mind I'm thinking, I've just been to Hollywood. I've just had a tremendous standing ovation, I don't need you! Go and sod off! And she did.

A few days later, or it could have been weeks, a researcher from the Terry Wogan show rang and said, 'We want to get you and Mark together on the show because *Oliver!* is going to be on this Christmas and we'd like to see what you are both up to today.'

Just the usual bollocks and so I said, 'Yeah, yeah, that's no problem. I'll do that!'

So as I'm living on my own again in the bungalow, I thought, yeah, that'll be nice. I'm getting work now on British TV and everything's coming up roses.

I thought, I must make sure that I keep my drinking to an absolute minimum for the TV show. And I think I was mad enough – no, I think I was just about sensible enough – at the time to try and work out in advance, say three or four weeks beforehand, what I was going to wear on TV. So I got all that planned and made sure it was all clean and ready.

At the time me Mum and Dad were in a bungalow just around the corner and they'd only been in there about eighteen months. During these last few years my Mum's health weren't that brilliant, which I'd say was a mixture of worrying about me and Arthur and her asthma which was made worse by running up and down the stairs in Hanworth Road. They decided they would get a bungalow, and sold the house to their next-door neighbour. He was a lovely Indian guy who'd always said to me Dad, 'Give me first refusal if ever you move,' as he wanted to expand his house to keep pace with his family.

Just after I'd come back from the charity show in Beverly Hills, me Mum was taken into hospital into the Intensive Care Unit having had an asthma attack. Of course, I would go in and see her with me Dad and Arthur; and she was in there for about a week to ten days, something like that. It was awful to see because she just had tubes everywhere, and in Intensive Care Units nobody looks like they're ever going to come out of there alive! But she overcame all that and came home.

Then the week before the *Wogan* show, I was at home on my own, pissed, when I had a phone call and it must've been about 1.30 in the morning and it was Arthur on the phone. He'd got divorced and moved back with me Mum and Dad when they moved to the bungalow. I thought, what the fuck's he phoning me for at this time in the morning?

Arf said, 'You'd better get round here!'

'Why?'

'It's Mum, she's died and I need help with Dad!'

It didn't sink in just what had happened. It's amazing how your adrenalin can sober you up temporarily, and literally within minutes I'd got dressed and sobered up enough to get in the car and drive round the corner. When I got into the house, they were in the bedroom with Mum.

'What happened Arf?' I said in a voice that didn't quite sound like my own.

'Well, Dad came and woke me up and said Mum's dying!'

Arf had got up and tried to see what the score was but I think by then she'd already died. It was her asthma. So Arthur was trying to comfort my Dad and saying, 'We've gotta get this organised. We've got to call an ambulance.'

By the time I got there, he had done all that and I was just trying to console Dad and we were all trying to console each other basically. They were taking her jewellery off and Dad was so obviously distraught; he was taking her rings off and having a bit of difficulty getting them off. 'I'm not going to leave these on for anyone to take,' he kept saying. That sticks in my mind like yesterday.

The ambulance came and they said, 'We're very sorry, but she's died. There's nothing we can do for her. We'll take her to the hospital and you can come with us, or you can call the hospital in the morning and they'll tell you what you need to do.'

It was decided that we weren't going to go to the hospital and they took her away.

After they'd gone, I suddenly became aware of the period of time that had gone, maybe half an hour or an hour, and not for any of that time did I think about booze at all. The news seemed to shock my body out of its usual reaction because, with anything else, I would've been saying, 'Get me a drink!'

Having said that, within half an hour of the ambulance going I said to Arf and Dad, 'There's not much point in us all sitting up all night. We might as well go to bed 'cos things will have to be organised tomorrow. And it's a week before Christmas as well!'

As soon as I went home, I then drank a lot very quickly.

Before this night, I don't think I could've cared about myself to any large degree because of what I was doing to myself; and now Mum had gone, I just slipped further down the ladder, closer to hell. If ever I'd stopped and questioned myself before about, 'Why don't you stop all this drinking? It's not doing you any good,' it simply didn't seem to matter now. I felt I just wanted to be with Mum. I thought, I'm not really bothered any more. I don't care about me! If I felt this once, I must've felt this God knows how many times over the next period of time.

I poured a drink and several more and waited for it all to disappear.

Through the haze, in my mind, I saw Billy, in Chiswick one Christmas. Billy would always think that the paper chains and tinsel were really forest vines and that they could easily hold his weight. Of course, when he'd take a leap at them, they'd snap immediately and he'd fall flat on the floor, splat! Then he'd look at you as though he was thinking, that was bloody stupid! You should've warned me about that! Both of them did try and jump on the Christmas tree. Bluebell didn't like the pine needles and gave up straight away, whereas Billy did try to nick the fairy off the top and nearly pulled the tree over in the process. He gave it up as another bad job. It was funny though, I remembered.

'*Oh Mum.*'

I woke up at some time, retching and shaking, and reached for a glass of vodka to make me feel better. As the tremors reduced I noticed another fag burn on my arm. It looked sore, but I couldn't feel it. I saw the butt lying next to a burnt hole on the sofa. I brushed it away.

I can't remember when I called Lisa, but it was either as soon as I got home and had a drink, or it was that following morning. I started apologising for the way I'd been behaving and said that me Mum's died. She said how upset she was for me. I remember her sending flowers to the funeral, but she didn't come. I didn't ask her to come back.

Mum knew that I'd been booked to do the Wogan show, and when it was and all that; and initially I said, 'I don't want to do it now!'

Arthur and me Dad said, 'Well no, because Mum would've wanted you to do it so you've gotta do it for Mum. Don't do it for yourself, do it for Mum!'

'Right, okay, fine, I'll do it!' I said.

The show was on the Wednesday the 23rd and I thought, who would I want to come with me to do this? Within forty-eight hours of Mum dying I spoke to Gay, and it's the only time I ever did it, but I asked her if she'd come with me. She said yes.

When I got up that morning I said to myself, I mustn't have more than one drink during the day before I go to the show. I also thought that, when I get in the green room at the studio, I will only have one drink there.

It was going to be a difficult day as me, Dad and Arf had organised to see Mum in the chapel of rest that day. All three of us went together to see her and I was completely gutted now. Seeing her in the coffin, that was awful; and I certainly cried all the way back. In fact I started crying as soon as I saw her and I think the others had tears in their eyes, but they weren't making a noise like I was. By now, this was like four or five days after she died and I was well into my drinking.

But I tried to stick to my resolution of that morning, and I remember having one, albeit a very large drink, the equivalent of at least four in a pub, before getting the car to go and pick Gay up. I had the car pick me up and then, because the Wogan show was done at the theatre on Shepherd's Bush Green, I went via Chiswick to pick her up and then on to the theatre.

When we got to the theatre, I had one glass of white wine in the green room; but, as I had to get there a good two hours or so before the transmission, it was a very large one. The amount that I had been drinking was enough to intoxicate a small elephant, and on the programme it proved that because I was slurring my words. But I was glad that I did it because I know me Mum would've wanted me to do it and not cancel it.

The show was going out live and me and Mark were stood in the wings waiting for the cue to go on, when someone tapped me on the shoulder. I turned around thinking, who the fuck's this? because we were about to go on in a couple of seconds, and it was Rolf Harris. He was also guesting that night and, God love him, he said, 'Jack, please accept my sincere condolences. I've just heard about your mother passing away. I'm ever so sorry, mate!' I must have looked a bit shocked because he then said, 'You'll be alright, you'll be fine,' as me and Mark were walking on. I'd never met him before; I'd seen him on *Crackerjack* years and years ago when I was a stand-in for the games on the show, but not to talk to.

I tried to pull my mind back to the present as we sat down on the sofa with Terry. The usual topics were covered: my height, did we still enjoy watching the film and what our memories were. I talked about smoking the herbal tobacco and did my wallet gag. Terry then touched on *Pufnstuf* and *Melody*, and then came the difficult question of what we were up to now. Me and Mark both started bullshitting like it was going out of fashion: I talked of a pilot for an American series, and Mark said he was focusing solely on his karate. And all the time I was thinking about how soon I could get home and catch up with my drinking.

When we came off, someone said to me, 'I'm sorry… we knew your mother had passed away this week… we'd said to everybody not to mention anything. We're sorry…' Maybe they thought I would throw a wobbly for Rolf saying something just before I went on.

'Oh… I… it doesn't matter…' I stumbled. I was finding it difficult to focus. 'It was nice of him… I'm sure he just felt it was the right thing to do,' I said, recovering slightly. It *had* been a nice thing to do, I just found it difficult to hear it within thirty seconds of having to walk on stage and be the chirpy Jack Wild. As soon as it was all over I dropped Gay off at Chiswick and went back home. I think the show went alright, but I couldn't really be sure.

So that Christmas, considering these two things, me Mum dying and my alcohol problem, *was the worst year, the worst Christmas for me ever!* And that was 1987; and so, that's that.

*

From when me Mum died everything went downhill. I was drinking so much by the end of 1987 that my body couldn't keep down any solid food at all. For the next six or seven months I basically just had liquids: a mixture of Lucozade, milk and alcohol. That's what I lived on and I wouldn't eat at all. I went down in weight to something like six and a half or seven stone.

I'd constantly have an alcoholic drink within three foot of me, twenty-four hours a day. I'd drink vodka, vomit, fall unconscious, come round and drink some more vodka. To some people, after throwing up, they would then say, 'Stop! I'm not having any more until I feel better. I won't smoke, I won't eat, I won't drink!' But it didn't matter to me. No sooner had it gone up and I'd thrown it down the loo, than I'd poured meself another vodka and Coke and drunk that to make me feel better. All I was doing basically was anaesthetising myself. The time of day had no meaning to me; the TV was on twenty-four hours a day. I'd often fall asleep, and forget to take my injection. Sometimes my sugar levels would get so low, I would become unconscious and either me Dad, Arthur or Bob would turn up and save me. They'd take me to the West Mid Hospital where I was becoming almost a regular. It was just an insane lifestyle because you couldn't do anything whatsoever.

Lisa came to visit me in hospital. I was very weak and could hardly stand, but I said to her, 'If you don't bring me some vodka in, I'll sign myself out of here!' I remember Gay one time coming to visit me at the hospital with the geezer that was living with her. I got upset at seeing her and was telling her that I still loved her. She said something to the effect of, 'Don't be so stupid! You've got Lisa there, she's looking after you!'

After each hospital stay, when I'd finally get home, I'd pour several drinks to make up for lost time. I'd play Joe Cocker's 'Give Peace a Chance' and I'd have it blazing out so loud that no word or thought could penetrate my world. Any thought the alcohol couldn't dull, the music obliterated instead; oblivion was mine.

Although 1987 had been a dreadful year, in more conscious moments I also reflected it had been good in the sense of how the Americans reacted to seeing me after so many years. Their response had made me feel twenty feet tall. So, in the new year of 1988, I said to myself: what's the point of me having this bungalow when I'm obviously gonna get a phone call from Spielberg and I'll be back working in the States all the time? It's not practical for me to own something that I can't lock up and leave for any length of time, I continued, so in theory it would be better to buy a flat; so why don't I do that, I asked myself; and as I couldn't fault my reasoning, I set about organising it.

As I was going to get a flat now I obviously couldn't keep Jaeger, because she was too big. So I sold her to someone who went in Arthur's pub. I think he gave me fifty quid for her and, with that, I bought a few drinks. Around this same time I also got back with Lisa because we were supposedly getting on better, and she came back to my bungalow. It didn't take long, however, before Lisa thought, oh, he's not gonna get better, he said he was going to stop drinking and he hasn't.

A lot of the time I wouldn't be getting up out of bed. It'd go through phases where we'd have an argument and I'd just say, 'Well, go back to your fucking mother. Stop nagging me! I've got my drinking under control, bugger off then!' and if that happened once during our relationship, that must've happened a good half a dozen times at least.

When she'd gone home to her mother's, then I would live in the bed and not get up at all. The floor slowly disappeared under the accumulation of I don't know what and I didn't much care. A narrow winding path stretched between the loo and the bed, but even that at times was obscured. I'd only get up and get dressed if I had to go out and get some booze or sign on.

I was also throwing money away like it was going out of fashion; I didn't have a care in the world. In reality I didn't have a penny in the world except what was tied up in the bungalow, but I just kept spending the money I didn't have. If there was a new gadget on the market, I'd phone up, order it and have it delivered to my home. For a good six months, I literally wouldn't know what was arriving at the front door from one day to the next. I bought nearly everything that was on sale in 1988, whether it was silk-imitation plants, exotic lamps or a rather large leather seal. Rubbish basically. I also changed cars by the week. I convinced the bank to lend me money against the house and bought a Porsche, although I couldn't actually afford the petrol to put in it. Reality was escaping me.

Then I said to Lisa, 'You've got a really naff car; if I put the Porsche in for part-exchange, we can both get a good car each.' So I put that in part-exchange for a 2-litre Ford Capri automatic for her and had my first Rover 2600 SDI. Then when I told her to bugger off, of course, she left in the two-and-a-half-grand car, and I thought, for my pride, I can't ask for it back!

That Porsche was the best car I ever had and yet I don't really remember driving it.

Still, I didn't need her because I was popular in the States; and I didn't need money in the bank, because I had equity in the bungalow. So, to progress my Stateside plan, I got a valuation on the bungalow and they said I could sell it for somewhere around a hundred and twenty to a hundred and thirty thousand. I'd bought the bungalow for seventy-five grand with a ten grand mortgage, so in my drunken state I thought, great! I'll buy meself a flat with that and I'll be able to buy that outright!

What I hadn't taken into consideration was the running costs of my lifestyle at that time, buying all this stuff with no means of paying for it, and it was just building up and up. So, when I did sell the bungalow for a hundred and twenty thousand, and I was waiting for it all to go through, I hadn't done my sums correctly and I paid dearly for it. It is the ultimate irony of being given so much when you have everything and given nothing when you have nothing. I had no experiences to draw upon on how to make things right as I couldn't remember not being famous and moneyed. All the people who had helped me when life was easy weren't around. I made some bad decisions – I made some terrible decisions – and was too drunk to learn from the consequences.

During this time, two of Arthur's friends from the pub, I forget their names, needed somewhere to stay and I let them move into the bungalow with me for about six or eight weeks. The same day they arrived, so did a silver space pen that could write upside down (certainly a wise investment), and Lisa with another row about drinking. She had contacted Carole Collins saying, 'Look, he's drinking too much and I don't know what to do.'

Carole had said, 'Well, a friend of ours has helped alcoholics; he used to be an alcoholic himself. Why don't we arrange to get him involved and see if he can help Jack?'

The guy's name was Nick Charles, and at first when Lisa suggested arranging for him to come and see me at my bungalow I said, 'No! I'm not interested, it's all under control!'

This argument went on for several weeks until I was so fed up with it, in the end I gave in and said, 'Alright, bring him down!'

You can tell how low I was feeling because I didn't even bother getting out of bed when he turned up. Obviously I was pissed when we spoke, but he told me what he could do for me.

'Well, I'm not ready for it,' I said, and that was that; I dismissed it totally. I thought he'd left and that the matter was closed.

I sold the bungalow in the June of 1988 and bought a flat in Sheen Court, Richmond. It was a two-bedroomed, first floor flat with a balcony, which I bought for £87,500. I moved into Sheen in the September with the help of Arthur. My solicitor from Pattmans took care of everything with regards to the two properties, and I'd also given her the list of all my debts.

I hired a skip to put all the crap in that I didn't want to take to the flat. It'd been arranged that I'd hand over the keys to the property at midday, but I was so pissed I was maybe four or five hours behind of what I should've been; I hadn't filled up the van and I was still eating my lunch in the middle of the lounge when they turned up at twelve. Quite rightfully they were well pissed off.

I just said, 'I'm sorry, but we got a late start and we'll be out as quick as we can.' I gave them a set of keys and said, 'I'll give you the other set as soon as I've got my last things out of the house.' They left and I finished my lunch.

I moved to Sheen Court, eventually, and things carried on as before. I was drinking so much, I couldn't really drink any more than I was at this stage. Nick Charles's name kept coming up all the time, but I just wasn't interested. I had more important things on my mind.

When I'd moved to Richmond I'd bought a foot-long *Hypostomus plecostomus*, a large catfish that had a big sucker on the front. I needed to clean the fish tank out and wanted to do it properly. I had decided to take the catfish back to the shop in Sheen where I bought it from so that they would look after it while I cleaned the tank out. I planned to catch it and take it back in a bucket. But Christ, it took me about an hour and a half to catch it. It was only in this three-foot tank, but it was that slippery to get hold of; it was insane. I'd also had problems with a freshwater crayfish that I'd given far, far too much food to, and I'd made a complete cock-up with some petrified wood; and everything takes so much longer when you are drunk.

With all this going on I didn't really have time to deal with this Nick Charles and his rehab programme. Life, of a sort, carried on, but his name still kept coming into the conversation. One day I caught sight of a corner of something jutting out from a pile of rubbish. For some reason I pulled it out and turned it round to read:

> Alcoholics Victorious believes that alcoholism is an addiction. The alcoholic is an individual who cannot, as a matter of willpower alone, control his drinking. Because of this loss of control, the alcoholic is almost always the last to realise drinking has become a serious problem in his life. In fact, he develops a complex system of rationalisations, justifications, and deceptions in defending his use of alcohol, and slowly, over a period of time, a denial system emerges that makes it almost impossible for him to recognise the reality of his condition. Drinking is no longer a matter of choice, but a matter of need. The individual is slipping into a physical and psychological dependence or addiction.

I pushed it back under the pile of rubbish. I wasn't an alcoholic, why couldn't anyone get that? I needed to go out to buy some more fish food and booze so I picked up my keys and left.

I didn't know at the time, but Nick Charles had arranged with a guy at his church in Heston for the parishioners of St Leonard's to pray for me from that September in 1988. And despite my lack of interest, Nick Charles also started coming round and telling me what he could do for me. He said if I stopped drinking he could get my career back on track. He suggested, then Lisa nagged me, to have a chat with somebody from AA. Eventually I gave up and to shut them up said, 'Alright, I'll go and see him!'

We met at my flat, drove to Richmond Deer Park and walked half way around the park chatting. I must've walked about five or six miles that day. We talked about drink and how it had affected him and that he'd been sober for three or four years. He was only a young guy and he asked me if I'd ever been to an AA meeting.

I told him of one meeting I went to where this woman had started drinking heavily after her husband died and she'd been left on her own. She'd said that they'd never had children, but they had a parrot and she used to give the parrot as much as she drank herself. When she got sober she said she now feels so bad about it because she felt she was, in a way, killing her baby. As I was telling him, it reminded me of *Flight of the Doves* and the guy getting this pigeon pissed in Galway. That must have been a hundred years ago.

'She said that the parrot became addicted,' I continued, 'and if it didn't have a slug of vodka in its water, it'd behave not very nicely – and apparently this parrot did talk as well. I should've asked her if it actually talked as though it was drunk. "My name's Polly and I'm an alcoholic!"' I said.

I don't think he thought it was funny.

I didn't mean to offend anyone; it was just the AA thing didn't seem to work for me, although it obviously had done for her and for him too. We walked a little further, but it seemed like a waste of time. I just had so little in common with this guy, apart from the drink problem, although that actually was a great deal because that was my whole life at the time.

I think basically when I first went to the AA programme at Broadreach, the one thing I couldn't understand, or accept for that matter, is: how can someone's 'higher power' be just *anything*? Any object, anything mechanical, or anything unproven? I could understand the unproven thing because you have that with all the different religions; the belief is the thing. But I couldn't understand how a lot of people say, 'Well, I'm sorry, but that light bulb over there is my higher power!'

Or 'That candle that I've got in the bathroom is my higher power!'

Or 'The number 47 bus is my higher power!'

I thought, that's for nutters that is! Give me something that I can relate to, that I can believe in! That'll be my higher power! Perhaps I had to go to something Christian, because that's how I'd been brought up. I'm not saying to go to church every week necessarily, but to try and lead a Christian life. Perhaps this half-formed thought prepared the ground for Nick's next visit.

In Christmas '88 Nick came and saw me again in the flat in Sheen. He'd brought a Good News Bible with him and said, 'Why don't you have this and give it a read?'

I must've been that desperate to get over this problem that I had with my drink as he convinced me to buy it off him; I felt I had tried everything else.

He said, 'What I do is buy these books to read with it. They're called *Every Day With Jesus* and *Daily Bread*; they come out four times a year so they cover each day of a three-month period. I find that this helps me a great deal to read it.' Each page has a daily thought and a couple of verses from the Bible to have a read and see what you can make of it. It asks you to see if it has any relevance to you and your life so far, or what you think it means to you as an individual.

Nick also talked again about Alcoholics Victorious and said, 'Their meetings aren't big meetings like AA where it can be anything from a dozen people to five or six hundred; it's very much a smaller, personal type of therapy. I find it helps me, although it isn't my main thing within my sobriety. If ever you want to go to this AV meeting, come with me and I'll take you.'

As he was leaving he said, 'I always read my Bible once a day, if only for my little section from *Every Day With Jesus*. Just read that and take that in and think about it, because that's all I do.' And he said 'I try!' which was what I liked. He didn't say 'I succeed!' or 'I am!'; he just said, 'I try my best to lead a Christian life.' I thought, at this stage, I've tried everything to stop and I'm not capable of stopping drinking on my own. I have tried and it ain't worked. Before he left he wrote a message in the Bible saying: *Dear Jack, I hope this is the best buy you ever made! Nick Charles, 30ᵗʰ December 1988.*

I don't know if I wanted to stop drinking, but I think I was feeling ill enough to say that, 'This can't go on indefinitely because I'm obviously killing myself and I'm a bit fed up with it now.' And this guy, if nothing else, he gave me hope. He made me think he could help me get back to working, being sober and enjoying my life; so I thought, well, I'll try that then.

I think, strangely enough, I was actually more after the work than I was the sobriety. Getting my career back on track was the carrot for me because, at this stage in my life, I had so little self-worth. I really didn't give a fuck about myself and about the way I was feeling on a day-to-day basis at all. But I so, so missed performing and pleasing audiences. I don't think for a minute I missed the fame aspect of it at all because I could really take that or leave it, having had it. I think what was more important to me was the audience's reaction to my work.

Obviously, somewhere in my subconscious I must have wanted the sobriety and thought that the only worse it can get from this is dying, but I can't remember thinking that that clearly. It was always very much fifty per cent of me wanted to stop drinking but fifty per cent of me wanted to continue, and it was like one half of my brain was having a battle with the other half, saying 'I'm right!' and the other saying 'No you're not, I am!'

It was like a see-saw: one day it'd be, 'I must stop drinking!' and the next day, 'No, you're not that bad, have another vodka!'

That's what it was like and very rarely would I have two lots of twenty-four hours where I'd feel the same. Psychologically I wasn't in a fit state to say, 'I know what I wanna do. I'm going to stop drinking because I'm killing meself. Bollocks to you lot who want the vodka!'

But there was never that clarity.

After getting this Bible I thought, well, what I'll do is read it with my breakfast every day before I get a newspaper and hopefully that'll set me up for the day then! I bought the other books that went with it like Nick said to help me with the readings and I found that a bit comforting.

I also tried to cut down on my drinking and I tried to limit myself to a quarter of a bottle of vodka a day. That was still nearly two bottles of vodka a week. I really did try very hard to do that, but I got to the point where I wasn't getting drunk enough to forget whatever it was that I wanted to forget, which was mainly the fact that I wasn't working. I couldn't really see far enough ahead.

Nick said, 'If you wanna have a drink, pick up the Bible and look for a passage that you can relate to and then as soon as you find a passage you can relate to, you can put the book down. The chances are by then you'll have stopped thinking about wanting to have a drink. That thought will have gone because you will have felt that you have just gotten something out of the last ten or fifteen minutes; you've been looking for something and you've found it.'

Another thing that Nick said to me was, 'Look, if you fancy a drink, get on the phone to me, call me. That's when I want to speak to you, that's when I can help you. And take that thought out of your mind so you can think about something else.'

At the start of 1989 I would then speak to him on a daily basis. He encouraged me to call him every day and he'd say, 'It doesn't matter if you are feeling bad, it doesn't matter what time of day or night it is, call me because I'm here. If it's five o'clock in the morning or two o'clock in the morning, phone me and I'll talk you through it.'

At the time, in lots of ways, he seemed like 'the human saviour' for me because he'd done it himself; if anyone could help me, I suppose I felt he could.

Having nagged me to meet him, however, Lisa now didn't seem to like Nick and we argued about him constantly. She was well into spiritualists, and before this I had been and tried all that with her, especially after me Mum had died, and I must admit I did get comfort from what the people were telling me. Looking back on it, it was blatantly obvious to me that they were telling me what I wanted to hear, and that's why I was pleased, and that's why I was comforted by it.

So my views had changed; I now thought that spiritualists weren't a positive thing at all. Lisa railed against Nick and his ideas, but I wouldn't let that affect my belief in Nick and the Bible. I said, 'Well, look, you know, if I'm gonna get better, which is what I'm gonna have to do, I'll try this. But *I* don't believe it one hundred per cent; I'd like to believe it one hundred per cent, but I actually don't at this stage, so the worst that can happen is that I can prove that the big book is full of bollocks, there's nothing in it, it's just crap! That's the worst aspect of it and I will continue drinking because it isn't the way, so I haven't got anything to lose. I'll either get *that*, and I will have proved something else that I was thinking was right; or I will be proved wrong, but I will be fit and I won't have a drink problem, so how can I lose?' She looked blankly at me and this blinding piece of logic.

I'd read somewhere that if you flick through the Bible and stop at any page and then read that page, you'd always find something that you could relate to. And during these first three months I'd get the Bible to see if it worked. I did that at least four or five times a week, and every time I found something relevant for me. Well, that made me think there's got to be something in this because it goes against the odds to find something every time.

I'd now started on a daily basis to consciously say to myself, I've got to cut down, it'd be much better if I could do without this. Nick said, 'You've got to take control of your life because, at the moment, the booze is controlling your life and nothing else. If you don't get rid of that demon, you'll only go to one place and that is down and there's not much further for you to go!'

In lots of ways he repeated what I'd been told by doctors and that is that dying through alcohol abuse is a bloody painful way to die! It's not a case of one minute you're okay and the next minute you're dead. It's a very slow and painful death. I knew the pain of having pancreatitis in Poland, and apparently a lot of people can get water on the brain through alcohol abuse. They become like a vegetable; and, when they get to that stage, they wish they could have the strength to kill themselves because there is nothing, and you are just wasting away. You have to be looked after by everybody because you can't go to the loo, you can't dress yourself, you can't do anything.

Even when I came back from Poland and was told by the doctors, 'Almost every system in the body can be negatively affected by alcohol: see a psychiatrist!', I thought, they don't know what they're talking about! I know what I'm talking about. I know how I'm feeling. I've got it under control!

So although I'd heard it all before, when Nick told me what he'd gone through himself as an alcoholic, it seemed to be, it sounds mad, but it seemed to be closer to home. He used to do a cabaret act with his wife Lesley Roach who went to Barbara Speake's. So he knew all about the business, he'd been through all the drink problem and come out the other side.

At Broadreach none of them were in the business apart from Beechy Colclough who'd been in a band, but he wasn't my counsellor there. I could relate to where he was coming from when he would sit and talk in group therapy sessions about his experiences, and so there was a kind of an understanding. I would think, yeah, I know where you're coming from because I've been there, I've felt like that, I've done that! With my counsellor I could only respect her knowledge in alcoholism, but that other connection wasn't there.

In that way, Nick Charles was very much the right person at the right time for me. I suppose, whether consciously or subconsciously, I was searching for an easy way of getting over this problem. He'd been through it himself and knew all the ins and outs of it and how an alcoholic's mind worked. He also knew it from a performer's point of view, and performance was the light for me.

I was sick to death of being sick and close to death. I felt very weak, and I knew this could not go on indefinitely without disastrous results. My desire to work helped me to survive. I always have believed that everybody is on this Earth for a reason and for each individual, for them to have a happy life, it's important for them to find out what that is. Then, as long as it's not illegal, pursue it, and make your own destiny. It's just that, with a belief, everything becomes easier. I believed my reason was to entertain people and I thought Nick Charles could help me get back on track; that was the spark.

I don't remember when Nick first started talking about the fee for his services. When we first met I understood that he was a friend of Carole's, that he knew about people with drink problems, and that he could help sort them out for me. I was told he just wanted to talk. I suppose it was naïve to think he would want to spend all this time with me for nothing.

After a few months, he'd started to talk about how he could help me with my career, my debts and my sobriety. When I showed signs of starting to think the way he was explaining to me, and after I'd bought the Good News Bible from him, he said what he could do for me and that he would charge a fee for this.

I must admit, I was a bit surprised; but by then I think I'd been hooked on what he'd promised because, up until this stage, nobody would've even taken time to talk to me to any large degree; I'm not surprised because I was really pissed. Nick said his plan was to remortgage my flat, to help restructure my debts and to free up money to pay him. John Daly offered me a loan from Hemdale, but Nick didn't think this was a good idea.

'It'll obviously have to be done through solicitors so that it's all legal, but I will want £10,000 to get you back on the road to stardom again,' Nick said.

Anyone who works with alcoholics knows how helpless an alcoholic is when he's a practising one and how they will do or give anything to get an easy way out of their problem. Even so, I'm sure I would've said first of all, 'Well, I can't pay you 'cos I haven't got any money!'

'We can work all that out with me going through all your finances and sorting it out with your solicitor. It can all be organised!'

I must've said, 'Well, if you can do that, then yeah, I'm in agree-ance with that.'

I would've paid whatever price he'd have said, I was that desperate.

I gave him all my contacts and he did write lots of letters to people: he wrote to David Puttnam, he wrote to Marty Krofft, he wrote to John Daly, telling them that I was under his control. He told them that he was responsible for all my future work, that he was going to get me sober and that I was going through his programme.

So I carried on with his programme. I was still drinking: probably about a quarter of what I normally was, but still too much. I weren't drinking first thing in the morning, and I'd go through much of the day without a drink, but have maybe a quarter of a bottle of vodka at night. It was a tough time; I was always battling with it. Especially if I was out and about, every time I would pass an off-licence or somewhere that sold booze I'd be saying to myself, I could go in there and have one, no one would know. No! I mustn't do that. Stop thinking about that!

I still felt that I needed quite a lot of alcohol to get through the day and, having cut down, I now didn't think I had enough to cover me through the whole day. So in the car I would have miniatures of vodka, thinking that no one would be able to smell it. I kept two miniatures in each glasses case, but I'd have at least eight glasses cases in the car. One day I'd got up and was driving over to Nick and I can't remember what was going on in my head but I'd decided that I needed a drink. So I pulled over into a side road, pulled out one of the miniatures and drank it. I then lit up a fag, squirted some mouth spray into me mouth, turned the car around and went off. At this time, my car exhaust was blowing. I just didn't have the money to fix it, but I knew I would have, with my next giro. Within two or three minutes of my pit stop I was waiting to turn left at these traffic lights when I looked in my mirror and there was a copper on a motorbike directly behind me.

Oh fuck it! I thought. The exhaust!

The exhaust was coughing and spluttering, so I lit another cigarette in case he was going to pull me over and I found my mouth spray, giving it a blast of that as well to combat the double vodka. I tried to turn left, but he put his lights on as soon as he heard my exhaust and followed me around the corner.

'That's it! He's pulling me over!'

Just the one miniature would have put me on the limit, even if I hadn't had anything previously, so obviously I would have been well over the top now. I thought, be calm, get out and speak to him!

'Do you know why I've pulled you over, sir?' he said.

I tried to talk slowly and clearly, so as not to slur my words.

'Well yeah, I think so: my exhaust is blowing a bit. I'm gonna get it done later on today or tomorrow.'

'Well, I'm sorry, but I can't let you get away with it. It's far too loud, so I'm going to have to book you.'

I tried not to exhale because I thought, if he smells the booze I'm done for!

As he was writing the ticket out, he looked up and said, 'Oh, you're a naughty boy, aren't you?'

I thought, he's smelt my breath, and said as casually as I could, 'Oh, right. What else have I done then?' I must've looked as guilty as hell.

'Look at your tax disc!' he said, having clocked my road tax which was out of date. Thank fuck for that, I thought.

'Oh that! Yeah, I'm getting it done at the end of the week; but if you're doing me for that, it's a fair cop, that's alright!' I said, rather too pleased for the circumstances. I got the two tickets in the one day then – a fine for the exhaust and an endorsement for the tax – but I could've easily got done for drunken driving as well.

I was well pissed off when I drove over to Nick Charles to see him. I think this was probably the first time that I ever had a drink within an hour of actually being in his company. He'd often tell me that he'd got other people going through his programme and that he could tell when they'd been drinking because he'd been through it himself and knew all the lies; and I thought, yeah, but you ain't caught me!

The day, however, was to get even worse. Nick had said to me several times: 'You look like you're still living in the seventies, it's no good. You've got to be up to date.' But today he went one step further: 'We should change your image; I think you should have your hair permed!'

I nearly turned white.

My initial thoughts were Leo Sayer or Michael Jackson and I thought, I can't be having with this! I'm gonna look like a bloody gonk! I'm not gonna look nice whatsoever!

He talked of relaunching my career and fresh starts. 'Let me do it for you; we'll have new photographs done and I'll get you an agent!'

How could I refuse?

Lisa went ballistic! She thought I'd gone over the last ladder of being sane. She thought I'd cracked, but at the time I was ready to try anything to get back to work.

Nick and his colleague Teresa said they knew enough about hairdressing and that one of them was going to do it, and one of them was going to take the photographs. They got on with their creation and I had to sit there with all this aluminium foil on my head like a turkey at Christmas.

'When I take it out, if you don't mind, close your eyes until I've done it all,' Nick said. I closed me eyes and when he said, 'You can open them now; have a look and tell me what you think,' I looked into the big mirror in front of me and my mouth dropped to the floor.

'Bloody hell!' I said. 'That'll never bloody work!'

We took the photographs in Inwood Park near their house in Hounslow, but I can't tell you how pissed off I was. I was disgusted totally! I thought, what's me Dad gonna say with this? What's Arthur gonna say?

At the time, I was enjoying wearing hats; but, because my hair was all bouncy and sticking up now, my hats would sit on my hair, not on my head, and bounce along. It was like on a cushion of air and looked totally stupid!

One of the lucky recipients of this startling new look was a guy in America called David E. Willard. He was involved in a production of a movie entitled *The Lonely One* that was scheduled to start shooting in mid-July of 1990. He said the main office was at the MGM/Disney Studios in Florida, but material should be sent to him at his trailer in Oregon. We had several letters from him requesting all sorts and of course Nick's eyes lit up when we got a positive response. He asked for lots of photos and a recent videotape, and eventually we heard that I'd been cast in the lead role.

I still craved alcohol in every moment.

It was a daily battle and I lied constantly to Nick about drinking. I was trying to cut down, but not really succeeding. Although I thought I was getting a bit better, in the long run I wasn't; I was still drinking far too much and still killing myself. It was like saying, 'If I cut both me arms and both me legs off, I'll bleed to death, but if I cut just me arms off, I'll live twice as long as I would if I cut them all off!'

I was reading the Bible every day with my little passage from *Every Day With Jesus* and trying to learn something from it and take it on board. I thought, it's giving me immediate comfort, but it's not lasting all day: I need much more of it somehow; and I kept saying to Nick over a period of a couple weeks that I would like to go to this AV meeting and see what it's all about. Nick had initially suggested Alcoholics Victorious and I'd said no, but now I really wanted to go. Maybe I'd thought that going through his programme I would be alright, but for me to bring AV back up again I must've thought by now that what I was doing wasn't working. I think he didn't take me straight away because he wanted me to quit drinking through his own programme as well, but in the end I'd pestered him so much he agreed to take me.

He said, 'There's only about six or seven of us who attend this particular meeting. It's an offshoot of the AA programme. It follows all the principles of it with the Twelve Steps. The only thing it differs in is that the God of your understanding at AV is the Christian God and it can't be anything else.'

He also told me another member of the industry went to this AV meeting and he was a guy called Anthony Marriott who wrote *No Sex Please, We're*

British. 'He's been sober for a long, long while now,' Nick said. I thought, well, that's someone again in the business who I'll have a lot in common with.

The meeting was held every Friday night and run by the vicar from St Nicholas' church in Hayes. I don't actually remember drinking on the day of the meeting, and I went there and had a thoroughly enjoyable evening. Everybody seemed so, so, truthful. There weren't any of this 'I've got a worse story than that to tell you about my alcoholism.' Occasionally, you do get that in AA meetings and sometimes it does become hard to distinguish between what is the truth and what is fantasy.

I also got a great deal of comfort from Tony Marriott, not only because of the business connection, but because he seemed a lovely guy; he talked about how he'd gone through it all, how he'd recovered and how much better his life was without it.

I did feel funny at the end of the meeting when they all said they would pray for God to cure me of my illness. And they did the 'laying of hands' on my head thing before I left to go home.

As me and Nick were driving back, he asked, 'How do you feel about it?'

'That was amazing,' I said, 'because I met six new people who all seemed lovely. I'm really glad I went, because I think I could get to enjoy that on a weekly basis.'

The other thing that I learnt at the meeting was that they always prayed by themselves when they were at home at night before going to sleep; like, thanking Him Upstairs for everything during the day. I thought, I'll try that as well; and I went to bed thinking, well, that was really good!

I got up on the Saturday morning and it was a busy day; nothing in particular, but out and about doing food shopping and so on. It was four o'clock in the afternoon before I realised I hadn't thought about having a drink all day.

I must've gone past so many different places where they sold booze and I didn't look for, or think about, vodka or beer or any form of alcohol at all. It felt as though the word had been erased from my brain. This had never, as long as I could remember, ever happened to me before. I'd been out since ten o'clock, God knows how many places I must've passed and not even thought about it; in six hours!

'Bloody hell! This is amazing!'

I just remember feeling so flabbergasted that I hadn't thought about it. I couldn't believe what had happened in the last six hours. Now the thought of booze was back in my head I suppose I could have started wanting it again; but I thought, well no, I've done without it for the last six hours, I can do another six.

Another six hours later, at ten o'clock at night, I thought, oh, this is good this! I've enjoyed today and I didn't think I could've coped. I'm gonna do another six now: I'm going to bed soon, so see how I feel in the morning!

In the morning I got up and said, 'Well, I didn't have any bad dreams or think about booze at all!' From then on it was like a constant; it wasn't a battle any more. That element of the fight had disappeared completely. I thought, this is great, this! I'm cured, I must be cured! I must be! I don't feel like I want one at all! I was totally gobsmacked. I couldn't believe my luck in what had happened.

At the following meeting they weren't necessarily surprised, just so pleased for me. And it just became the norm then to go there every week and talk about what's gone on during the last week, and then if anyone would come and have a specific problem that they'd had during that week, we'd talk about it and try and help each other through it.

I must admit, from that first meeting there, almost overnight or certainly over that weekend anyway, I lost my dependency on Nick. It disappeared as quickly as it arrived. I didn't feel I depended on him to stay sober. I'd now got this meeting to stay sober and I was getting stronger by the hour, by the day.

It's funny looking back on it, but as soon as I became sober I was so a hundred per cent definite on my feelings for everything and everyone around me. Prior to that, it was a very foggy existence for me. There was only that clarity on the night after I'd met these half a dozen people and listened to what they had to say, on the 3rd March 1989. I wrote on a piece of paper under that auspicious date: *I had a drink problem for fourteen years. Looking back, five years I didn't know it, and nine years I thought I had it under control.*

I'd spent three months reading the Bible, I'd attended this meeting and now I was free; sure of my feelings, myself and everything around me.

My sobriety within Broadreach hadn't given me the same sort of clarity. Then, I was going through the process of the AA programme which means that you have to make amends for what you've done. Part of what I felt I'd done was ruin a diamond marriage, so the natural conclusion for me at that time was to mend that relationship. Now, my feelings were that the thing with the letters had happened for a reason, and having come through that, I was now a stronger person and going to get on with my life. In the clear light of day, I wasn't in love with Gay any more.

I was now only in love with myself and staying sober. That's what I was in love with. And that sounds bollocks, but that's the only way I can describe it. It was one thing that Lisa could not accept in our relationship, that my sobriety was the most important thing in my life. It was more important than my Dad and Arf, and it was certainly more important than Lisa: and she couldn't accept that. I said, 'You come second, but my sobriety has to come first. You've got to understand that!' but she couldn't. She sought comfort elsewhere, and the relationship ended.

During this time Nick would be saying, 'Now that, after a month, we've got you sober, you do understand that if I'm going to get you an agent, it would be very unfair if you went back to drinking because not only will you be letting yourself down, but you'd be letting me down, you'll be letting my programme down, you'll be letting your Dad down, you'll be letting everyone down; so just bear that in mind.'

He asked John Daly if he had any ideas about agents and finding work for me. John was very positive and said he had a couple of film parts lined up for me, and gave us a couple of addresses of agents, but we didn't get any takers on that level and the film parts didn't happen. Then Nick said he knew a guy who worked at London Management for Kenneth Earle, who was one of the top guys at London Management at that time.

So a few months into my sobriety we went to see Phil Dale and Kenny Earle and they seemed very positive. I was only drinking non-alcoholic beer, and that was only whenever I wanted one. I felt quite happy doing that and didn't treat it as a substitute for the real thing as I had done before. Kenny was lovely and took me on. 'Yes,' he said, 'we'd like to help you get back working again, so let's see what we can do and we'll take it from there.'

I was so, so, pleased. My hopes then were all based around the fact that I've got a new agent working for me, I'm sober, and I've just got to keep sober now; and if the last few months are anything to go by, it's a completely new life. I thought, I'm so much happier now, and because I've got my faith, I believe I can deal with anything that the world wants to throw at me.

I continued going to AV every week, thoroughly enjoying every minute of it. I carried on going to the meeting until it closed down when the vicar was retiring and moving elsewhere. Before it closed down, the vicar asked me, 'Would you be interested to share your story with my parishioners, about how you overcame drink with the help of God and Jesus?'

And I said, 'Yeah, I'm up for that.'

Then Malcolm, who came to the AV meetings, started one up himself in Teddington and I would attend that occasionally. It was only for that first year at Hayes that I felt I *needed* to go to the meetings. After that I felt strong enough within myself not to, but I carried on because I enjoyed it; and because, like AA meetings, a lot of the people go there not just for themselves but to help others, and that's how I treated AV.

Another plus side of being sober was that I could learn how to use my video camera that had sat in a box for two years. Tony's brother-in-law had the same model as me and showed me what to do. I started to really enjoy using it, but then because money was short I ended up having to sell it for £300 barely used; I'd paid £1,200 for it. I made a better deal on my Rolex that I'd bought for £90; I sold it for £1,800. It was a good profit, but didn't really help the money situation. I also pawned my wedding ring; the pawn shop was burgled and my ring went with it.

I tried to sort my life out after all the years of drunkenness, but it wasn't easy. Apparently the alcohol levels in blood are graded as Sobriety, Euphoria, Excitement, Drunkenness, Stupor, Coma, Death. I'd hovered around the later stages for such a long time and it's hard to make good decisions in that state. I became concerned that I'd signed all sorts of things that perhaps I shouldn't have. I was also worried about the agreements I'd made with Nick while I was still pissed. I managed to pay him £6,000 out of the ten and it was agreed that he would get the rest at a later date when I started working or sold the flat.

With AV to keep me sober and my agent looking for work, I spoke to Nick less and less. I suppose it's similar to this scenario of changing addictions, going from one to another, and that maybe I'd become addicted to Nick for a short space of time. I'd believed in what he'd promised me, but it became obvious that although he was sending out lots of letters, he weren't actually getting anywhere and at that time he wasn't that much better with words than I was really. Nothing had come from the supposed film in the States. In the end it seemed to be just a con and the guy just a nutcase. Nick sent an awful lot of material and photographs of me with curly hair to the guy in 'Trailer No. 1, Oregon', but no film came.

As soon as I started getting input from London Management, it was obvious that they knew so much more about the business than Nick did; and, although Nick may have had good intentions, he did not have the knowledge and expertise. And I lost faith in Nick very, very, quickly.

London Management asked me to get a new set of proper photographs done and asked me about Nick. He was styled as my publicist; but now I'd got an agent, I didn't need a publicist, so what's the point in having to pay someone's wage to do a job for you when you don't actually need it? Money was tight and I didn't have any to spare to give him. So, to me, it seemed insane to carry on paying that bill when it wasn't necessary. The longer I kept him on, the more money I would've been paying him; I already had paid him six grand and I owed him another four. I said all this to London Management and they questioned lots of things like, 'What did he actually do for this money?' I told them and they seemed a bit sort of shocked and they said, 'You should get an inventory of what he's done for you.'

Nick was also beginning to annoy me in his attitude; he seemed to think he was God in lots of ways. Like, he'd put the work in and now he could call the shots and make me do whatever he wanted me to. He said he didn't like the way I looked now the perm had grown out, that he didn't like the new photographs, which would never work, and he went to my agents to tell them so. I felt like he thought he owned me. My agents *did* like the new photos and I felt I must trust them as they were my management now.

Later, I approached Nick and said I'd been advised by London Management that I needed proof of his work for me, for the amount of money that I paid him for tax purposes. Well, this got right up his nose and he went very, very, quiet and I probably didn't hear from him for a good six months. Not that I had anything to speak to him about really. I was going to my AV meetings and kept in contact with London Management.

He sent a document to me some time in 1990. He wasn't very happy about what had gone on. He spelt out what he felt he had done and sent examples of letters he'd written to prove that he'd earned the money that he'd got from me. I thought the letters weren't very professional. There was also the curly-haired photograph captioned JACK WILD TODAY AFTER THOUSANDS OF INJECTIONS OF NICK CHARLES. There were other photographs as well. It came to light that, on our first meeting in the July when I was pissed, he was taking photographs of me laid drunk on the bed, and taking pictures of what the loo looked like with me throwing up, and the general state of the place, and me.

I was fuming about that. I thought it was totally out of order to come into *my* home and take such personal photographs of me when I was so vulnerable. I wanted the negatives back, but he never sent them.

I suppose it had been coming for some time, but that was really the end. I didn't speak to him after that and he didn't contact me again.

And really, for this six grand, he sent out maybe a hundred or so letters, all in the hope of getting me some work which failed miserably. He permed my hair and made me look like a gonk, and I had new photographs taken by his friend.

But six thousand pounds, in my opinion, was well spent for his advice and support, the phone call to London Management and, most importantly, the introduction to Alcoholics Victorious, because that's what stopped me from dying! AV took away my battle, and from that day to this that's how it's been. What price for that? So, if anything, I got off lightly: I haven't got any complaints.

Chapter 24

M Y FIRST JOB AFTER GETTING SOBER was for a TV show called *The Bill*. I started the first day of filming on the last one or two days of August, so I'd only actually been definitely sober for six months. I was still drinking non-alcoholic lager, and I felt, as long as I don't do anything more than that, there's no reason why I should come unstuck. The Guinness Brewery had brought out a non-alcoholic bitter called Smithwicks which was really gorgeous, but it was more popular up north and difficult to get down in London. I'd scour the shops for it and I was well pissed off when they eventually stopped making it; but nothing would send me off course.

My episode in *The Bill* overran and my scene was cut before broadcast; but at least I was back in front of a camera again, almost exactly a decade after *Alice*, and I got a nice letter from them afterwards.

More work came in the New Year: I was booked to do a musical in the West End called *Heaven's Up* to start in the autumn, and I got the part of Much, the miller's son, in *Robin Hood: Prince of Thieves*, to start filming in late summer.

I was going to be busy that Christmas with *Heaven's Up*, and so not available for panto, but Dave Lee booked me for Christmas '91 to do *Snow White and the Seven Dwarfs* at the Lyceum Theatre in Crewe. He'd forgiven me for the Canterbury disaster six years before when I'd been sectioned during rehearsals. He was pleased I was sober, and I was so pleased to be trusted again. 'Thanks for giving me another chance, mate!' I said; 'I'm so sorry about last time, but I won't let you down again.' I also apologised to Sally Thomsett when I saw her again, a good few years after that. I was doing a TV show in Southampton and I apologised to her for putting her through all the aggro I must've done. She told me that a TV presenter took over from me, but in the first week of the show he had broken a leg and had to be replaced as well!

My first day of shooting for *Robin Hood* was on a Friday, out near Hemel Hempstead somewhere. Friday was AV night. I'd said to them the previous week I would do my best to get there: 'If we finish early enough, I'll come to the meeting and let you know how it all went.' I didn't feel I needed to; I wanted to share it with them. I did the day's shooting, drove back to Hayes and got to the meeting half an hour late.

'How did it go, Jack? How did it feel being your first film back?' they asked. I felt fine. I hadn't been nervous at all. It was almost like, being sober, I felt that much more confident because I was not missing a trick of what was going on. I was conscious of everything around me, where the camera lens was at any given time and what I had to do.

I met Daniel Peacock on the first day and he was great. He played Bull, and I had my main scene with him. We shared a dressing room, which was a caravan but it had everything in it: a hi-fi, a microwave, a TV, everything. It was almost like a Winnebago, but without an engine. We said to each other: 'Well, if the film is gonna be like this and we've got one of these for the location shooting, it'll be very nice thank you very much!'

We didn't; we only had that on day one and after that it really did vary. That first day was the best we ever had. The worst was the pokiest little corner of a normal-size caravan split into six or seven different cubicle-type rooms with a mirror and lighting and that was it. More often than not, that's what we had, and all the Merry Men would be in together. We all knew each other so well after the first week and it really was a helluva happy gang.

One of the Merry Men was an actor called John Dallimore, a lovely guy with a very characterful face. Wardrobe had given him this big long wig to wear that went way down past his shoulders; we nicknamed him 'Mother' and he lived up to his name. His character became the main cook in the camp. Whenever we were playing games he would be keeping the scores, and if we couldn't make our minds up what we were going to do, we'd always ask Mother.

With all the hanging about, I don't know whether it was Mother who suggested it, but someone came up with the idea of a dice game called 'Zilch'. I've forgotten the actual rules, but it's a fabulous game. It made a change from playing the usual card games to make the time go quickly when we weren't working. We used to play that for money, and some days you could earn lots of money and some days you could lose lots of money. We'd only play a pound a game, but with say fifteen of you playing, that was fifteen quid a game and you might get through fifty games during the day. Nobody took it deadly seriously;

obviously it was lovely if you won over the period of a day, but it wasn't the end of the world if you lost because there was always the following day to try and recoup. I probably broke even over the length of time and on the odd occasion I'd come home with an extra hundred quid or so in my pocket.

It was so good to be working again, and working with such fabulous people. I'd been sat alone at home for so long and I'd missed the camaraderie of work. We were stuck together for great long periods and me and the Merry Men had an hysterical time.

We were in the middle of the New Forest somewhere down near Bournemouth and we were shooting this scene where Robin Hood has just come back from the Crusades. He gives a speech to the Merry Men saying that we should take up arms against the Sheriff and are we men or mice and all that. The first rehearsal of such a big, long speech is quite an ordeal for an actor to know it and deliver it to the rest of the cast. Kevin Costner rehearsed it once and said to the director, Kevin Reynolds, 'Ah, hang on! I'm gonna go and get… I'm not getting this. I'm gonna get some motivation. I'll be back.' And walked off into the bushes.

He disappeared from view for a matter of a couple of minutes before making his way back carrying a twig. He was tapping his hand with it, and came back to Kevin Reynolds. 'Right! I've got it now,' he said, shaking the twig.

After that, in any scene with the Merry Men, there'd always be one of us who'd say to the rest, 'I'm just gonna get my motivation!' and disappear into the bushes. There was an unspoken contest as to who would come back with the biggest piece of wood, to then continue working. It amused us for the whole time we were making the film, and you wouldn't come back until you'd found a bigger stick than whoever had done it previously. It always guaranteed a laugh between us Merry Men.

I reflected that, as a working child, I'd had people around me to take the responsibility, so in many ways that's why I had treated it as a game. When I became an adult, I didn't have anyone to take the pressure off of me and I didn't realise soon enough that it was a job to be taken seriously. I created my own, quite possibly flawed, moral code: things had got in such a mess. Now, doing *Robin Hood*, there seemed to be a balance; we worked hard and had fun too. The pressure wasn't on me. It was on Kevin. I recognised it, remembered it, but didn't want it.

We were shooting another scene in the same location where we were all in hiding ready to ambush whoever is coming along. They'd found this tree, maybe three or four foot in circumference, with a completely hollow trunk. They wondered if they could get one of the Merry Men inside. Kevin Reynolds thought it was a great idea and, as I was actually the smallest of the lot of us, it was down to me.

'Can you get in there?'

'Well, I'll give it a go,' I said.

The hole for me to get in was about eight or nine foot off the ground, so they put a ladder down for me to climb up and rigged somewhere for me to rest on while I'm stood inside the tree. With me and me weapons, there weren't a lot of room to move about. I was up there for about thirty or forty minutes while they set up all the lighting and the camera and all that. They kept saying while all of this was going on, 'Are you alright up there? Can we get you anything?'

'No, I'm alright, I'm fine!' I shouted down.

When they were ready to shoot it, they said, 'Well, it's almost lunchtime now, so we'll have an early lunch today and we'll come back and film this immediately after eating.'

I was stood in this tree and watching everybody packing up their gear and waiting for someone to come over with a ladder to help me get down, but nobody was taking a blind bit of notice of the fact that I'm half way up this tree. And everybody buggered off!

I didn't want to make a song and dance of it if it wasn't necessary. I thought I'd give them the benefit of the doubt and expected one of them to turn back and say, 'Oh hang on! We've forgotten Jack up in the tree. We'd better get him down so he can have some lunch!' but nobody did. By now they were about seventy or eighty foot away, but easily within shouting distance, so I started shouting.

'Oi, I'm still up 'ere. C'mon! I want some lunch!'

A couple of the crew came back.

'We done you like a kipper that time, didn't we?' they said as they came and got the ladder up, and then got me down. It had all been a joke. They'd said to themselves, 'Let's see how much shouting and screaming he'll do when he realises that we're leaving him there.' They explained this, beaming at me, as they got me down. We shot the scene after lunch and apparently it looked good, although I don't actually remember seeing it in the final edit. It was a great film to work on, a great team and everyone worked so hard. I was proud to be part of it.

The attention to detail was amazing, and the care and high production values really reminded me of working on *Oliver!* The production team faithfully reproduced twelfth-century Britain from the sets and weaponry to the right type of vegetables, the right size of pigs and the right breed of geese.

The costumes were also beautifully made and then battered to death to look as if they had really been worn. Apparently they 'done them in' with a cheese grater!

My costume, however, was presenting me with a bit of a problem. When we first started, they gave me these suede knee-length boots that didn't have a sole, just a piece of suede, so it was just like running around in your socks. They were expecting everyone to run around the forest as though they'd been living in it for fifty years and it's all fully carpeted with Axminster. Now, I have ridiculously tender feet and always have had (me muvva was the same!) and there's me, tip-toeing, saying, 'Oh, oh, oh... Oh, oh, oh!' How was anyone going to believe I'd been living in a forest for forty years looking like that? So I said to Wardrobe, 'You've gotta give me some kind of soles or something!'

And they said, 'Well, we don't have your small size here, but if you've got some old sneakers you can bring them tomorrow.' These sort of welly-type suede things that they'd given us were so big, I could easily wear a pair of sneakers inside of them, so that's what I did the following day. Thankfully, on the first day, it was all pretty still stuff in the forest and I didn't have to do any walking or running. Everyone else was walking around as though they'd been doing this all their life, but their feet weren't made of flesh like mine.

Then we had the battle scenes! Because the Merry Men were in the movie throughout, we had to learn how to use a bow and arrow; and if we weren't in a scene, we'd be off on the side being taught how to shoot. We were also taught how to club and pierce and generally maim for particular battle scenes. Once it had been decided what sort of weapon you'd be fighting with, we'd learn how to use it properly so we could make it look as though we knew what we're doing with it. That was interesting because I'd never done that before and I thought it would be a piece of cake, but it ain't.

We were on location at Burnham Beeches in Buckinghamshire filming this bit where our camp in the middle of the woods is under attack. There were a lot of extras involved in the battle scenes who weren't actors, which can rub pro actors up the wrong way. Someone said there were ex-bouncers from nightclubs, boxers and wrestlers! These were heavy dudes we were up against. The trouble is, when these extras are told to do something, they do it one hundred and ten per cent as though their life depended on it: which is what annoys actors because, after all, we are just making a movie. *I* have to wear sneakers in my suede wellies, for goodness' sake!

So, we were getting ready to do this bit where these people come and attack the camp, and they said to us actors, 'Now, you've got your bows and arrows and over there is the area where we want you to aim the arrows at!' They were pointing to anywhere between a hundred and two hundred yards away. Our initial thoughts were, well, we'd better be careful because we don't want to injure anyone, so we're purposely not aiming at any individual as we're shooting it; but there's these bastards on the other side of the hill who are aiming directly at us without any thought of whether they're gonna hurt anyone or not – they're doing it for real! They were fearless; if they were told to jump off the tallest tree they could find, they'd go and do it without question.

It was the same in another scene I did with this guy who had a big club with spikes on it. We were trying to work out little bits of choreography, and I said to him, 'If you wanna come and take a blow at me and move out of the way, and then I'll come and go to hit you and I'll pull a punch, and then you can go down…'

Well, this guy comes at me with this axe club thing and he's trying to kill me: no such thing as pulling punches and aiming to just miss, he was aiming for my head. 'This is outrageous. One of us is gonna die here!' I said as I tried to duck.

With all the extras for the battle scenes, a greater pressure was also put on the dressing rooms. The caravans had been divided by these flimsy partitions, and this one particular day I was getting changed while the others were sitting outside playing Zilch. The walls were so thin that I could hear extras selling drugs to each other in the other bit of the caravan. One of the Merry Men then fancied a go and went in to get some.

I could hear all this going on, and when we came out of the caravan together I thought, I can't be having with all of this!

Costner hadn't been over to England much and there'd been rumours that his marriage was in trouble, so the paparazzi were everywhere trying to get pictures of him. Christian Slater, who played Will Scarlet, had just come out of a drying-out clinic and had minders on the set to make sure that he didn't relapse into whatever his addiction was. And there's me, just over a year of being sober, and within six foot of me there's drug dealings going on.

It was a difficult situation. I was frightened of someone putting two and two together and making five and involving me because I'm that close to it. So I said to one of the Merry Men, who'd been and had some of this cocaine, 'Look, I'm sorry, but this is far too close to me and I can't afford any bad publicity as I'm only just getting my career going again; if you're gonna do that, please make sure that it's nowhere near me.'

'Sorry mate!' he said. 'I didn't think it through. Yeah, I'll do that.'

And fair do's, he kept it well away from me and I never saw it again after that.

As producers were beginning to trust me again to be able to do my job, I didn't want them to be given any reason to doubt me. You have to be so aware of what's going on around you. There was a public right of way only fifty yards from the set and anyone could have actually got a picture of me passed out on the forest floor and come up with the wrong idea. I was only asleep. The British Academy had invited me to go to a special screening of *Oliver!* in Hollywood; Morgan Creek (the production company) had agreed, but insisted that I be back on set on the Monday morning. So I flew out on the Saturday and back the next day; I didn't spend twenty-four hours in LA before coming home. Back on location, what with getting up at five o'clock in the morning and working till late, and trying to recover from jet-lag, I'd tell the guys, 'This is where I am, so wake me up if we're needed,' because I'd be laid on the floor in the undergrowth, fast asleep. It took me until Friday before I felt back to normal.

Apart from the suede boots, my other costume challenge was my mediaeval camouflage. In one scene me and Danny are trying to collect donations for passing through Sherwood. We jump out of the bushes aiming our bows and arrows at Maid Marian and ask for some money. Marian then grabs me around the neck, sticks a knife at my throat and says, 'You stunted scum! How dare you attack us?'

'It's me job, m'lady!'

'Your job? And who is your employer?'

'Robin Hood!'

'I insist on seeing him at once!'

But that last bit, we had to keep stopping filming because when Marian had collared me from her horse, the horse must've been hungry because it kept turning its head to have a nibble at my camouflage. I was held between the two of them. We all started giggling and if that happened once, it must've happened half a dozen times. The prop men had to keep restocking my camouflage after every take, and there is a quick shot of it having a munch in the finished film.

Having gotten so friendly with Danny, we'd had some ideas about the first bit of this scene where Bull and Much first come up against Maid Marian. The way it was written, in the original script, was with a very American sense of humour. We thought this short conversation between two bumbling outlaws had many possibilities so we said to Kevin Reynolds, 'Look, we think this scene can be so much better in the same space of time; can we sort of mess about with the dialogue?'

'Yeah, if you want; come back to me with what you think is right guys!' he said. He was working on an extremely tight schedule, but he always gave the impression of complete calmness and was so lovely and open to different ideas.

Danny had written a lot of stuff for TV so had enough experience writing-wise, and I think I had enough experience comedy-wise over the years, so we went back into our caravan and worked out what we thought we might do.

Me and Dan were so much happier with what we came up with, but because we'd made quite a big thing about the fact that the scene could be so much better if it was rewritten, we did rehearse quite a bit between ourselves to make sure it worked. We rehearsed it one more time:

'Much!'

'What?'

'You take the one on the left!'

'Which one's left?'

(He waves his right hand and I say)

'Which one are you taking?'

'Whaddya mean, which one am I taking? If you're taking the one on the left, I'm taking the one on the right!'

'Which one's the one on the right?'

'The one next to the one on the... Bollocks! We'll just jump out and grab 'em!'

'Now?'

'Now!'

'Yeah right, that's it! That's how it works, let's go!' we said and went back and performed it for Kevin Reynolds.

'Yeah, that's great guys! We'll keep that and use that then!'

He didn't make any adjustments or changes and let it play just as we'd rehearsed it.

I think a lot of tinkering with the script was going on anyway. We'd heard Kevin Costner talking to Kevin Reynolds when we were filming the 'motiv-ation' scene about how he saw it, and Costner certainly changed some of his lines from the original script. Alan Rickman wasn't happy with his dialogue as the Sheriff either and rewrote most of his as well, so we weren't the only ones doing it.

It was lovely to be given so much creative freedom and Kevin Reynolds asked us to improvise on several occasions. We shot this bit by a waterfall in Yorkshire, a really lovely place it was; and we're leading Maid Marian to Robin coming down this hill, and Kevin said, 'I want you two to ad-lib giving excuses for what's happened, because don't forget you've been beaten up by two women and you are arguing between yourselves.'

We decided to argue about the number of people involved in the fight, eventually claiming to have been beaten up by 'fifteen large, big lads'. Kevin was very happy with what we came up with and they kept it all in the film.

It's so important to an actor to be given that freedom and confidence, and Kevin and Kevin created a great atmosphere on set. I could understand why Sean Connery had come in to do Richard the Lionheart as a favour to Kevin Costner. They'd already done a film together, and he did one day's shoot on *Prince of Thieves* and gave his fee to charity. It reminded me of all those years ago when Stratford Johns and Frank Windsor came in to shoot the end of *Government Inspector*.

One weekend Kevin Costner hired a cinema in Leicester Square for the cast and crew to see a preview screening of *Dances with Wolves*. We filled the cinema and we were just gobsmacked because, from what we'd seen of him on the set, it was like looking at a different person. The talent was just flowing out of him, particularly from the directing point of view. It was very surprising, and after we'd seen that, our respect for him went up very high.

One of the first scenes we shot was of me and Danny walking back into camp. It was a wide shot and Kevin Reynolds said to me and Danny, 'You two are walking back from an escapade in the woods. You can be talking amongst yourselves about whatever you like, and I want you to walk over to the camp fire to either help with the cooking or ask about when dinner is going to be.'

We started doing it and got onto the subject of animals in the forest and what would we be eating if we were living there. I said, 'Squirrels is my favourite snack!' and Danny started arguing, saying, 'They aren't as nice as rabbit!' This seemed to please the director; and then, as we were breaking for lunch, the sound guy said, 'We need to get a wildtrack of you arguing with each other as you were walking along, because you were so far away from the camera, we couldn't get it; so can you do a bit of ad-lib and we'll dub it on later? Can everyone stand still while we just do this wildtrack please?'

So everybody stood there waiting to go for lunch, and it felt a bit daunting because we knew that everybody was going to be listening and looking at us and it's not as though we'd had time to talk about it or rehearse it...

'Quiet please! Roll the tape! Running; right, go!'

I accused Danny of stealing my last squirrel, eating it, and not asking if he could have some. That, and the fact that he never offered me any of his rabbit. I can't pronounce my R's so it just sounded quite accidentally the right animal to be talking about. We argued for about two minutes or so.

'Okay, that's enough. Thanks very much, gentlemen,' the sound guy said; and quite unexpectedly, we got a round of applause from everyone. For some unknown reason we seemed to have timed the conversation for the length that they wanted to record because we concluded as they said, 'Yeah, that's fine, thank you!' so we couldn't have timed it or planned it any better. We were quite chuffed about that. After that, if anybody was arguing on the set the topic of 'squirrels' would be thrown in and it became a running joke for a while.

The filming overran by a few weeks and because I was already contracted to do *Heaven's Up*, I had to leave. It meant that they had to rewrite what was planned for my character, as originally I was going to be one of the men rescued from the hanging at the end. I think they cut out some of what I'd already shot to make it all make sense. Had it been on time, I would have been okay to finish the movie and then, within a week or two, start rehearsals for the musical; but because they ran behind schedule, I missed out on the end. And that was a shame really.

So I started rehearsals for *Heaven's Up* with Patrick Cargill and Mike Berry at the Playhouse Theatre just off the Strand. It was the stage version of the well-known story of Captain Beaky and his Band, and I played Reckless Rat.

We had about a month's rehearsals and I had one main song in it which was a duet with me and Timid Toad, Jenny Galloway. It was a fabulous variety-type song, very vaudeville; she was quite a plump young lady and a lot of fun to work with. We did a bit of dancing as well and I wouldn't say it was a showstopper, but I think we did it really well together. We thought it was certainly one of the best songs, although I loved most of the songs in it. They all had so much charisma which fitted the colourful characters in the play so, so well.

It was directed and choreographed by Wendy Toye and she was fantastic. She must've been seventy if she was a day and she was so nimble on her feet. She choreographed the Royal Ballet or something outrageous like that. She was a tiny lady, quite slim and incredible.

If I was driving to the theatre I would almost go past where Mike Berry lived, so I would often pick him up and take him home at night as well. He'd been a pop star in the sixties and was a lot of fun to work with. The show was written by Jeremy Lloyd who wrote loads of TV sitcoms. I met him quite a few times during the rehearsals and the run. He was a really nice guy and came to the theatre a lot to give us all support, but it wasn't incredibly well received and we didn't get great reviews. It was a shame really that the show didn't run longer because it was a great family show. Musically speaking, it had every type of song you could think of – ballads, pop, country and western, knees-up-type songs, reggae, vaudeville, songs for all tastes – and had a very magical atmosphere that ran through the whole show. The audiences that came all seemed to love it judging by their responses during the run. And, to me, that is my greatest accomplishment: making people happy. Overcoming drink was hard work, but didn't give me as much satisfaction.

It wasn't a critical success, but I didn't mind. I'd enjoyed doing it and I had my two greatest loves – my work and my sobriety. I was so much happier now than I had been when I was drinking; there was no sense of reality then. It had been a long road to get here, but here I was. Over the years people have tried to blame my battles on my early success as a child actor, but I just don't see that. I'd have been an alcoholic no matter what career I had chosen; and, rather than my success unbalancing me, I think it balanced me out. Without it I would have been capable of anything, even murder. Some of my family ended up on the wrong side of the law, and I think I would have been there too if it hadn't been for my success; my success saved me rather than destroyed me.

So this seems a good place to end it – a new movie coming out and working in a West End musical. Of course, things got worse after this, then better, then worse still, then better. That's life innit? But as I write, I'm in my sixteenth year of sobriety and I'm still working – not too bad eh?

Epilogue

by Claire Harding-Wild

THIS IS WHERE JACK WANTED HIS BOOK TO END. He planned to go on and write a second book about his oral cancer and the loss of his voice, but he died before it was possible. We worked on this book together over several years. All the material was there when Jack died: it just needed rearranging, editing, and, in certain sections, writing out from transcripts Jack and I made as we recorded him talking about his life. So this is Jack's book, how he wanted it to be.

I hope he is pleased.

We met in 1995 in *Jack and the Beanstalk* in Worthing. I was an acting ASM and he was the star of the pantomime, playing Simple Simon. I had booked my digs with a reluctant landlady. 'I've got *Jack Wild* staying with me... Well if you've really got nowhere else to stay... Well, make sure you walk quietly past his door... and have your breakfast first so as not to disturb him...' The name didn't mean anything to me, but I thought if he demanded such treatment he must be an arse. He didn't and he wasn't.

We got on tremendously well from the start; he was fun, strong, kind and generous and I adored him from the first moment he popped his head round the kitchen room door. 'Any chance of a coffee please?' he asked, grinning.

We were pretty much inseparable from then on, and we were eventually able to get enough money for a mortgage on a house together, moving out to a village in Bedfordshire. We worked together whenever we could. If one of us was away working on a show, the other would nearly always be there too, working on this book.

After *Prince of Thieves*, as he said, things got a bit worse for a while: he had just received an eviction notice for Sheen Court and didn't get solvent until 2003. But throughout the challenges he kept on working. He had screen roles in *Basil*, *Archangel Night Out* and the TV series of *Lock Stock*. On stage, he was in *Snow White*, *The Wizard of Oz*, *The Angel* and an Ugly Sister two years running in *Cinderella*. We appeared together in several shows including the short-lived musical *Virus* and a tour of *The Lavender Hill Mob* in 2002.

By the time we were touring in the *Mob*, Jack was already undergoing treatment for his oral cancer, which was diagnosed in 2001.

One of his happiest experiences, not long before his operation, was the *Oliver! After They Were Famous* reunion programme filmed in May 2004. He said it was like a meeting of a dozen Del Boys! Their joy at being reunited was palpable. I was with him during the weekend's filming and when he said, 'This is better than winning the Lottery,' he meant it; and he had done the Lottery religiously every week since its inception. He said it was like your most favourite, your most fun year, condensed into two days, with the absolute delight of being reunited with the people you love.

Two months later, in July 2004, Jack had his tongue and voice box removed.

We were booked to appear in panto at Worcester that Christmas, and we did; I was Prince Charming and Jack played a silent Baron Hardup (the Ugly Sisters not letting him get a word in edgeways). Having that contract to fulfil, and not wanting to let his audience down, was very important to his recovery and became the fixed point for which he resolutely got better. At the end of the panto, in January 2005, however, we knew his cancer had come back.

*

'I don't bloody know, darlin', you tell 'em.'

We are doing a press conference for 'Oral Cancer Awareness Week' and Jack's just been asked a question. He has had his voice box removed and cannot speak so I'm meant to be lip-reading and translating for him word for word.

He has been asked a question about his treatment, and it's not exactly that he doesn't know, it is rather that he is disinterested in his treatment and indeed his illness, and wants me to say something appropriate; so I do.

Jack never really saw himself as sick and gave the management of his cancer over to me like outsourcing an undesirable element of his life. I stayed with him twenty-four hours a day while he was in hospital; and so successful was Jack's ability to disengage from his illness that, when a nurse told me that I couldn't stay with him overnight in ICU, despite the fact that Jack was connected to a ventilator, several drips and drains, and a catheter, and despite having just gone through eight hours of surgery, Jack said, 'If she can't stay, I'm not staying either!'

The nurse recognised that Jack meant every word, and I stayed.

That's not, however, to diminish the pain that Jack went through or the extraordinary strength and amazing spirit that he showed throughout his illness, so much so that even when he had died, I sat beside him for the next ten hours thinking that he really, really might just come back. As Jack said, 'My body is alright, it's just my neck's got to come off.'

We were married on 7ᵗʰ September 2005 and Jack died at home, just before midnight on 1ˢᵗ March 2006.

In that pantomime where we met, there were several shows a day at varying times; and one day Jack went missing. He missed the half, he missed the fifteen, and at the five we were all worried. Someone was dispatched to run along the seafront to find him, and they held the curtain for as long as they could.

Well past 'beginners' they said I would have to go on for him. I wasn't an understudy, so hadn't learnt any of it; but these things are possible in panto, and it was potentially my big break. I got into costume with stage management, wardrobe and cast fussing around me, but in truth I wasn't worried. Front of house made the announcement that unfortunately Jack Wild wasn't going to be appearing today (a disappointed groan from the audience) and assurances made that people could get their money back. Sound had just fixed on my head mike… when Jack popped his head around the door of the dressing room.

'Hello,' he said.

His costume was pulled unceremoniously off me, and the head mike was ripped from my head and restored to its rightful owner. Jack was grinning and laughing and apologising and I stood there in my knickers in his dressing room as an army of people bustled about and ushered Jack onto the edges of the stage.

''Ere, have you told them anything?' he asked.

'Yes, we said you weren't appearing tonight, Jack.'

'Oh, okay,' he said, and entered downstage left to an enormous cheer.

'Hello,' he said to the audience. 'You didn't think I was coming, did you? Well, sorry about that. I forgot we had this show, and I was just getting a burger. Sorry.' The audience loved him.

And so did I.

Afterword

Jack was destined for stardom the moment he lit up cinema screens around the world with that unforgettable impish grin. He became the boy that every parent wanted to mother, every girl wanted to marry and children wanted to emulate. I so remember my son Harry, now a West End musical all-rounder, at the age of three bouncing around our living room in a battered top hat singing 'Consider Yourself' in perfect harmony with the soundtrack; not long before Jack died I showed him video footage I'd taken, which amused him hugely.

In 2002 I cast Jack and his wonderful Claire in my adaptation and production of *The Lavender Hill Mob*. Even though his cancer was beginning to rob him of most of his speech Jack still had a quality that made his presence an unforgettable joy. When his voice box was finally removed making it almost impossible for him to work again, I had a notion of adapting *Three Men in a Boat* for the stage, and have Jack play a silent Montmorency – he was blessed with such expressive eyes, and his diminutive size would have made him, I think, the perfect dog! Sadly, this was never to be as he died before I finally got the production off the ground, although I did dedicate the published version to his memory.

I remember way back Jack saying he was worried about writing his memoirs because of being unable to remember anything, especially the periods he was in Hollywood. 'I was so fuelled with drink and various other things, that I honestly can't recall much.' I suggested he just left those pages blank. 'Trouble is,' he replied with a mischievous grin, 'that would account for most of the book, and who's going to buy a blank book?' Well, thanks to the extraordinary dedication and patience of Claire Harding we do have a book, a fine book and a joyous portrayal of Jack's brilliant and often heart-breaking life and career. I shall always remember him with huge affection and be forever grateful for the chance of working with him.

Clive Francis
October 2016

Acknowledgements

J ACK INTENDED THE EARLY VERSION OF THE BOOK to be dedicated to the staff of the West Middlesex Hospital 'for keeping me alive!' He was a regular visitor there when drink and diabetes were close to killing him in the eighties.

My grateful thanks go to Billie Hayes and Clive Francis who kindly contributed their memories to the foreword and afterword and provide two very distinguished 'bookends' to Jack's career.

Thanks, too, to Dexter O'Neill and his colleagues at Fantom, for their perseverance and enthusiasm in getting the book to you. Editor Phil Reynolds has been careful to keep the sense of how Jack wrote and zealously checked a variety of obscure details, including discovering that someone Jack thought had died in the eighties is still, at the time of writing, going strong.

The BBC Script Archives at Caversham were very helpful in tracing an accurate chronology for Jack's early TV career, enabling me to identify specific shows, some of which Jack had forgotten. The staff of Westminster Reference Library also provided useful resources; and a very detailed picture of Jack's career can be found on the new official website **jackwild.info** which is an ongoing project to document Jack's life and work.

The late Charles Vance was the producer who cast Jack and me in the pantomime when we met, later brought us into the very happy experience of *The Lavender Hill Mob*, and wrote the most affectionate tribute to Jack in *The Stage* newspaper.

Lastly, my thanks to Richard Burnip who tirelessly has worked as sounding board, subeditor and factfinder extraordinaire.

Claire Harding-Wild
October 2016